WAKE UP!

Our Old Beliefs
Don't Work Anymore!

Praise for the previous edition…

"Andrée Cuenod has written a remarkable book for anyone on a spiritual quest to determine how they, as an individual, fit into the Whole of what we know as humanity. She discusses in depth the factors that have influenced us, with an emphasis on religion and science. She covers the perspectives of ancient sages to modern philosophers. "This is not a book to read and put aside, but one to keep as a reference for your own exploration." ~ Nancy Cox

"Dee shakes us awake to Be in the Holy Space - to Be what we want to see in our world and in fact to Be the Shift.
Read this book and you will look at your life in a whole new way."
~ Carol Wassmuth

"I enjoyed reading all of the historical background info for each of the sections that followed…. [And] I am so impressed with the details that you included and how you were able to tie it all together. I appreciate how your mind works … it's amazing! … I commend you on the fulfillment of an important soul purpose and sharing your gifts with humanity." ~ Linda DeMont

"It is obvious that years of research and thinking went into the creation of this book. Questions of why we are here on earth at this present time and what is the best way to live happily with ourselves, others, and the planet are fully covered. Viewpoints of the scientific, religious, philosophical, and historical, are given as they have appeared throughout the ages along with the questions they have brought up.
"I know the writer personally, and can honestly say that she is one happy person. So her personal beliefs are working for her. Maybe you too will 'Wake Up' after reading her book." ~ Sharon Casteel

"Visionary Andrée Cuenod writes, '…our world problems continue to worsen, with money, self-interest, and a need to control determining our decisions and behavior, bringing us to the brink of extinction on which we teeter. We must change. And we can.' How? 'We must first raise our individual consciousness to a higher level, which will then raise our collective consciousness.' And how to do all that is superbly covered, by this seer's far-reaching new book, *WAKE UP!*…

"If your schedule only permits you to read one book this month, let it be *WAKE UP!* You will agree, 'We see that we are all, everything, ONE; that we are eternal spirit beings enjoying physical human existence on Earth.' This reviewer knows that a good book is easy to read. But a great book is that and one that teaches and challenges. Such is *WAKE UP!* And when you read it, you will find not only a well written book, but a well-researched book and you will nod in agreement." ~Richard Fuller, Senior Editor, ~Metaphysical Reviews

"I felt this book was very much an eye opener. It really does not try to change ones beliefs, but gives an individual a new outlook on what is happening and how one should maybe look at things a little differently. I believe the author has done a great job of presenting these facts." ~Nanlee Hall

"Andrée Cuenod's new book, *WAKE UP!* presents a wide spectrum of ideas and information. ... I am impressed and instructed by her ability to synthesize information and draw original, thought-provoking conclusions from her many years of research. Her work on Intelligent Design, taking the concept far beyond limited fundamentalist Christian thinking ... Cuenod has convinced me that evolutionary theory needs to be re-examined in the light of new information from biologists. The consciousness and intelligence of individual human cells, she writes, suggest the breakdown of rigid Darwinian notions about genes being independent from the influence of environment ...

"Her own views about the rapidly spreading 'New Thought' movement, with its emphasis on spirituality over ideology, are creative, insightful, and in keeping with the growing awareness that spirituality and quantum physics are compatible. ... Her conclusions move beyond a new ideology, which is not what she's about. Instead, her aim is to 'help us reclaim our spiritual roots, move from separation and competition to unity and cooperation. . .'To that end, she offers not only insights and theory, but practical means by which we can transform the planet into a place that is safe and nourishing for all beings. The alternative is simply unthinkable: we must grow in consciousness or die in ignorance." ~Barbara Wilson, PhD (Comparative Literature), author of *The Wind is the Breath of God.*

WAKE UP!

Our Old Beliefs Don't Work Anymore!

(a guide through these changing times)

by

Andrée Louise Cuenod

Portal
Center
Press

WAKE UP! Our old beliefs don't work anymore! 2nd edition
© 2020, Andrée Louise Cuenod

First edition published in 2013 by Portal Center Press,
©Andrée Louise Cuenod; ISBN: 978-1-936902-10-1

Cover photo by Jane Salmons, TwoFishPhotography.

Quotations from *The Starseed Transmissions, an Extraterrestrial Report*, by Ken Carey (c)1982. Used with permission from Ken Carey.
from *God is a Verb* by Rabbi David A. Cooper, © 1997. Used by permission of Riverhead Books, an imprint of Penguin Group (USA) Inc.
from *The Jesus Mysteries* by Timothy Freke and Peter Gandy, © 1999. Used by permission of Harmony Books, a division of Random House, Inc.
from *Creative Evolution, a Physicist's Resolution Between Darwinism and Intelligent Design*, by Amit Goswami, © 2008. Reproduced by permission of Quest Books, the imprint of The Theosophical Publishing House (www.questbooks.net).
from *The Theory of Evolution: History of Controversy*, an audio course, by Edward J. Larson, © 2002. Used by permission of The Teaching Company, a Limited Partnership.
from "Mysticism of Physics," by David Lewis, *Atlantis Rising*, Nov-Dec, 2008. Used with permission from Atlantis Rising.
from *Spontaneous Evolution, our Positive Future*, by Bruce Lipton and Steve Bhaerman, © 2009, Reprinted with permission from Hay House, Inc.
from *The Lost Gospel: The Book of Q & Christian Origins*, by Burton L. Mack, © 1992. Reprinted by permission of HarperCollins Publishers.
from *Life and Teaching of the Masters of the Far East*, Vol II © 1927, by Baird T. Spalding. Used with permission from DeVorss Publications, (www.devorss.com).
from *Edgar Cayce and the Kabbalah*, by John Van Auken, © 2010. Used with permission from ARE Press.
from *Newsletter, April 5, 2009* by Neale Donald Walsch. Used with permission from Neale Donald Walsch.

Published by Portal Center Press
www.portalcenterpress.com

ISBN: 978-1-936902-36-1

Printed in U.S.A.

This book is dedicated to all the wonderful friends who, by reading and commenting on versions of my work, helped me get this book together. They generously gave of their time and energy:

Maurine Leonard, wise and spiritual by intuitive osmosis, without seeking;

Elizabeth Klungness, editor extraordinaire;

Margaret Cuenod, theologian and my aunt

Nancy Cox, spiritual microbiologist;

Carol Wassmuth, Sharon Casteel, Linda DeMont, and

Sharon Phipps, my spiritual sisters.

A special thank you to Dr. Ruth L. Miller, my editor at Portal Center Press, who helped me with this final version. As it turned out my "finding" Ruth was the real turnaround in getting this book ready for publication; she couldn't have been a more perfect editor.

Publisher's Note

When the world seems to be falling to pieces around us, this book is a godsend. The result of the author's own heart-driven search for answers, it addresses the most important questions facing humanity today: *Why are we in the mess we're in? What's really going on? How do we find a way out of it?*

We at Portal Center Press knew, when Dee Cuenod brought the first manuscript to us seven years ago, that we would have to publish at least some of it, simply because this kind of overview of what's been going on was so badly needed at that time in humanity's history. And that is so much more the case today!

Dee has created an almost overwhelming compilation of the roots of the distress our culture has been suffering for so many years. She's also given us potential healing points. She's done so, not as a piece of academic scholarship—she's very clear that her years working in academia were as a planner, not a scholar—but as a heartfelt plea to all of Western culture to stop relying on explanations of our world that may not be true.

She has used endnotes and a detailed bibliography to point the reader to resources that she herself found helpful as she wandered through this vast landscape of historical developments in science, religion, philosophy, education, and social norms. We hope you, the reader, will check them out yourself.

As you go through the book, even if you don't always agree with her, you'll find, as we did, many points that resonate with your own wonderings and concerns—along with some intriguing questions to explore and useful ideas for how to find your own way out of what she so aptly calls "the mess we're in."

Ruth L. Miller,
Managing Editor, Portal Center Press

CONTENTS

FOREWORD	i
PART ONE: THE LEVEL OF CONSCIOUSNESS THAT BROUGHT US TO THE MESS WE'RE IN	1
Our Beliefs and Their Effects	2
Assessing Our Beliefs	3
Materialist Beliefs vs. Spiritual Metaphysical Philosophies	5
The Power of Belief	7
Power and Energy in the Human Experience	10
Yin & Yang: Receptive & Creative Energy	10
External Power and American Fear	12
Religious Beliefs	13
A Bit of Religious History	14
The Non-Spirituality of Fundamentalist Religion	15
Undoing the Mess: Religion	19
Scientific Beliefs	21
Mainstream Science	21
Science's Materialist Background	22
Our Choices and Science's Responsibility	26
Undoing the Mess: Science	27
Academia's Influence on Our Beliefs	29
A Narrow Focus	29
The Accepted Line of Thought	31
Public School Education	34
Academia & the Media	35
Undoing the Mess: Academia	35
Shifting Into Higher-Level Beings	39
PART TWO: WHAT'S BEHIND OUR PREVAILING BELIEF SYSTEMS	41
Today's Predominant Belief Systems	42
Western Religions and Their Beliefs	49

The Development of Judaism	51
The Development of Christianity	57
Splitting Christianity	64
Comments & Questions: Western Religious Beliefs	76
Beliefs of Western Science	84
Earth's Development	85
Biological Evolution	86
The Fossil Record	95
The Role of Genetics	98
Comments & Questions: Orthodox Science	100
The New Sciences: Quantum Physics	103
The New Science of Epigenetics	106
The Noetic Sciences	107
Comments & Questions: New Sciences	108
Conclusions: Science	109
Intelligent Design: A Bridge Between Science And Religion?	114
Today's Intelligent Design Movement (IDM)	116
Is ID Science or Religion?	117
Arguments Against Design	119
Teaching the Controversy	120
"The Wedge"	121
Comments & Questions: Intelligent Design	123
Conclusions: Science & Religion	126
PART THREE: PERENNIAL WISDOM – OUR ROOTS IN ANTIQUITY	**133**
Perennial Wisdom	134
Ancient Civilizations: New Light on Their Age and Sophistication	138
Our First Civilizations	139
Atlantis and Other Possibilities	143
Extraterrestrial Influence or Circular Evolution?	146
Continental Drift	147
Comments & Questions: Ancient Lore	153
Our Long-Lost Spiritual Roots	157
The Mysteries	158
Actual Pagan Beliefs	160
Recapturing and Reconstructing Ancient Wisdom	165
Comments & Questions: Ancient Wisdom	167

Gnosticism: What Christianity Could Have Been Had It Followed Its Own Mystery Tradition — 171
- *Gnosis*/Knowledge vs. Belief/Faith — 172
- Who Were The Gnostics? — 175
- Relation to the Hindu Vedas — 176
- Comments & Questions: Gnosticism — 176

The Jesus Story: A Mysteries Myth? — 179
- The Jesus Mysteries — 179
- Comments & Questions: The Jesus Story — 182

PART FOUR: MORE PERENNIAL WISDOM - TODAY'S NON-ORTHODOX METAPHYSICS — 183

Spiritual Metaphysical Philosophies (Metas) — 184
- Common Meta Beliefs — 187
- Comments & Questions: the Spiritual Path — 190

Metaphysics in the New Sciences: Proposals to "Save The World" — 192
- A Quantum Proposal for Intelligent Design — 192
- Cooperation in Evolution — 196
- Purposeful Evolution — 197
- Comments & Questions: The New Sciences — 198

Evolutionary Spirituality and Enlightenment: Andrew Cohen & Ken Wilber — 201
- Andrew Cohen's Teaching — 201
- Ken Wilber & Levels of Consciousness — 204
- Pierre Teilhard de Chardin — 206
- Sri Aurobindo — 207
- Comments & Questions: Evolutionary Spirituality — 208

Edgar Cayce's Christian Mysticism — 211
- Evolution/Involution — 212
- Cayce's Story of Our Beginnings — 212
- Reason for Being — 213
- Karma: Meeting Self — 214
- Levels of Consciousness — 215
- Comments & Questions: Edgar Cayce — 215

Helena Blavatsky's Theosophy — 217
- Blavatsky's Teaching — 217
- Monads, Mind, and Levels of Consciousness — 218

Comments & Questions: Theosophy	221
Kabbalah: Jewish Mysticism	223
Kabbalistic Teaching	224
Shattering the Vessel	225
Reincarnation, Resurrection, and Awakening	226
Levels of Consciousness	228
Comments & Questions: Kabbalah	229
The Starseed Perspective: An Extraterrestrial Report	231
Comments & Questions: Starseed Transmissions	234
PART FIVE: WHAT IT'S ALL ABOUT—MY PERSONAL PHILOSOPHY OF LIFE	**237**
My Personal Belief System	238
What Is God?	240
What Are We?	242
Did We Err?	243
To What Extent Are We Divine?	245
The Why of It All	246
A Story of Our "Creation" and Evolution	247
The Story	247
Beyond the Story	255
How It All Plays Out	258
The Big Why	259
Seeming Evil	261
Extensions of Our Soul	261
Planning Our Plays	262
Enlightenment	268
Karma	271
Comments & Questions: My Philosophy	272
Consciousness	275
A Nonphysical Quality	275
What Is Consciousness?	277
Consciousness, Conscious, or Intellect?	278
Four Levels of Consciousness	280
Monism	285
Comments & Questions on My Personal Belief System	286

PART SIX: WHAT WE DO NOW	289
How We Get From the Outer to the Inner	289
Our Destiny	290
Shifting Our Beliefs and Behavior	292
Cooperation and Unity or Competition and Division?	292
Not the End But a Shift	294
The Shift	295
Balancing Our Energy and Restoring Our Relationship with Nature	296
A Spiritual Renaissance	299
Wake Up! Shift Your Consciousness	302
Change and Transformation	303
A New God and A New Spirituality	303
We Won't All Shift at Once	305
Experiencing the Light	307
Being the Shift	312
Afterword	316
APPENDIX A	323
Comparisons of Levels of Consciousness	323
APPENDIX B	324
Time Line	324
APPENDIX C	327
The Botanical Society of America Statement on Evolution	327
APPENDIX D	331
American Association for the Advancement of Sciences Board Resolution on Intelligent Design (ID) Theory	331
BIBLIOGRAPHY	333
CONTINUING THE CONVERSATION	345
ABOUT THE AUTHOR	346

FOREWORD

> No problem can be solved from the same level of consciousness that created it. ~ Albert Einstein

> Are we physical beings yearning for a spiritual experience or are we, at the core of our existence, conscious and immortal beings evolving a physical experience? ~ Edgar Mitchell, Apollo 14 astronaut

> We can only succeed in achieving world peace if there is a spiritual renaissance on this planet.
> ~ Dag Hammarskjold, 1950s Secretary General of the United Nations

Einstein and Hammarskjold shared their above wisdom over sixty years ago and Mitchell asked his question about thirty years ago, yet there is little indication that we've even thought about their profound words. Instead, our world problems continue to worsen, with money, self-interest, and a need to control determining our decisions and behavior, bringing us to the brink of extinction on which we teeter. It all must change. We must change. And we can.

Together, the above quotations are the theme of this book.

There is no doubt in my mind—and probably in yours too—that we must find a way to effectively address our dire world problems, but how? We can't just *say* we're going to address our problems from a new level; it doesn't work that way. We must first raise our individual consciousness to a higher level, which will then raise our collective consciousness.

Once we're living at the higher level, we will function from it, then we can raise our collective consciousness and will be able to resolve our problems with new, heart-based thinking. How do we raise our consciousness? By realizing who we truly are.

We each need to answer Mitchell's question and, if necessary, change from believing we are physical beings to *knowing* (intuitively) we are conscious and immortal (spirit) beings. We each must purposefully set the beliefs that condition our attitudes and determine our level of consciousness. Our ancient ancestors can help us define who we are individually, and by reclaiming their wisdom—our nearly lost roots—we can bring forth Hammarskjold's spiritual renaissance in humanity collectively.

It's important that we understand our personal role in the collective change, and commit to helping it come about. The noted cultural anthropologist Margaret Mead said: "Never doubt that a small group of thoughtful, committed citizens can change the world. Indeed, it is the only thing that ever has."

Many years ago, I began asking questions like Mitchell's. I wanted to understand who I am, where I came from, why I am here, why life seems filled with so much suffering, and what will happen when I die. Notice that when I began my quest, most of my questions centered on me. The more answers I got, though, the more aware and disturbed I grew about our Western culture's obsession with materialist values and its callous disregard for the welfare of other people, other creatures, and our environment. I became concerned that life was so hard for so many people, that so many were starving, and that there was so much fighting and death in the world. I've since realized that the closer we come to awakening to our shared spirituality, our Oneness, the less self-absorbed we are, and the more compassionate, caring, and concerned we are for the wellbeing of all life on Earth. So, I've made it my life's mission to help others raise to higher levels of consciousness.

Our beliefs determine our individual level of consciousness, and we are unable to see and understand what goes on at higher or even parallel levels. For example: Someone at a militaristic level cannot relate to a pacifist's way of thinking; the clear-cutting logger can't accept what the environmentalist stands for; the right-to-lifer cannot tolerate the abortionist. And the reverse is also often true.

But higher levels of consciousness enable more expansive beliefs through which to understand and be more tolerant of others' views, without feeling the need to agree with them. Also, we must look at each problem only in context with the whole. We need to change how we see the world and all life in it. We created our problems at a materialist, linear, separate, piece-by-piece level, and can solve them only from a higher, holistic level, which I contend is spiritual. If we are to understand each other, we must each proactively raise our consciousness toward the spiritual.

Our various belief systems answer Mitchell's question differently, and in that fact lie the major differences in our ways of approaching life. The belief systems that say we are physical beings (materialist) have ruled for two millennia, bringing us to today's deplorable world conditions. Those systems that say we are conscious and immortal beings (spiritual) existed before Christianity did its best to eradicate them, and now hold keys to renewed ways of living and resolving our world problems. These differences, I believe, constitute the most crucial issue today, one we must address before we can create a better world. Please understand, I'm not saying higher spiritual levels are "better" than lower materialist levels; they just serve different purposes at different times. They are higher or lower only because their adherents' energy fields vibrate at different frequencies.

Materialism and Spirituality

More and more people today realize that the materialism of our Western culture has become harmful to life on Earth. But most can't imagine that our worldview can change; it seems so overwhelmingly entrenched, change seeming so hopeless.

That's why I've written this book. I believe we can change our worldview by replacing our materialist beliefs with spiritual beliefs, and, in effect, creating a new culture.

This may seem as though I advocate discarding scientific beliefs as materialist in favor of religious ones as spiritual. But I mean, we must replace the materialist beliefs of both science and religion with spiritual beliefs, some of which are religious, some scientific, some ancient, and many perennial.

Materialists say matter is all that is natural and this physical life is the only reality. This view is held by atheistic scientists, certainly, but also by most fundamentalists of Western religions. It says everything is separate and fighting to survive, so features competition, conflict, and insensitivity, including an inability to identify with any other person or creature. Seeing humanity as the acme of life on Earth, it allows humans to abuse other Earth inhabitants rather than ensuring the wellbeing of all life.

The spiritual way says God consciousness is all there is, and everything is spirit; matter isn't real, only seemingly so. Nothing is separate; everything is interrelated, interdependent: the Oneness of God. This in one form or another was part of the esoteric teachings of all ancient religions, traditions, and philosophies. It is held today by Eastern traditions, aborigines world-wide, spiritual metaphysical philosophers, and a growing number of quantum and noetic scientists. Viewing all life as one, it emphasizes unconditional love, harmony, holism, cooperation, and well-being for all, putting our heart on equal footing with reason.

Most spiritual philosophies and religious traditions have, at their esoteric core, taught that "God is One." But, different teachings understand it differently. Fundamentalists of the Western religions of Judaism, Christianity, and Islam take it to mean there is one supreme being, who is God (this is called monotheism).

The more spiritual of most other traditions—ancient and modern, Eastern and Western—although often treating the sun, elements, animals, and their heroes as embodiments of deity, imply there is only One: God; all, everything, is that One (this is called monism or pantheism). If they have many deities, they see them as expressions or faces of the One. That One is not a being but is the "ground of being." This seems to be the defining difference between Western religions and nearly all other spiritual philosophies and traditions.

Despite their obvious differences, fundamentalists of both Western religions and science perpetuate the materialist belief system. Fundamentalists are those who emphasize belief in the literal truth of their Holy book and those who rigidly adhere to a set of basic principles in science. Western religions also have mystical branches and teachings, but their adherents are relatively small in number, and their beliefs are not accepted by the orthodox, so, although I mention them, I write mostly about the norms that dominate our culture. Science, too, has its mystics, and I do write about them, contrasting their thinking to the orthodox view.

Religion and Spirituality

Humanity in Western culture is very religious, but largely lacking in spirituality.

Many people would say religion and spirituality are synonymous, but also many view them as different, yet not necessarily mutually exclusive. Western Fundamentalist religion expresses creed, dogma, and ritual in institutional and congregational systems. It reflects the biblical perspective of God as a separate, supreme, human-like—emotional, demanding, vindictive, male—being, creator of the universe, Earth, humans, and all other creatures, each as a separate physical entity and apart from Him. Spirituality relates to God as love and higher intelligence that is in, encompasses, and interconnects everything, all as One. Spirituality is philosophical and introspective, not doctrinal. It is personal, something we individually commit to as an on-going process of life and take with us everywhere. Religion often requires that worship be done in a certain way and usually in a specific place. Religion's focus is on morals and ethics, our behavior in daily life. Spirituality involves meaning and purpose in life, and encourages compassion and kindness in our attitudes and conduct toward all life.

If we consider spirituality internal and religion external, there is no good reason for them to be at odds; they can surely be complementary, addressing different issues and satisfying different needs. One who is religious can also be spiritual, and vice versa. Religion provides for an external expression of one's internal spirituality and a community in which to enjoy it. Many people comfortably combine their religion and their spirituality.

Today's Western culture formed its worldview over the last two thousand years through Bible-based religion, and further molded it in the last three centuries by classical science. It no longer works well for us. Our culture is out of control, with a few, driven by greed, controlling and running rampant over the many, and a large share of the many striving to become part of the few, wanting to enjoy the luxurious life style of the few, and misguidedly believing only personal power and wealth bring happiness.

Belief and its Power

The "power of belief" in everyday life is a popular topic today, with spiritual teachers talking about it and noetic scientists proving that what we believe creates our experience. This has for many years been one of my basic truths, and why I focus on our beliefs as what must change if we want our world conditions to change. Our materialist beliefs created a view of reality that is false. New beliefs will create new experience, and if those beliefs are spiritual, our reality will naturally be filled with love, compassion, and harmony, raising our consciousness to higher levels.

Our individual beliefs are the power behind the creation of our world as we experience it. They determine what we think about ourselves, resulting in our attitudes and behavior toward everything in life. By our collective thoughts, intentions, and behaviors, our culture has created our world conditions and problems, and only it can remedy the situation. But our culture is not an entity; it is made up of individuals, whose personal beliefs collectively define it.

A Shift

Contrary to appearances, humanity is currently in the throes of a shift that is raising our collective consciousness to a higher level, permitting a new, heart-based, harmonious, cooperative reality. That shift got well underway in the 1960s and is now in full swing as the greatest evolutionary advancement in human history. Some people say December 21, 2012 was when the shift occurred, and maybe it did on a subtle level. I have always seen it as an ongoing process of enlightenment in a journey toward awakening from the ignorance that keeps us stuck in materialism, not something that occurs suddenly. Cosmic events coming together with the winter solstice of 2012 facilitated the process—the universe doing its part to help us shift. But we didn't suddenly shift into kind behavior, needing first to understand what such a shift means to us and our individual responsibility in fulfilling it. We must take certain steps toward the return of spirituality to our beliefs and our worldviews. Once we've accomplished the spiritual renaissance, our behavior will naturally follow our heart.

Buckminster Fuller sagely said, "You can never change anything by fighting the existing reality. To change something, build a new model that makes the existing model obsolete."[1]

This Book

I offer this book to further a more integral understanding of life on this planet. While I point out the fallacies of the materialist belief systems, I give you a spiritual view of life on Earth to replace the outmoded, false, materialist picture. This spiritual view sees harmony and love in our lives and peace and wellbeing in our world for all life. It also emphasizes the perfection of everything as it is. Everything that has occurred in the last two thousand years, including our self-absorbed ways, was completely appropriate for our experiences and spiritual growth of that period, just as strong spirituality was appropriate for many prior to this Age of Darkness now ending. An immediate re-birthing of our spiritual knowingness is needed to bring us into the Age of Light in ways needed in our new growth experiences.

People speak of healing humanity and our world. But, we don't need healing—we aren't sick or broken—we are simply in the process of changing direction.

Now that we've had all that experience and growth through materialism and its negativity and problems, it's time for a different type of growth experience. In our new experience, we will be more holistic in our approach to life, with greater balance between masculine and feminine ways of expressing, and be more reverent of all life. It's time for Western religions to reclaim our spiritual roots, as some religions, many metaphysical philosophers, and some parts of science are already doing.

Metaphysics is the philosophical study of reality beyond and including the physical. I further define it adding the spiritual, because the people and philosophies I want to highlight take a spiritual perspective in their approach to the metaphysical, while most academic metaphysicians avoid the spiritual in their teaching. My shorthand term for spiritual metaphysicians and their philosophies is "Metas."

Although sketchy, what we know about the beliefs of our ancient ancestors shows a far deeper spiritual wisdom than we've been taught about them by theologians, scientists, and historians. It's clear that before Christianity, spiritual traditions existed everywhere throughout humanity. With the recent resurfacing of numerous ancient texts and new interpretations and better understanding of previously known texts, the wisdom of the ancients is re-emerging. This is part of the spiritual renaissance, aiding our shift in consciousness. It's a case of the old adage: "When the student is ready, the teacher will come."

Integral philosophy is a major alternative thinking process rapidly spreading worldwide, led by such luminaries as Ken Wilber and Don Beck. It's an approach to life that uses systems theory to examine things holistically. It sees all life in cooperation rather than in competition and fighting to survive. It also integrates science, religion, and spirituality into a more complete view of life on Earth than we are seeing now. Only through an integral approach can we understand our life and effectively resolve our world problems.

The ancients possessed integral wisdom, wisdom we need to reclaim. We can see integral thinking in quantum and the noetic sciences and in the more mystic traditions worldwide. It must be a normal part of our thinking in all our enterprises. But, being able to see life in an integral way in itself requires being at a higher level of consciousness than materialism allows. Once there, though, integral philosophy raises one's consciousness ever higher.

This book is an integral approach to life that brings science and religion together through spirituality. Its intent is to help those who want such help to attain higher levels of consciousness.

I've organized this book into six parts to depict our beliefs in terms of their importance to our shift in consciousness.

Part One introduces the way life appears to us through our current beliefs and the level of consciousness from which we created our world conditions. It looks at religious, scientific, and academic contributions to the mess we're in today.

Part Two examines our Western culture's predominant beliefs, those of religion and science—our materialist level—so we can better see the beliefs from which we need to move away. It relates the story behind the story of each, and how we got to it, not to condemn it but to illustrate its limitations. Then it looks at Intelligent Design as a possible bridge between science and religion.

Part Three focuses on the perennial wisdom of our ancient ancestors as some of the beliefs we might move toward.

Part Four contains more perennial wisdom, but of today not yesterday. It shows how the more mystical new sciences, along with today's Metas, are reclaiming our nearly lost spiritual roots, while integrating scientific and spiritual beliefs.

Part Five presents a personal spiritual view of life, what it all truly is as I see it. It includes a "creation" story, application of this philosophy to our everyday life, and discussion on consciousness as our Oneness.

Part Six concludes the book with discussion about the shift, our destiny, ideas of what we do now to effect the changes we want in our world, and how we get from the outer to the inner.

Throughout the first two parts of this book I draw your attention to what I see as the limitations and falsities of the materialist belief systems, depicting them as I see them rather than as their promoters want us to see them. I have drawn from considerable research of both academic and alternative sources to present as objective a picture of those materialist belief systems as possible, given my obvious bias.

In examining the prevailing Western belief systems, both materialist and spiritual, we'll get each system's take on some big issues of life, and see how each answers Mitchell's question. To see what we've been without for two millennia, we'll consider ancient civilizations, their antiquity, sophistication, and spiritual beliefs. We'll view them from a perspective of circular evolution.

Rather than provide explicit details of the many various belief systems, I have tried to paint an overview picture of each, giving the flavor of their set of beliefs and in some cases differing interpretations and arguments against. Sometimes I felt the words of my sources would do that best. I give you dates, not for you to remember but to provide an idea of relative time. To help those who want to further pursue a belief system or particular point of view, I provide references to my sources and a bibliography of all the books, audio/videos, magazines, and newsletters from which I drew information. I've added others I enjoyed in my research for this book that you too might enjoy.

I offer you my philosophy because, while it has similarities to many Metas—such as Gary Zukav, Neal Donald Walsch, Andrew Cohen, Deepak Chopra, Gregg Braden, and Wayne Dyer, as well as ancient philosophers Pythagoras, Socrates, Plato, and Plotinus, later philosophers Sri Aurobindo and Pierre Teilhard de Chardin, and new scientists such as Amit Goswami and Bruce Lipton—it has some new concepts you might enjoy. And, it puts our scattered spiritual intuitions into a cohesive, comprehensive, and wholly positive picture of our existence.

I explain the shift, our individual role in it, and how it serves our destiny as the basis of our thinking shifts from materialism to spirituality, the outer to the inner. To help individual seekers in their enlightenment and personal transformation, their shift, I offer a way to gather one's own "truths" and to consciously receive constant inner, higher guidance.

If anything in what follows doesn't interest you, skip it. I'd rather have you keep going than get bogged down by something tedious and lose interest altogether. You might consider skimming rather than skipping, since each belief system is approached in an uncommon way and you could learn something important to you.

Who am I that you should want to pay any attention at all to what I have to say? Nobody. And you shouldn't, necessarily. But think what you would miss by not reading this book: religious wisdom gleaned through sorting out the chaff of Western religious dogma and distorted accounts of history; scientific wisdom with a focus on the noetic and quantum sciences that are transforming conventional materialist sciences; resurfacing ancient spiritual wisdom; wisdom from several modern Metas. Add in experiential wisdom of nearly ninety years of human life and intuitive wisdom from forty-five years of in-depth communion with my personal source of knowledge and wisdom, and you get the soup of this book. I have done the research and synthesizing to integrate science, religion, and spirituality into a holistic picture of life on Earth.

I don't personally claim any of this wisdom. I believe that all wisdom is available to everyone who wants to know. I only want to share my good fortune with you in hopes that you will find some morsel of value to you, and to give you a possibly different way to view life on Earth, yourself, and God.

Often it's not the actual words of information or insight which cause an "aha," but what a word or phrase triggers in us individually to help us "remember" a truth. We all, very early in our circular journey, knew all, but purposely forgot it to better experience this human life.

I will be telling you a lot of strange things in this book, things you may never have read or heard about before, things you may never even have thought about before. But don't take my word for their truth. Find out for yourself. Quietly go within and ask your higher guidance what to believe. We are beginning to remember.

Our higher Selves (often unbeknownst to us) are helping us do that; they're helping us change our beliefs and worldviews to the extent necessary. They are helping us raise our consciousness through enlightenment.

Making conscious and constant contact with that "voice within" and letting it guide one's life is the single most valuable and important thing anyone can do in this life. And it's not hard to do. Nor does it take years of practice; it merely takes sincere commitment. One has only to open communication between their self and their inner, all-wise, unmanifest soul-Self, and never again feel alone or fear anything. Each and every one of us will eventually make the connection and remember who we really are, when we are ready.

Humanity in general needs radically new belief systems, and the chaos of change is needed to birth the new culture and make way for a cooperative, peaceful, and love-filled world. More and more people today are seeing the light of spirituality and moving toward it.

It's an exciting time to be living on Earth, a time of great change, wonder, and joy. I am so glad to be here now and a part of what is happening! I hope you are, too. Are you ready to wake up?

---

[1] Fuller, R. Buckminster, *Critical Path*. Cambridge UK: St Martin's Griffin, 1962.

PART ONE: THE LEVEL OF CONSCIOUSNESS THAT BROUGHT US TO THE MESS WE'RE IN

No problem can be solved from the same level of consciousness that created it. ~ Albert Einstein

Our Beliefs and Their Effects

Introduction

Our individual beliefs make us who we are. They affect how we perceive and face our world and determine how we view ourselves, resulting in how we treat our neighbors, other cultures, and other beings. They influence our political, economic, and social values and concerns: our worldviews. They define whether we consider the world population a global unit or separate pockets of people and creatures different from us and not our concern. Most of today's conflicts have arisen because of differences in beliefs.

As he gazed at Earth on his trip back from the moon, astronaut Edgar Mitchell had a momentous shift in consciousness. In an instant he "understood that the major crises of our times are due not to aspects inherent in the external world, but to flawed and inadequate worldviews."[2] He founded the Institute of Noetic Sciences (IONS) to address this issue as part of an exploration into the nature and potentials of consciousness. "Noetic," as defined by IONS, is "'inner knowing,' a kind of intuitive awareness—direct and immediate access to knowledge beyond what is available to our normal senses and the power of reason."

Our beliefs, attitudes, values, assumptions, and ideas form our worldviews, creating the general way we see ourselves and the world we live in. IONS researchers studying this issue add:

> People's worldviews therefore influence every aspect of how they understand and interact with the world around them. Worldviews profoundly impact individual and shared goals and desires, shaping perceptions, motivations, and values both consciously and unconsciously. Worldviews inform human behavior in relationships and choreograph individual and social reactions and actions every moment of the day.[3]

We cannot merely correct the flaws, however, but must replace our harmful worldviews with radically new heart-based ones. We must realize that the damage we've done to our world, to its creatures, and to ourselves results from the self-absorption of our predominant worldview. We must take responsibility and behave differently. If we don't like what we see in our world, it's up to us to change it by being what we want to see. We focus our attention on a higher level and bring it into our reality, knowing we can, and thereby enable our world to reflect that higher expression.

In that way, we will create a new culture and a new world.

A spiritual worldview is to the predominant materialist worldview what Copernicus' heliocentric position was at the time to the Aristotelian belief that Earth was the center of the universe: hated and rejected by the ruling purveyors of the old belief system.

Well-entrenched beliefs are hard to change, but change them we must.

Our individual beliefs make our personal worldview. By beliefs, I mean all beliefs, about ourselves and our capabilities, about how and from where all that's physical came into being, and about other cultures and our own culture. Some are religious, some scientific, some spiritual, some historical; some are empirical and some have no basis in fact. Some relate to our health and aging, some to ourselves in relationship with other people. Some involve our ethnicity, our country, our government, our environment, our gender, our sexual orientation.

Often what we believe conforms to the beliefs of others, instilled in us as children through family members, teachers, places of worship, our ethnic, racial, or economic environment, our peers, and our experiences have conditioned many others of our beliefs. Our beliefs are all interconnected, and are based on a single premise: how we individually see ourselves and all in existence, as either material or spiritual, separate or One, mortal or eternal.

Assessing Our Beliefs

We each need to honestly assess our worldview to see if it is in fact heart-based; then, if it isn't fully, work on changing the beliefs that define it, perhaps coming to a new realization about our self, life on Earth, and God. We need to examine our beliefs.

We need to answer Mitchell's question: Are we separate mortal physical beings fighting to survive or are we eternal spirit beings co-creating physical experience through which we learn and evolve?

In *Spontaneous Evolution*, cell biologist Bruce Lipton and Steve Bhaerman ask: "[W]hat if our belief system about life is wrong?" They write that what we need is a "spontaneous remission of civilization," and they go on to say that to do so

> ...necessitates that we individually and collectively reexamine many of the fundamental assumptions our civilization accepts as true. Those beliefs we find inadequate or incomplete must be revised so that the new awareness is incorporated into civilization and becomes our new way of life. ... we must empower ourselves with the knowledge of who we truly are. [Then,] we can rewrite our destiny.[4]

Many people, especially those who have in recent years become disillusioned with religion, haven't defined their beliefs. For many, it's a case of knowing more what they don't believe than what they do. But, since our beliefs truly do determine how we see the world and react to it, we can no longer afford not to know, at least in a general way, what we believe. Our world and fellow Earth inhabitants need us to know, now. We each need to determine what we want to believe about the big issues of life and answer Mitchell's question.

Defining my truths has been very stabilizing and freeing for me. Knowing what I believe has given me a peace about life and death, and has raised my self-esteem and my confidence. I can enjoy life, cope with its challenges and disappointments, and truly be afraid of nothing. I can love unconditionally, knowing we are all One.

This is not to say one's beliefs should be rigidly fixed, but only that they might be generally formed. Then, remaining flexible and open enables one to expand one's beliefs on a solid foundation, so they can evolve.

One reason I accept my spiritual beliefs as valid is that while I received them intuitively from my higher Self, I have since found that they conform remarkably to the wisdom of our ancient ancestors. I find also that nearly all contemporary spiritual teachers are saying many of the same things, things they, too, have understood intuitively, gnostically, noetically, mystically. Each of us is interpreting those truths from our own experience, expanding and putting our own slant on them. This indicates to me that spiritual truths are resurfacing in every way possible and at this time, because we are ready for them.

Our beliefs are personal, even when we put our faith in what someone else believes. And ours are the only ones we can control. Only by seeing that our own beliefs are heart-based can we then be and behave in ways that might positively influence others.

By being individually spiritual in our beliefs and raising our own level of consciousness we will collectively lead humanity's consciousness to the spiritual and a higher level of being.

There's a difference between being self-absorbed and being concerned with our degree of enlightenment and level of consciousness so we can help the whole of humanity evolve. Being self-absorbed is part of a materialist belief system in which one's care and concerns are basically only for one's own happiness and survival, without regard for those of others.

Pursuing one's own enlightenment in an effort to raise one's consciousness is spiritual and, although still focusing on the self, enables us to see all life as One, not separate, and fosters concern for the whole of life.

Materialist Beliefs vs. Spiritual Metaphysical Philosophies

The Western World has had two millennia of religious influence and about three hundred years of orthodox science. Together, they have provided a backdrop for wonderful growth experiences, and were completely appropriate for our experiential needs throughout the previous age. Now, though, we are moving onto a different path, and those old perceptions can't satisfy our new needs. It's time to wake up to who we really are and begin to see life differently. We are expressions, faces, manifestations of the One, yet, we are also individual beings, experiencing physical life in individual ways. We need to understand both of these aspects of ourselves to know who we truly are.

Western spiritual metaphysical philosophies, expressed by the people I call "Metas," represent a variety of spiritual teachings with many similarities. All have far more spiritual beliefs than either of the materialist belief systems. Most Metas—including those called "occult"[5] or "New Age"[6]—express beliefs that are similar to those of the classical Greek philosophers whose spiritual teaching stemmed from earlier Egyptian mysteries and still earlier Mesopotamian spirituality. It is that wisdom we need to reclaim, understand, and make our own.

Before science came into its own, philosophy was at the top in Western as well as Eastern cultures. To philosophers, philosophy is profound musing on the big issues of life. To opposing philosophers and non-philosophers, it's someone else's opinion.

Philosophers of the Greek classical period, when the ideas of Pythagoras, Socrates, Plato, and Aristotle reigned supreme, considered nearly everything of importance today: mathematics, astronomy, physics, chemistry, zoology, medicine, law, politics and government, history, logic, ethics, metaphysics, the spirit realm, and our origins. Their work formed the basis of Western thought on almost every subject. Before Pythagoras (6th century BCE[7]), the wise were called "sages," which was interpreted to mean those who knew. Pythagoras coined the word philosopher, which means "lover of wisdom" in Greek, which he defined as "one who is attempting to find out."[8]

Materialist Beliefs of Western Religions and Sciences

As it gained more and more power, the Christian Church became ever more domineering, seeking to control the thinking of all people everywhere. Philosophers and scientists were no longer permitted, under penalty of death, to express anything that didn't conform to the Roman church's teachings. Prior to becoming a separate discipline, late in the 1700s, science was one of many branches of philosophy, called "natural philosophy," with theology also a part of philosophy; and the men who studied and taught these subjects were members of the Christian clergy. With this history, it's easy to see why natural scientists, once free, removed themselves far from anything implying religion. Claiming the physical for its realm, science banned God, or anything "supernatural," from the picture.

Bible-based, fundamentalist Christianity, with its belief in God as a human-like being who created everything physical, has always been materialist. It teaches that the Genesis story of creation is literally true, that every creature on Earth came out of the earth or the seas, and that Adam was created from the "dust of the ground"—and Eve from Adam's rib. All were creations and had no prior existence.

The scientists who established materialist science had this same Judeo-Christian foundation and lived under the intellectual control of popes and bishops.

When we understand that, we can begin to see that Western fundamentalist science and religion are more alike than either would like to think. We can see why materialism, rather than spirituality, has been the dominant belief system of our culture.

The Power of Belief

Although spiritual traditions and teachers have never lost sight of it, quantum and noetic scientists have recently begun to realize the power of belief. The fact that science is finally learning of it is significant, because once science propagates an idea, the public at large, informed by the media, is more apt to accept it.

TV programs such as *NCIS*, *CSI*, and *Bones*, demonstrate nightly how unique our individual DNA is, yet geneticists have recently realized that our beliefs have actually determined and can change our DNA pattern. Reportedly, only 7% of our DNA has been thought important in defining our physical makeup, with the remainder considered "junk DNA." But, scientists are beginning to see the significance of the 93% portion, saying we, what amounts to, program those genes with our beliefs. Those genes determine our health and who knows yet what else.

Think what this means. For one thing, we don't have to be in pain or sick if we don't want to. What we've been taught and programmed to believe about our mental, emotional, and physical health and our aging is false. We no longer need believe that as we chronologically age our body deteriorates. Every cell in our body is replaced annually, and doesn't have to be replaced with the same conditions.

Nor do we have to accept that physical and mental conditions are hereditary. If we believe these new ideas to be true, we can change whatever abnormality intrudes in our body, or in our thinking.

Exciting! Several books and audio/video presentations cover this, so I won't go further into it. Check out Bruce Lipton, Wayne Dyer, Gregg Braden, or Deepak Chopra for more details on this issue.

The important thing is, we can change our old beliefs. We don't have to keep them. They were useful yesterday, but may no longer be valuable or even valid. As we gain new beliefs, we can release old ones;

we can change our reality, if we want to. Check out the work of Ruth L. Miller for processes.

Our media all too often use sensationalism and scare tactics, focusing almost entirely on the horrific in an effort to get our exclusive attention. They play up disasters and distort events and people's words. Little of what they present accurately represents the facts, so who can tell what's fact or fiction? Yet, in an environment of fear, we raptly hang onto their every word as if true and valuable. They tell us how to behave and what to eat. And we do what they say.

They are irresponsibly greedy for higher ratings that draw advertisers to create a higher bottom line. We are stupid to permit them to control us. Reading the newspaper every morning, listening to the news whenever driving, and watching TV news every night fills us with negativity and makes us fearful.

Think about all this. If our beliefs truly do create our reality, what are we doing to our world by paying any attention to the media? We certainly couldn't be putting much positive influence out there to be reflected in our world. So, we are perpetuating a world that reflects the media's fearful sensationalism.

No matter what we say about something, what we believe about it determines how it affects us. For example, we may say we feel fine, but if at the same time we think "I wish!" or "except for...," what do you think will be our truth? We may pray for peace, but doubt it can ever be—and *voila*, we still have war! When we pray, if we doubt that the outcome will be as we wish, our wish will seldom come true. If we are sure of the outcome, we don't think to pray for it. So, nearly all of our prayers concern things we have doubts about, and can't help being self-fulfilling prophecies, This is why prayers of gratitude are encouraged over supplication prayers.

For more than a century, New Thought churches have taught the power of belief, through the "power of positive thinking," "mind over matter," and more, using affirmations in their practice. When accompanied by conviction, affirmations are very effective, so long as they are phrased in the present and as already fact, and are accompanied by consistently seeing no other possibility as reality. They are possibilities awaiting acceptance, making them our experience. The new sciences are putting a new intellectual acuity to this vital issue and are arriving at the same conclusion as the New Thought teachers, but with scientific proof that suggests that we truly are creating our experience.

---

² Mitchell, Edgar, quoted in "Worldview, Transformation, and the Development of Social Consciousness," by Marilyn Schlitz, C. V. Mandala, *The Noetic Post Journal*, Fall/Winter 2010. Petaluma, CA: Institute of Noetic Sciences.

³ Schlitz, Marilyn; Mandala, Cassandra Vieten; and Elizabeth Miller, "Worldview Transformation, and the development of social consciousness," *The Noetic Post Journal*, Fall/Winter 2010. Petaluma, CA: Institute of Noetic Sciences.

⁴ Lipton, Bruce and Steve Bhaerman, *Spontaneous Evolution, Our Positive Future*. Carlsbad, CA: Hay House, Inc., 2009.

⁵ The term "occult" means "hidden" and, while traditional Christians have given it a shade of evil, was once simply referring to the wisdom which only those who had been trained to understand had access to. In that sense, we could say that for most people, computer science and quantum mechanics are occult teachings.

⁶ The term "New Age" pertains to beliefs and predictions about a coming era, or Age of Light, in which cooperative spirituality, rather than competitive materialism, is the norm.

⁷ "BCE" means "before the common era," formerly called BC ("before Christ"). The years are numbered in the same way.

⁸ Higgins, Frank C., *Ancient Freemasonry*, quoted by Manly P. Hall in *The Secret Teachings of All Ages*. New York: Tarcher/Penguin, 2003.

Power and Energy in the Human Experience

Introduction

Humanity's energy is out of balance in its masculine and feminine expressions—not male and female; it isn't about gender. Instead, it's an influence in our collective unconscious causing us to believe and behave in certain ways as we go about our daily lives.

Yin & Yang: Receptive & Creative Energy

We all have both masculine (left brain, creative/expressive *yang* in Chinese Taoist tradition) and feminine (right brain, receptive/nurturing *yin*) expressions of energy. A long time ago, humanity's energy shifted away from the sacred feminine, causing us to experience the negative conditions of an off-balanced masculine state, including anger and aggressive behavior, resulting in abuse, genocide, and war. Individually, we've become fearful, defensive, and greedy, so emphasize competition and winning. We need to feel superior to and in control of others to feel safe. We seek power and wealth to insure survival in the greatest comfort and luxury.

The masculine, while strong and inventive, when over-balanced instills a reliance on intellect to the exclusion of intuition, and causes an emphasis on material possessions over spiritual expression: the outer over the inner. It supports militarism and incites crime, substance abuse, and political and economic corruption. It encourages a frenetic life style, and entails self-absorption, causing us to enjoy luxuries without regard for the cost to anyone or anything else. Decisions are made on the basis of profit and loss. Out of balance, the left brain process limits our thinking to a linear, materialist belief system, and brings out the overactive, rigid worst in us. When that happens, fear rules.

Too much feminine energy causes excessive emotion, indecision, submissiveness, and a focus on superficial beauty and intuition, rejecting anything intellectual or active. Life may appear calm only when it is dull and unproductive. When that happens, inertia rules.

In a balanced state—which the Taoist philosophy and indigenous cultures encourage—we are strong yet gentle, compassionate, kind, considerate, caring, and nurturing; flexible yet decisive, fair, and just. We're interested in what's good for all life on Earth and cannot even consider inappropriately harming another being. We're not critically judgmental, but peaceful, and open to spirituality. We draw equally from intuition and intellect, and are interested in learning. We're creative, inventive, and curious. Our emotions are on equal footing with reason. The outer is balanced by the inner. Love, as a powerful way of being, rules.

While the energy imbalance isn't determined by what gender our bodies are, it has influenced how we behave as women and men. In the over-balanced masculine state, a few men have dominated this world patriarchy for over two millennia. Their way is control, power, greed, and aggression. They have taken whatever they wanted without regard for the wellbeing of any other life on Earth or our environment. They fight for what they want, and against what they don't want.

They even seek to achieve peace through might; the stronger they are the more powerful and less vulnerable they feel. Their superior-seeming facade often hides a low self image, over compensating for the feminine traits that they perceive as inadequacies. They have brought us to the mess we're in.

Until fairly recently, women accepted that masculine dominance in our lives as a matter of course. Some still encourage it and some have chosen to emulate men in those over-balanced masculine ways.

Women in the patriarchal culture tend toward the feminine state, being more compassionate and nurturing than men. Instead of fighting, these women are more apt to seek peace through understanding and communication. They are more likely to care about the plight of others, are more holistic in their thinking, and are more spiritual.

Such women must now come forward to be leaders around the world, in business and in government. And, as leaders, they must let their feminine energy rule along with their masculine energy, in balance.

Men and women think and approach issues differently. But that doesn't mean one way is necessarily better than the other, they're just different. When one way dominates over the other, problems occur. We need both, balancing each other in full cooperation, to solve our world problems and make peace a reality.

Men whose energy is more balanced, who are in touch with their feminine side as well as the masculine, must also rise to the top. Bringing the compassionate ways of the feminine into the masculine hierarchy, together they will turn humanity around and stop patriarchal dominance and its destruction.

External Power and American Fear

Spiritual philosopher Gary Zukav says in *The Seat of the Soul* that our problems today stem from essentially two conditions: a perceived need for external power and a continual state of internal fear. He says that we live in survival mode, having been taught that it's normal and expected, believing we must control our environment and everyone around us. Our perceived security depends on our ability to control others. But we also are afraid of losing our power and control, not convinced we truly have either.[9]

Nationally, power struggles reinforce our insecurities, making us paranoid, so we look for enemies everywhere. Controlled by masculine energy, we Americans manufacture needs for greater might and greater wealth. We seek self-sufficiency and isolation to negate dependency. Rather than freely sharing our abundance, we are protective of what we have. Individually, our life is one competition after another, as we strive to be better than others. We seek wealth and amass material possessions so we can enjoy and show off our success, hoping to gain respect, even love. We feel powerful when we control another person. We're really scared children, trying to bolster a low self image. We haven't yet realized that love begins at home—in ourselves—and that the more we give the more we have to give.

---

[9] Zukov, Gary, *The Seat of the Soul*. New York, NY: A Fireside Book, Simon & Schuster, 1990.

Religious Beliefs

Introduction

Nothing has had as much influence on human experience as our religious beliefs—with mixed results. While much good has been done in the name of God, overwhelming evil has also been committed. Torture and genocide run throughout the history of Christianity, and much of the hatred and strife in the Western world today exists because adherents of different belief systems, even though they worship the same God, think only their beliefs are the true beliefs and only they are the true worshipers. Too many people have fed others to lions, stoned, burned, flogged, racked, and otherwise terrorized them—all because those others didn't conform to their beliefs.

The pilgrims who came to America did so for religious freedom, yet today religious intolerance runs rampant. Many people believe that if we don't join them in their beliefs we are at war with them. One might think that by now we would have learned that nothing can be solved through violence; yet the twentieth century was the bloodiest in history. Why haven't we found other ways of resolving differences, become more tolerant of our differences?

If the early Christian bishops had been less ambitious in achieving a universal institutional church or the Roman church had been less ruthless in gaining and maintaining its sovereignty, our world today would be less harsh. Had the teachings of Jesus prevailed as the Christian focus instead of miraculous stories about him, the Christian Bible might be understood today as being in accord with other ancient wisdom and our society might be very different. Spirituality might be filling us with compassion and tolerance.

If we were as creative in ways of resolving differences as we are in coercing conversion of dissidents, we might have a peaceful world today.

A Bit of Religious History

Until about 3500 BCE[10], women and men were equals in both their communities and activities. Then a new breed of men began diminishing women, even becoming abusive. Woman was often made the brunt of ridicule, scorn, and debauchery instead of a symbol of life, nurturing, and wisdom. Out of this new way of being the Hebrews created a patriarchal religion; Christianity carried it further and Islam further still, with men and masculine energy dominating *their descendants and converts ever since.*

*Before Ch*ristianity, most people had rituals, but not creeds and dogma. The people we call Pagans were not philosophical in their spirituality—that was limited to the intellectual elite. Appeasing the gods was important to the welfare of the community or empire, and failure to do so was seen as putting them in peril, so the leaders insisted on some worship of the gods, but religious tolerance was the norm.

Exclusive beliefs and dogmas entered the picture with Christianity and then Islam. Neither Jewish nor Eastern nor aboriginal traditions try to impose their beliefs on others.

Spiritual "Mysteries" existed in the pre-Judaic Pagan world and on into the common era (CE[11]), but their teachers were very selective of whom they initiated into those mysteries. The mysteries appealed to more serious and spiritual thinkers, like Pythagoras, Plato, Siddhartha Gautama, and Jesus, and they have continued into the present day, despite Christianity's efforts to eradicate them. Eastern spiritual traditions prevail strongly, and Western Metas are growing, with both groups reflecting wisdom common to the ancient Mysteries.

Almost two thousand years ago, the Roman church denied our spirituality and gave us patriarchal dogmatism based in fear and control. It instituted what many theological scholars now call the "Christ myth" and slaughtered as heretics and witches its Gnostic and Pagan competition who didn't accept that myth as fact. In their exclusivity and through their missionary practices, the Roman Catholic (which means "universal") leaders, and later Protestants, all but wiped out indigenous belief systems, worldwide.

Divisive fear- and guilt-driven dogma set modern humanity up for its competition- and conflict-orientation and judgmental tendencies.

Teaching that God is separate from the created world, Judaism, Christianity, and Islam caused humanity to see all life forms on Earth as separate entities, creating an "every person for him/herself" mentality and fostering a "survival of the fittest" approach to life.

Yet their guidance wasn't all bad. It gave us order, focus, and support, leading to many of the laws of the land we now follow. It gave us an almost touchable God to worship, fear, and love. It provided a structure and focus around which communities functioned socially, and it led to the founding of the United States and to its development as a nation and world leader.

Today, Biblical Christians[12], sometimes called Fundamentalists, dominate religion in America, and their involvement in politics makes their influence on American society substantial, but not necessarily in the best interests of life on Earth. They have taken their Roman roots to the extreme, calling all personal spiritual influences and intuition Satanic. Their leaders have convinced millions of American Protestants that the Bible is completely factual and error-free and is what God wanted us to know. Many of those leaders abuse their influence, imposing their own greed-driven, self-centered, ultraconservative political views on those who blindly follow them. Sadly, those views often run counter to basic human rights and well-being, and are destructive to Earth's finely-tuned eco-system.

The Non-Spirituality of Fundamentalist Religion

In mulling over the non-spirituality of the fundamentalist religions, I realized their foundation was materialist, not spiritual. When they came out of Egypt, the Israelites had only the barest memory of their forefathers' religion and learned only the outer, exoteric experience of Egyptian religious practice. They likely hadn't been privy to the spirituality of the inner, esoteric Mysteries, so didn't experience the spiritual wisdom of the ancients as they formed their new religion. As a result, their God, expressing human-like emotions and needs, was more human than spiritual.

By the time of the Roman empire, most Jews expected their Messiah to come and re-establish their material kingdom in Israel. Their scriptures reflected the mythic stories of surrounding cultures, and they focused on appeasement of their God through hundreds of laws of conduct in everyday life which they attributed to the man who led them out of Egypt, Moses.

Religious Fundamentalists and Metas

The Jews who founded Christianity had this materialist base and rejected the spirituality of other groups of Jesus followers. The founding apostle Paul's letters make it clear, and the church fathers apparently agreed, that their new religion would be more attractive to the Pagan public if they based it on myths and concepts familiar to the public, rather than the laws of Moses or the ancient Mysteries. They were probably thinking that the illiterate masses wouldn't understand spirituality, possibly not understanding the concept themselves. More than that, spirituality is a personal experience rather than a group one, so can't be easily shaped and controlled by ruling powers.

This non-spirituality explains many differences in worldviews between religious fundamentalists and Metas. To the fundamentalists, for example, we originated here on Earth. To the Metas, our origination is in the consciousness we call spirit.

This difference affects our views of both life and death. If we believe in the eternal life of our soul, we view salvation and ascension differently than do those who believe that at death we lie in a grave awaiting judgment, hoping to be saved and bodily resurrected, based on our beliefs and actions.

Biblical literalists view life and death as solely in God's purview, so they oppose abortion and euthanasia, even as they approve of war. Metas don't believe in death other than of our outer shell and ego, taken on for use in our experience of life on Earth. To Metas, our home is in spirit, from which our inner being has come and to which it will return, as a conscious, immortal, spirit being. Most Metas therefore view all of us as expressions (or extensions) of what is called God and, on some level, in control of both our life and our death, seeing no need for salvation other than perhaps getting free from cycles of reincarnation.

While Biblical literalists interpret the Bible as giving them dominion over Earth and all its creatures, Metas see themselves as caretakers enjoying the privilege of joint tenancy with other beings who are also aspects of the One.

Ethics and Morality — Social, not Spiritual Issues

While humanity might benefit from a check on its ethics and morality, much of Western religions' energy has been devoted to those issues, yet they have failed. And they don't take responsibility for that failure.

High ethical and moral standards can't be imposed from without, but must come from within. Such behavior is natural to individuals with self-respect and a supportive belief system.

Insisting we all were born with a sinning nature, power-driven Christian leaders imposed strict moral values on us, made us feel guilty, and damaged our self-image. If we were more spiritual, understanding ourselves to be true "children of God" and as the founding apostle Paul tells us "joint heirs with Christ," our self-respect would be higher and so would our ethics and morals.

Moreover, with higher self-respect would come less judging and less need to impose ones moral values on others. Spirituality, therefore, fosters the nonjudgmental acceptance of love for everyone as they are.

Interpreting Scriptures

The Hebrew Scriptures, Christian New Testament, and Islamic Qur'an were all written and canonized to satisfy the practical, more than spiritual, needs of institutional religions as they were forming. The books of the Bible were organized during Roman Emperor Constantine's Nicene Council to provide a common doctrine or dogma that would set the Christian Church as an institution of the Roman Empire and maintain power for its bishops. Some parts were used to support the patriarchy, while others were used to emphasize morality and are often used today to judge people as "sinners." Other parts of the Bible, which could be interpreted more spiritually, are largely ignored within fundamentalist and "mainline" churches.

It's said that esoteric truths are hidden in the symbolism of biblical myths, the messages behind the words. If that's so, then literal reading of biblical scripture is a deterrent to understanding spiritual "truths." For example, in saying "Seek ye first the kingdom of God" (Luke 12:31), Jesus, knowing God's kingdom is within each of us, is imploring us to go within to find God. The great Hindu teacher Ramana Maharshi said: "The whole of wisdom is contained in two biblical statements: 'I am that I AM' and 'Be still and know that I am God.'"[13]

There are also different ways of understanding ancient wisdom stories. For example, describing the creation of Eve from Adam's rib could have been a way of relating the diminishing of our feminine energy. Adam may initially have been the embodiment of a balance between the masculine and feminine, and creating Eve from Adam's rib signifies the separation and subsequent dominance of masculine energy. Maybe these varying interpretations explain why there are two versions of human creation in Genesis, causing us to wonder and seek understanding.

Religious Tolerance

While many of us believe in religious tolerance and would like to see all peoples everywhere free to worship as they please, it's important to understand—without agreeing with—those who oppose it.

Fundamentalist Jews, Christians, and Muslims each believe wholeheartedly that they—and only they—have the correct point of view; only they behave justly; only they will survive the coming apocalypse and end-time judgment. Fundamentalist Christians and Muslims both believe that religious tolerance is in opposition to everything they stand for. For Christians, this is a carryover from early bishops' efforts to make Christianity universal by "winning souls to Christ" and to gain and maintain power by being exclusive. For Muslims and Christians alike, it's a matter of salvation: only those who follow their path will be saved.

Christian and Muslim fundamentalist leaders are therefore understandably threatened by religious tolerance, and can't afford to accept it—their livelihood and power are at stake. If, for instance, hell is removed as a threat and anyone can go to heaven, who needs a savior? Why would anyone need to be baptized? Why follow Christianity?

Other traditions, as well as mystics within Christianity, Islam, and Judaism, teach that there are many roads to God, and it doesn't really matter which one a person takes, only that they take one.

We are all unique individuals who live under a huge variety of conditions and circumstances. We have grown up in different cultures, nations, and levels of wealth and poverty, education, and health. We each have needs that are different from others' needs, and we don't think or react to our world alike. Our differences enrich humanity, so we would be wise to appreciate our diversity.

Wisdom is all around us, but we must look with open minds and hearts. When we do so, it seems possible that each system of belief has only a portion of the story of God and humanity, and only by learning about and understanding all of them might we get the whole picture.

Undoing the Mess: Religion

We need religion to serve as an expression of spirituality that helps humanity off its path to destruction, not a continuation of the religious intolerance that fostered today's conditions. Instead of fostering discrimination and bigotry, we need religions that are supportive of all people in all situations and behaviors.

Too often people who need moral support from a church get ostracism, even excommunication. Infractions of church rituals and dogma are often considered greater sins against God than disobeying the Ten Commandments, and both are often emphasized by Christians over the love-and-forgiveness teachings of Jesus. Rather than idolizing those who showed them the way, religions might teach the ideals that their way-showers taught and demonstrated.

A place of worship should never fail an individual or society. Religion must become an accepting, harmonious source of help to those in need of kindness, solace, nonjudgmental acceptance, and a nurturing community. Everyone should be able to expect unconditional kindness, compassion, and emotional support in their sacred places—the congregations as well as their leaders.

Rather than judgmental moralizing, religions might better concern themselves with spiritual interpretation of scriptural symbolism and ancient wisdom, and with helping people find meaning and purpose in their lives. Religion's job could now be to unite the inhabitants of this world in peace, understanding, and love. They could preach concern for the environment and inter-species respect and care.

They might focus their efforts on creating a unified world community concerned with inter-cultural, inter-racial, and inter-faith peace and understanding. Some do now, through such organizations as the Interfaith Alliance and the International New Thought Alliance. Interfaith seminaries training and ordaining a new type of minister are emerging all over, from New York City to Portland, Oregon, from India to Jerusalem. In *Beyond the Indigo Children*, P.M.H. Atwater says:

> They are taking us toward honoring the underlying truth found in all religions, fusing feminine and masculine polarities, and making plain

that a religion that cannot be questioned is a religion of man, not of God.[14]

You may think my indictment of fundamentalist religions is judgmental, but I'm only stating the facts as I see them, and don't mean to suggest blame. They have provided the perfect foundation for our growth of these past two millennia. But, now we need to move away from materialist beliefs. To help us do so, I thought we would benefit from seeing the fundamentalist religions in a more objective light than they present themselves. So, that is my aim both here and in the religious perspective in the next part.

Reverend Jim Rosemergy (of the Unity Institute) expressed my feelings when, as related by Atwater, he said: "I long for the day when the statement, 'Our God is love, our race is human, and our religion is oneness,' is more than the musings of my mind, but is the creed of the heart of the human family"[15]

---

[10] "BCE" means "before the common era," formerly called BC ("before Christ") in the social sciences.

[11] CE is the abbreviation for "Common Era," which replaces A.D. (anno Domini, meaning "year of our Lord") in the social sciences.

[12] "Biblical Christian" is an umbrella term I use for Protestants who say they read the Bible literally, constituting a religion in America of over 42 million people, and as many as 159 million worldwide.

[13] Quoted in *The Essence of Wisdom*: words from the masters to illuminate the spiritual path by Stephen Mitchell. NY: Broadway Books.

[14] Atwater, P.M.H., *Beyond the Indigo Children*. Rochester, VT: Bear & Co., 2005

[15] Rosemergy, James, quoted by P.M.H. Atwater in *Beyond the Indigo Children*. Rochester, VT: Bear & Co., 2005.

Scientific Beliefs

Introduction

The term "science" as used in this book includes the academic sciences, governmental military sciences, independent laboratory development and research, and corporate product development. It may be theoretical or applied, addressing the physical, life, or social sciences, and includes the mainly applied engineering and health sciences.

All of our things—technologies, pharmaceuticals, weaponry—are produced through applied corporate or military science. Theories, research, discoveries, and testing pertaining to our understanding of the universe and forces governing it, Earth, and all life, are generally the purview of secular academic science.

"Orthodox" is an umbrella term I use for materialist academic physical sciences based on the classical Newtonian view, as well as the life and social sciences applying Darwinian evolution theories. I often substitute "mainstream," "conventional," or "Darwinism" for orthodox. I call "alternative" those scientists whose beliefs are unorthodox.

Mainstream Science

Influenced by Cartesian ideas, 17th-century Newtonian physics set the doctrine that all that exists is material and directed by a few physical laws of nature. That understanding saw the solar system and life on Earth as machines, like clockworks, but in time came to see them as without a designer or creator.

Naturalism and materialism became the foundational beliefs of Orthodox science. Naturalism insists that all beings and events in the universe are natural, with no supernatural influence, and can be fully understood through scientific methods. Materialism says matter is the only reality, and all beings, processes, and phenomena can be explained as manifestations of matter.

While physics and the other "hard" sciences are based on Newton's theories, Charles Darwin's "natural selection" theory was the foundation for the life and social sciences.

These theories are the bases for most science done in the last hundred and fifty years. In its extreme, this form of science is held like a religion, referred to as "scientism," defined derogatorily by science philosopher Massimo Pigliucci as

> an ideological position implying that science is the only key to solve any problem worth addressing, and that, given enough time and resources, science in fact will solve those problems.[16]

Believers in this "religion" are atheists who insist there is no direction or creator, no supernatural laws or processes, no life after death or pre-life, and no reason for our being here; everything happens randomly by chance. Matter is all that's real. This view, still predominant in our Western culture, is my focus when considering the belief system associated with modern science.

Science's Materialist Background

Had it not been for their restricted Christian foundation, scientists' view of what is natural might be very different today. Indeed, most of our beliefs about life might be very different.

The scientists who formalized natural science in the 1700s, sometimes called the Age of Reason, started with the materialist foundation and consciousness of the Christian culture in which they were raised. Rejecting the Genesis story as irrational, most also excluded the only supernatural element in the religion from which they were breaking away: God. From this base, they became thoroughly indoctrinated in the belief that every form of life came out of the earth and was separate and fighting for survival.

Fact or Faith?

Orthodox scientists would probably deny that theirs is a belief system, insisting instead that it is acceptance of evident facts. But some of their basic theories seem as much a matter of faith as of fact. Consider, for example, the ideas that:

- All matter and energy exploded into being in one Big Bang;
- Life occurred on Earth by spontaneous generation from inanimate matter;

- New species, even new genera, develop from existing species through random genetic mutation;
- All species evolved from one primordial form, their physical bodies built up in an additive process.

They believe these assumptions to be true, but are they?

The scientific method involves a constant expansion of the realm of knowledge. Each successful experiment is expected to lead to new questions; new knowledge is gained, new theories are accepted, and new possibilities become evident. Often the new information completely contradicts the assumptions of previous generations. Then, as Thomas Kuhn tells us in *The Structure of Scientific Revolutions*, even when thoroughly tested and proven, much of the newest scientific thinking is not accepted by old guard scientists who have come to depend on their old beliefs. This leads to an ongoing tension between those who cling to what was once considered to be true and those who accept what must now be understood as basic premises.

The Applied Sciences

We know much more now than the first scientists who broke away from the Roman church, in large part because of the discoveries and theories of mainstream science. And applied science, the use of those discoveries and theories in industry, has made life so much easier, more enjoyable, more productive, longer, and healthier, has brought world populations closer together, and made the universe more accessible.

Unfortunately, though, there's also a downside to applied science's contributions. For one thing, it's much easier to kill each other in very large numbers. And, while many of us enjoy an easier life, portions of humanity are exploited and our environment is being devastated.

Applied science's improvements have not been uniform throughout humanity, creating huge gaps between those who prosper and those who have little. Whole segments of humanity have been ignored, because to provide for them wouldn't be profitable for the industries using the science. Much of what has been accomplished has been done irresponsibly out of greed, leaving Earth's natural resources diminished, her ozone damaged, her air and water polluted, and dump-sites strewn over her surface with toxins that may never be eliminated.

Technologies are far ahead of our ability to know how to responsibly use them, and we've no idea how to dispose of the toxic residue from our industries' production of them or of our discards. These effects of our ignorance and indifference have the potential to destroy all Earth inhabitants. They have destroyed many other life forms, and put more at risk daily. We've allowed it.

Indifferent to these side-effects, we buy ever more industrial products and innovations without demanding environmental protection, human and animal rights, or corporate responsibility. Because we enjoy what the applied sciences provide us, we ignore the misbehavior of the corporations that promote them.

So applied science has helped foster the negative aspects of capitalism that make us self-absorbed, fearful, and greedy. It has encouraged us to be materialist, with an emphasis on owning "things" that ultimately get discarded and become toxic waste. The destruction is almost impossible to conceive. We may have to lose it all before we wake up.

Traditional Science

Secular academic science, the purveyor of materialist science, has also influenced our worldviews in negative ways. Its focus on "survival of the fittest" has encouraged a masculine mindset and survival beliefs that cause us to be self-absorbed, so we put ourselves above all else. They cause us to be fearful and protective of what we consider ours, and dictate our need to control our environment and everyone in it. They make us possessive and militant, individually and nationally, and direct us toward amassing arms, wealth, and possessions to give us a sense of security. When we don't succeed, we become angry, belligerent, and abusive. We abuse substances to ease our pain of failure, and we hunger for control and power.

Science's tendency to dissect things into independent parts has substantially affected our worldview in both scary and faulty ways, as well. In *The Holographic Universe,* Michael Talbot says that quantum physicist David Bohm "believes that our almost universal tendency to fragment the world and ignore the dynamic interconnectedness of all things is responsible for many of our problems," not only in science but in our lives and our society as well. For instance,

> ...we believe we can extract the valuable parts of the earth without affecting the whole. We believe it is possible to treat parts of our body and not be concerned with the whole. We believe we can deal with

various problems in our society, such as crime, poverty, and drug addiction, without addressing the problems in our society as a whole.... Bohm argues passionately that our current way of fragmenting the world into parts not only doesn't work, but may even lead to our extinction.[17]

Orthodox science contends that a handful of material laws govern the physical and explain all its processes through a research method based on taking things apart, called reductionism.[18] But, the Tibetan spiritual leader known as the 14th Dalai Lama tells us:

> In this view many dimensions of the full reality of what it is to be human, art, ethics, spirituality, goodness, beauty, and above all, consciousness, either are reduced to the chemical reaction of firing neurons or are seen as a matter of purely imaginary constructs.... The problem is... with the contention that these data alone constitute the legitimate ground for developing a comprehensive world-view or an adequate means for responding to the world's problems.[19]

He wonders if humanity is clear about the place of science in our life, what exactly it should do and how it should be governed. "[U]nless guided by a consciously ethical motivation, especially compassion," its effects may cause great harm. New technologies

> ...create new conditions and ...give rise to new ethical and spiritual challenges, the emergence of new reality.... What matters above all is the motivation that governs the use of science and technology, in which ideally heart and mind are united.[20]

The New Sciences

Fortunately, less rigid and more expansive sciences are strengthening and changing the ways scientists view life. Noetic biologist Bruce Lipton says that applying reductionism to world problems "has hastened our apparent demise." He adds:

> It's a simple fact that society cannot sustain itself by continuing to adhere to its current worldview. So leading-edge research is questioning fundamental assumptions long held as dogma by conventional science.[21]

In *Spontaneous Evolution,* Lipton and Bhaerman tell us that quantum physicist Max Planck

...also questioned the emphasis on reductionism, saying that in order to understand the nature of the Universe, we must abandon reductionism and, instead, turn to holism, wherein everything interacts with everything else.[22]

In the mid-1950s, physicist Hugh Everett introduced a theory dealing with vertical time, in which there are layers of parallel universes. With experiences awaiting our focus, these "choice points" keep us from being locked into any particular outcome.

Computer-scientist-turned-spiritual-teacher Gregg Braden tells us we can claim the experience we want: "We can focus our awareness in vertical time to make the quantum leap from one road to a new road of our choice."[23] The Hebrew prophet Isaiah, says Braden, wrote of two different futures for humanity—one leading to utter annihilation, the other to fulfillment and awakening—and may have been letting us know we aren't tied to only one destiny. We are at that crossroads and must choose.[24]

Braden adds that Einstein believed that time is not at all what it seems. "Time," Einstein said,

> does not flow in only one direction. The future simultaneously exists with the past. In this moment, time exists in many possibilities, each with a different outcome or potential.[25]

Lipton and Bhaerman write that "Einstein showed that atoms are actually not made out of matter, but consist of nonmaterial energy."[26] They say this means that the long-standing beliefs of Newtonian science—that matter, or "physical objects," is the foundation of all that exists—is "an elaborate illusion!" In contrast, they tell us, "Einstein's unified theory proposed that the Universe is one indivisible dynamic whole wherein all physical parts and energy fields are entangled and interdependent...."[27]

Our Choices and Science's Responsibility

Science has given us the tools to bring about the biblical Armageddon, either through world warfare or as the result of environmental ruination. But neither scenario need occur. We are beginning to wake up and realize where we are headed, with many of us choosing a new path, turning toward spirituality and seeking enlightenment, shifting our consciousness.

It's not science in general I criticize as harmful, but rather any greed-driven applied science and rigidly materialist mainstream orthodox science. We need the responsible technological advancement and skeptical, critical examination of all forms of science, unfettered by preconceived ideas. But we also need the wisdom and compassion of spirituality to balance the knowledge, invention, and application of the sciences—our heart and head in balance.

Undoing the Mess: Science

To move toward a solution, money and the mega-corporations' profits must no longer dictate how we acquire goods or address our problems and needs. Industrial, applied scientists and the corporations that hire them must think beyond profit motivation, and academics must think beyond the doctrines of Orthodox science. Academic scientists have to allow themselves to investigate the spirituality of ancient cultures, and thereby enable us to better understand our life and learn of the ancients' biodegradable, nontoxic, sustainable technologies (some based on archeology and some intuitively reported) so that applied science can replicate them. Science (all forms) must be ethical in its research and must take responsibility for its products and its influence on humanity at large.

Scientists must allow themselves to go beyond orthodox theories. After all, what is natural and what is supernatural? Do we really know? Isn't it possible that the supernatural is only the natural not yet understood?

Most of us can probably agree that politics and the special interests of a greedy, power-hungry, self-serving few must be put aside, with consideration given to the greater good for all Earth inhabitants. We must find ways to stop pollution, poverty, exploitation and abuse of any segment of our world community, and squandering of natural resources. We can no longer afford to think only of ourselves, our creature comforts, and our status in the community. We must consider the good of all worldly inhabitants.

If we were willing to give up the larger luxuries and change our lifestyle, we could end the pollution and abuse committed in their making. Those of us who have a lot could share with those who have little. We could put effort into providing equal opportunities for all humans for food, clothing, education, good health, dignity, and prosperity. We could care, and we could recognize the importance of self respect, and foster and nurture it in our fellow humans.

We can't and shouldn't be forced to do these things, but we might want to do them. If we don't care about others, we might at least realize that our current behavior and attitudes are ensuring our own eventual demise. But also, as we become more spiritually oriented, we will be ever more heart-centered. Then to do such will be our natural inclination. Recognizing our Oneness, we will care about others as ourselves. We need to see all life worthy of our care and concern. And, it's essential for our survival that a goal of highest quality of life for all begins to replace profit as our new bottom line.

---

[16] Pigliucci, M. "The Sin of Scientism" *Skeptical Inquirer,* Nov-Dec, 2003. Amherst, MA: CSICOP

[17] Talbot, Michael, *The Holographic Universe.* New York, NY: HarperCollins, 1991

[18] Reductionism is the attempt to explain all processes by the laws that chemists and physicists use to interpret inanimate matter; also a procedure or theory that reduces complex data or phenomena to simple terms.

[19] The Dalai Lama, *The Universe in a Single Atom.* Morgan Road Books, 2005.

[20] Ibid.

[21] Lipton, Bruce, "Embracing the Immaterial Universe," *Shift: at the Frontiers of Consciousness*, December 2005-February 2006. Petaluma, CA: Institute of Noetic Sciences.

[22] Lipton, Bruce and Steve Bhaerman, *Spontaneous Evolution, Our Positive Future.* Carlsbad, CA: Hay House, Inc., 2009.

[23] Braden, Gregg, *Speaking the Lost Language of God.* Niles, IL: Injoi Corporation, 2004.

[24] Ibid.

[25] Ibid.

[26] Lipton, Bruce and Steve Bhaerman, *Spontaneous Evolution, Our Positive Future.* Carlsbad, CA: Hay House, Inc., 2009.

[27] Ibid.

Academia's Influence on Our Beliefs

Introduction

Much of my very fulfilling career was in academia where I was responsible for academic planning on my university campus (UCLA), so I have a certain understanding about American education I would like to share. I believe secular university academia must take responsibility along with fundamentalist religion and science for our current worldview and resulting problems.

Although different from the previous two subjects in that it isn't in itself a belief system, academia's influence on our beliefs is enormous. Academia teaches teachers how and what to teach, business people how to conduct business, other professionals how to perform in their chosen area of expertise, and researchers how to conduct experiments, report findings, and investigate others' conclusions in their field. It gets us at all levels, from the time children start school to when medical practitioners, lawyers, and other professionals begin their careers, and Ph.D.s go into teaching and/or research in higher education, industrial laboratories, or business.

With all that influence, the expressed beliefs of instructors and professors affect us at all levels and facets of society, at least to the extent we take them in and make them our own.

I had hoped, since it has been many years since I left it, conventional academia would have mitigated its narrowness, exclusivity, and materialist science's dominance, but everything I read and hear as I write this says otherwise. So, I will relate what I understand to be the case. Of course, since my observations are general, there are many exceptions, hopefully more now than earlier.

A Narrow Focus

While religious doctrines are the bases for theological academia, science is the ideal of secular academia. Secular higher education has taught orthodox scientific theories as the only way to think since the late 1800s, and American public school science classes have taught them since the 1960s. Most scientists today base their work on them, taking them for granted, without question. Most other disciplines automatically apply the Orthodox science line of thought and method in their own work. So, despite the fact that quantum scientists of the early 20th century, such as Albert Einstein and Max Planck, were convinced that material form is illusion and should be understood holistically, most scientists still cling to the reductionist-materialist view and continue to study and conduct research piecemeal.

As a result, by the time most students reach the dissertation stage of their Ph.D. programs, academia has channeled them into an extremely narrow focus within their specialty, within their subject, within their field, within their discipline. Then those with Ph.D.s carry that narrowness into their chosen professions. A university biologist, for example, can spend his or her entire teaching and research career focused on a single genus, such as finches or wheat, and never see the larger picture. While there are individual and institutional exceptions, that narrowness is so ingrained that many professors know or care little about other subjects.

Geologist Trevor Popp reports that, in *Science Matters,* professor of earth sciences Robert Hazen blames scientists for the profession's insistence on niches. Universities and high schools teach one science at a time, which means most biologists lack a basic understanding of physics, most astronomers don't know much about genetics, and so forth: "Even the highest-level scientists are illiterate in the most abysmal way."[28] Popp says Hazen believes "the goal of general science education should be to enable specialists and lay people alike" to

> read the newspaper—read about environmental issues, energy issues, a new medical advance, the discovery of a fossil whale—and put that into a broad context of historical relevance, so that these new discoveries fit into a bigger matrix... of knowledge.[29]

Academia's narrowness has become the predominant way of Western thinking, causing a narrow worldview and approach to problem solving. While a few interdisciplinary subjects, such as ecology and cosmology, have formed to consider a broader, more holistic picture, most of us are stuck in a symptomatic, piecemeal, Band-Aid approach to problem solving, generally, as in health care.

Surveys taken in the late 1990s found that only seven percent of American adults are scientifically literate. In *The Myth of Scientific Literacy*, Morris Shamos says he "is pessimistic" that

> the traditional approach to science education, with its... tendency toward compartmentalization by sub-discipline, could boost the scientific literacy level to a level sufficient to sustain intelligent public debate over an issue like global warming....[30]

Philosopher Buckminster Fuller says:

> Of course, our failures are a consequence of many factors, but possibly one of the most important is the fact that society operates on the theory that specialization is the key to success, not realizing that specialization precludes comprehensive thinking."[31]
>
> We are at an age that assumes the narrowing trends of specialization to be logical, natural and desirable. ... [H]umanity has been deprived of comprehensive understanding. Specialization has bred feelings of isolation, futility, and confusion in individuals. It has also resulted in the individual's leaving responsibility for thinking and social action to others. Specialization breeds biases that ultimately aggregate as international and ideological discord, which, in turn, leads to war.[32]

A perceptive and wise man, Fuller!

We will never understand our life from a narrow focus, and won't resolve our world problems except holistically, across disciplines. Far too much information is available now to stick to a narrow focus and detail orientation. We can't see the big picture from a level of minutiae and reductionist materialism; it's not possible to achieve a new level from which to understand our life and address its problems effectively.

The Accepted Line of Thought

Establishment academics limit what is "acceptable" to study or teach, denying altogether alternative or unorthodox positions. These academics consider themselves the intellectual elite, and if it's not orthodox, it has no value. Even some ideas acceptable within traditional academia, orthodox scientists in academia negate. They ignore most engineering, for example, because it's an applied science. Interdisciplinary fields of study such as earth sciences or cybernetics are often looked down on by faculty in traditional disciplines as too general. They also look down on the arts, business schools, and teacher education—they don't rigorously follow the method and principles of orthodox science.

There is also always a currently accepted line of thinking, such as Darwinian and Newtonian materialism. Academia is built on a hierarchy of professorships, and any idea at variance with the prevailing position of those at the top is at least tacitly discouraged. Also, academia is a very prestige-oriented community—"publish or perish" is the rule. As a result, professors are apt to be secretive about their research, lest someone were to publish their idea before they do. This means sharing of ideas and open discussion amongst peers is not common practice—there's very little "collegiality" on most university campuses. As a result, new ideas and direction in related fields or disciplines may not be known about, much less considered.

Once academics accept a theory, they are slow to accept new ones or evidence that would make them rethink what they consider to be fact. To avoid being ostracized by their peers, most academics think and work hard before proposing a new theory. For example, as amazing as it seems, even Albert Einstein added a constant to one set of equations that would support the prevailing view of a static universe. It took over ten years for Edwin Hubble's proof of continued expansion to change the minds of orthodox science. Einstein said later that changing his equations was the "biggest blunder" of his life.

The Influence of Outside Funding

One reason for academia's adoption of orthodox science's views is funding. Beyond faculty salaries, academic research gets little or no state support, so all secular universities rely heavily on federal and private grants, contracts, and donations. The sciences, in particular, rely on grants from federal agencies and contracts with private research corporations, both of which are very specific as to what they will and will not support. For example, according to retired chemistry professor Henry H. Bauer, "Since corporate scientific organizations also control the funding of research, by denying funds for unorthodox work, they function as research cartels as well as knowledge monopolies."[33] The National Science Foundation provides funds in a similar fashion, and the Pentagon funds a great deal of science from a militaristic orthodox perspective.

An institution's ability to attract top faculty and researchers depends on both its reputation and its relationship to funding agencies. Also, top candidates for faculty teaching and/or research positions have to bring with them the ability to attract outside funding. If an institution and its faculty want federal and corporate funding—and they all do—they have to toe the orthodox line. All of this keeps academia focused on maintaining the conventional status quo. So, to a large extent, funding agencies actually determine academic study and what the public gets through education.

Avoiding the Supernatural

If their materialism isn't true, what can the orthodox replace it with that doesn't involve what they consider the supernatural?

Dean Radin, senior researcher at the Institute of Noetic Sciences, reports in the film, *What the Bleep Do We Know: Further Down the Rabbit Hole,* that academic science holds that a belief in the supernatural stems from a lack of education (equated in the academic mind with a lack of intelligence). Not until later, pursuing their own interests, might tenured professors think beyond academic constraints, but apparently not openly even then. Radin says many academics are secretly interested in paranormal sorts of things, but have to keep such interests to themselves because the current academic climate discourages them from openly discussing them. Only those willing to risk ostracism come out. He says that when more open, we may find that more than half of academia is interested in the paranormal or supernatural.[34]

If that happens, what's acceptable will change.

Consider how academia's avoidance of the supernatural affects its general application. In medicine and psychology, near-death experiences (NDEs) are scorned as just instances of the brain seeking oxygen; children who have "imaginary" friends, as well as UFO abductees, are discouraged from talking about their experiences, a stance harmful to the psychological wellbeing of people with those experiences, whether adults or children.

How will we ever know the truth of such issues from a closed position? To avoid dualism, scientists study consciousness only as a product of activity in the material brain. With this approach they will never understand it or life generally.

Public School Education

American students are poorly educated in comparison with students in the major countries around the world. But rather than find ways to improve students' education, many schools have instituted ways to enable ill-prepared students to graduate, slanting the statistics to show improvement. In the process, limited funds are shifted away from helping dedicated students learn more.

Allowed to twitter, text, or talk on their phone in class, many public school students are more interested in playing than in learning; the classroom environment is often anything but a learning one. What does all this say about our nation's future? It must change.

Teachers can't possibly convey all knowledge to all students, and shouldn't try.

It's a mistake to underestimate any student's native intelligence. Today's youth may know better than the adults around them what they need and from which subjects and approaches they could gain the most benefit. Students could be encouraged to participate in curriculum planning, at least to give input to it.

We are reportedly experiencing a remarkable evolutionary advancement, in which the majority of children born since around 1980 are more intelligent and more assertive than previous generations. Many are said to have come into this life remembering their spirituality and remain in conscious touch with the spiritual longer than their predecessors, and indefinitely if encouraged to do so.[35] They may have trouble reconciling orthodox science with their own knowledge of the spiritual, so, orthodox science, closed against anything supernatural, may cause a decline in science students.

Most academics don't take such reports seriously because they run contrary to orthodox evolutionary theories. This seems especially sad considering the intelligence that could be put toward a sustainable future through science, as well as greater understanding of the workings of matter and what truly is natural. The new sciences may well attract these youths, and benefit us all. The academic establishment would do well to examine the empirical evidence, even if it's not academic, regarding today's youth.

Humanity is evolving into higher level beings. In the popular literature they're sometimes called "indigo children" or, for more recent births, "crystal children." Each new generation may be more intelligent—or have different kinds of information access—than the previous one. Students are often more intelligent than their teachers—not a comment against the teachers—the best of whom accept that fact and are willing to help students learn rather than try to teach them.

Until this issue is effectively addressed throughout the system, students will continue to challenge their teachers, and our youth will continue to be poorly educated in public schools. Many disruptive students have been erroneously diagnosed with attention disorders and given drugs to calm them. They're not sick, they're bored. They may need only to have their minds stimulated.

Academia & the Media

The many forms of media, like academia, are extremely influential in our culture—too often in ways not beneficial to life on this planet. Again, like academia, the news and related media largely dictate our "knowledge" of science and our views along political, economic, health, and human rights lines; they add substantially to our worldviews. What academia doesn't directly teach us, the media provide indirectly. And because they consider academics "the authorities" on everything, mainstream media promote orthodox academia's materialist view of life, acting almost as academia's continuing education arm.

That materialist view is not only limited, but could well be false, giving us at most half the picture. To understand ourselves and Earthly life, we must expand our knowledge and our thinking more generally to include the supernatural or spiritual. I believe the spiritual will eventually prove to be the more natural. But without examining it, we'll never know!

Fortunately, there are audio/video production companies focusing on the work of "independent scholars" and "alternative researchers", which at least open the door for some consideration of different assumptions.

Undoing the Mess: Academia

To the extent that orthodox science influences academia and that academia influences us and our belief systems, people in our culture will not understand our life. Mainstream science insists that, to be science, a study has to rely solely on observations, evidence, or experience with naturalistic explanations. But so long as they deny anything outside those parameters mainstream scientists will never fully understand life on Earth. Without that understanding, destructive worldviews and our global ills will continue until we destroy all life.

To end this pattern, learning and study must not be limited in any way. A new kind of teacher and new methods are needed, so teacher education needs to change substantially. Teachers at all levels, from kindergarten through the doctorate, must be open to learning new things, even if it's from their students. They have to encourage their students to think outside the proverbial boxes of conventional thinking. A little humility on the part of professors and teachers would help; they don't have to have all the answers.

To better respond to the needs of tomorrow's children, secular academia must completely revamp itself at all levels. The educational system must become flexible and responsive, itself evolving. We've had such an explosion of knowledge in the last fifty years that minutiae don't need to be taught—they can be found on any cell-phone with access to Google, Yahoo, or any other search engine. Rather than trying to be "current" in teaching, perhaps teachers could direct students to internet updates, controversies, and alternative views. Instead of relying on outdated textbooks, maybe the internet should be students' source for information.

Public education might better emphasize breadth rather than depth, which can always be gained through focusing one's individual interests and life pursuits. Students might be exposed to ranges of ideas without delving deeply into any.

Academia may not realize its sphere of influence, but it must do so and be more responsible for the content and nature of its teaching. Academia must lead humanity into a new openness, with innovative, visionary, and holistic paradigms for understanding life on Earth. Once we understand life, we will more easily deal with our world problems and not create such dire ones in the future.

A New High School Philosophy Class

Rather than high school students being prepared for college, careers, or employment, their interests and imaginations could be piqued. They could be taught to enjoy learning and how and where to learn more about what interests them. High school education might be understood as introductory—to knowledge generally and to adult life. Ideally education would be holistic, viewing the big picture and crossing disciplines, and could be problem-solving and project-oriented, in which students learn in context with some aspect of life, situation, or problem.

As an example, I propose a new high school course on our belief systems, covering the big issues of life philosophically. Although philosophy is not currently a high school subject, such a course might be very appealing to the youth of tomorrow.

Darwinists and creationists battle over what's taught in public school science classes about our origin and beginnings. And, since we need to better understand each other, a class on these belief systems could well accomplish the goals I'm suggesting.

The course could let students examine from many perspectives some fundamental philosophical issues, such as: the nature of reality—is it strictly material or might it be spiritual? Does God exist, and if so, as a being, principle, higher intelligence, or...? What is our relationship to that God? Did our world come into being with cause and purpose or by happenstance? From where and how did matter arise? How did life on Earth in its various forms, especially human, come about and develop? Does our life have purpose?

The views must represent nonacademic as well as academic approaches and take into account ancient wisdom, metaphysical, physical, "supernatural," and "natural" perspectives.

Comparative discussion might be the meat of the course. It could be required for students going on to college, and might be offered without grading or credit as an option for those who don't need or want credit, encouraging some students to take the course when they might not otherwise.

In a section of comments from teenagers in *Beyond the Indigo Children,* P.M.H. Atwater quotes a sixteen-year-old, Tori:

> ...I don't want to know what they are teaching us in school, all the useless information that is drilled endlessly at us, all the information that we regurgitate on tests. I don't want to know that! I want to know why we can't go inside a black hole, and do other life-forms exist? I want to know if there is a God and what created stuff in the beginning?

What made it all start? Where the hell did matter come from? Questions are the main thing in my mind lately, and I can't get them answered.[36]

Students needn't wait for college to study philosophy—and in fact they are studying it all the time, without the tools to assess their findings. What better mechanism is there for stimulating young thought processes, especially about such important and popular subjects and prevalent questions?

Besides, they won't get the more esoteric philosophies in today's college environment. This course would be offered to them at a time when their minds are inquisitive about big issues, and they may be seeking direction and their own belief system. They could be asking the same questions we adults are, and likely several more.

Most teenagers have no idea what they want to do with their life. This course could excite their interest and help them find direction. And, it would introduce students to the spirituality of the ancients as well as modern Metas. It would not muddy the waters between church and state, because it would be an academic course *about* religion and spirituality, as well as science, not a devotional one.

---

[28] Popp, Trevor, "America's Double Trouble" *Science & Spirit,* Sept-Oct, 2007, quoting Robert Hazen, *Science Matters*

[29] Ibid.

[30] Ibid.

[31] Fuller, R. Buckminster, quoted by The Quotation Page at www.quotationpage.com, 2016.

[32] Fuller, R. Buckminster, *The Wellspring of Reality*, quoted by Wikiquote at http://en.wikiquote.org, 2016.

[33] Bauer, Henry H., quoted by Trish Riley, "Why the Bleep?! *Shift*, December 2005 to February 2006. Petaluma, CA: Institute of Noetic Sciences.

[34] Radin, Dean, interviewed in *What the Bleep Do We Know: Further Down the Rabbit Hole*. DVD by Captured Light & Lord of the Wind Films, 20th Century Fox Home.

[35] Carroll, Lee and Jan Tober, *The Indigo Children, the New Kids have Arrived*. Carlsbad, CA: Hay House, Inc., 1999.

[36] Atwater, P. M. H., *Beyond the Indigo Children*. Rochester, VT: Bear & Co., 2005.

Shifting Into Higher-Level Beings

This Part One has been a brief introduction to the world of beliefs in which we live today and the level at which we created our world conditions and problems—at least as I perceive it all. Not wanting to put energy into the negative aspects of our current reality, I have skimmed over our deplorable world conditions and focused on what I see as their causes. Only by understanding those causes will we realize what must change to remedy the situation. It will take commitment and concerted effort to make the needed individual changes, but then together as a new culture we can change our shared reality and the reality of all humanity.

Gary Zukav writes about what we are becoming as we shift our consciousness and leave the old survival paradigm behind. In *The Seat of the Soul* he uses the terms "five-sensory" and "multi-sensory" to describe these states, saying one is not better than the other, one is just more appropriate now as we evolve into higher level beings.

> The experiences of the multi-sensory human are less limited than the experiences of the five-sensory human. They provide more opportunities for growth and development and more opportunities to avoid unnecessary difficulties.[37]

So long as we think we have to control our environment and our relationships, we live as five-sensory humans and miss opportunities for development as multisensory beings. Moving into a multi-sensory view, we realize we are leaving behind the limited view of materialism. We are growing into an expanded understanding of evolution, through which our values and behavior are changing into love for all Earthly life. Altruism, denied by Darwinian science, is seen as a deep truth.

When we, over-balanced in masculine energy, limit ourselves to the five-senses, the basis of life is fear, and power to control the environment and those around us seems essential. Anything we fear to lose (such as money or our precious things) is a symbol of external power, as are all perceptions of greater or lower personal value.

Zukav writes that our five-sensory human perception causes us to believe "we are alone" in a physical universe, but

> From the perception of the multi-sensory human, the physical world is a learning environment that is created jointly by the souls that share it, and everything that occurs within it serves their learning.[38]

Humanity has evolved to where we are by sensing our external world in primarily five-sensory ways. Our institutions—social, economic, and political—reflect our understanding of power as external. We believe our happiness depends on others, externally. But we can't heal the insecurity underlying the perception of power as external by accumulating external control or wealth. That perception brings only pain, violence, and destruction.

Outgrowing the five-sensory state of consciousness, we are moving rapidly into a multi-sensory state in which we see that real power comes only from within and can't be gained in external ways. We are realizing also that happiness is internal rather than external, and that control is completely unnecessary. We're beginning to understand that the basis of all life is found in balanced masculine and feminine energy, which will enable the shift in our consciousness from five-sensory to multi-sensory. Deeper, multi-sensory understanding leads to authentic power that doesn't judge what it encounters, and sees meaningfulness and purpose in the smallest details.

As we undergo the constant changes natural in this life, we evolve. Our beliefs evolve. Our worldviews evolve. Our world conditions evolve. But the direction of our evolution is entirely up to each of us, individually. In the process, it's useful to keep in mind that the gamut of belief systems is not an either/or between science and religion, religion and spirituality, spirituality and science, matter and consciousness; there is always a continuum between extremes, each segment helping to define the others.

---

[37] Zukav, Gary, *The Seat of the Soul*. New York, NY: A Fireside Book, Simon & Schuster, 1990.
[38] Ibid.

PART TWO: WHAT'S BEHIND OUR PREVAILING BELIEF SYSTEMS

> Are we physical beings yearning for a spiritual experience or are we, at the core of our existence, conscious and immortal beings evolving a physical experience?
> ~ Edgar Mitchell, Apollo 14 astronaut

Today's Predominant Belief Systems

Introduction

The main theme of this book is Edgar Mitchell's question (quoted on the first page of this section), to which he answers: "Historically humankind has behaved as though it believes the former, but it seems to me all the evidence points toward the latter."[39] Our diverse belief systems answer the question differently, creating major differences in our worldviews and behaviors.

This part of the book examines in some detail the historical basis and justification for the belief systems that are predominant in America today and apparently most influential to our Western ways of life, those of religion and of science. The focus is on their fundamentalist beliefs, because those extremes have had the greatest influence on our culture and its materialist worldviews.

Both are rigid in their beliefs and closed to spirituality. They battle for supremacy, yet neither is plausible today and may have outlived its usefulness. Both systems, though, have more expansive mystical arms which can certainly be seen as spiritual.

We can't be simultaneously materialist and spiritual in our beliefs; they are philosophical opposites. Actually, they are complementary, separately serving humanity in their own way and time. Neither has been able to stand alone in this experiential theater we call Earth. They could have, but with little benefit, so no purpose would have been served. Nor can they now peacefully co-exist, since materialism by its very nature is divisive, competitive, and conflict-oriented. We've lived with near-exclusive materialism for almost two thousand years, and it's time now for the pendulum to swing to the other side and give us a chance to enjoy our spirituality as an enlightened culture.

Since the materialist views are the ones whose influence we must diminish if we are to become more spiritual, we'll examine their failures, fallacies, and falsities. We need to see how untrue the picture is that the materialist belief systems have painted for us, see them for what they truly are, to know what has to change. So, what you'll find in this book is not their stories, but new stories about them. You'll see a story of each you may not have seen or heard before, and certainly not from them. These presentations include evidence and conclusions drawn from both academic and alternative sources, with my comments and questions. I offer these to help you understand people with these beliefs and to help you form or reinforce your own belief system from an informed position.

NOTE: I invite you, as you read, to question each view, especially my depiction and reaction to it. None is without bias. Keep in mind that a quote from one source is that source's opinion or reading of the available facts, and there are other people who would say it quite differently or disagree entirely. Most of the time these would be differing interpretations of evidence or texts slanted by the author's own particular biases. Please be mindful, too, that no radical view fully represents its larger body; there is always a continuum of ideas and beliefs between extremes, each helping to define the others.

No matter how objective I've tried to be, I chose my sources and what I cite or summarize through my biases. I make no apologies. I only caution you to consider this as you read what follows and suggest you let your heart, mind, and soul help you evaluate each belief system. I know you can intuitively sense for yourself its pertinence to your personal belief system, whether it be set, developing, or freely open.

After examining the two dominant belief systems, we'll look at Intelligent Design (ID) theories to see if something there can't bridge the gap between science and religion. While the current ID movement seems to be controlled by Christian creationists, many of its questions about orthodox science appear worth serious consideration.

Distinguishing Science from Religion

Let's begin with a little history depicting the influences that led to the delineation and polarization of religion and science. The story begins with the classical Greek philosophers of around 300 BCE who greatly influenced the emerging Abrahamic religions (Judaism, then Christianity, then later Islam—all descended from the original patriarch, Abraham) and continued to influence much of the philosophic and intellectual thinking of those religions throughout their subsequent development. Plato and Aristotle, in particular, heavily influenced Christianity, and

Aristotle further influenced and has been thoroughly studied in Judaism and Islam; for centuries Muslim theologians have compared the teachings of Aristotle to those of Islamic prophets.

In the early years of the Roman church, science and religion were one and the same. Through the medieval period, the teachings of Plato and Pythagoras were part of the advanced education offered through the church. Then, from the early 13th century, when Thomas Aquinas established the University of Paris, and through the centuries prior to the European Enlightenment in the 18th century, Christianity was married to Aristotelian ideas. Indeed, the Church considered Aristotle's hypothesis that Earth was the center of the universe and of a nature different from the heavens, his theories of matter and form and of cause and effect, and his ideas of morality to be almost as sacred as the texts from the Bible.

The Aristotelian philosophy sees everything in form as separate and independent. For example, to Aristotle (384-322 BCE), the form and color of an apple exist within the apple, while to his teacher Plato (424-c347 BCE), the form comes as a blueprint from the world of Ideals, from the intelligible (implicate, unmanifest) to the sensible (explicate, manifest), a model which is consistent with modern quantum theories. It was also Aristotle's idea that life came out of "dead matter," a notion science still clings to.

Aristotle was a major contributor to modern scientific thinking, delineating formal logic, pioneering the study of zoology, and developing a basic form of the "scientific method," which later scholars, notably Roger Bacon in the 1200s and Francis Bacon in the 1600s (unrelated), refined. Still, some scientists feel that academia's insistence on ignoring Aristotle's errors held science back. Bertrand Russell noted: "[A]lmost every serious intellectual advance has had to begin with an attack on some Aristotelian doctrine."[40]

Science today, although truly only in existence since the European Enlightenment of the late 1600s and early 1700s, can thank the classical Greeks for so much of their foundation. Pythagoras, for all intents and purposes founded mathematics with his reverence for numbers and his geometric theorem. Heroditus fathered history, Democritus formulated atomic theory, and Heraclitus began the thinking that led to our current laws of thermodynamics. Plato's demiurge myth can be seen as a precursor to quantum thinking, and he was a major contributor to medieval spiritual philosophy as studied at institutions such as the school at Chartres. Aristotle gave scientists their empirical and experimental methods. Theirs was "the irrepressible, inexhaustible *eros*, or desire, to understand the Universe, and thereby to understand man's place in it."[41]

Thanks to the Roman church's efforts to control the minds of humanity, scientific thinking that seemed to contradict church doctrine was not openly pursued again until at least the 16th century. And then, of course, first Copernicus and later Galileo ran into a churchly brick wall in their efforts to propose something different from the Church's geocentric belief. Throughout the late "Christian Era" (roughly from the 1200s through the mid-1600s), scientific developments had to be kept secret. Science, considered the "antithesis of scripture" by the Inquisition-dominated Roman church, was banned for several centuries and people were executed for expressing unaccepted scientific observations in public.

The only schools were operated by the churches, and scholars, generally, were members of the Christian clergy until Isaac Newton, near the end of the 1600s, became the first non-cleric mathematics professor at Cambridge University.

Development of Science

Nicolaus Copernicus (1473-1543), a Catholic cleric, was the first person to formulate a comprehensive cosmology which displaced the Earth from the center of the universe. For his own safety, he kept his book, *On the Revolution of the Celestial Spheres*, secret for decades and published it just before his death. It's regarded as "the starting point of modern astronomy and the defining epiphany that began the scientific revolution."[42]

Another cleric, Galileo Galilei (1564-1642), whose work with optics supported and elaborated on Copernicus, was prosecuted by the Inquisition as a heretic. Forced to recant, he was sentenced to life under house arrest and told to neither hold nor defend that position. Despite this suppression, both men added measurably to the development of modern science.

René Descartes (1596-1650) learned from Galileo's experience not to go public with his scientific beliefs, so most of his works were published only after his death, and were banned by the pope thirteen years later. Considered the "Father of Modern Philosophy," Descartes is also credited as the father of analytical geometry, and as the first philosopher to provide a framework for the natural sciences outside of Christian doctrine. The Stanford Encyclopedia of Philosophy says that by separating mechanistic and materialist processes from beliefs, "he offered a new vision of the natural world that continues to shape our thought today."[43] He also argued for the existence of God, basing those natural processes on God as the creator of all matter and its laws.

Descartes aimed to replace all the main parts of Aristotelian physics, but refrained from directly attacking the Aristotelian position, since it was accepted in university education and strongly supported by orthodox theologians, both Catholic and Protestant. In particular, he believed that Aristotle's manner of perceiving truth through the senses was basically flawed; for him intellect alone provides truth (expressed in the famous line, "I think, therefore I am").

Seeming almost quantum in his thinking (except that to him, mind and matter were the only reality), Descartes denied the existence of space separate from matter, and hypothesized that our surroundings are composed of many small parts of various shapes and sizes. In his model, these parts are not connected but are themselves surrounded by "intervals," which, although possibly appearing as voids, are not empty but are filled with what he called "extremely subtle matter" through which light communicates. Color, for example, he said, is not a quality of matter, but is seen through light reacting to the spinning motion of surrounding particles in response to the form's shape and transmitted to the eyes and then perceived by the mind; the spinning motion, jiggling the retinal nerves, directs the brain into perceiving a specific color.[44]

Although he officially subscribed to the biblical story of creation, Descartes hypothesized that

> the universe began as a chaotic soup of particles in motion and that everything else was subsequently formed as a result of patterns that developed within this moving matter....[45]

His primary contribution to modern science, though, is that he established the basis of dualism, the split between mind and matter, including the body. To Descartes, there are

> three substances, each characterized by an essence. The first and primary substance is God, whose essence is perfection. ... The other two substances, mind and matter, are created by God and can only exist through his ongoing act of preservation....[46]

He said that the essence of matter is extension: its shape or form. In contrast, he went on, mind's essence is thought, and human minds have two faculties, which he called intellect and will. He equated soul with mind, and held that only humans have souls, saying:

> ..souls account for intellection and volition, including conscious sensory experiences, conscious experience of images, and consciously experienced memories...[47]

For Descartes consciousness was the "defining property of mind... the substance in which thought immediately resides; ...all thoughts are, in some way conscious." Some modern scholars, seeing this interpretation, wonder "If mind is thinking substance and thoughts are essentially conscious, is consciousness the essence of thought?"[48]

With Descartes leading the way, natural scientists decided that two entirely different substances—mind and material—could not interact. They accepted Descartes' atomistic components of matter, and his ideas that modes of intellect are of the material brain and that animals (at least nonhuman animals) are machines. These ideas eventually led to modern science's current stance of material monism: matter, to most modern scientists, is the one substance that is the basis for everything; even thought, emotions, imagination, and consciousness are understood as functions of the material brain and its associated neural network.

Isaac Newton (1642-1727), though he refused to be ordained, which was the historical condition of teaching mathematics, was also a believer in God as the designer and creator of everything, but he modified Descartes' ideas with his own theories of light, motion, and the laws governing matter.

Descartes was a philosopher and much of his thinking lacked empirical proof, so his model was easily challenged. Newton's theories, however, were developed in the language of mathematics and empirically supported, so have been favored as the basis for modern physics and chemistry.

The Roman church's religious authority began crumbling in the mid-1700s, especially in France, where natural philosophers were seeking materialist explanations for life. Scientists focused on how the universe, Earth, and its hugely diverse life had emerged. The scientific community began collecting and studying fossils, forming theories of evolution, creating methods for studying empirical evidence, and testing their theories.

This European Enlightenment was not merely a scientific revolution but was a culmination of both intellectual reason and challenges by Protestants to Roman Catholic rule and dogma and in opposition to intolerance and abuses in both Church and State. It was, as Immanuel Kant put it: "the emancipation of the human consciousness from an immature state of ignorance and error."[49]

Even so, until scientists in the 19th century decided against it, design of all life by higher intelligence was, for all intents and purposes, taken for granted.

Now, let's get to the specifics of the prevailing belief systems of our times. These are the systems that have sent us into wars, encouraged exploitation of the environment, and focused on our material existence in self-absorbed ways. We must move away from them if we are to raise our level of consciousness and create a better future for all life on Earth.

---

[39] Mitchell, Edgar, *Science of Mind* magazine, 1992.
[40] Bertrand Russell, quoted in the article "Aristotle," Wikipedia.com
[41] Drew, Jean F. "The 'Cartesian Split' Is a Hallucination; Ergo, We Should Get Rid of It". Posted June 12, 2005. Freepublic.com, 2011.
[42] Quoted in an article, "Nicolaus Copernicus," on Wikipedia.com
[43] Hatfield, Gary. "René Descartes," *The Stanford Encyclopedia of Philosophy*, stanford.edu, 2008.
[44] Ibid.
[45] Ibid.
[46] Ibid.
[47] Ibid.
[48] Ibid.
[49] Kant, Immanual, in Roy Porter, *The Enlightenment*, Google Books, 2001.

Western Religions and Their Beliefs

Introduction

In Europe, the Americas, and other urban centers dominated by our Western culture, no other belief system has been as influential as that instilled by Christianity. No book has been as important to so many people for so many years as the Christian Bible. Every ancient culture had a creation myth, many similar, but the Bible's account is the one most familiar to us in the Western world. That story, from Hebrew Scripture, is not considered mere myth or metaphor by millions of American fundamentalist Christians, but for many generations has been seen as a factual account of what occurred in the beginning. That view is the primary focus of this religious perspective.

In the Beginning

To see the creation story of Western religions, one need only read the beginning verses of Genesis, the first book of Hebrew Scripture, the Christian Old Testament, and the Islamic text called *The Torah of Moses*. Although you probably know the basics, I'll give a brief summary, because there are some details I want to pursue.

Assuming God as a given and without definition, the story covers six days of creation. After creating heaven, earth, and the seas and separating light from the darkness, God asked the earth to bring forth vegetation, Then He created the sun, moon, stars, seasons, days, and years, and asked earth to bring forth fowl and the seas to produce sea creatures. On the sixth day, God had earth bring forth every other living creature. Finally, still on the sixth day, God said to another, unidentified, god: "Let us make man in our image, after our likeness…. So God created man in his own image… male and female created he them…." He told them, as he had done with all creatures, to be fruitful and multiply. But to Adam and Eve he also said: "fill the earth and subdue it; and have dominion over the fish of the sea, and over the fowl of the air, and over every living thing that moveth upon the earth."

The second chapter has God resting, and elaborates on God's making of man and woman, with God forming man from "the dust of the ground" and breathing life into his nostrils to create a living soul. God then puts the man into the newly planted garden, surrounding him with every tree pleasant to sight and good for food, including both the tree of life and the tree of knowledge.

As the story goes, God gave Adam the job of caring for the garden, and told him he could eat freely from every tree, except that of knowledge; eating from that tree would bring his death. He gave Adam help from all the beasts and fowl and ordered him to name them.

God then put Adam to sleep and removed one of his ribs from which he made a woman. The woman, Eve, was beguiled by the serpent to eat the forbidden fruit. When Adam also ate the fruit, an angry God told Eve he would greatly multiply her "sorrow and conception," and added: "in sorrow thou shalt bring forth children; and thy desire shall be to thy husband, and he shall rule over thee." God also gave Adam a good tongue lashing. Then, saying, "[T]he man is become as one of us, to know good and evil," God sent Adam from the Garden of Eden, lest he take also from the tree of life and live forever.

Christians consider Adam and Eve's yielding to the serpent's temptation by eating the forbidden fruit their "fall" or "original sin," the cause of human suffering to be the rule on Earth. Christian Fundamentalists (both Catholic and Protestant) teach that all humans have been saddled with that suffering and that we all have inherited Adam and Eve's sinning nature. As our birth affliction, we are separated from God and vulnerable to Satan's influence. We suffer and we sin.

In 1650, Ireland's Archbishop Usher calculated from biblical details that Earth's creation occurred on October 26, 4004 BC (BCE). Accepting this date, biblical literalists believe Earth to be only 6,000 years old; some arbitrarily allow up to 10,000 years.

God, Dominion, and the Flood

Thanks to literal reading of Hebrew Scripture, we view God in our image, after our likeness, a person with human emotions, who is demanding and vengeful. While leaders of some Christian denominations see a more expansive and spiritual vision of God, biblical literalists hold tenaciously to this personified view.

Other ancient creation stories deal with humanity as just another part of creation; only Genesis implies we were the purpose of creation and gives us dominion over every living thing on Earth.

These differences make other cultures more in tune with and reverent of other Earthly creatures. This biblical story causes us to misread dominion and subdue, and believe it is our birthright to dominate and abuse other life and devastate Earth rather than be responsible caretakers. Muhammad's interpretation of Genesis expressed in the Qur'an, says: "All nature has been made subservient to humanity, which may *exploit* it and benefit from it" [emphasis mine].

The existence of evil in this world is an issue that confounds most of us. According to Genesis, God later had a problem with it as well. The multitude of descendants of Adam and Eve had become filled with evil. Regretting having made humans, God decided they all had to die, as well as all land and air creatures. He would start over. He would cause a lengthy torrential downpour, creating a deluge over all the land. As an afterthought, God chose the righteous Noah and his family to be the only human survivors. And, to enable life of every kind to begin anew at the end of the flood, God instructed Noah to build an ark in which to safely house a pair of every living land creature to ride out the storm and survive the tumultuous waters of the great flood.

The Development of Judaism

To understand the hugely influential Abrahamic religions, we need to look at least briefly and objectively at their beginnings and at the writing and selection of texts that came to be the canon scriptures on which those religions were based.

In ancient times, throughout the Middle East, women and men were equals. Women were autonomous, owned property, sat on governing councils, served in courts of law, and often worked alongside men. In many lands, sovereign rule was passed down through matrilineal descent. Women were valued for their insight and authority, especially to do with "unseen" matters, knowing the mysteries of life, and how to invoke the primal elements and energies of nature. They passed that knowledge down to other women, along with, as Judith Duerk relates in *Circle of Stones*, "how to align with the eternal flow of those energies, within and without."[50]

Then, with the arrival of horse-riding warrior-kings, things began to change and laws were written taking away women's rights of inheritance. Control over their property, finances, and legal affairs was given to men related to them, and in some places women were considered property.

> The serpent, venerable symbol of wisdom and nobility, became ... a target for humiliation and derision, treated as a symbol of woman's folly, evil, cunning, and lust. This ancient symbol of life was abased as that which tempted Eve, and through Eve, all of humankind, into sin and death.[51]

No longer revered, woman's wisdom was now ridiculed. Woman's instincts and intuition were rebuked. In this environment the Israelites built a patriarchal way of life that evolved into Christianity and later Islam.

The Hebrew religion was the first strictly monotheistic religion, with belief in only one true God. All other religions in urbanized cultures of the first millennium BCE, were polytheistic, with two or more gods. Having fled Egypt where the Mystery tradition and panentheism (belief that the universe is all God manifesting in different forms) were strong, Israelites acknowledged the existence of numerous gods. But they chose one God to single out for their worship, whom they called YHWH, holding their God as greater than all the others. They wrote the name as an unpronounceable set of consonants and referred to their god as Adonai ("Lord"), because they believed it irreverent to speak the name aloud.[52]

The Israelite elite chose YHWH because of His covenant with Abraham, promising that his descendants would occupy the "land from the river of Egypt unto the great river, the river Euphrates" as found in Genesis, 15:18. Later, to unify their disparate tribes and distinguish themselves from other cultures, their oral traditions were begun to be written down in the 9th century BCE.

They conceptualized their God as having human personality but without ordinary human limitations, and didn't define or limit Him in myths, as did their Pagan neighbors. YHWH was also different from Pagan gods in that He cares about human struggles and behavior, making humans seem important to Him. Historian Kenneth Harl says this was a new concept in peoples' perception of Deity. A new religion was thus defined.[53]

In 586 BCE, after seizing Israel and Judah, Babylonian King Nebuchadnezzar destroyed Jerusalem with its temple and deported the ruling classes to Babylon. During their 47-year exile those literate elite Israelites re-defined their religion and practices, re-conceptualized their God, edited existing scriptures, and wrote new ones, including (scholars now believe) Genesis. They made YHWH transcendently omniscient, omnipotent, and omnipresent, rather than part of nature or merely an exalted human being like Pagan gods. Pagan gods were related to place: empire, land, or city/state; but the Israelite God's covenant had been made with the people of Israel regarding their right to live in a particular land, not merely to manage the place where they lived.

When the exiles were returned to Jerusalem, they rebuilt their temple, and focused their religion on the sacred scriptures, both Torah (the first five books of what Christians call the Old Testament) and Talmud (the explanation of those books written by later rabbis) as their way to understand divinity and their relation to it.

For all the millennia since, Israelites have believed the world would soon come to an end. At that time people everywhere would be judged and the righteous saved. Most Israelites did not believe in an afterlife, but that those who had faithfully read Scripture and followed the Laws would be saved and be given sovereignty over Israel as their kingdom. In later years, they expected a Messiah from the lineage of King David to reign. The idea was part of their identity, and daily prayers remind Israelites, even today, that their true home is Zion (the hill of Jerusalem on which the city of David was built) and the messiah is coming to reclaim it for them.

They believed their sins would be redeemed by living in accordance with the Laws of Moses. The 613 laws outlined in the Torah include the Ten Commandments, circumcision, abstinence from eating certain foods, avoidance of "unclean" peoples and things, observance of specific days in specific ways, procedures for handling debts, servants, and bondservants, rules for managing houses, land, and animals, and ceremonial rituals. They are very specific rules for behavior and difficult to follow in their entirety. But because YHWH had made His covenant with Moses and given him the Laws by which He wanted His people to live, those Laws were sacrosanct. Adherence to them would demonstrate the Israelites' righteousness as their part of the covenant, and would guarantee their salvation as a kingdom. The laws became a very important part of Hebrew religion.

By the beginning of the 1st century BCE, the Greek Empire had spread east to the border of India and included the Syria/Palestine region surrounding Jerusalem. As a result, many Israelites became Hellenized, living more by Greek Pagan religion than by Hebrew laws. Hellenists had oral traditions of mythic stories about personified gods with names and faces. The myths gave gods and goddesses human emotions and depicted them romancing each other, killing each other, battling for superiority and possessions, behaving in sexually promiscuous ways, marrying siblings or cousins, making them anything but ideal role models.

But, by making the gods and goddesses seem human, those stories made them accessible to the illiterate public. Many were originally based on real people, deified through myth and made powerful through fantasy. Although this practice is polytheistic, in the teachings of their Mystery traditions each culture's many gods and goddesses were understood as the many faces of their one God.

Throughout the ancient Mediterranean region peoples lived for centuries by this religious system. But while most Pagans understood their myths to be stories or symbols and metaphors for higher spiritual truths, Israelite elites chose to think of their myths as historical fact, giving them leverage in gaining obedience to their laws, as well as distinction, meaning, and purpose.

This insistence created a creed and dogma, which was essentially new in religion. Israelites formulated their religion around the existence of evil and suffering, but their commonplace existence had to be explained if belief in one supreme, all-knowing, all-powerful God was to be accepted. God's wrath in the Eden story gave a rationale for suffering, and the serpent explained evil. The covenant between Moses and YHWH gave Israelites a set of laws that they understood to be God's rules for avoiding evil and overcoming suffering.

Their concept of evil derived from Zoroastrianism, which had flourished throughout the Persian Empire from the first millennium BCE and continued in the region into the Common Era. The Zoroastrian scripture, the *Avesta*, set the dualistic belief that life is a constant struggle between good and evil. The great Persian Zoroaster had rejected the pantheism of Indo-Iranian Vedic beliefs and singled out one of the ancient deities of

Persia, Ahura Mazda ("the wise Lord"), as the one supreme God who is manifest in Earth in two forms, one of which is the source of the evils humanity experiences.[54]

This religion, too, was tempered by Hellenistic beliefs during the Greek empire's occupation of Persia, and flourished until bowing to Islam in the 7th century CE. The tradition thrives today among the not quite three million Parsees in India and Persian immigrants in the U.S.

Both religions had chosen a single male God for their worship, eliminating the Goddess figure present in all Pagan traditions and Mysteries.

Hebrew Scriptures

I said earlier that part of Genesis elaborates on the creation of man and woman by describing the use of Adam's rib to create Eve, because that's what it seems to do. But biblical scholars suggest that those verses reflect distinct versions of the creation story written by two different individuals or schools. Although originally attributed to Moses, Genesis and the other four books of the Hebrew Torah (known as the Pentateuch to Christian scholars) are now thought to be composites from several scribes written over many centuries. Modern biblical scholars, studying textual variations in Hebrew Scripture (such as use of YHWH for God versus the plural *Elohim*) have identified distinct versions attributable to at least four separate sources, referred to by scholars as E, J, P, and D.

Scholars believe the E source (using Elohim, possibly polytheistic) represented the "earliest traditions" in the Hebrew Bible. The J source (use of YHWH in its German form, Jehovah) was "passed on by authors who had a powerful sense of the Monotheistic God," Kenneth Harl tells us. The P (Priestly) tradition possibly came from the literate elite during their exile in Babylonia and later, who also put the documents in their final form. The D tradition, based on Deuteronomy, gave "another vision of the godhead, and influenced the later narrative books."[55]

Once written down, Hebrew texts were preserved in loose parchment scrolls for the next several centuries by a series of scribes. Some, instead of making perfect copies of the text, inserted their own ideas. Some certainly made copying errors, the ancient equivalent of "typos," mistakes in copying that could have changed the meaning entirely. It's also possible that, since Hebrew was written without vowels and could mean something different depending on orally or mentally inserted vowels, misinterpretations abounded.

In *Who Wrote the Bible?* Richard Elliott Friedman identifies each writer's contribution, showing it to be complete in itself. He illustrates each author's slant on history, with each writing from his own perspective and including material that would serve his own purposes, some of which may have been merely to glorify the scribe's ancestor, whether Moses or Aaron, or his king, Solomon or Josiah. Penance rules were set down through stories depicting God's punishment for infractions.[56]

Since the discovery of the Dead Sea scrolls—Hebrew and Aramaic writings dating back to the early Roman empire that include all books of Hebrew Scripture except Esther—it's now clear to scholars that "God did not hand down the Bible in its present form."[57] Scholars now believe that its content and structure were adapted from earlier texts to meet their community's social, political, personal, and devotional needs.

It seems obvious that much of that Scripture followed a pattern similar to the oral and written religious traditions of their neighboring cultures. Israelites surely borrowed the flood theme from Egyptians, who, in turn, probably borrowed from the more ancient Sumerians. Their flood myth was written in the story of Gilgamesh in about 2500 BCE, in which the Noah character is called Ziusudra, a man who was befriended by the god Enki and advised to build an ark.

The Jewish religion was designed to serve specific needs and purposes, and has undergone many reformations since the rabbinic sect of scripture scholars gained leadership over Jews, canonized the full set of writings that make up the modern Hebrew Bible, called the TaNaKH,[58] and formalized Judaism in 220 CE. Most of those rabbis didn't believe in resurrection or ascension, so they rejected the concept of reincarnation as taught by Pagans and initially favored by both Israelites and Christians. "The TaNaKH is almost exclusively concerned with life in this world," says professor of Jewish thought Shai Cherry.[59] He explains that among the rewards for following the laws of the Torah is that the Israelites will

> ...continue living in the Land of Israel and not be dispossessed. This is the Torah version of immortality. Nowhere in the TaNaKH, is there a promise of reward in the afterlife. There are a few verses that mention the afterlife, [such as] 'Everyone who dies, good or bad, goes to Sheol ... bowels of the earth.'[60]

When biblical texts refer to resurrection, says Cherry, it is

> understood as a metaphor for the political resurrection of the people of Israel. Immortality of the soul appears nowhere in the TaNaKH. The words that are translated into English as 'soul' or 'spirit' mean other things in biblical Hebrew.[61]

In short, Hebrew-speaking people wrote Genesis, but they interpret it very differently than Christians do.

Each religion or denomination interprets their scriptures to suit their specific needs. For the authors, as well as subsequent editors, scriptures reflect the needs of peoples in their particular time, and circumstances in formulating religion to work for them. Christianity, and later Islam, built on these roots and traditions.

The Development of Christianity

It's not enough to look only at our beginnings in considering a belief system. The perspective resulting from a particular take on our beginnings is what is significant in defining a worldview that affects us today. For Christians, the Genesis story, important though it may be as the foundation of their beliefs, is only the start. How they interpret that story and add to it with stories, tenets, dogma, and traditions of their own is what defines Christianity and its individual denominations, which heavily influence Christians' worldviews.

The early fathers of Christianity added the life, teachings, death, and resurrection of Jesus, first as God's only Son, then as God incarnate, to the base of Hebrew Scripture. They created stories about him, dubbing him "Christ" (Greek for Messiah, meaning "anointed one."), and giving him a virgin birth, a reason for his execution (atonement for humanity's sins), and bodily resurrection to demonstrate his specialness to God. The stories about Jesus were written into scripture, then taught as factual accounts. Later bishops interpreted both sets of scripture to form their unique dogma, creed, and tradition, and canonized their Bible.

Religious studies professor Bart Ehrman relates that Jesus, his disciples, and their followers formed a minor sect of the Jewish religious community in a remote, poor, and small section of the eastern Mediterranean area, and were persecuted as blasphemers by orthodox Jews for claiming Jesus was the Messiah.[62] Thoroughly Jewish, Jesus and his disciples probably saw themselves, not as starting a new religion, but as clarifying to peasants the wisdom of the pure Jewish religion.

The Apostle Paul's Role

It was a Greek Jew, Paul of Tarsus (in Hebrew, Saul, 10-68 CE), born and raised in Asia Minor (now Turkey), who set about creating the new religion. According to the New Testament, Paul persecuted Jesus' followers in the early 30s, but after converting to belief in Jesus became the central figure in the formation of Christianity.

It's clear from reading his letters that Paul wanted a religion that would pertain to everyone and be maintained, so he focused his efforts on people in urban centers, where literate leaders could teach in his absence. He was not alone in spreading the teachings of Jesus, but it's worth noting that other known Christian texts were written only after he began writing letters to his churches.

While he wanted to keep Hebrew monotheism, he had to give both Jews and Gentiles an easier way to attain salvation than obeying the difficult laws of Moses. His religion had to respond to the issues of suffering and salvation, but differently than the way the Jewish religion did. It had to be different from Pagan myths but with enough similarities to be attractive to gentiles as potential converts. He had only to create a story about Jesus, the man, as Christ and special to God, with powers like the demigods of Pagan myths.[63]

Prior to his conversion, Paul had been a devout Pharisee, that minority sect of strict observers of the Mosaic laws referred to in the gospel stories who believed in an afterlife and the resurrection or ascension of the body at death, at least for special god-men. In his letters he described a spiritual revelation telling him that Jesus, although having died on the cross like a criminal, was resurrected by God, thereby demonstrating his importance to God.[64]

Since Paul believed the end of the world was imminent, he thought he had to found as many churches as possible, as quickly as possible. His was a personal religion rather than a community or empire-related one, so he converted gentile (non-Jewish) Pagans of all classes to his religion.

Paul's Christ myth spread west into what would become the European countries and Great Britain. Europeans centered in Rome (now Italy) and in Lyons (now France) were far removed from the birthplace of the Christ myth that Paul encouraged. They believed it to be the true account of Jesus and formed their new religion around that teaching. His myth also spread to Egypt where it integrated with Egyptian Paganism and likely formed what became Gnostic Christianity.

It's conceivable that Paul wrote or commissioned the gospel of Mark, setting the stage for the other three gospels and Christianity as a religion.

Paul proclaimed that Jesus had, through resurrection, overcome the forces of evil by overcoming death. He then declared it was Jesus' "death and resurrection that could bring salvation for the sins of the world." This meant that salvation applied to everyone who believed in Jesus' death and resurrection. Ehrman explains that Paul felt,

> If Jesus was really raised from the dead, he was obviously not the one cursed by God, but the chosen one of God. And that must mean that his death was according to the plan of God, which in turn must have meant that Christ did not die for his own sins... but for the sins of others.[65]

With these tenets as his base, Paul interpreted insignificant passages in Hebrew Scripture about a sufferer and martyr to have prophesied Christ, the Messiah, as the redeemer/savior rather than king.

Paul largely failed in his efforts to win Jewish converts to his new religion; Christianity was to them a confusing and heretical doctrine of a failed Messiah. But when he turned to gentiles, Paul at once achieved extraordinary success, and founded one church after another in Syria and Asia Minor. Paul started the "Christ myth" and greatly influenced the nature and direction of the Christian Church and Bible to support it. In fact, 13 of the 27 books of the New Testament have been attributed to Paul or were largely about him, including the book of Acts.

He created a religion about Jesus rather than one based on Jesus' teachings, which may have been immaterial for his purposes. And, for all we can tell, he may not have known any of Jesus' teaching. Scholars are certain Paul did not know Jesus, and that none of the biblical gospels is an eyewitness account. They were written in Greek (Paul's language), not the Aramaic of the disciples, decades after the events they describe, and they may have been given the authorship of disciples to give them authority and imply historical validity.[66]

Formation of a Universal Church

Judaism and Christianity were institutionalizing churches and canonizing their scriptures in the first few centuries of the common era. Both, heavily influenced by social and political issues, needed to be different from other religions in the area, including each other, and both chose to be monotheistic and patriarchal.

Hundreds of documents were circulated within the Christian community during those years describing Jesus, his life and his teachings. With wide variations existing in both Hebrew and Christian scripture, early Christian bishops and priests offered a wide range of interpretations of biblical passages and fought among themselves for recognition.

Egyptian theologian Origen (185-235CE) compared and integrated six sets of scripture, a total of 50 volumes that took him 27 years to complete. His version was favored for centuries.

Much of the philosophic debate that kept Christianity in turmoil during the 3rd and early 4th centuries centered on the godliness of Jesus. Origen's position had been that when Jesus was referred to as *Logos* in Greek ("Word" in English), it indicated he was subordinate to the Father, but a "mirror image of Him in the world." In the accepted translation of John 1:1, the "Word" was not only "with God," but "the Word was God."[67]

Egyptian Bishop Athanasius argued that based on that passage, Jesus was "God on earth," while the Libyan priest, Arius, disagreed, saying that "if the 'Father begat the Son,'... then, he that had been begotten, had a beginning of existence." He said Jesus "became perfect God," and set a pattern for people to follow.

The arguments ended when Emperor Constantine called the Council of Nicea in 325 CE, and required the attendees to develop a single canon, or set of texts, as well as to compose and then sign a common creed. After a year of debate, Arius and two bishops refused and were excommunicated from the new Roman church. In the process, politically inspired alterations are said to have excluded at least 45 entire books from the Christian New Testament. But Constantine received his canon, and the Nicene Creed that resulted declared Jesus Christ to be both God (as the Word) and the Son of God (as flesh, or human form).[68] Christianity was now universal.

Reincarnation: No Longer a Christian Tenet

A hundred years later, in 451CE, the Council of Chalcedon clarified the doctrine of Jesus as Christ consisting of one person with two natures: true man and true God. This "Doctrine of the Incarnation" states that "...as the Son of the Father, Jesus is truly God, while as the son of Mary, he is truly human."[69] This was the basis for the "3-in-one" trinity doctrine that followed (In contrast to the Jewish trinity of God as omniscient, omnipotent, and omnipresent).

Without a visible Emperor-God to justify their power as the official religion of the Roman empire, the early bishops tied their power directly to their new Lord, Jesus, by way of the disciple Peter. They interpreted Matthew's "rock" as Peter, commissioned by Jesus to build his church: "And I say also unto thee, that thou art Peter, and upon this rock I will build my church..."[70] This idea that Peter was effectively the first Pope and that the early bishops of Rome were his successors became the basis for what is called "apostolic succession:" an unbroken chain from Peter to the present.

Because the Nicene Creed said that Jesus had died and resurrected only once, the bishops conceived of human life as a once-only event, and abandoned the Pagan reincarnation belief. As a result, two books were omitted from the New Testament then being compiled, because they alluded to successive lives.

Then, in the 500s, an ecumenical synod condemned 15 of the propositions in the early bishop Origen's work, 4 of which alluded to reincarnation.[71] This effectively killed any remaining Christian belief in reincarnation, and supplanted it with emphasis on Jesus' resurrection being possible only as God.

Still today, although most of Christianity doesn't teach it as a tenet, several passages in the New Testament imply reincarnation, possibly left in as oversight from earlier texts. A commonly used example is:

> Jesus asked his disciples, saying, 'who do men say that I, the Son of man, am?' And they said, 'some say that thou art John the Baptist, some Elijah, and others Jeremiah, or one of the prophets'.[72]

Differing Histories

The Roman Church would like us to believe that its orthodoxy had from the beginning been the view taught by Jesus and his apostles and never deviated. The Church wants us to see others as latecomers with a corrupt minority view. This became the accepted position when, commissioned by Constantine, a church father named Eusebius wrote the first history of Christianity in a ten-volume work entitled *Ecclesiastical History*, which is still in use today. This view was held unchallenged for 16 centuries, until the discovery of other early Christian writings. At that point Walter Bauer published a critical appraisal of the biases expressed by Eusebius. In his 1934 text, *Orthodoxy and Heresy in Earliest Christianity*, "Bauer maintained," says Ehrman, "that Eusebius had not given an objective account of the relationship of early Christian groups but... had rewritten the history of Christianity."[73]

Until fragments of manuscripts were found in the late 19th and early 20th centuries, the Eusebius history was the only version available. Then, in mid-20th century, the Nag Hammadi codices (generally Gnostic) were found in Egypt and translated, and they supported Bauer's position. Scholars now say a remarkable diversity existed among Christian groups of the 2nd and 3rd centuries. Also, by examining newly discovered fragments of 1st-century manuscripts (Bauer's work begins with the 2nd century), scholars further substantiated the diversity.

Paul's letters in the Bible, instructing several church officials how to deal with heretic Christians within their ranks, also support Bauer's position. As Ehrman points out, those were churches Paul had founded, so we can safely assume that other churches had even greater problems with non-orthodoxy.

Each group had authoritative books (there were over 30 separate gospels at the time of the Nicene Council) they used in support of their own perspective that they claimed represented the view of Jesus and the apostles.

Bauer says that in some communities some of what the orthodox called heresies were not that at all, but were probably "the only form of the new religion" in those areas.[74] He claims that what is now orthodoxy was originally just one of many forms of Christianity in those early centuries. The Constantine-appointed leadership was able to wipe out its opposition, then rewrote its history to appear as though its doctrine had always been the majority view. Texts supporting other views were systematically destroyed or not copied, so didn't survive. But Bauer found traces of earlier conflict everywhere he looked, indicating "the earliest attested forms of Christianity are in fact nonorthodox."[75]

According to Bauer, Christianity in the second century in Egypt was mostly Gnostic, in Asia Minor mainly Marcionite, and wholly Ebionite in Syria-Palestine. Ebionites combined faith in Jesus with strict adherence to Jewish Laws, and considered Jesus a man, not a god. Gnostics believed Jesus was a man with an immortal soul and that Jesus' death on the cross did not describe his literal dying, but symbolically represented a profound mystical truth.[76] Timothy Freke and Peter Gandy write: "To imitate Jesus was not to court martyrdom, but to die to one's own lower self and resurrect as the Christ within."[77]

Marcionites denied Christ's humanity, believing him to be fully God, and condemned the creator God of the Old Testament. Marcion wrote *The Antithesis*, in which he contrasts the love, mercy, and kindness of Jesus' Father God with the wrathful, murderous, vengeful, and demanding God of Hebrew Scripture. He declares, "they can't be the same... there was a second God, the true God."[78]

Emperor Constantine created the Roman church to spread a unifying religious influence throughout the Empire. The Empire by then stretched from the Black Sea in the east, south through Egypt, west along and on both sides of the Mediterranean, throughout southern Europe to Scotland and north to the Rhine River in Germany. And Constantine's Roman Christianity was something new in religion: exclusive, demanding devotion to its one God, strict acceptance of its creed and dogma, and adherence to its rituals. As a result, it destroyed nearly all other religions in the Near East and Europe, except Judaism.

The Emergence of Islam

In the 7th century, Arabs formed the Islamic religion based on teachings of the prophet Muhammad. The Qur'an, meaning "the reciting," contains revelations given Muhammad and memorized by disciples through recitation of oral teachings. Although they use both the Hebrew Scriptures and the Christian New Testament gospels, because Muslims believe all other scriptures had been corrupted, the Qur'an (which has been called "Allah's final word to mankind") "supersedes and overrules all previous writings."

To Muslims, Allah is one, without partners, and decrees whatever he pleases; they call this "kismet, the doctrine of fate. 'It is Allah's will.'"

The Qur'an describes Jesus as a prophet who was taken up to heaven without dying.

Muslims believe that at the end time, "the dead will be resurrected" and Allah will judge each person, sentencing them to either heaven or hell, the latter being for anyone who opposes Allah and his prophet Muhammad. Following the Five Pillars of Faith as spelled out in the Qur'an is how Muslims earn this salvation.[79]

Splitting Christianity

From the 4th century on there were eastern and western divisions of the Roman church. Constantine relocated his capital to what was then Constantinople, known later as Byzantium and now Istanbul, Turkey, even though he set up his new church headquarters at the traditional seat of spiritual power for the empire: the Temple in Rome. Then, as the Roman empire was falling, the Roman church became the only cohesive structure in what was left of the western empire, and in 800CE, the Pope gave rule over western Europe to Charles the Great (*Charlemagne*) of France, who renamed it the Holy Roman empire.

By the 11th century, the differences between the Byzantine version of Christianity and the Roman version were so great that, no longer content with the Church of Rome's rule, the eastern block of churches in Turkey, Greece, Egypt, Russia, and other eastern states divested itself of that rule. They wanted only to preserve doctrine they had understood from the outset. Believing the Roman church to be changed and heretical and that their own version of several conceptual issues reflected the true traditions, they called themselves "Orthodox." Greek and Russian Orthodox churches later became independent.

The Renaissance and Reformation of the 15th and 16th centuries led to the formation of several Protestant denominations, including the Lutherans and Calvinists. Although not intending to break from the Roman church, Martin Luther began the Reformation in Germany and it gained momentum throughout Europe with people who were dissatisfied with the Roman view on many issues.

Rome's insistence on total control of all matters doctrinal, as well as supreme political power and authority over all Christendom, were two reasons that both Eastern Orthodox and European Protestants broke away from the Roman-ruled church. Both groups felt that the Vatican had gone too far in developing dogma from application of certain tenets not mentioned in the Bible.

Disputed concepts include humanity's inheritance of sin, the basis for salvation, and the Roman-ruled hierarchy based on apostolic succession. Eastern Orthodox, believing "all bishops share equally in the apostolic succession," rejected the supremacy of the pope. Others didn't want to adhere to such regulations as confession of sins and priestly celibacy. As evangelical pastor Fritz Ridenour relates in *So What's the Difference?* some Christians also objected to the Nicene Creed and the Trinity doctrine as later additions not expressed in the Bible. Reformers rejected Roman additions to their practices, arguing for a church that based its doctrine on strict adherence to biblical teaching.[80]

Protestants wanted to be able to study the Holy Scriptures—a practice that was frowned on in the Roman church. In fact, that text was considered unnecessary by the Roman church, even being classified "potentially heretical" by the keeper of the faith, the Holy See. Protestants wanted to interpret the Bible, reading it for themselves in their own language rather than getting only snippets of the Latin text from poorly educated priests. A German priest and doctor of divinity, Martin Luther, was the first to translate the New Testament into the vernacular (German), just about the time that Herr Gutenberg was inventing the printing press. This meant that suddenly virtually every household could have a copy of the sacred writings of Christianity and Judaism to study.

The King James English version was completed in 1611, and is used today by conservative English-speaking Protestants.

The Roman church continued to use only the Latin version of the Bible until, under Pope John XXIII in 1964, English and other local languages were first used for the mass. Roman Catholics are still not permitted personal interpretation of the Bible. The Roman church wants its constituents to believe that only apostolic bishops or their appointees (priests) are guided by God to true interpretation.

In predominantly Protestant colonial America, the Bible became the primary text for teaching reading and for supporting family spiritual life. In most of the colonies, each town had its own community church, often served only occasionally by visiting preachers. This situation lasted well into the 1800s, and is wonderfully described by Ralph Waldo Emerson, Mark Twain, and others.

Late in the 19th century, several American women began to form their own religious denominations. Perhaps the most unusual was Mary Baker Eddy's Church of Jesus Christ, Scientist (Christian Science), remaining, through its newspaper, *The Christian Science Monitor*, a major presence in the world today. Several of her students went on to form organizations of their own. One of them, Emma Curtis Hopkins, formed a seminary and taught thousands of people to become healers and teachers, many of whom founded their own organizations, which, together, became known as the New Thought movement. These, including Ernest Holmes' Science of Mind or Religious Science (now called Centers for Spiritual Living), and the Filmores' Unity, tend to be more spiritual in their teaching than more traditional and more literal denominations.

Today, Christianity is two billion strong and has over 1,500 denominations. A great variation in beliefs and teachings exists among them, even among its fundamentalists—those who say they are reading the Bible literally.

Fundamentalist Christian Beliefs - Biblical Literalism

Evangelical Protestant Christians, the most radical American fundamentalists, are staunch creationists and, although materialists, are strong opponents of evolutionism. They are literalists who believe that all words in the Bible are true, and error free. Most congregations, and the ministers that lead them, are judgmental of moral values that differ from their perceived Bible-based values.

They view the idea of spirituality as of Satan, and see themselves in a "war" against "New Age" spirituality in particular. They are very conservative politically (the "religious right") and are nationalists, strongly opposed to global-unity considerations. They view Earth, her natural resources, and other Earthly creatures as ours to dominate and freely use as our God-given right, as written in Genesis. Clearly, these extreme beliefs are not held by all Christians, nor possibly all evangelicals, and may be held by only a minority in countries outside the United States, but they're a major influence in American society.

Many fundamentalist Christian denominations teach that their church—and only theirs—is where congregates can find the living God. The leaders are conduits to God, and let their congregation know what

God wants of them. Note though, God's "wants" almost always relate to church laws and rituals (devised by church fathers to keep their congregants in line).

"Biblical Christians" is a term applied to a myriad of American churches, each with its own reading of the Bible. They are lumped together by biblical literalism and basic doctrines centering around Jesus' death and resurrection. Although very literal in their interpretation of the Bible, evangelicals also adhere to the Nicene Creed and the Trinity doctrine, and believe in both heaven and hell as actual places. Ridenour says that biblical Christians recognize the words in the Bible alone as the only ones from God and, "...the only infallible rule of faith and practice." Only those scriptures are "God-breathed" and complete. The Holy Spirit guided the authors to write what "He wanted written." Of the New Testament gospels, he says, "the writing was done either by eyewitnesses or by people very close to those who actually knew and lived with Jesus."[81] These beliefs cause evangelicals to deny the validity of religions that don't exclusively and literally follow the Bible in the same way they do.

The Christian believer, guided by the Holy Spirit, Ridenour claims, "searches seriously and carefully for the meaning of the Bible on its own terms, not changing its meaning to fit the times."[82] One supreme and sovereign God created the universe and Earth from nothing, and we are his crowning creation. Biblical Christians believe Christ is God, and that he died for our sins. By nature, all humans are sinners, and our only hope of salvation is faith in Christ's resurrection. He goes on to explain that "The reason for our spiritually dead condition is the sin of the first man, Adam," who, although made in God's image, willfully "disobeyed God."[83] So, according to Christian doctrine, although we too are created in God's image, because Adam represented all humanity and sinned, God counts the whole of humanity sinful for all time.

People object to the doctrine of Jesus' virgin birth, Ridenour writes, because it's like "pagan (polytheistic) stories of heroes who were half god, half man." There's an "enormous difference," he claims, between the pagan and biblical stories. In pagan stories "there is gross physical cohabitation of a god with a human being," while in the biblical account, "Mary is simply informed.... There is no suggestion that Jesus is half God and half man."[84] (Enormous difference?) Theologian Wayne Grudem elaborates: "the virgin birth made possible the uniting of full deity and full humanity in one person."[85]

The significance of Jesus' resurrection to biblical Christians, says Ridenour, cannot be overstated. "It is absolutely nonnegotiable." Jesus "conquering death" by resurrection

> ...proved He was God.... Mohammed is dead. Buddha is dead. Confucius is dead. But the Bible affirms that Christ is alive; and because He lives, the Christian will live also, eternally.

In an interesting aside, Freke and Gandy tell us that:

> The original version of the gospel of Mark, the earliest account of the Jesus story, did not include the resurrection at all.... Mark's gospel ended with the women finding the empty tomb....[86]

Ridenour also says "Although we are far from what He intended us to be, [God] loved us and sent His Son to die for us." Having been "brought into a correct relationship with God" through Jesus' sacrifice and payment for our sins, biblical Christians hold "justification by faith" as their primary doctrine, becoming a Christian is a personal transaction of faith between the individual and God. "When you, as a sinner, turn to God through Christ, amazingly (and inexplicably), your guilt is wiped out as well." Christ will return at the end time to judge the dead as well as the living. He says that for anyone to claim (as do Jews, Muslims, Catholics, and some Protestants) they

> can *earn* their own salvation is to say that God is something less than perfectly holy, and this is to say that God is less than God...
>
> Christians do good works not to *earn* salvation but because they *have* salvation....
>
> Moral truth, in particular, is absolute because God has pronounced it so. The Ten Commandments are not the 'ten suggestions.'[87]

Papal Primacy and the Means of Salvation

Until the late 19th century, all popes held their authority by virtue of the bishops, and had to ask for approval of any change they wanted to make. In 1870, however, Pope Pius IX, reportedly through subterfuge and coercion, obtained a 49% agreement of the First Vatican Council and declared the pope infallible.[88]

Pope Benedict XVI issued a statement in 2007 saying that Christ established only one Church here on Earth. The other communities, he said, "cannot be called 'churches' in the proper sense because they do not have apostolic succession—the ability to trace their bishops back to

Christ's original apostles." He points out that since they have apostolic succession, the Orthodox are "churches," but, in not recognizing the primacy of the pope, lack something so are "defective." Other Christian denominations are "not true churches... but merely ecclesial communities and therefore do not have the 'means of salvation.'"[89]

Eastern Orthodox Christian Beliefs

Eastern churches differ greatly from both Catholics and Protestants in their view of sin and salvation. The Orthodox (215 to 260 million worldwide) believe that mankind, instead of inheriting Adam's sinful nature, inherited "mortality and corruption." They believe Christ's experience was a "victory over sin and death," and along with "God's grace" enables man to "obtain theosis" and "become god." They justify this by citing several passages in the Bible; one of which reads: "God granted to us His precious and magnificent promises, in order that by them you might become partakers of the divine nature" (2 Peter 1:4). Bishop Athanasius explained: "God became man so that men might become gods.... [T]o be deified is to become a partaker of the divine nature, but you are not changed into a divine being."[90]

Christian Patriarchy vs. Union of Goddesses With Gods

Pagans and Gnostics worshiped both masculine and feminine divinity. While Pagan deities were given mythic personalities and adventures, they represented principles or forces.

All truly ancient traditions balanced the masculine and the feminine, but when Western religions settled on one God to worship, they deliberately made him male and without a partner. Judaism under Moses and confirmed under Nehemiah, then Christianity, and Islam a few centuries later, chose to be patriarchal. They permitted only men to be receivers and imparters of the word of God, as rabbis, priests, imams, ayatollahs, bishops, and popes. Scriptures of Western religions were written to support their patriarchy. Eve was made subordinate to Adam by being created from his rib, and was blamed by Christians for their "original sin" and "fall" from grace.

Women were made subservient to men. It became biblical law for women to obey men.

Many early Christians were adamantly against women in the Church, even though women likely were Jesus' staunchest supporters. Paul writes in his letter to the Corinthians: "

> Let your women keep silent in the churches; for it is not permitted unto them to speak, but they are commanded to be under obedience... And if they will learn anything, let them ask their husbands at home....[91]

In her book, *The Gnostic Gospels*, Elaine Pagels says that Paul

> ...argues from his own—traditionally Jewish—conception of a monotheistic, masculine God for a divinely ordained hierarchy of social subordination: 'as God has authority over Christ,' he declares '...so man has authority over woman: man... is the image and glory of God; but woman is the glory of man....'"[92]

An early bishop, Tertullian, said a woman was banned from speaking in church, "nor is it permitted for her to teach, nor to baptize, nor to offer (the Eucharist), nor to claim for herself a share in any masculine function—least of all, in priestly office." In 1977, nearly 2,000 years after this position was set in motion, Pope Paul VI "declared that a woman cannot be a priest 'because our Lord was a man'"! Throughout many of those intervening years, unable to countenance independent women, the Church slaughtered at least tens of thousands—some say millions—of women as witches.

In most Pagan myths, both male and female gods share the power. In fact, Egyptian pharaohs only held power as couples: man and wife or brother and sister, or both. But, as Pagels says, the "God of Israel" has the power alone.

> [T]he absence of feminine symbolism for God marks Judaism, Christianity, and Islam in striking contrast to the world's other religious traditions, whether in Egypt, Babylonia, Greece, and Rome, or in Africa, India, and North America, which abound in feminine symbolism...."[93]

By contrast, Gnostic mythology includes God the Father, God the Son, and the Mother Goddess Sophia as Wisdom/Spirit.

Destroying The Opposition

The originators of orthodox Christianity wanted a catholic (which means universal) religion for everyone. Gnostic teachings were too esoteric and enigmatic, so didn't serve the originators' need for a Roman religion to bind the Roman empire together. The early bishops decided that Paganism and Gnosticism had to be eradicated for them and their church to succeed. And with Emperor Constantine's conversion of the Roman empire to Christianity, they gained the forces of the empire to enforce their exclusivist hatreds.

Through adaptation and adoption, village after village and kingdom after kingdom were brought into the fold. Then, following the collapse of the empire, by means of Inquisitions and Crusades, fifteen hundred years were bloody with the deaths of millions of heretics, witches, and political enemies: anyone perceived to be threatening to the universality of Christianity. Such killing was for the "Glory of God," despite the biblical commandment to not kill.

The Church was above the law.

The Church was the law!

Then it rewrote its history.

The Christian Bible Evolves

While fragments of canonical texts exist from the 2nd and 4th centuries, nearly all existing manuscripts date from the Middle Ages.

Ehrman says "we don't have the original texts of any early Christian book," and no two of "the 5,400 copies... of the New Testament, many fragmentary... are exactly alike in their wording, except for the smallest fragments. Scribes changed the text so extensively."[94] Even using computers, he says,

> Nobody has been able to count all the differences among the manuscripts yet.... We do know that the differences number in the hundreds of thousands. There are more differences among our manuscripts of the New Testament, than there are words in the New Testament.[95]

Most of the differences, though, are misspellings, which, for the most part, don't alter the meaning of their passages. Changes were probably also intentionally made, some to make more sense to the scribe and some to actually change the sense of the text.

George M. Lamsa (1892-1975), who grew up in the Assyrian Church of the East, believed that the Peshita (a form of Aramaic) version of the New Testament was the original text and that the Greek version was translated from it, corrupting the gospel texts. He also claimed that although much of the Old Testament was written in Hebrew, the original had been lost and the present version was re-translated from the Peshita. Lamsa produced his own translation of the Bible, *The Holy Bible from Ancient Eastern Manuscripts*, commonly called the "Lamsa Bible."

In 1989, the Christian Research Institute (Evangelical apologetics research ministry) published a review of Lamsa's Bible concluding that: "Lamsa promotes metaphysical, not evangelical teachings which have led him to inaccurate interpretations and translations of portions of the Bible...."[96] (While I haven't read the Lamsa Bible, I thoroughly enjoyed his *Gems of Wisdom* (published by Unity School of Christianity), which is definitely more metaphysical than evangelical.)

Studying the New Testament along with other writings of early Church fathers has given biblical scholars the picture they now have of early Christianity. In 1988, after centuries of rigorous study, scholars came to a major understanding about the gospels and the infancy of Christianity. Years of trying to determine the order in which the four evangelical gospels were written paid off with the realization that Matthew and Luke both borrowed from Mark for their narratives, so Mark had to have been written first. John had its own story line, and probably came later. Most scholars now believe that Mark was written in the 70s CE, Matthew in the 80s, John in the 90s, and Luke in the 120s.

Assuming the gospels were designed to narrate the life and miracles of Jesus as the Messiah, scholars were confused by the blocks of sayings attributed to Jesus in both Matthew and Luke. The real break-through came, though, when they noticed that in addition to their story line agreeing only when it followed Mark's story, Matthew and Luke both contained groups of sayings not found in Mark, many of them identical. This suggested they both had also used another source.

Then, with the 1977 English translation of the Gnostic Gospel of Thomas, which was found in the collection of codices at Nag Hammadi in Egypt, a "sayings" style was identified as another type of writing used besides the narrative style.

By isolating groups of sayings used in Thomas and in the New Testament, scholars revealed what they think of as a separate document with its own story of Jesus, his teachings, and his followers. They call it "Q" (short for Quelle, meaning "source" in German), which is assumed to have been lost or destroyed sometime during the 2nd to 5th centuries CE when the Church destroyed so many Gnostic texts.

"[T]he narrative gospels prevailed as the preferred portrayal," writes New Testament scholar Burton Mack in *The Lost Gospel, The Book of Q & Christian Origins,* "and the sayings gospel finally was lost to the historical memory of the Christian church."[97]

The idea that something like Q must have existed was developed by nineteenth-century Protestant scholars who, claiming "Catholic religion was a pagan adulteration of true Christianity," sought "the historical Jesus." They hoped to show that

> Catholic Christianity [was]... a historical development that veered away from the original intentions of Jesus and the earliest forms of Christian community and faith."

They wanted to put Protestant Christianity at the beginning to support their claim that theirs was the "true form of Christianity.[98]

Since the gospels were the only account of Jesus' life and that beginning, those scholars began comparing their stories. They noticed the gospels' descriptions of the same events did not agree, and also distinctly resembled Hellenistic Outer Mystery teaching, especially in their myths of a dying and resurrecting god-man.

That Protestant effort culminated in Karl Ludwig Schmidt's 1919 book, *The Framework of the Story of Jesus*, in which, Mack tells us, he shows "that all the connecting links between the smaller stories in Mark were of Mark's own doing. ... Mark's gospel was a fiction."[99]

Q is significant regarding the origins of Christianity because it dispels a trust in the narrative gospels as historical accounts of the founding of the Christian Church. Q relates an earlier history that doesn't agree with the narrative gospel accounts, and shows the gospels to be, as Mack says, the "results of early Christian mythmaking."[100]

Mack tells us that some of Jesus' disciples deified him and became preoccupied with the story of his miracles, never identifying with his esoteric teachings. Other disciples considered Jesus a teacher of great ancient wisdom, and to them, Jesus taught what he had learned in the Mystery schools he had attended in his travels through Egypt and the Far East.[101]

The mythology of the New Testament, Mack says, came out of congregations in Syria and Asia Minor, formed by Paul. This myth drew from Hellenistic myths and shifted those groups' focus from Jesus' teaching to the person of Jesus as the familiar figure of a dying and resurrecting god-man. It ultimately led to many differing mythologies and brought about the narrative gospels.[102]

The Q people, he goes on to say, "were not Christians. They did not think of Jesus as a messiah or the Christ," and didn't view "his death as divine, tragic, or a saving event," or even that he had been resurrected. He was a wise teacher. The Q people weren't involved in Paul's Christ cult, so were not Christians, but were "Jesus people," and had no interest in starting a new religion.[103]

These scholars realized the Christian gospels hadn't shifted in content from apocalyptic narrative to wisdom instruction, as they had thought. Wisdom teaching had come first and was corrupted into an apocalyptic narrative to support the social values of an institutional church.

They also found that more than a third of the sayings are also in the Gnostic Gospel of Thomas, and that a majority of those sayings parallel what they've assumed must be the earliest Q sayings. This puts the Thomas people early in the Jesus movement and associated with the Q people.

When examined in light of the structure of Thomas' Gospel, this suggests that the Gnostic gospels were written before the narrative ones, and could indeed have been eyewitness accounts by disciples, as they claim.

The Gospel of Thomas uses dialogue in presenting the sayings of Jesus, with the disciples asking questions and Jesus answering them. That format, says Mack, "allows Jesus to instruct the inner circle in the true meaning of his teachings while also allowing the other disciples to represent views the Thomas people have rejected as wrong."[104]

Thomas's gospel relates the "highly metaphoric and largely enigmatic" mystic wisdom of Jesus to certain of his disciples in private, teaching that "true knowledge is self-knowledge.... [T]rue self-knowledge is a state of... being in touch with a noetic world of divine light and stability."[105]

Mack explains that the rejected "gross misunderstandings" show two kinds of concerns. One is about the future and the "kingdom," when it will come, what it will be like, and if they will be permitted entrance. He says that in all instances in the Gospel of Thomas Jesus tells them "they have completely misunderstood his teachings about the kingdom. The kingdom, Jesus explains, is already present, and if they knew who they were,... they would know not to ask."[106] The other kind relates to "ritual behavior," with disciples wanting "to know whether and how they should fast, pray, give to charity, wash, diet, and whether circumcision is required." He tells us that "Jesus treats their questions as silly, but takes the occasion to turn the ritual reference into a metaphor for contemplative self-awareness for his true disciples."[107]

At the Nicene Council called by Roman Emperor Constantine to establish the tenets of his new empire-wide religion, texts chosen for the New Testament were drawn from a huge body of literature. The intent was to serve the aims of the bishops in forming a universal church with themselves as leaders and their instruction as the only truth. The narrative gospels were chosen to provide a historical point of origin that supported the bishops' institutional claims and

> pictured Jesus preparing his disciples for leadership in the church he came to inaugurate.... [T]heir primary function as narratives was to create the illusion of a chain of tradition that not only linked Jesus with the epic traditions of Israel but also with the disciples as the apostles of the church.[108]

Selection of the narrative gospels over the sayings gospels was also because they were more easily read, with entertaining stories for the public. Gnostic gospels, by contrast, are difficult to read because they were written for Gnostics familiar with Jesus' esoteric teaching, some in need of specific answers.

It was important to the bishops attending the Nicean Council that Jesus be seen as fulfilling the divine intention of Hebrew Scripture, and that it be read to anticipate the Christ. From the Old Testament, bishops arranged the order of the TaNaKH to "end with Malachi," so the Hebrew epic announces a messenger to come, flowing into the New Testament, with "John (or Jesus) saying that Malachi's prophecy is coming to pass..."[109]

Mack concludes: "Q is the best record we have for the first forty years of the Jesus movements." It shows the narrative gospels aren't historical accounts, but "are imaginative creations."[110]

Comments & Questions: Western Religious Beliefs

Notice that God created Earth and planted it with vegetation before creating the sun, moon, and stars, which not only made Earth the center of the universe but the purpose of creation.

Although God—and someone else—made man, he had the earth and the sea bring forth all other creatures. This suggests that all living things originated in and of the earth. And Chapter Two specifically has God forming Adam from "dust of the ground," while Chapter Three has God saying Adam was to "till the ground from whence he was taken." God also breathes a "living soul" into Adam, implying a life force with no pre-existence.

Why did God put the tree of knowledge with Adam in the Garden if he didn't want him to learn of good and evil? Was it a test? Did God create Adam and Eve with flawed character that caused them to disobey his explicit instructions?

The whole Garden of Eden, with its trees and the serpent, I feel, is metaphorical, symbolic of the dualistic nature of Earth life in contrast to life in spirit. Eating the apple was acceptance of intellect and, in effect, separated humanity from God, the spiritual, and thrust them into a world where good and evil were theirs to choose between. In fact, according to Ridenour, Jews believe we are "not born good or evil," but are "born free to choose between the two."[111]

Another metaphor, Eve's being created from Adam's rib, was put in to solidify patriarchy by decreeing women's subservience and reliance on men for everything, including their life. Notice the author had God tell Eve her husband was to rule over her.

Sin and Salvation

Genesis portrays Adam and Eve eating the apple and making God angry, and has them multiplying to populate the Earth, but doesn't call them sinners. Those events have been interpreted by Christians to imply that all humans inherit Adam and Eve's flawed nature, so are sinful. The early Christian patriarchs probably thought long and hard on this issue. Without original sin and our inheritance of that flawed nature, we would have no need for a savior, no need for a church to enable our salvation and eternal life in heaven. When the gospels talk about Jesus' death on the cross, they don't claim he died for our sins; that was something Paul applied to his death to create a reason for people to be baptized into Christianity. Paul's letter to Romans is the Church's source on this issue. It says "Wherefore, as by one man sin entered into the world, and death by sin, and so death passed upon all men, for all have sinned".[112]

If God cleansed Earth of all evil with the great flood by killing off all humans and starting life over after the flood with the righteous Noah, why would we still be considered inheritors of Adam and Eve's sin? Why did we need a savior in Jesus Christ to take away our sins by dying on the cross? If we inherited knowledge of good and evil, that doesn't make us sinners. In fact, if God really said, "Behold, the man is become as one of us, to know good and evil," doesn't that imply we, too, are gods, or at least as gods? In fact, didn't Jesus say so? And, if Jesus' death redeemed our sins, why are we still considered sinners? Why are Christians made to feel guilty?

The fundamental question one has to ask about Christianity is: if we were created in God's image, how can we be flawed? Why are we not, as Ridenour says, "what He intended us to be"? In two tries?—the first in the early chapters of Genesis and the second after the flood!

If we have salvation already and don't earn it by our behavior, why will Christ return to judge us? Is the salvation we've been given somehow in jeopardy? I don't know how believing we can *earn* salvation makes "God less than God," but I would think that saying that we are less than what God intended us to be and are flawed from birth is demeaning God, saying that God wasn't able to create perfect people.

Why do fundamentalist Christians put so much emphasis on the Ten Commandments and other Hebrew laws rather than on the teachings of Jesus? Didn't Jesus say there are no greater commandments than to love God with all our heart, and to love our neighbors as ourselves?

Interpreting the Bible

Biblical Christians typically say the Bible should be read word for word as truth without interpretation. But, I don't see how that's possible. Most churches provide interpretation for their followers, and offer Bible study classes to explain how their denomination interprets scripture. Prospective members are required to attend indoctrination classes before being granted membership. Preachers, whether in church, on radio, or television, constantly offer specific interpretation of scripture. Most people who faithfully study the Bible do so from the point of view of the religious denomination to which they belong. Given the differences in beliefs expressed by the various denominations, each practicing its own version of Christianity, how can there be only one way to read the Bible?

I have interpreted many passages in the Bible in a way that's quite different from the way most fundamentalist churches do, and I would guess that's true of many other people. Each of us sees what we want, expect, or need to see. We have our own beliefs, which affect how we read all wisdom books and how we view others' beliefs. So, how can anyone believe the Bible doesn't need interpretation?

Besides, it would be virtually impossible for the average lay person to search for the meaning of the Bible on its own terms. It's only natural to have one's own circumstances in mind while perusing the Bible for words of wisdom. Isn't that what the searching is about? There are numerous contradictions in the Bible, and many of the sayings and parables of Jesus are not easily understood on face value, their meaning needing explanation. Maybe that's why they get little use. Even in regard to the godliness of Jesus, the gospels aren't clear that Jesus was God, or the Nicene Council and Creed wouldn't have been necessary.

Notice that the defining tenets of each denomination deal with the godliness of Jesus, the fact or not of his virgin birth, death, and resurrection, the salvation of humankind, and practices and traditions of church organization. None has to do with any teaching of Jesus. While this could mean all denominations agree when it comes to those teachings, it could also mean the teachings aren't nearly so important to them in defining their denomination.

The teachings require specific interpretation to be understood so are often ignored. None of this deals with the Bible's metaphors and symbols, which may well be the most important today.

Comments on Christian Doctrine

Doctrine is no more uniform today among the various denominations than it was during the formative years, when Christianity was being designed to meet specific needs and to be acceptable to Pagan gentiles of the Roman empire. Do we have the same needs today?

In taking the Bible literally, Christian fundamentalists follow the narrative stories about Jesus as factual, paying little attention to his wisdom. They may never know the spirituality rejected by the church fathers to fulfill their agenda for an institutional church to control the ignorant masses, and so they allow themselves to be part of today's ignorant masses.

While scholars have long known some of this history, much has surfaced, been translated, or is being better understood in only the last few decades.

It's our loss that the 19th-century Protestants who looked for the historical Jesus were so blinded by literalism that they stopped their quest rather than modify their beliefs to conform to what they found. They apparently were correct: Roman Catholicism was an adulteration of true Christianity that had veered away from Jesus' original message. Had they been less literal and more open to the spirituality of Jesus' esoteric teachings, they might have reclaimed our spiritual roots—of course minus the wisdom of the Gnostic gospels not yet discovered at that time.

Whether the stories about Jesus are true historical accounts or Christian mythmaking is not important. Those who wrote both the Hebrew and Christian bibles had wisdom to impart, wisdom we should understand and cherish. The Christian religion has so much to give, were it to embrace its own spiritual roots. Were it to restore the image of Jesus as a teacher, pick up the Gnostic gospels, and use his sayings' wisdom as its teaching, it could be a wisdom religion for the future.

There's no reason to continue the separation of the Mystery traditions, or of secret societies: outer and inner, exoteric and esoteric, public and intellectually elite. Religions can certainly now openly have both basic and higher-level teachings, allowing congregants to go as high as they choose.

Since I emphasize Jesus' teaching over stories about him, let's see some of those teachings. In *Life and Teaching of the Masters of the Far East*, Baird Spalding reports that the ascended master Jesus he met in Tibet spoke about many things beyond church doctrine. Summarizing and extending his biblical teachings, Jesus says:

> The sum of... every condition, every form, every being is the One Infinite Cosmic Principle, God, whether it be individuals, worlds,

planets, stars, atoms, electrons, or the most minute particle. All together make One Infinite Whole, the body of which is the Universe; the Mind, Cosmic Intelligence; the soul, Cosmic Love....

It is the Law that in Principle we live, move, and have our being. Thus, when we wish to come in contact with God, we do not think of something away from us and difficult to attain. All we need know is that God is within as well as all about us and that we are completely included in God; that we are consciously within the presence of God, and are present in God, and in command with full power. Thus we need not pause, we need not ponder; we take the path directly to God within....

God is the principle behind everything that exists today. The principle behind a thing is Spirit; and Spirit is Omnipotent, Omnipresent, Omniscient. God is the one Mind that is both the direct and the directing cause of all the good that we see about us. God is the source of all the true Love that holds or binds all forms together. God is impersonal principle.... God is the Life itself and that life never dies.... God is a loving, all-giving Father-Mother....

God is never wrought up, nor angry, nor cast down. God never destroys, nor hurts, nor hinders one of His children or creatures or creations. If God did these things, He would not be God. The god that judges, destroys, or withholds any good thing from his children or creatures or creations is but a god that is conjured up by man's ignorant thinking; and you need not fear that god unless you wish to do so.

The divinity that shapes your destinies is not a mighty person molding you as a potter moulds his clay, but a Mighty Divine Power—within and all around you, and around and in all substance—which is yours to use as you will....

The Truth is, "All is One:" One Spirit, One Body, the Great Lord Body of all humanity. The Great Love, Light, Life of God completely amalgamates that body into One Complete Whole....[113]

---

[50] Duerk, Judith, *Circle of Stones, Woman's Journey to Herself.* San Diego, CA, Lura Media, 1989

[51] Ibid.

[52] Ancient Hebrew was written in only consonants, so YHWH was given vowels by German scholars and possibly spoken as Yahweh. Since in German, the Y is

pronounced as a J and W as a V, it was pronounced as "Jahveh" and later written as "Jehovah." Scholars believe it was spoken only by the high priest at certain times, which is why it's not spelled out in the Hebrew Bible or the Old Testament.

[53] Harl, Kenneth W., *Origins of Great Ancient Civilizations*. Chantilly, VA: The Teaching Company, 2005.

[54] *Phillip's Atlas of World History*, edited by Patrick K. O'Brien. London: George Phillips, 1999

[55] Harl, Kenneth W., *Origins of Great Ancient Civilizations*. Chantilly, VA: The Teaching Company, 2005

[56] Friedman, Richard Elliott, *Who Wrote the Bible?* New York, NY: HarperCollins Publishers, 1987, preface.

[57] Nelson, Craig, "Dead Sea Scrolls continue to mystify, mesmerize," *The Sunday Oregonian*, April 8, 2007

[58] TaNaKH is an acronym for the three sections of the Hebrew Bible: Torah (Pentateuch), Nevi'im (Prophets), and Ketuvim (Writings).

[59] Cherry, Shai, *Introduction to Judaism*. Chantilly, VA: The Teaching Company, 2005

[60] Ibid.

[61] Ibid.

[62] Ehrman, Bart D. *From Jesus to Constantine*. Chantilly, VA: The Teaching Company, 2004

[63] Ibid.

[64] Ehrman, Bart D. *From Jesus to Constantine*. Chantilly, VA: The Teaching Company, 2004

[65] Ibid.

[66] Ibid.

[67] Robinson, Barbara, "Christianity Today and Yesterday," *Venture Inward* November/December 2003. Virginia Beach, VA: Association for Research & Enlightenment.

[68] Ibid.

[69] Cary, Phillip, *The History of Christian Theology*. Chantilly, VA: The Teaching Company, 2008

[70] Matthew, 16:18

[71] Robinson, "Christianity Today and Yesterday," *Venture Inward*, November/December 2003. Virginia Beach, VA: Association for Research & Enlightenment.

[72] Matthew, 16:13-14

[73] Ehrman, Bart. *Lost Christianities*. Chantilly, VA: The Teaching Company, 2004

[74] Quoted in Pagels, Elaine in *The Gnostic Gospels*. New York, NY: Random House, 1979

75 Ibid.
76 Ehrman, Bart D. *From Jesus to Constantine*. Chantilly, VA: The Teaching Company, 2004
77 Freke, Timothy and Gandy, Peter, *The Jesus Mysteries; Was the Original Jesus a Pagan God?* New York: Three Rivers Press, 1999
78 "Marcionites," *Funk and Wagnalls New Encyclopedia*, on *Infopedia* CDROM Funk and Wagnalls Corp, 1996
79 Ridenour, Fritz *So What's the Difference?* Ventura, CA: Gospel Light, 2001
80 Ibid.
81 Ibid.
82 Ibid.
83 Ibid.
84 Ibid.
85 Gruden, Wayne quoted by Fritz Ridenour in *So What's the Difference?* Ventura, CA: Gospel Light, 2001
86 Freke, Timothy and Gandy, Peter, *The Jesus Mysteries; Was the Original Jesus a Pagan God?* New York: Three Rivers Press, 1999.
87 Ridenour, Fritz, *So What's the Difference?* Ventura, CA: Regal Books from Gospel Light, 2001.
88 Baigent, Michael, *The Jesus Papers*. New York: HarperCollins Publishers, 2006
89 "Pope: Other denominations not true churches, Benedict issues statement asserting that Jesus established 'only one church'." MSNBC Interactive, 2007. www.msnbc.msn.com/id/19692094/?GT1=10150
90 Ridenour, Fritz, *So What's the Difference?* Ventura, CA: Regal Books from Gospel Light, 2001.
91 2nd Corinthians 14:34-35
92 Pagels, Elaine, *The Gnostic Gospels*. New York, NY: Random House, 1979.
93 Ibid.
94 Ehrman, Bart D., *Lost Christianities*. Chantilly, VA: The Teaching Company, 2004.
95 Ibid.
96 "George Lamsa Translations." Wikipedia.com
97 Mack, Burton, *The Lost Gospel Q and Christian Origins*. San Francisco, CA: HarperSanFrancisco, 1993.
98 Ibid.
99 Ibid
100 Ibid
101 Ibid.
102 Ibid.
103 Ibid.
104 Ibid.
105 Ibid.

[106] Ibid.
[107] Ibid.
[108] Ibid.
[109] Ibid.
[110] Ibid.
[111] Ridenour, Fritz, *So What's the Difference?* Ventura, CA: Regal Books from Gospel Light, 2001.
[112] Romans 5:12
[113] Spalding, Baird T., *Life and Teachings of the Masters of the Far East*, Vols. II & III. Camarillo, CA: DeVorss & Company, Vol. II 1927, revised 1944; Vol. III 1935.

Beliefs of Western Science

Introduction

The second major belief system in the Western World today is that of mainstream Orthodox science, which uses Newtonian physics and Darwinian organic evolution to define what is natural. I think of it as a "belief" system because orthodox scientists believe their theories to be the only truth, but are unable to prove their basic materialist theory that matter is the only thing natural and the basis for all reality. Nor can they falsify what they deny: the existence of supernatural forces and principles (the spiritual) as agents in the creation of the universe, Earth, and all life. Theirs are unsubstantiated beliefs, so we must treat them as such.

The fundamental doctrine of orthodox science is totally materialist, seeing matter (including measurable energy, as interchangeable with matter) as all that exists. In this doctrine all animals, including humans, are little more than organic machines, like the workings of a clock, built up part by part (naturally, randomly, without a designer). Our physical brains are responsible for all we think and do, including consciousness, reasoning, and imagining; mind is a function of the brain. The doctrine permits no cause, purpose, or meaning to our existence or to evolution; it says that life appeared on Earth by spontaneous happenstance and has evolved through the processes of random genetic mutation, without direction.

Comprehending this belief system is no simple matter, for, while it has a basic creed, it also has many variables and is in constant flux; and, as we saw earlier, defining science itself is complex. In what follows I describe concepts and theories that are to some extent under dispute. There will always be disputes within science; that's the nature of scientific investigation. Scientists develop and test their hypotheses, then publish their readings of the empirical evidence, mathematical computations and analysis, and personal conclusions.

These are then challenged and picked apart by other scientists, some of whom approach the same data or mathematics from different angles and arrive at different conclusions. As new evidence is found, new experiments produce new findings, and new theories are proposed, old theories and concepts may be challenged anew. This part of the scientific process helps scientists work out bugs in their theories and solidify those aspects that stand the test of peer scrutiny.

Much of the current body of science has undergone this process and is no longer disputed. I have included some of it in the following presentation, which summarizes current thinking in several natural, biological, and physical science fields based on sources within their ranks. I offer comments and questions.

Thanks to the classical Greek thinkers, the fathers of the Renaissance (Copernicus, Galileo, Descartes, and Newton), and all those involved in the scientific revolution of the European Age of Enlightenment, science broke away from religious domination and formed its own disciplines during the 1700s. Throughout the 19th and 20th centuries, then, science burgeoned. Scientists were finally able to freely think, theorize and hypothesize, test their theories, and openly publicize them.

And those scientists whose theories were the farthest removed from Church dogma drew the most attention. Early in the 20th century, using Descartes' reasoning and claiming the physical for its realm, science deliberately took God or anything supernatural out of the picture, settling on naturalism and materialism for its orthodox dogma. Although their forefathers more or less took for granted the existence of a creative God as the benevolent designer and creator of the universe and all its life, the new scientists of the late 19th and early 20th centuries wanted to draw a strict mechanistic, materialistic, and naturalistic picture of the universe and its life.

But have they proven it?

Earth's Development

Physical scientists who are proponents of "classical Newtonian" physics, geology, astronomy, cosmology, and chemistry believe our universe was created nearly fifteen billion years ago (bya) by a spontaneous explosion. (From here on I will be using the abbreviation "tya" for thousand years ago, "mya" for million years ago, and "bya" for billion years ago.) In 1927, Georges Lemaitre posited that at one time the universe was infinitesimally small (likened to a period at the end of a sentence) and infinitely dense. George Gamow added that the primeval atom suddenly exploded from that dense state into a primordial soup of quarks and elemental particles of mainly hydrogen and helium. Fred Hoyle derisively called this the "big bang," and it stuck.

These scientists believe that particles hurled into space began cooling, enabling protons and neutrons to congeal into complex structures that eventually condensed into stars, solar systems, and galaxies, creating the universe. Ten billion years later, our sun was formed and its gravity attracted groupings of particles that eventually became Earth and other planets, set in nearly perpetual elliptical orbits.

Biological Evolution

According to this model, one billion years after her inception, planet Earth developed life. How? Louis Pasteur, 19th-century founder of microbiology, disproved Aristotle's theory that life emerges out of "dead matter," saying: "living things come only from living things and like produces like." Unable to create life themselves, scientists still don't know how life began in that ocean so long ago. Some scientists think life began on land instead of in an ocean. Others, concluding life could not have arisen on Earth spontaneously, believe it must have originated in outer space and floated down to Earth. But, Francis Hitching says that if amino acids had somehow escaped being burned up in Earth's atmosphere and had reached the ocean, there would not have been enough energy beneath the surface of the water to activate the needed chemical reactions. Water, he says, actually "inhibits the growth of more complex molecules."[114]

This model says that about 3.5 bya the first photosynthetic microorganisms came to life. Cyanobacteria (blue-green algae) appeared around 3 bya, and a few million years later began to oxygenate the atmosphere, changing Earth forever.[115] Paleontologist Douglas Erwin says: "the first cyanobacteria turned carbon dioxide into oxygen and set off a revolution that completely changed the chemistry of the oceans and atmosphere." Most species, he says, "modify their environment and this often changes how selection affects them...."[116]

Oxygen is a major element in the makeup of things on Earth, and when combined with two parts of hydrogen it is water (H_2O). Atmospheric oxygen is generated through photosynthesis by chlorophyll in green plants. The chlorophyll in leaves takes light energy from the sun, carbon dioxide from the air, and water from the roots to make sugar and release oxygen, a constant level of which is sustained across the planet by all the plant life, together. Numerous chemical reactions are involved and the oxygen produced sustains nearly all life on Earth—without it most organisms would die.

Orthodox science says that the process moved very slowly. According to their model, the primordial single-celled micro-organism, similar to modern bacteria, began life and, through a splitting process, populated the ocean with single-celled organisms. Then after many hundred million years, a single-celled organism merged with another cell to form a two-celled organism, then those cells combined with others, and on and on. Sexual reproduction was introduced when two forms of algae combined their DNA, and it continued for more hundreds of million years. During the next several hundred million years, cell groupings became ever more complex, forming a variety of marine invertebrates, and finally fish—the first vertebrate, or creature with a backbone. About 500 mya, some groupings of cells got onto land as land plants and scorpions—the first air-breathing animals. Amphibians and forests began about 350 mya, and reptiles and very small mammals emerged 200 to 300 mya.

The model goes on to say that as life forms became ever more complex, some of those cell groupings got carried away with the vertebrate idea and formed dinosaurs. It wasn't until the end of the Jurassic period (213-144 mya) that some groupings of reptiles sprouted wings and took to the air as birds. After that, whales and very large land mammals, such as the mammoth and mastodon, which are early versions of the elephant, came into being. The last 65 million years have brought advancement of mammals and flowering plants.

This science seems to paint a pretty complete picture of the development of life on Earth, but cosmologist Robert Jastrow says the fossil record of the first billion years "contains no trace of these preliminary stages in the development of many-celled organisms."[117] "[B]acteria and single-celled plants [were all that existed] until about a billion years ago," he says, when "the first many-celled creatures first appeared on earth."[118]

Biologist L. L. Larison Cudmore points out in *The Center of Life* "that present-day single-celled organisms are not the simple forms science thought, but are wonderfully complex": Many can

... catch food, digest it, get rid of wastes, move around, build houses, engage in sexual activity, ... with no tissues, no organs, no hearts and no minds. ... Many are able to take silicon and oxygen from seawater and build beautiful, extremely intricate glass houses.[119]

Zoologist Ernst Mayr writes in a *Scientific American* article: "[A]lmost every component in modern man's belief system is somehow affected by Darwinian principles." He also says that "No educated person any longer questions the validity of the so-called theory of evolution, which we now know to be a simple fact."[120] And paleontologist Steven Jay Gould said that "Everyone knows that evolution is true; the issue is how it occurs."

Gould and Niles Eldredge proposed that new species were only rarely the product of gradual, linear evolution. They say that stability or stasis is the norm until a major event in the physical environment triggers rapid speciation, at which time a new species "suddenly" appears.[121]

Pre-Darwinian Theories

Let's backtrack a little and look at what some theorists before Darwin posited regarding biological evolution. George Buffon (mid-19th-century) suggested that "species devolved from a few ancestral types" into new, more complex species through gradual inheritable changes.[122] Jean-Baptiste de Lamarck theorized that traits acquired through the course of a lifetime could be inherited, and formulated the first comprehensive organic evolution theory. He imagined an "ongoing, spontaneous generation of simple living organisms," through a natural electricity, or energy, which would continue to act on formed species to gradually develop ever greater complexity. With changes in environment over time, new conditions would require new behaviors and new abilities, so new species would develop from old ones. [123]

Lamarck held that in order to survive, organisms had to change to keep pace with environmental changes. Giraffes, for example, stretched their necks reaching for food at ever higher levels, with each generation of offspring having longer necks. Likewise, organs that organisms stopped using would shrink, like the human appendix. He also believed that as they adapted to their environment, organisms were driven "inexorably upward from simple forms to increasingly complex ones...."[124]

Arguing against those theories, Georges Cuvier, a Christian and ardent anti-evolutionist, attributed the creation and destruction of species to huge land upheavals and floods, what he termed "catastrophic extinctions." He was the first to relate fossils to the living organisms they seemed to be most like, and oversaw the first comprehensive collection of fossils and biological specimens, effectively founding modern biology.[125]

Studying fossils and biological specimens, Cuvier concluded there had been "no significant changes in living organisms over time or during recorded history." Instead, he "found sharp breaks in the fossil record corresponding to epochs of geologic history," not gradual development, and surmised that environmental changes must have somehow made it impossible for extinct species to survive. To him, "each succeeding layer of rock strata contain[ed] a distinctive array of fossil types," which he saw as indicating "systematic development over time," with invertebrates coming first, then fish, then reptiles, and finally, mammals. Species, he noticed, seemed to remain constant throughout their lives, and were often suddenly replaced by considerably different forms.[126]

Cuvier's "correlation of parts" theory said that every animal organ is functionally related to all its other organs and that an animal's anatomical form is determined by its functions and habits. He believed that "any significant change" in the delicate interactions within each species would make their survival impossible. Cuvier read the developing fossil record to show that "species breed true to type, with only superficial variations." The origin of new species through evolution was, he said, therefore impossible.

However, by establishing the field of paleontology and the science of comparative anatomy, Cuvier unwittingly advanced the theory of evolution. In the mid 1800s, the more religious of Cuvier's followers theorized that Earth had undergone numerous floods and ice ages that shaped its geologic features, each followed by God's (or some vital source in nature's) creation of new life modeled on previous viable life forms. This theory gave Christians the means to reconcile the fossil record with the Genesis story, by equating the days of creation with geological ages, so was called the "day/age" theory, or "catastrophism." To Cuvier's Christian followers, "...the Intelligent Design of each species... proved God's existence"[127]—a position maintained by today's proponents of Creationism and Intelligent Design.

Soon though, intense research worldwide filled in the fossil record, and the breaks Christians had relied on to prove repetitive creative intervention seemed less dramatic than they had earlier, and the new fossil record was read to favor gradualism over catastrophism. Also, geologic research showed that the most common rock forms were igneous rather than sedimentary: They came from volcanoes and Earth's inner core instead of being spread by flood, as Cuvier had supposed.

This supported Charles Lyell's "uniformitarianism," which all but denied that catastrophes had occurred and put an end to Cuvier's eminence. Lyell's theory is that physical, chemical, and biological processes now at work on and within the earth have operated uniformly over the course of Earth's existence and account for all geologic changes. Gradual geological change suggested that organisms would need time to adapt to a changing environment, and uniformitarianism provided the time.[128]

Darwinism

Evolution, as taught in public high schools, colleges, and universities today, is often referred to as a form of Darwinism, updated by genetic mutation theories to neo-Darwinism. It encompasses a number of specific theories, most of which were not Darwin's.

Educated in the various evolution theories of his day, British naturalist and breeder of domesticated animals, Charles Darwin (1809-1882) became convinced that natural evolution was responsible for all existing species of plants and animals. An essay written in 1798 by Anglican cleric Thomas Malthus on human population gave Darwin the breakthrough idea he needed to understand how evolution worked on species. Malthus maintained that because the human population was far greater than the food supply could sustain, only the fittest could survive. And even then the population had to be limited by natural occurrences such as famine and disease and by social actions such as war.[129]

Darwin saw that, when applied to all plants and animals, survival-of-the-fittest enabled some species to continue on while others became extinct. To him, changing environments brought about slow, progressive changes in species, then gradually, given the time which the uniformitarian idea allowed for, created new species.[130]

In synthesizing those theories, Darwin held that existing species of living organisms evolved in a lengthy, ever more complex, but undirected chain from previously existing species. This he depicted like a tree, with numerous branches, its seed a single cell. Darwin's contribution was that evolution occurred through gradual, slight, random, changes by adaptation, what he termed "natural selection," through a dynamic that's often referred to as "survival of the fittest."

In *Ever Since Darwin*, Steven Jay Gould says that Darwin felt that natural selection is the creative force of evolution: not only the destroyer of the unfit, but also the builder of the fit. For natural selection to be creative, variation must be random, not pre-directed in favorable ways, as in Lamarckism. Variation must also be small in relation to all of the change in producing new species. "For," he stated, "if new species arise at once, then selection has only to remove former occupants to make way for an improvement that it did not manufacture."[131]

Worried about acceptance from his scientific peers, Darwin spent decades developing and debugging his theory, trying to supply an answer for every conceivable question or objection anyone might have. Also, because his wife was a devout Christian and he knew his theories would refute the biblical creation story and upset her, Darwin held off publishing his beliefs for more than two decades, then referred to himself as the "Devil's Chaplain."[132]

Gould gives another reason for Darwin's postponement:

> [H]e espoused but feared to expose something he perceived as far more heretical than evolution itself: philosophical materialism—the postulate that matter is the stuff of all existence and that all mental and spiritual phenomena are its by-products. No notion could be more upsetting to the deepest traditions of Western thought than the statement that mind—however complex and powerful—is simply a product of brain.[133]

Evolution has no purpose, no direction, and does not necessarily lead to higher things, says Gould. "Matter is the ground of all existence; mind, spirit, and God as well, are just words that express the wondrous results of neuronal complexity."[134]

Darwin was forced to publish *The Origin of Species* when, in 1858, British naturalist Alfred R. Wallace sent him and others in the field a thesis stating the same theory of evolution as his, arrived at independently. Darwin simultaneously published both Wallace's thesis and an abbreviated one of his own, to be followed the next year by his book, filling in the details. Although his theory agreed with Darwin's, Wallace drew a different conclusion from it: that "God guided the process of evolution as his instrument of creation."[135]

Darwin began his *Origin* by looking at variation under domestication, and proceeded to natural variation. For example, we know from the experience of breeders of pedigreed dogs that certain features can be modified and perfected over several generations by intentionally selecting them.

Domestic breeding for variety and perfection is common to many industries. Thoroughbred horses are bred for speed in racing, dairy cows for high milk production, and watermelons and grapes are made seedless for enjoyable eating. Darwin argued that the process breeders and farmers manipulate occurs naturally over time, responding to gradual changes in the environment. "Therefore, each generation will improve adaptively over the preceding generations, and this gradual and continuous process is the source of the evolution of the species."[136]

Species living on the fringes of their environment, Darwin observed, spread out and adapt to new surroundings. Only changes that help a species survive would themselves survive, to be added to by the species' next improvements. Each adaptation occurs through species' intra-breeding over several generations. According to Darwin's theory, over many hundred million years and generations of slight beneficial modifications, groupings of cells formed into organisms that adapted to new environments. Weaklings were gradually weeded out to allow the most adaptable to develop according to their environmental, nutritional, and sociological needs.[137]

Darwin surmises in his second book, *The Descent of Man*: "All the organic beings which have ever lived on this earth have descended from some one primordial form."[138]

Human Evolution

After much debate, Darwinism was finally generally accepted in the 1930s, with evidence in both the fossil record and in living organisms that seemed to support its theories. Humans though, were initially excluded from the evolution mechanism as being sufficiently different from apes for us to have evolved from their line. Indeed, evolutionists still hope a missing link will be found indicating Homo sapiens and apes came from a common ancestor.

Darwinists believe that humans are the pinnacle of natural selection. They believe that we have evolved through all the various stages of creature development to the most complex of species. They believe this, because we resemble chimps, and also because our body chemistry and DNA are like that of other animals. To orthodox scientists, once mammals began developing, it was literally only a matter of time before one in the primate family (apes and monkeys) found a need to stand up, to reach higher-growing berries or to use its arms to carry its young. The first hominid,[139] paleontologists now say, appeared on Earth more than 7 mya and began the process of evolving toward what we see as human characteristics, bone structure, and behavior.

The first evidence of a hominid was found in Germany in 1856, a Neanderthal skeleton whose massive bone structure and extensive arthritis led to many illustrations of our ancestors as large, bent over creatures with little use of their hands. Since it had a brain slightly larger in size than humans, archaeologists felt that *Homo neanderthalensis* must be an offshoot, and could not have been the missing link between humans and apes with much smaller brains. Fossil remains of hominids who walked upright and had smaller brains and human-like teeth were found in China throughout the early 20th century. Then, in the 1950s, East Africa became the major source of hominid fossils when paleontologists found several, slightly different pre-human fossils, the oldest dating to 6mya.[140]

These convinced scientists that human evolution fits a Darwinian pattern: an upright posture allowed bigger brains, an open larynx permitted language, and freed-up hands enabled tool use. Although fossils have been found that appear to have characteristics similar to both hominids and chimps, no definitive link has been found. And with larger brains than ours, Neanderthals don't fit the Darwinian model.

In 2001 paleontologists found a human-like skull in Kenya, Africa they've dated to between 4.2 and 3.5 mya. This would coincide in time and location with the famous Lucy, yet the new skull is sufficiently different from Lucy's to be identified as a new pre-human species. This is a problem for scientists, because they believe different species of one genus would not develop at the same time in the same place. The theory of natural selection requires different environments for speciation—the 14 species of finches on the limited Galapagos Islands notwithstanding. An area could at different times have different environments (such as: during one of many ice ages and after the thaw) that would produce different species to meet different environment-induced needs.[141]

In 2002, anthropologists found the skull of another new pre-human species in Chad, Africa.[142] My web-surfing produced only two updating references. One was an article dated 10/2002 on the Science Against Evolution web site, which claimed: "Chad Man is just the latest in a long line of fossils that evolutionists hoped would be the missing link, but turned out to be just another extinct ape."[143] The other was a Chinese web site, dated 2005, announcing: "Chad Man confirmed as 1st hominid." The latter also said that Chad Man was 7 million years old and believed to be our earliest ancestor yet found.[144]

Existence of very small humans living in the South Pacific between 95 tya and 13 tya puzzles scientists, because they had believed Neanderthals were the only species of our relatives to co-exist with us for any duration. Now they see that these "Hobbits" may have co-existed with us for probably their whole existence.

Although they had very small (grapefruit-size) brains, they were "evidently smart enough to use fire, make tools, and hunt, challenging existing notions of the relationship of brain size to intelligence." They also had watercraft, and possibly language. Michael Lemonick writes that they "represent an entirely new twig on the human family tree."[145]

To understand the development of any species, science relies heavily on patterns of migration. Most paleoarchaeologists believe that humans evolved from primates in East Africa, a "fact" that influences their analysis of the movement of humans throughout the world—both sequence and timing.

Anthropologists concluded that about 50 tya the human brain mutated, allowing for an entirely different line of evolution from that of any other existing species. We developed the ability to know ourselves and think rationally. We evolved into self-aware, intelligent, discerning beings, able to reason and create.

Scientists wonder what occurred to cause our ancestors to become more socially complex, to express in drawings, adornments, and in language, to become so creative in their ways of living.

Orthodox science says we began to use symbolic thinking only about 40 tya, with the emergence of Cro-Magnon man in Europe. Yet, carved jewelry beads strung together, and other decorative elements, as well as well formed hearths were found in 2004 in Africa, and dated to at least

75 tya. These, it seems, would indicate self awareness and some sort of social development, suggesting we likely were more civilized a lot earlier than most scientists have believed. Because of numerous such discoveries, many scientists now think we may have acquired consciousness over 120 tya rather than only 50 tya. Some say 200 tya.

To many orthodox scientists, consciousness is merely synaptic activity of our physical brain. Even love, to Darwinists, is only some sort of atomic combustion. We are each only a bag of bones, muscles, tissues, nerves, and "selfish genes" (a term coined by Darwinist Richard Dawkins). To those scientists, thinking, imagining, dreaming, loving, and interacting are things we've learned to do over the last 120 thousand years in order to survive. But what is consciousness and how did we acquire it?

That's what scientists want to know. (We'll see much more about consciousness throughout what follows.)

Altruism and "Selfish" Genes

In *On the Origin of Species* Darwin said:

> Natural selection can produce nothing in one species for the exclusive good [altruism] or injury of another; though it may well produce parts, organs, and excretions highly useful or even indispensable, or highly injurious to another species, but in all cases at the same time useful to the possessor."[146]

Darwinists such as Dawkins, believe that "selfish genes," are altruistic only to the extent necessary to enable their species' gene pool to evolve and survive.

The Fossil Record

Although biologists assert that a great many findings from the study of animal fossils and ancient animal forms support Darwin's theory of evolution, the fossil record doesn't directly show the gradual changes in species as they grow into higher level species.

Most species appear to have come into existence suddenly, with almost no links evident between species on a single branch of a genetic tree, let alone from one branch to another. A huge diversity exists with almost no fossil evidence to indicate how or why those sudden, drastic changes took place.

In *Origin*, Darwin expressed concern about missing links between species and the lack of transitional forms within species or genera:

> [W]hy, if species have descended from other species by fine gradations, do we not everywhere see innumerable transitional forms? Why is not all nature in confusion, instead of the species being, as we see them, well defined?"[147]

He couldn't account for the lack of transition fossils and believed the fossil record to be incomplete. How, he also wondered, can we account for the fact that when species are crossed, their offspring are sterile, but when varieties within a species mate, their fertility is unimpaired? He saw other problems, too:

> Can we believe that natural selection could produce, on the one hand, an organ of trifling importance, such as the tail of a giraffe, which serves as a fly-flapper, and, on the other hand, an organ so wonderful as the eye? To suppose that the eye with all its inimitable contrivances for adjusting the focus to different distances, for admitting different amounts of light and for the correction of spherical and chromatic aberration, could have been formed by natural selection, seems... absurd....[148]

Today's vast fossil record tells a different story from what Darwin supposed. It indicates an explosion of fully developed complex sea creatures appearing in the Cambrian (nearly 600mya) ocean, with no prior fossils to suggest slow formation from any predecessor. Those creatures were invertebrates, some with hard outer shells, and included snails, sponges, starfish, and jellyfish. The fossils indicate that each species appeared abruptly, fully formed, then continued with little change for several hundred million years before some became extinct. They also show that some of the oldest creatures were more complex than some more recent ones.

Science occasionally discovers an intermediate, or subspecies but, according to Darwinian theory, says physicist Amit Goswami, many thousand intermediates should have been discovered by now and "That hasn't happened." He found "only about fifty cases of intermediates in the entire fish-amphibian-reptilian lineage of about forty-two thousand species." So, he says, the fossil gaps raise legitimate doubts about the veracity of Darwinism as "a complete theory of evolution."[149]

Historian Edward Larson tells us that Gould and Eldredge termed the missing-link phenomenon "punctuated equilibrium," saying that only rarely would gradual, linear evolution produce new species. They felt that stability existed until a major environmental event triggered rapid change and a sudden eruption of new species. One species stops, or continues as it is, and another starts, fully formed and more advanced, with organs and features specialized to meet a new or different set of needs. They deduced that because sudden drastic changes punctuated lines of species, gene pools spontaneously underwent leaps in evolution.[150]

Such rapid changes, without the necessary time to produce fossils, would justify and explain the absence of demonstrable links between related, yet different species. New species may have been better adapted to survive an environment drastically changed by a sudden natural catastrophe, such as radiation from sun spots, a volcanic eruption, or an earthquake. Catastrophes thus again are considered potentially beneficial to the development of new species, enabling new characteristics to be suddenly established as most useful for survival.

In his article "Should Evolution be Taught?" natural scientist John Moore covers the results of an extensive study conducted jointly by the Geological Society of London and the Paleontological Association of England. He explains that 120 scientists, all specialists, were involved in the study, and prepared 30 chapters in a work of over 800 pages to present the fossil record for plants and animals divided into about 2,500 groups. Moore reports that "Each major form or kind of plant and animal is shown to have a separate and distinct history from all the other forms or kinds," with groups of both plants and animals appearing suddenly in the fossil record.

"Each species is as distinct at their first appearance as they are now," Moore says. "There is not a trace of a common ancestor, much less a link with any reptile, the supposed progenitor."[151]

Darwinist Dawkins admits that many major invertebrate groups are found in the Cambrian rock strata in "an advanced state of evolution, the very first time they appear." But, he says, Darwinists believe this shows a "very large gap in the fossil record, ... due to the fact that, for some reason, very few fossils have lasted from periods before about 600 million years ago."[152]

The Role of Genetics

Gregor Mendel (1822-1884), experimenting with pea plants, demonstrated the idea that new species are hybrids of old ones, and developed a theory that both parents contribute traits to offspring through a process that's governed by fixed laws of dominance and recessiveness. Hugo DeVries (1848-1935) then posited a theory in which species develop from preexisting species through chance inheritable mutation of dominant traits, creating a distinct breeding population, with recessive traits held in abeyance for future use. These ideas supplanted the previously held notion of blended acquired traits. It also led to the modern evolutionary synthesis and the abandonment of the Lamarckian theory of biological evolution which said that when an individual changes the way the body is used, those changes are passed on to future generations.

When Francis Crick and James Watson determined the shape of the DNA molecule in the 1950s, their observation that the flow of information is only "one way, from the genes to the proteins; never the other way" became "*the* central dogma of molecular biology." Based on this doctrine, since the environment of the cell affects only the proteins of cells, data from the environment can't be "communicated to the genes [located in the nucleus and] involved in reproduction." This means environmental adaptations must be left out of the hereditary loop. This says that "genes are the only entities that can carry heredity information."[153]

Recently, there's been data that suggests that, rather than taking many generations to effect a change, some changes occur almost immediately, and their mechanism in the species' genes is very different from what Darwin supposed—and apparently Crick and Watson as well.

Groups of scientists, studying various species over time, observed changes almost before their eyes. Finches on the Galapagos Islands were discovered to evolve, "from one year to the next, as conditions on the island swung from wet to dry and back again," writes Matt Ridley.[154] Also, fish who have adapted to diets in different habitats were found to be using the same gene to thicken their jaws as the finches to make their beaks deep and wide to better crush large seeds. Such changes imply that species do pass on physical modifications resulting from diet and environmental changes, resurrecting Lamarckian evolution theory in a new form.

Cellular mutations, geneticists claim, come about through modifications of individual genes. Genes actually are sequences of four chemicals along the strands of DNA molecules: Adenine, Thymine, Guanine, and Cytosine, represented by their initials in most gene maps as A, T, G, and C, in the nucleus of individual cells. These chemical letters are strung along the DNA molecule in varying combinations. Mutations are changes in the sequence, or changes in which individual genes may be "switched on or off."

"[E]very organism carries the chemical code for its own creation inside its cells, a text written in a language common to all life," says Ridley.[155] The differences between species, most biologists agree, are the result of accumulated changes in sequences on the DNA molecules that make up the genes. They say that combinations and modifications of these sequences have been the process by which both extinct species and those we see today have come into being.

Gene sequences are not, however, unique to a species—humans share over 98% of our genes with chimpanzees and nearly as many with other mammals—it's the duration of the period that they're switched on or off and their interaction with other genes that determine the characteristics that define the species. For example, the same gene enables humans to speak with words and a canary to sing so beautifully. A single gene determines the length of both a mouse's and a giraffe's neck—it's just switched on longer in the giraffe than in the mouse. The genes that build the bones in fish fins is also the pattern that assembles the limb in a bird or any land-living animal, the sequence is just switched on at different times in the development process for the different species.

In only the last decade, as scientists have compared the human genome (the total pattern of genes in a species) with that of other creatures, they found: "we inherit not just the same number of genes as a mouse—fewer than 21,000—but in most cases the very same genes." Ridley concludes: "Just as you don't need different words to write different books, so you don't need new genes to make new species. You just change the order and pattern of their use...."[156]

Orthodox scientists accept the process of mutation to explain sudden appearance of new species from previously existing ones. But, mutations of any kind are relatively rare, and are said to be harmful in a ratio of about 1,000 to one that benefits. [157]

Our bodily cells each seem to have a specific job to perform (as skin, heart, lung, brain, or kidney, etc.) and each is replaced annually by another cell somehow knowing how to continue the job. Geneticists believe that cells know and remember their differences from other cells and pass on their knowledge to their replacement cells in the cell-division process.

According to journalist Lynn McTaggart, writing in *The Field:*

> Most biological explanations of the great mysteries of living things attempt to understand the whole by breaking it down into ever more microscopic parts. Bodies supposedly take the shape they do because of genetic imprinting, protein synthesis and blind mutation.

She adds that

> British biologist Rupert Sheldrake has mounted one of the most constant and vociferous challenges to this approach, arguing that gene activation and proteins no more explain the development of form than delivering building materials to a building site explains the structure of the house built there.[158]

Comments & Questions: Orthodox Science

It's hard to imagine how infinitely dense that infinitesimally small primeval atom would have to have been to erupt in that big bang and produce this infinitely huge universe.

And once the Earth was formed, how did all those photosynthetic reactions come about to produce oxygen, one reaction at a time? What sustained atmospheric oxygen for two billion years before plant life? Perhaps it took those single-celled microorganisms two billion years to sufficiently multiply while creating their own life sustaining oxygen.

From where did that first single-celled life originate? In *Origin*, Darwin admits: "Science as yet throws no light on the far higher problem of the essence or origin of life" ("from one primal organism"). Darwin said that 150 years ago, yet science still simply does not know how life began.

What would make outer space—as some suggest—a more feasible origin of life than Earth? Wouldn't everywhere present the same problem of how life could occur spontaneously?

Those invertebrates of the Cambrian explosion had to have developed in synergistic patterns. They had reproduction and elimination systems, outer protective shells, and they could see and propel themselves. How did they get so fully formed and capable?

Hundreds of step-by-step mutations would have been required in their separate development.

I can see how improvements might take place through natural selection within a family or genus of species, but there seems to be no connection evident between different genera. And interbreeding produces infertility, as when a horse mates with a donkey and produces an infertile mule. It doesn't matter whether evolution is considered gradual or jolted by sudden mutations; science is unable to support evolution from one species to another different species. The branches on its tree of life don't connect.

How did complete populations of species (such as dinosaurs), scattered around the world, become extinct, despite differences in their environments? How did a weak, unfit species (apparently, since they died out) manage to get spread to distant areas of the world in the first place? The scorpion is thought to have been the first land creature, yet has changed very little since its inception. It can't see well and has to touch something to know of its presence. Why hasn't it either reached a higher level of perfection or become extinct?

Does uniformitarian geology explain the development of fossils? The normal processes of death cause decomposition and eventual disintegration, not fossils. As I understand it, only sudden catastrophe produces the upheaval and pressure needed to over time create fossils. Also, as a basis for Carbon-14 dating of rock strata and fossils, uniformitarian geology dictates orthodox time lines. The orthodox assume the strata they examine were all produced by time alone, and date their artifact contents accordingly. Cataclysmic geology, however, would (and often does!) date the same strata and their treasures as considerably more recent in time. Yet uniformatarianism is still the conventional belief today.

While evolution is often equated with Darwin's theory, to do so is erroneous, since evolution can be observed in nature without applying Darwinian theories. Darwinism seems to account for only the gradual improvements in species, not the rapid development of new species, as in the Cambrian explosion.

Darwinian theory says that, like all species, we humans originated as a single cell and gradually built up one cell addition at a time, being modified by favorable mutations, to invertebrate marine life, to fish, to reptiles, to mammals, to primates, then to the magnificent and complex masterpieces of human form and intellect we have become. Step, by step, each of our organs and each of our systems (endocrine, reproductive, respiratory, cardio-vascular, digestive, neural, etc.), along with our skeletal structure and muscle and tissue covering, had to develop almost as a separate entity, yet symbiotically, to work together as they do. Each had to have had its own distinct, individual reason for being. Each step also had to occur simultaneously in at least two of each species and of opposite sexes, and they had to get together to procreate, and each step also had to have been beneficial to the species survival. Finally, our brains had to develop consciousness so we could become what science refers to as "modern humans." Absolutely mind-boggling!

Conventional science pictures us as evolving from primates to very primitive human-like beings to modern humans, because that's what they expect to see, not because the evidence affirms that view. The orthodox don't find hard evidence of sophistication in our early ancestors because that sophistication was way beyond what those scientists are prepared to see. The minds of those scientists are stuck in an antiquated paradigm that prejudices their understanding of life on Earth. So, when they find hominid bones that don't fit their preconceived human evolution pattern, they merely identify those bones as belonging to another pre-human species, a relative on a slightly different branch of life's tree, like Neanderthals.

How is it determined how long genes are switched on, or which ones are switched on at all, to produce a favorable part of a form?

Although extensive and thoroughly analyzed, the fossil record still shows the breaks that concerned Darwin, and hasn't produced the missing transitional links. While genetic research has provided rationale for some aspects of natural selection, it has also provided a mixed bag as to whether environmental adaptations are hereditary, and has falsified much of Darwin's theory concerning new species. If alive today, would Darwin still propose gradual natural selection evolution in the development of new species?

Many of science's basic theories have been accepted as fact, not because they have been proved beyond doubt by evidence or repeated testing, but because they seemed to either make sense to a majority of scientists or filled in some gaps in science's previous picture of the development of life on Earth. The only thing wrong with this is when scientists claim these theories are "fact."

What do you believe? What if the development of new species actually took place in another dimension and only emerged physically when observed—in the same way that waves change to particles in quantum physics?

The New Sciences: Quantum Physics

Although most scientists are mired in the materialist paradigm, quantum scientists have expanded scientific thinking way beyond the material, and some have gone undeniably into the spiritual.

The word "quantum" means "a discrete quantity" in Greek, so it seemed appropriate to describe what goes on at the subatomic level. When Planck received his Nobel Prize as the father of quantum theory in 1917, he astounded his colleagues with the following mind-blowing statements:

> ...There is no matter as such. Matter doesn't exist the way we think it exists; our world isn't solid. What we see as matter originates and exists only by virtue of a force.... We must assume behind this force the existence of a conscious and intelligent Mind. This Mind is the matrix of what we see as matter.[159]

Physicists have since confirmed that an unseen force, or field, of what they call "nonlocal" (meaning present everywhere) energy surrounds and permeates everything, all the time. Retired quantum physics professor Amit Goswami explains that unlike atoms, which are strictly physical, quanta are the core of everything everywhere, material and nonmaterial.[160]

To quantum scientists there are no fixed objects, but rather "probability patterns" or sets of interconnections that reach out to other interconnections and form what we perceive as matter and energy. While quanta make up the "field of possibility" or "ground of being," an observer is necessary to manifest them.

Expressed mathematically by John von Neumann in 1955, the realization that consciousness is necessary for the collapse of the possibility wave into matter has been repeatedly validated in the famous "double-slit" experiments with light photons.[161]

Physician T. Lee Baumann describes these experiments in his book *God at the Speed of Light,* reporting that, when observed, photons (and electrons, protons, and entire atoms) always instantaneously change from their normal state of waves to particles. He says light

> exhibits an uncanny and unexplained awareness, or consciousness, of its surroundings.... At the time of observation, the wave collapses into a particle. At this moment, the state of the entity changes into what we recognize as "reality."[162]

Journalist David Lewis reports that the current understanding among physicists is that an electron can be both a particle and a wave at once, with differing characteristics.[163] In her book *The Quantum Self,* physicist-philosopher Dana Zohar calls them "wavicles" and says they seem to choose whether to appear and act like a particle or wave depending on the experimental apparatus being used, and sometimes on the expectation of the experimenter.[164] This tells us, Lewis says, that: "matter is defined by conscious perspective rather than being fixed or finite." [165]

Lewis writes that Einstein "suggested that matter is inseparable from an ever-present quantum energy field, that it is a condensation of that field and... the sole reality underlying all appearances."[166] According to Lewis, Einstein said: "What we call matter is energy, whose vibration has been so lowered as to be perceptible to the senses. There is no matter."[167]

Lewis also says that David Bohm, a protégé of Einstein, found that

> electrons act as parts of an interconnected whole... [I]t is ultimately meaningless to see the universe as composed of parts, or disconnected, since everything is joined, space and time being composed of the same essence as matter. A subatomic particle, then, does not suddenly change into a wave; ...it already is a wave sharing the same *non-space* as the particle. Reality, then, is not material in any common sense of the word. It is something far more ineffable. [168]

"Physicists," Lewis says, "call this *non-locality*. Mystics call it *oneness.*"[169]

Described in the book *Wholeness and the Implicate Order,* Bohm "developed, in fact, a holographic model of the universe, where the whole can be found in the most-minute part..." He realized that subatomic quanta are conscious. This means, says Lewis:

> [E]verything is conscious, even inanimate objects and seemingly empty space, the very definition... of mystical or spiritual reality.... Space,

then, is not empty, but filled with highly concentrated conscious energy, the source of everything in existence....[170]

In the quantum world, everything is interconnected relationships.[171] Experiments prove that without an observer, the universe exists only as a possibility. Understanding this, in 1995, Goswami posited that the entire big bang of the universe existed only as an abstract potential until "life somehow evolved to the point that consciousness, as sentient being, came into existence." In the moment of that being's observation, the entire universe suddenly manifested physically. For the universe to exist, he says, a conscious being must be aware of it.[172] But, he explains, it isn't "our ordinary individuality" from which we choose to shape our material reality; it's from the Oneness of our cosmic consciousness.[173] His book, *The Self-Aware Universe,* is an explanation of how this works.

Goswami is one of the scientists who participated in the movie *What the Bleep do We Know!?* He was raised in the Indian Vedanta tradition, but says that becoming a physicist led him to forsake his spiritual upbringing and buy into the strictly materialist belief system, until a friend gave him an "aha," saying:

> ...[C]onsciousness is prior to experiences. Your scientific blinders keep you from understanding. Underneath, you believe that consciousness can be understood by science, that consciousness emerges in the brain, that it is an epiphenomenon. Comprehend what the mystics are saying. Consciousness is prior and unconditioned. It is all there is. There is nothing but God.[174]

To orthodox science, consciousness and self are nuances of matter, referred to as "epiphenomena": enhancements of matter. For orthodox scientists, Goswami says, "explaining consciousness is a matter of understanding how the brain behaves as a complex material machine." But, in Eastern traditions "a transcendent consciousness... is the ground of all being and all else is epiphenomena, matter and self included."[175]

Goswami's "aha" changed his belief system into one that integrates into physics the "monistic idealism" of some spiritual traditions. He now asserts that it's consciousness which transforms the possibility wave into actuality. Quantum physics, he says, provides an opportunity to "recognize that consciousness plays a major role in shaping reality...." To his fellow scientists, he says:

> Perhaps the greatest challenge of living in the world today is compartmentalization, torn as we are between two competing worldviews—one the godless, rationalized creation of the old separatist Newtonian science, the other the spiritual knowledge that resonates abidingly in our hearts.... When the quantum is added and integrated into the Newtonian worldview, you not only have a new, more complete worldview, you have integrated your spiritual heart with your scientific head.... The new science within consciousness acknowledges the role of consciousness... found to be quite consonant with the ancient vision of spiritual traditions....[176]

Quantum physics has been verified with unprecedented precision, yet, while very much a part of it, Einstein is said to have hated it, claiming that if its theories are true, "there is no more science,"[177] in the classical, orthodox sense. Einstein was both a scientist and a mystic; he said: "The world as we have created it is a process of our thinking. It cannot be changed without changing our thinking." He also said:

> A human being is part of the whole, called by us "Universe," a part limited in time and space. He experiences himself, his thoughts and feelings, as something separated from the rest—a kind of optical delusion of his consciousness. ... Our task must be to free ourselves ... by widening our circle of compassion to embrace all living creatures and the whole of nature in its beauty.[178]

The New Science of Epigenetics

Many cell biologists refute the Crick-Watson theory and the "selfish gene" concept. Noetic cell biologist Bruce Lipton says that for fifty years geneticists, looking piecemeal and misunderstanding the workings of a cell, have been separating proteins from their genes, discarding the proteins, and studying only the genes. The orthodox belief says that the nucleus of a cell is its command center or brain, but Lipton's research shows that when the nucleus is removed from the cell, the cell still functions as before, so the nucleus can't be the command center. As it turns out, the nucleus is the reproductive system of the cell, while the cell's membrane is its perception unit, its brain, receiving signals from its environment and sending its own signals to proteins which convert them into behavior. Genes, he says, do not self-activate, but are activated by the signal from the cell's membrane brain. And the membrane is responding to electrical signals, from chemicals and electrical fields—both of which are a function of emotions, which are based on perceptions and beliefs. This means, he says, that belief and perception—our interaction with our environment—control our behavior.[179]

Although most biologists still contend that genes within the DNA molecule determine our structure and our behavior, Lipton says that the proteins manufactured and utilized in the cell, not the genes, provide for both our structure and our behavior. And while DNA contains the blueprints for the protein, the signal from its environment—its perception—activates expression of the gene, so belief controls genes, not the other way around.

Based on this research, Lipton portrays the universe as "a cooperative venture comprised of all living organisms," and adds, "cells and organisms are integrated communities that are physically and energetically entangled within their environment." Evolution, instead of being random, is seen as a mutual development process. Mutations are purposive, adaptive in response to their environment.

In this new approach, called epigenetics, it's understood that our beliefs activate genes and when necessary, rewrite genes. By adjusting our perceptions and the beliefs on which they and our emotions are based, we can actually rewrite our genes and behave in new ways.[180]

The Noetic Sciences

The noetic scientists' view of life on this planet is very different from the orthodox view. The word "noetic," like gnosis, is a process of "inner knowing," and when Edgar Mitchell formed the Institute of Noetic Sciences, he knew he would be challenging traditional science. But he was determined to bring the scientific method to the study of consciousness.

Bruce Lipton explains that the noetic sciences are holistic, transcending the parts to see the whole. For example, examining the cell as a whole unit, its parts and overall functions and processes can be integrally understood better than examining the parts independently. Besides, each cell has system parts identical to its body, such as endocrine, respiratory, neural, and digestive, all better understood as a whole rather than built up as parts. Lipton adds: "the noetic vision emphasizes that life is derived from an integration and coordination of both the physical and the immaterial parts of the universe." He writes:

Noetic science recognizes that the structure of the universe is made in the image of its underlying field. The physical character of atoms, proteins, cells, and people are controlled by immaterial energies that collectively form that field. The cellular community comprising each human responds to a unique spectrum of the universe's energy field. This unique spectrum, referred to by many as soul or spirit, represents an invisible moving force that is in harmonic resonance with our physical bodies.

This is the creative force behind the consciousness that shapes our physical reality. Noetic consciousness reveals that collectively we are the "field" incarnate. Each of us is 'information' manifesting and experiencing a physical reality....[181]

Comments & Questions: New Sciences

Is observation by consciousness how we individually create our own reality? By mentally or emotionally focusing on the possibility of something, whether out of desire or apprehension, we observe it and manifest it—we make it real?

Baird Spalding reports a talk given to a group of engineers and scientists in the late 19th century by the ascended master Jesus that seems to describe this process that is remarkable for its time. Jesus says:

> It takes a true motivating thought, focused on a central absorbing point or ideal to bring forth or accomplish; and you, as well as all mankind, can become that motivating center. Not one thing comes forth unless man first expresses the ideal.

> This is the principle back of the endless array of life and manifestation that you see all around you, and includes your own life, together with that of every existing thing, as every existing thing has life. Ere long science will give you ample grounds for saying that things are not material; as science will soon see that all things can be reduced to one primal element containing innumerable particles universally distributed, responding to vibratory influences, and all in perfect and absolute equilibrium or balance.

> Hence it follows on mathematical grounds alone that it took some definite movement, some initial action, to draw together the infinite particles of this all-pervading universal natural substance, in order to bring them into form as selective objects.

This, then, is not a material universe as you have thought; that is only your definition of it. It came forth from spirit, and it is spiritual if you will define it as such.[182]

Goswami's understanding of the implications of quantum physics is apparently a minority within a minority. That is, most of academic quantum physics, a minority within the sciences, is still very materially oriented, focusing on the measurable level, not the immeasurable level. The spirituality Goswami and others have brought to quantum physics with its concept of consciousness as the ground of being is also very rare.

I was first introduced to Goswami through the movie *What the Bleep Do We Know!?* which reflects some of his ideas. Since I found his thinking very similar to my own, I use him to represent the quantum perspective. This may not be very illustrative of the field, but since my intent is to further spirituality, not orthodox science, it serves my purposes. I thought you should know this.

Conclusions: Science

Although both orthodox materialist and quantum sciences took hold in the early 20th century, orthodox materialism became the preferred mainstream science. Yes, it had been formulated over the course of the previous two centuries, and quantum physics was a new realization of Plato's ideas. But here we are, nearly a hundred years later, and the orthodox position prevails, even though so many of its theories are not supported by current empirical evidence, and quantum theories are. Is this mere academic obstinacy?

As Thomas Kuhn writes in his 1962 landmark book *The Structure of Scientific Revolutions*, science "does not progress via a linear accumulation of new knowledge but undergoes periodic revolutions." These "paradigm shifts" abruptly transform the science of particular fields, rather than science as a whole—as in the scientific revolution of the Enlightenment. In the course of doing their "normal science," scientists hypothesize and conduct research to elaborate on a paradigm. Some of their research results in failure, but are not seen as failure of the paradigm but as mistakes on the part of the researchers. As these failures accumulate, they eventually reach a critical mass and cause acceptance of a new paradigm based in the old paradigm modified by the anomalous results of the "failures."[183]

We can see from Kuhn's work both why many scientists have not denounced the classical Newtonian-Darwinian paradigm and that a new paradigm could be gaining the critical mass necessary for a new scientific "paradigm shift."

The problem with this mode of change is that it's extremely slow. It's said that on average it takes a new idea nearly 50 years to be accepted into mainstream science and up to 75 years for a book written about it to become a standard reference. This obviously means that at any point, scientific education is truly obsolete.

I believe that integrating orthodox, quantum, and noetic sciences would better direct all scientists to a more full understanding of life on Earth, with science and spirituality in balance. I am hopeful that Goswami's and the noetic version of science will one day prevail as mainstream academic science.

---

[114] Hitching, Francis, *The Neck of the Giraffe*, quoted in *Life - How Did it Get Here?* Brooklyn, NY: Watch Tower Bible and Tract Society of New York, Inc., 1985

[115] "Photosynthesis," Wikipedia.com: http://en.wikipedia.org, 1/26/2009.

[116] Erwin, Douglas H., Quoted in "Darwin Still Rules, but some Biologists Dream of a Paradigm Shift." *The New York Times* on line, New York: New York Times, http://www.nytimes.com/2007/06/26/science.

[117] Jastrow, Robert, S. *Red Giants and White Dwarfs*, 1979, quoted in *Life - How Did it Get Here?* Brooklyn, NY: Watch Tower Bible and Tract Society of New York, Inc., 1985

[118] Jastrow, Robert, S. *The Enchanted Loon: Man in the Universe*, 1981, quoted in *Life - How Did it Get Here?* Brooklyn, NY: Watch Tower Bible and Tract Society of New York, Inc., 1985

[119] Cudmore, L.L. Larison, *The Center of Life*, quoted in *Life - How Did it Get Here?* Brooklyn, NY: Watch Tower Bible and Tract Society of New York, Inc., 1985

[120] Mayr, Ernst quoted by Karl W. Giberson & Donald A. Yerxa in *Species of Origins: America's Search for a Creation Story*. Lanham, MD: Rowan & Littlefield Publishers, Inc., 2002

[121] Gould, Steven Jay, quoted by Karl W. Giberson & Donald A. Yerxa in *Species of Origins: America's Search for a Creation Story*. Lanham, MD: Rowan & Littlefield Publishers, Inc., 2002

[122] Larson, Edward J., *The Theory of Evolution: history of Controversy*. Chantilly, VA: The Teaching Company Limited Partnership, 2002
[123] "Early Concepts of Evolution: Jean Baptiste Lamarck," UC Berkeley Education Dept. online at http://berkeley.edu/evosite/history/evol, 2011
[124] Ibid.
[125] Larson, Edward J., *The Theory of Evolution: history of Controversy*. Chantilly, VA: The Teaching Company Limited Partnership, 2002
[126] Ibid.
[127] Ibid.
[128] Ibid
[129] Ibid
[130] Darwin, Charles, *On the Origin of Species*. United Kingdom, 1859
[131] Gould, Stephen Jay, *Ever Since Darwin, Reflections in Natural History*. New York: W. W. Norton & Company, 1977.
[132] "Introduction to Darwin," Great Books edition. Chicago IL: Encyclopedia Britannica for the University of Chicago, 1952
[133] Gould, Stephen Jay, *Ever Since Darwin, Reflections in Natural History*. New York: W. W. Norton & Company, 1977.
[134] Ibid.
[135] Bechner, Morton O., "Darwinism," *The Encyclopedia of Philosophy, vol. 2*. New York: Macmillan, 1972
[136] "Darwin's Theory of Evolution." *Funk and Wagnalls New Encyclopedia, on Infopedia* CD-Rom by SoftKey Multimedia Inc., 1996
[137] Darwin, Charles, *On the Origin of Species*. United Kingdom, 1859
[138] Darwin, Charles, *The Descent of Man*, quoted by Ridley, Matt, "The Darwin Bicentennial - Part Two, Modern Darwins," *National Geographic*, February, 2009. Washington DC: National Geographic Society.
[139] Hominids are species in the primate family, upright-walking and relatively large-brained, including modern humans.
[140] Larson, Edward J., *The Theory of Evolution*. Chantilly, VA: The Teaching Company Limited Partnership, 2002
[141] Dorfman, Andrea, "The Gang' Hits Again," *Time* magazine "Paleontology": New York: Time Inc., April 2, 2001
[142] Neimark, Jill "Take Your Pick," *Science & Spirit* magazine, September/October 2002. Washington, DC: Heldref Publications
[143] Jones, Do-While "Chad Man," from "Evolution in the News," October 2002, published on the Science Against Evolution web site, 2005
[144] Home-Culture/Life/Edu-Culture News on News Guangdong, a Chinese web site, Headline, 2005
[145] Lemonick, Michael D., "Hobbits of the South Pacific," *Time*, magazine "Science," with reporting from Andrea Dorfman/New York and Eugenia Levenson/London. New York: Time Inc., November 8, 2004

[146] Darwin, *On the Origin of the Species*. United Kingdom, 1859
[147] Ibid.
[148] Ibid.
[149] Goswami, Amit, *Creative Evolution, a Physicist's Resolution between Darwinism and Intelligent Design*. Wheaton, IL: Quest Books, Theosophical Publishing House, 2008
[150] Larson, Edward J., *The Theory of Evolution*. Chantilly, VA: The Teaching Company Limited Partnership, 2002
[151] Moore, John M., "Should Evolution be Taught?," *New Science,* 1983, quoted in *Life - How did it get here?* Brooklyn, NY: Watch Tower Bible and Tract Society of New York, Inc., 1985
[152] Dawkins, Richard, *The Blind Watchmaker*, quoted by Phillip E. Johnson in "Evolution as Dogma: The Establishment of Naturalism," in *Intelligent Design Creationism and Its Critics*, edited by Robert T. Pennock. Cambridge, MA: MIT Press, 2001
[153] Goswami, Amit, *Creative Evolution, a Physicist's Resolution between Darwinism and Intelligent* Design. Wheaton, IL: Quest Books, Theosophical Publishing House, 2008
[154] Ridley, Matt, "The Darwin Bicentennial - Part Two, Modern Darwins," *National Geographic magazine*, February 2009. Washington DC: National Geographic Society
[155] Ibid.
[156] Ibid.
[157] *Life - How did it get here?* Brooklyn, NY: Watch Tower Bible and Tract Society of New York, Inc., 1985.
[158] McTaggart, Lynn, *The Field: The Quest for the Secret Force of the Universe*. New York, NY: HarperCollins, 2008.
[159] Planck, Max, quoted by Gregg Braden in *Speaking the Lost Language of God*. Niles, IL: Injoi Corporation, 2004
[160] Goswami, Amit, *The Visionary Window*. Wheaton, IL: Quest Books, Theosophical Publishing House, 2000
[161] For a highly effective illustration of how this works, see the "Dr. Quantum and the Double-Slit Experiment" segment of the video *What the Bleep? Further down the Rabbit Hole.*
[162] Baumann, T. Lee, *God at the Speed of Light*. Virginia Beach, VA: A.R.E. Press, 2001
[163] Lewis, David S., "The Mysticism of Physics," *Atlantis Rising*, November/December 2009;
[164] Zohar, Dana, *The Quantum Self,* London: Houghton-Mifflin, 1997.
[165] Lewis, David S., "The Mysticism of Physics," *Atlantis Rising*, November/December 2009;
[166] Ibid.

[167] Ibid.
[168] Ibid.
[169] Ibid.
[170] Ibid.
[171] In the movie *Mind Walk,* produced by Fritjof Capra, the physicist (played by Liv Ullmann) explains to politician (Sam Waterston) and poet (John Heard) that "We are all part of an inseparable web of relationships." Atlas Productions, 1995.
[172] Goswami, Amit, in an interview with Craig Hamilton called "Proof of the Existence of God," *EnlightenNext,* Fall/Winter 2001. Lenox MA: EnlightenNext Media.
[173] Goswami, Amit, *Creative Evolution, a Physicist's Resolution between Darwinism and Intelligent Design.* Wheaton, IL: Quest Books, Theosophical Publishing House, 2008
[174] Goswami, Amit, *Visionary Window, a Quantum Physicist's Guide to Enlightenment.* Wheaton, IL: Quest Books, 2000
[175] Ibid.
[176] Ibid.
[177] Einstein, Albert, taken from Goodreads Inc., © 2012, an internet source for quotes: www.goodreads.com
[178] Ibid.
[179] Lipton, Bruce, *The Biology of Perception* video, Spirit, 2000, Inc. Also in *The Biology of Belief,* Carlsbad, CA: Hay House, 2007.
[180] Ibid.
[181] Lipton, Bruce, "Embracing the Immaterial Universe," *Shift: at the Frontiers of Consciousness* magazine, December 2005-February 2006. Petaluma, CA: Institute of Noetic Sciences.
[182] Spalding, Baird T., *Life and Teachings of the Masters of the Far East*, Vols. I - V. Santa Monica, CA: DeVorss & Company, 1927, 1944
[183] Kuhn, Thomas, *The Structure of Scientific Revolutions,* Chicago, IL: University of Chicago Press, 1962.

Intelligent Design (ID): A Bridge Between Science and Religion?

Introduction

Creationism and scientism are both extremes, yet both greatly influence our Western society. They battle for supremacy from flawed positions, which makes their adherents defensive and dogmatic—each side fighting for not only their belief system's supremacy but for its very survival. The concept of Intelligent Design has been suggested as a bridge between science and religion, so let's consider it.

The idea of Intelligent Design (ID) has been around since Plato wrote of creation by higher intelligence. The creation story of every culture suggests design, with the biblical version reigning unchallenged in Western culture until Darwin wrote *Origin* as an argument specifically against design, claiming nature had no need for a designer. Today, Darwinism is still a major challenge to the design theories.

A verbal and legal battle rages today, with

> Foes of evolution... convinced that an America that embraces evolution will be an America that has lost its soul. Arrayed against them are evolutionists convinced that an America that does not embrace evolution will be an America that has lost its mind.[184]

The battle began in the U. S. when the space race following the Russian launch of Sputnik in 1959 led to a reform of public high school science curricula which made evolution the core of the life sciences.

A backlash by conservative Christians set off a deluge of laws to ban evolution in public schools. But in 1968, the U.S. Supreme Court ruled that an Arkansas anti-evolution statute "was in place for religious reasons and therefore established a state-endorsed religion in violation of the Constitution."[185]

Hydraulics engineer Henry M. Morris then convinced many conservative Protestants that the biblical creation account was "the only valid one based on scientific evidence." In *The Genesis Flood*, Morris and

John Whitcomb depict each day of creation in scientific terms, such as "energizing of the physical elements of the cosmos" on the first day, "formation of the atmosphere and hydrosphere" on the second day, while the "lithosphere," "biosphere," and "astrosphere" were affected on other days. Doing this also with the flood, they claim the supernatural processes God used in his creation of Earth are no longer operating, so are outside science's purview. The only way to learn of them, they say, is from reading God's Bible.[186]

Morris says a single flood, not evolution, layered all organic fossils. Rather than life evolving from simple to complex forms, the more mobile and intelligent forms of life were able to "run from the approaching deluge," escaping to higher ground. Marine invertebrates are

> ...found at lower elevations in each geological column, for the simple reason that they live at the lowest elevations and would be first affected and buried in a global cataclysm.... The sequence, then, is the result of ecological zonation and is exactly what a great flood would cause.[187]

Soon Biblical Christians were promoting Morris's "creation science" to be taught alongside evolution.[188]

To counter those teachings, the Botanical Society of America issued a statement on evolution that clearly explains the methodology used by scientists to prove or falsify their theories. It explains science's opposition to the inclusion of creation science in public education as unable to stand up to the test of that methodology. (See Appendix C for the BSA statement.)

Support for creation science in public school science classes grew until, in the 1980s, courts systematically ruled against it. The National Academy of Sciences influenced those decisions with the following:

> ...[C]reation science is not science, because it fails to display the most basic characteristics of science: reliance upon naturalistic explanations. Instead, proponents... hold that the creation of the universe, the earth, living things, and man was accomplished through supernatural means inaccessible to human under-standing.[189]

Finally, in 1987, the U. S. Supreme Court ruled against Louisiana's Balanced Treatment Act, saying: "No law was needed to teach scientific evidence for or against evolution... therefore, this law must have been passed to promote religion."[190]

Today's Intelligent Design Movement (IDM)

In the mid-1990s an American Intelligent Design movement (IDM) emerged, focusing on ID as a scientific alternative to Darwinian natural selection. A group called the Discovery Institute established the Center for Science and Culture (CSC) to house and formalize the IDM, mandating it to

> challenge materialism on specifically scientific grounds, to detect intelligent causes in natural systems, as well as apply the explanatory power of Intelligent Design to empirical problems in scientific research.[191]

The CSC's position is that "certain features of the universe and of living things are best explained by an intelligent cause, not an undirected process such as natural selection."[192] The Discovery Institute argues against the Darwinian position, saying it lacks plausibility.

> ...[S]cientists now realize that the structures that confer functional advantage on organisms are exquisitely complex and finely-tuned both spatially and temporally. Living things depend upon hugely improbable arrangements of matter: information-rich genes, complex three-dimensionally specified proteins, functionally integrated molecular machines and hierarchically-organized physiological systems and body plans... [H]ow do these complex biological systems, subsystems and components originate in the first place? The neo-Darwinian answer to this question—random mutations—now lacks all credibility in the face of the astronomical improbabilities associated with the structures that such mutations must build. Chemical evolution theories of the origin of life have likewise failed to explain how the complexity and information necessary to the very first life might have arisen from non-living chemicals.[193]

Mathematician William Dembski, a leading IDMer, says scientists worry that

> invoking design will stifle scientific inquiry, substituting a supernatural cause where scientists should be seeking an ordinary natural cause. By dogmatically excluding design from science, scientists are themselves stifling scientific inquiry.[194]

Richard Dawkins begins *The Blind Watchmaker* saying the complicated things studied through biology "'give the appearance of having been designed for a purpose.'"

Dembski adds that one of the discoverers of the DNA molecule, Francis Crick, says in *What Mad Pursuit*: "Biologists must constantly keep in mind that what they see was not designed, but rather evolved."[195] Why, Dembski asks, when empirical evidence suggests design, must science deny it? "[W]hy should design be barred from the content of science? Isn't it at least conceivable that there could be good positive reasons for thinking biological systems are in fact designed?"[196]

Is ID Science or Religion?

At a meeting of the American Academy for the Advancement of Science (AAAS), attorney Steven Gey said

> The idea that ID is science fails because the theory cannot be empirically tested, it does not appear in peer-reviewed journals and it is not accepted by the vast majority of scientists.... [S]cientists, lawyers and educators shouldn't care if ID claims it's doing science.... That's not the issue. The issue is: Is it religion?[197]

Shouldn't it really be, "Are they doing science?" What difference does it make who does it or if it's published, if it truly is science? The fact that ID is not accepted by the majority of scientists is not legally nor scientifically a valid argument; as we've seen, many theories take years, even decades, to be accepted by the majority of the scientific community—or more than a century in the case of quantum mechanics.

ID is not seen in peer-reviewed journals because Darwinists control those journals and won't print it. So, the only valid question is: Can it be empirically tested?

Complexity & Our Anthropic Universe: Evidence for Design

Dembski says yes to the above question and proposes a "specified complexity" filter of three criteria: contingency, complexity, and specification. If any one of the three is missing, he says, the event was the result of an automatic process, but if all three are present it would suggest design. He refers to biochemist Michael Behe's "irreducible complexity" theory, quoting him:

> An irreducibly complex system cannot be produced... by slight, successive modifications of a precursor system, because any precursor to an

irreducibly complex system that is missing a part is by definition non-functional.[198]

Ken Wilber, an integrating philosopher of science, gives an example of this kind of complexity, looking at wings evolving from forelegs. Saying it takes maybe "a hundred mutations to produce a functional wing from a leg," he adds that a half wing is no good as either a wing or a leg, and that this form of evolution works only when it occurs simultaneously in another animal of the opposite sex and the two get together and procreate. He writes:

> Random mutations cannot even begin to explain this. The vast majority of mutations are lethal anyway; how are we going to get a hundred nonlethal mutations happening simultaneously? Or even four or five, for that matter? But once this incredible transformation has occurred, then natural selection will indeed select the better wings from the less workable wings—but the wings themselves? Nobody has a clue.[199]

Darwinists believe that organs are built up "bit by bit," says Amit Goswami. But the human eye is so complex it would require "thousands of genetic" mutations, and to Darwinism would mean an alternative use for each. ID scientists estimated the number of multicellular species that have ever existed on Earth, figured the approximate number of "chance events" required to produce them, and showed that the required number is almost infinitely greater than the maximum number of events that could have been available.[200]

The almost unbelievably complex and symbiotic details necessary to produce life on Earth have convinced Antony Flew, formerly a leading atheist, to agree with American ID theorists who see "evidence for a guiding force in the construction of the universe."[201] His whole life has been guided by Socrates' principle: "Follow the evidence, wherever it leads." Evidence for an anthropic (human-centered, human-life-supporting) universe has led him to say that, while he still generally accepts Darwinian evolution, he doubts "it can explain the ultimate origins of life.... The only satisfactory explanation for the origin of such 'end-directed, self-replication' life as we see on earth is an infinitely intelligent mind."[202]

Neurobiologist George Wald, too, had believed "life arose by chance," but writes:

It has occurred to me lately that mind, rather than emerging as a late outgrowth in the evolution of life, has existed always as the matrix, the source and condition of physical reality—that the stuff of which physical reality is composed is mind-stuff. It is mind that has composed a physical universe that breeds life, and so eventually evolves creatures that know and create.[203]

The many conditions which enable and support life on Earth, especially human life, are further arguments for design. Over a hundred conditions symbiotically combine to allow life on Earth as we know it. A few such (anthropic) "coincidences" are:
- Earth's elliptical orbit of the sun and its tilt and revolution on its axis together create night and day, annual seasons, and varying climatic conditions.
- Earth's exact distance from the sun allows water to exist here.
- A smaller moon orbits Earth at the right distance to help stabilize Earth's tilt, climate, gravity, and ocean tides.
- Ozone gas surrounds Earth, and protects us from the sun's radiation, while Earth's magnetic core has the right elements to repel space debris.
- Because of sunshine on green plants, we have oxygen and food to sustain life around the world.

If any one of these conditions was off by only .01 degree, say most scientists, life on Earth as we know it would not exist. Astronomer Hugh Ross asks "How many coincidences does it take for one to say that luck has nothing to do with it, that someone has designed it this way?"[204]

Arguments Against Design

Bruce and Frances Martin at least use science to refute ID. Citing vestigial organs as evidence of living intermediate forms, they say faulty or inefficient design features show they are not intelligently designed. The useless appendix is infection-prone, leading to inflammation and potentially fatal appendicitis. Tails are useful to some animals and of no apparent value to such as the elephant, whose tail is small and wispy. "Tails are absent in adult apes and humans, except they appear in early embryos and are residual in the coccyx at the end of the vertebrae;" in some human babies a tail is clipped at birth.[205]

In 1995, the National Association of Biology Teachers wrote a statement to help biology teachers teach evolution:

The diversity of life on earth is the result of evolution: an unsupervised, impersonal, unpredictable and natural process of temporal descent with genetic modification that is affected by natural selection, historical contingencies and changing environments.[206]

Huston Smith (author of the iconic text, *The World's Religions*, originally *The Religions of Man*) wrote a letter to the NABT asking them to change their wording unless they could prove evolution is "unsupervised and impersonal." After initially voting to reject Smith's request, they reconsidered and overturned that decision, changing the wording accordingly.

Teaching the Controversy

Stephen Meyer, philosopher of science and Director of the CSC, wrote in 2001 to the Ohio State Board of Education:

When two groups of experts disagree about a controversial subject that interests the public-school curriculum, students should learn about both... teachers should not teach as true only one competing view... [but] should describe competing views to students and explain the arguments for and against... made by their chief proponents.[207]

Educators call this "teaching the controversy." But orthodox scientist Robert Camp says there's no "legitimate controversy: [The ID movement] is a political movement, begun and led by those outside the discipline... driven by theological imperatives."[208]

The Discovery Institute responded, saying that contemporary theories of ID are based on scientific evidence and analyses, not theological beliefs; and Center fellows are philosophers and scientists. In addition to biochemist Michael Behe's "irreducible complexities" thesis, others are making arguments for ID based on DNA encoding and on Earth's fine tuning for life. The Institute says "[S]cience-based design arguments would still need to be assessed" aside from personal beliefs. Motives don't matter in science. Evidence does."[209]

Is the IDM Christian Based?

Robert Pennock's anthology on Intelligent Design was put together to expose the ID movement's religiosity. It begins with philosophy professor Barbara Forrest saying "extreme right-wing fundamentalist organizations" fund over a million dollars a year to the CSC. She quotes Center director Phillip Johnson:

> If we understand our own times, we will know that we should affirm the reality of God by challenging the domination of materialism and naturalism in the world of the mind.... I have developed a strategy for doing this.... We call our strategy the "wedge."[210]

"The Wedge"

An internet search of the term "Wedge Strategy" uncovered a seven-page "Wedge document," along with responses to critics, and other documents on the Institute's position. The Wedge opens with:

> The proposition that human beings are created in the image of God is one of the bedrock principles on which Western civilization was built. Its influence can be detected in most, if not all, of the West's greatest achievements, including representative democracy, human rights, free enterprise, and progress in the arts and sciences.
>
> Yet a little over a century ago, this cardinal idea came under wholesale attack by intellectuals drawing on the discoveries of modern science.... [Humans were portrayed], not as moral and spiritual beings, but as animals or machines who inhabited a universe ruled by purely impersonal forces and whose behavior and very thoughts were detected by the unbending forces of biology, chemistry, and environment. This materialistic conception of reality eventually infected virtually every area of our culture, from politics and economics to literature and art....
>
> ...Materialists also undermined personal responsibility by asserting that human thoughts and behaviors are dictated by our biology and environment.... In the materialist scheme of things, everyone is a victim and no one can be held accountable for his or her actions....
>
> Discovery Institute's Center for the Renewal of Science and Culture [CSC] seeks nothing less than the overthrow of materialism and its cultural legacies.... and have re-opened the case for a broadly theistic understanding of nature....[211]

The Wedge's "Five Year Strategic Plan Summary" reads: "Design theory promises to reverse the stifling dominance of the materialist worldview, and to replace it with a science consonant with Christian and theistic convictions." It lists governing, five, and twenty-year goals, including: "To defeat scientific materialism and its destructive moral, cultural and political legacies. To replace materialist explanations with theistic understanding that nature and human beings are created by God" Two of its five-year goals are

1. to see Intelligent Design theory as an accepted alternative in the sciences and scientific research being done from the perspective of design theory;
2. to see the beginning of the influence of design theory in spheres other than natural science.

Its twenty-year goals include seeing ID "as the dominant perspective in science.'"[212]

Explaining that the Wedge document was written as a fund-raising tool, one response to critics reads:

> For many the scandal of the 'Wedge Document' is nothing more and nothing less than its mention of 'Christian and theistic convictions and our stated intention to support scientific research that is 'consonant' with such convictions... note first, that 'consonant with' means 'in harmony with' or 'consistent with.' It does not mean the 'same as.'"[213]

IDM's Religiosity

In *Mere Creation*, William Dembski says, "Intelligent Design... confirms that a designer of remarkable talents is responsible for the natural world. How this designer connects with the God of Scripture is then for theology to determine." Mere creation is aimed at "defeating naturalism and its consequences," in four ways:

> 1. A scientific and philosophical critique of naturalism... [identifying] the empirical inadequacies of naturalistic evolutionary theories and... [showing] how naturalism subverts every area of inquiry that it touches;
>
> 2. A positive scientific research program, known as Intelligent Design, for investigating the effects of intelligent causes;
>
> 3. A cultural movement for systematically rethinking every field of inquiry that has been infected by naturalism, reconceptualizing it in terms of design; and
>
> 4. A sustained theological investigation that connects the intelligence inferred by [ID]... with the God of Scripture and therewith formulates a coherent theology of nature.[214]

He adds that it will be theologians' task to formulate a theology that "makes sense not only of God creating, sustaining and acting in the world but also of God incarnating himself in Jesus Christ"[215] Along the same line, and possibly influenced by the nature of his audience, Dembski's 2000 address to National Religious Broadcasters Association also brings Christianity into play:

> ...Intelligent Design opens the whole possibility of us being created in the image of a benevolent God.... The job of apologetics is to clear the ground, to clear obstacles that prevent people from coming to the knowledge of Christ.... And if there's anything that I think has blocked the growth of Christ as the free reign of the Spirit and people accepting the Scripture and Jesus Christ, it is the Darwinian naturalistic view.... It's important that we understand the world. God has created it; Jesus is incarnate in [it].[216]

Comments & Questions: Intelligent Design

Both sides of this issue use flawed arguments. Regarding Morris' fossil layering in favor of creationism, one must ask: if so, why would fossil strata show marine life at the lowest levels? Why would a flood even affect marine life? On the science side, the fact that something is "inaccessible to human understanding" doesn't invalidate it; it merely means we don't yet understand it. I believe that when we come to understand our life on Earth, we will find that what we now consider supernatural is truly the more natural and that material existence is illusion.

When they stick to scientific arguments, such as complexity and the anthropic fine-tuning of Earthly conditions, ID supporters raise good questions and solid observations, worth serious scientific exploration.

Consider that the human body also is a finely-tuned cosmos of irreducible complexity. Every organ depends on the existence of other organs, glands, and their processes, working together cooperatively. Organs depend on the circulatory, digestive, and nervous systems as well as their body's outer protective facade, and couldn't exist without them. Our blood circulates to pick up oxygen from our lungs then flows to all parts of our body to energize every cell. As it travels, it gathers impurities and waste and delivers them back to be expelled as carbon dioxide. Intelligence keeps every bodily process functioning, including muscles working to pump blood, breathe, walk, talk, and chew without conscious attention.

Cells gather like an army to fight an invading alien and produce natural drugs to fight infection and maintain good health. Think of the systems enabling our senses. Can such wonderful processes be merely the result of a gradual build up of chance random mutations? Darwinism says each organ and each system had to develop bit by bit individually, and in other animals before becoming parts of our human body. It's incomprehensible!

While the Martins make good points in their *Skeptical Inquirer* article for the existence of intermediates as indicated by vestigial remnants, not nearly enough evidence of that type has been found to prove that stance. There could be any number of explanations for why animal features are the way they are.

To address one of their primary examples, the wispy tails of elephants are not altogether useless: they act as fly swatters and young elephants often stay in contact by holding on to a parent's tail with their trunk, possibly an essential nurturing mechanism for young elephants.

And regarding the human organ called "the appendix," a 2007 study at Duke University reported that the appendix produces and protects healthy bacteria in our digestive system that help to remove toxins and waste materials from our intestinal tract; those good germs also aid our immune system and help us assimilate nutrients, including B-complex vitamins.[217] The pineal gland, once considered a vestigial organ, is now known to be the producer of a variety of neuropeptides that affect cell behavior, including melatonin, a hormone that acts as a natural sleep aid, contraceptive, mood-enhancer, and infection fighter, and prolongs life.[218]

Maybe other apparently useless and poorly-designed features of life forms only seem as such because their use isn't yet known. Besides, who says design would have to be perfect initially? Why couldn't trial and error exist with design as with natural selection? And, if trial-and-error exists through natural selection, why doesn't the fossil record bear it out?

I can't help agreeing with Dembski: If something looks to be designed, what's wrong with examining it in that light? To disallow any scientific examination on the basis of separation of church and state puts blinders on the scientific community and imposes those blinders on public school children and the public generally. As Einstein is quoted as having said: "Science without religion is blind; religion without science is lame."

Orthodox science has imposed limiting parameters on its own thinking and examination, which doesn't seem very scientific.

Yet, while I agree with the ID supporters' scientific statements, I am horrified by the religious insertions. Parts of the Wedge Document and some of Dembski's words are anything but scientific. If ID is merely a tool of fundamentalist Christianity, I whole-heartedly oppose it. And despite Discovery Institute's qualifications and denials, it sounds like it intends to hold science to its own religious beliefs.

I don't want to see any religion imposed on American society any more than I want materialism forced on us. I strongly believe in our freedoms of choice, study, speech, and worship, and I don't want those freedoms infringed on. Religious convictions must never again dictate what is considered science. I don't want to see materialism replaced with anything but new theories proven through scientific methods. No one but scientists should dictate what defines science. If ID can be shown to be science, great.

Besides, no one religion can represent the diversity in our American pluralistic culture. We must come to terms with all of these issues, and find some way to integrate our acquisition of knowledge with our devotion and introspection in search of higher consciousness, all essential to understanding our life on Earth.

Were ID proponents to let theologians worry about the intelligence that is the designer, they and science generally would be better off. They make it a religious issue, and hurt their own cause and our pursuit of knowledge in understanding life on Earth.

I would love to see the ID supporters' scientific questions answered by impartial scientists, but I realize that in the current atmosphere they likely won't be. Since the folks who support ID are prone to bringing religion into their science, even broad-minded scientists aren't apt to consider ID theories as they are presented.

As a result, impartial investigation of life on Earth is nearly impossible. Gathering of knowledge generally, and the teaching of the sciences in particular, are currently distorted enterprises, limited to strictly materialist considerations: humanity's loss!

I would also like to see a scientific statement assessing the scientific validity of both the ID theories and the orthodox theories ID counters. But it must be from a scientific perspective, not a religious, atheistic, or anti-religion one; not even a spiritual one.

The 2002 AAAS "Resolution on Intelligent Design Theory" (in Appendix D) scratches the surface on this issue but neither invalidates ID theories nor addresses the issues those theories contest. It's just one more indicator that this battle is between opposing fundamentalists, not thoughtful researchers exploring the potential validity of theories of evolution and creation.

The concept of ID, with its irreducible complexity issue, seems a worthwhile scientific pursuit. Consideration of design in the processes of evolution could open science's collective mind to less limiting approaches to life than can be found within the confines of materialism and naturalism. ID without the religious implications could very well bridge the gap between science and religion, or at least smooth some of the rough edges. A little later, we'll see an Intelligent Design proposal from the quantum physics realm—one that just might fit that bill.

Conclusions: Science & Religion

The two approaches are not necessarily incompatible; only their extremes are. Yes, orthodox science and fundamentalist religion are irreconcilable, but they are the extremes and nowhere near all of either religion or the sciences. They're based in sand, rather than standing on a solid foundation, and needn't dictate our future reality. They had a job to do in the past, but we're moving beyond their materialism into a balance of more true and viable beliefs.

Millions of people worldwide are able to reconcile an acceptance of some evolution with theistic belief. Many scientists recognize that no matter how far scientific discoveries and theoretical insight can take us, in the end there is always the unanswered question: Who or what started it?

It seems obvious that a world in which spirituality (whether part of religion or independent) and science (whether part of academia or independent) joined forces would provide a more complete and true picture of life on Earth than is possible with the battling that they do now. We need spirituality to help us understand our inner world and science to better understand our outer world, and both—cooperatively, holistically, and integrally—to help us understand the relationship between the inner and the outer.

The inner and outer aspects of our lives are inseparable, making up the whole person, and only a holistic approach can truly help us understand both our uniqueness and our similarities, our relationships and our individuality. And such an approach has been demonstrated at numerous research institutes—such as IONS, the Heartmath Institute, and the California Institute of Integral Studies. They don't limit their investigation to one aspect or the other but integrate spirituality into science, and are open to new and different ideas. I believe they represent the science of the future.

---

[184] Giberson, Karl, "An evolving dialogue: The literature of America's creation-evolution controversy," *Science & Theology News*, July/August, 2004. Durham, NC: Research News and Opportunities in Science and Theology.

[185] Alspach, Kyle, "Creation v. Evolution through the ages," *Science & Theology News*, July/August, 2004, Durham, NC: Research News and Opportunities in Science and Theology.

[186] Henry M. Morris, quoted by Giberson and Yerxa, *Species of Origins*. Lanham, MD: Rowan & Littlefield Publishers. 2002

[187] Giberson, Karl and Donald A. Yerxa, *Species of Origins*. Lanham, MD: Rowan & Littlefield Publishers. 2002

[188] Principe, Lawrence M., *Science and Religion*. Chantilly, VA: The Teaching Company, 2006

[189] National Academy of Science, in a brief to the Supreme Court, as quoted in Phillip E. Johnson's "Evolution as Dogma: The Establishment of Naturalism," *Intelligent Design Creationism and Its Critics*, edited by Robert T. Pennock. Cambridge, MA: MIT Press, 2001

[190] Larson, Edward J., *The Theory of Evolution*. Chantilly, VA: The Teaching Company, 2002

[191] Giberson, Karl and Donald A. Yerxa, *Species of Origins*. Lanham, MD: Rowan & Littlefield Publishers, 2002

[192] Center for Science and Culture website: www.csc.org.

[193] Discovery Institute Website: www.discovery.org. Seattle, WA: Discovery Institute, 2006.

[194] Dembski, William A., "The Arrow and the Archer: Reintroducing Design into Science," *Science & Spirit* magazine, November/December 1999. Washington, DC: Heldref Publications.

[195] Ibid.

[196] Ibid.

[197] Gey, Steven, quoted by Jullia C. Keller and Thomas Jay W. Oord in "ID's legitimacy debated at Seattle meeting," *Science & Theology News*, Vol. 4 No. 8, 2004. Durham, NC: Research and Opportunities in Science & Theology,

[198] Behe, Michael, quoted by William A. Dembski in "The Arrow and the Archer: Reintroducing Design into Science," *Science & Spirit*, November/December 1999.

[199] Wilber, Ken, *A Brief History of Everything*. Boston, MA: Shambhala Publications, 2000.

[200] Goswami, Amit, *Creative Evolution, a Physicist's Resolution between Darwinism and Intelligent Design*. Wheaton, IL: Quest Books, Theosophical Publishing House, 2008.

[201] Ostling, Richard N., "Leading atheist now believes in God, more or less," *Science & Theology News*, January. 2005. Durham, NC: Research and Opportunities in Science & Theology.

[202] Flew, Anthony, quoted by Eric P. Olsen, in "'Where the Evidence Leads' Famous Atheist Switches Sides" *Science & Spirit* magazine, January/February 2008. Washington, DC: Heldref Publications.

[203] George Wald, quoted by Eric P. Olsen, in "'Where the Evidence Leads' Famous Atheist Switches Sides" *Science & Spirit* magazine, January/February 2008. Washington, DC: Heldref Publications.

[204] Hugh Ross, "Big Bang Model Refined by Fire," in *Mere creation: Science, Faith & Intelligent Design*, ed. William A. Dembski, Downers Grove. IL: InterVarsity Press, 1998.

[205] Martin, Bruce and Frances, "Neither Intelligent nor Designed," *Skeptical Inquirer* magazine, November/December 2003. Amherst, NY: CSICOP

[206] Smith, Huston, *Why Religion Matters*. San Francisco, CA: HarperSanFrancisco, 2001.

[207] Meyer, Stephen, quoted by Robert Camp, "'Teach the Controversy' An Intelligently Designed Ruse," *Skeptical Inquirer*, Sept/Oct 2004. Amherst, NY: CSICOP

[208] Camp, Robert, "'Teach the Controversy' An Intelligently Designed Ruse," *Skeptical Inquirer*, September/October 2004. Amherst, NY: CSICOP.

[209] Discovery Institute Website: www.discovery.org. Seattle, WA: Discovery Institute, 2006.

[210] Forrest, Barbara, "The Wedge at Work; How Intelligent Design Creationism is Wedging Its Way into the Cultural and Academic Mainstream," in *Intelligent Design: Creationism and Its Critics*, edited by Robert Pennock. Cambridge MA: A Bradford Book, MIT Press, 2001.

[211] "The Wedge Document," Discovery Institute Website: www.discovery.org. Seattle, WA: Discovery Institute, 2006.

[212] Ibid.

[213] Discovery Institute Website: www.discovery.org. Seattle, WA: Discovery Institute, 2006, response by author: Johnson.

[214] Dembski, William A., editor, *Mere Creation: Science, Faith & Design*, an anthology. Downers Grove, IL: InterVarsity Press, 1998.

[215] Ibid.
[216] Dembski, William A., talk at a meeting of the National Religious Broadcasters in Anaheim, CA, February 2000, quoted in *Intelligent Design Creationism and Its Critics*, edited by Robert Pennock. Cambridge MA: A Bradford Book, MIT Press, 2001.
[217] Gabbay, Simone, "The Functional Appendix: A Probiotic Factory," *Venture Inward* magazine, January/February 2008. Virginia Beach, VA: Association of Research and Enlightenment.
[218] Chapman, Carole A.P., *The Golden Ones: from Atlantis to a New World*. Mystic CT: CPS, Adult Imprint of Mystic Children's Studio, 2001.

PART THREE: PERENNIAL WISDOM – OUR ROOTS IN ANTIQUITY

> [W]e... find it difficult to recognize the plain fact that there has otherwise been a single philosophical consensus of universal extent. It has been held by... [people] who report the same insights and teach the same essential doctrine whether living today or six thousand years ago, whether from New Mexico in the Far West or from Japan in the Far East.
> ~ Alan Watts

Perennial Wisdom

Introduction

The more we learn about our ancient ancestors and their beliefs, the more clearly we see that our roots were very spiritual. We also realize that many of those beliefs are enjoying a resurgence of popularity in our Western society's quest for enlightenment and understanding of who we truly are.

The remaining parts of this book provide answers to our many big questions about life on Earth from various spiritual perspectives. In this part we'll visit our ancient ancestors, in the next part, today's predominant spiritual teachings, and in the final two parts my own spiritual metaphysics.

The ancients knew truths we are only now discovering, truths we can make our own and build upon. Spiritual metaphysical philosophies (Metas) of today and the new quantum and noetic sciences already benefit from ancient wisdom. In fact, the similarities between ancient beliefs and today's Metas are striking.

Seventeenth-century philosopher Gottfried Wilhelm Leibniz coined the term "perennial philosophy," and Aldous Huxley popularized it in his 1945 book *The Perennial Philosophy*. The term describes the spiritual wisdom of the ancients still in existence in Eastern traditions, aboriginal traditions worldwide, and esoteric societies, considered the mystical essence behind all great religions.

Ken Wilber says it is "the worldview that has been embraced by the vast majority of the world's greatest spiritual teachers, philosophers, thinkers, and even scientists."[219] Baird Spalding says in *Life and Teaching of the Masters of the Far East* that the ancient teachings showed the Masters "the way from the outer to the inner."[220]

While every culture has tales of their ancient past, conventional academics—philosophers, historians, anthropologists, as well as many life and physical scientists—have convinced us that those stories are only fantasies. And, under the control of the Roman church throughout the

Middle Ages, most of Europe was cut off from their cultural history, so prior wisdom and knowledge was almost entirely forgotten. Unable to remember the wisdom and technology of our roots, we must reconstruct them as best we can from bits and pieces found here and there.

From what has been reconstructed, we can see that the cultures in existence 2,000-5,000 years ago (such as the Sumerian, Egyptian, Anasazi, Vedic, and Chinese) did try hard to preserve the wisdom of their ancients and to leave tracks for future generations to follow. The Anasazi left us their petroglyphs and paintings. The Sumerians and Egyptians left us their inscriptions and paintings. The Vedic cultures and Chinese left us their written records on scrolls. Walls, columns, papyrus, leather, parchment, copper, pottery vessels, stone tablets—anything they could use to leave a record on, the ancients did. In later years the Mayans created their calendars and stelae, the Chinese recorded as the TAO the wisdom of the "Ancient Master" (which is what the words *Lao Tsu* mean), and the Greeks left a legacy of logical thought that we use extensively today.

Only in recent decades have some of these bodies of preserved wisdom been discovered, interpreted, and made public. So, today, we can know what some of our truly ancient ancestors knew—and could probably learn more if only conventional academia would open up and provide access to it.

It's clear to many scholars of ancient civilizations that ancient peoples throughout the world had beliefs that were predominantly spiritual. Only the Abrahamic religions developed fundamental beliefs which were essentially nonspiritual, and those religions, too, originally had and retain today spiritual branches. Native traditions worldwide are reclaiming their spiritual roots, some of which they've had to reconstruct after near eradication by missionary Christianity, both Catholic and Protestant. Our Western culture is experiencing a spiritual renaissance in which our nearly lost ancient roots are resurfacing and others are being better understood. Metas today all draw heavily from perennial wisdom—whether directly or because the wisdom is "out there" and available for anyone to intuitively draw upon for their enlightenment.

Conventional Wisdom

When conventional academics come across something that doesn't conform to their accepted view, they usually ignore it or relegate it to fantasy. Fortunately, many alternative researchers (independent nonacademics and maverick academics not limited by orthodox science theories and time lines) make it their life's work to look into such mysteries. Most academics avoid what is not backed by what they consider hard evidence, while alternative researchers are more willing to entertain ideas and value disconnected scraps of information in creating comprehensive explanations for things, and don't limit their thinking to current convention. We need both approaches, countering and complementing each other, to truly understand the nature of life on Earth and how we humans fit into the scheme of things.

Conventional academia says humans were beginning an agrarian mode only about ten thousand years ago (10 tya) and that only an agrarian mode encourages socialization and ultimately civilization. Their strict linear view forces them to believe that our first civilization was the Sumerian one, which arose not quite 6 tya.

Orthodox Egyptologists, therefore, believe the Giza Great Pyramid and sphinx were built only about 4,500 years ago. They also believe that early in their civilization, Egyptians were preoccupied with death and ensuring a good afterlife, and that the kings had the pyramids built as tombs for their final resting places where they could surround themselves with finery made of gold, silver, and lapis lazuli for their use in the afterlife. Being materialists, orthodox Egyptologists would never consider that the pyramids could have been built for any other purpose or that any from of spirituality could have been involved.

An issue that gives science many of its timing conclusions is the northern hemisphere's last "ice age" and its thawing. Geologists say that our Earth undergoes cycles of "glacial ages," and that the last of such ages centered in the northern hemisphere and peaked about 18tya (recently changed to 21tya). Then, northern hemisphere's climate began warming and melting its glaciers and ice sheets, raising sea levels world wide.

By 12 tya, much of the ice had melted, sea levels were high, and once again climatic conditions were more moderate. Conventional anthropologists are convinced that humans originated in Africa and ultimately began spreading out to hunt and gather in new territories. Unable to go great distances by boat, their travels were mostly on land, often following the seashore. Many scholars believe humans went first to what is now Europe, then to Asia and Australia. Others say it happened the other way around. Both say that humans entered North America where a land link still existed between Siberia and Alaska about 12 tya (updated to 13.4tya), and migrated south to populate the Americas.

Let's look now at our ancient ancestors and what some of them believed before institutionalized Christianity divested us of those roots. Let's see if our evolution might have been circular instead of linear. Let's see how our ancient ancestors might have answered Edgar Mitchell's question, and discover what a full-blown, concerted spiritual renaissance would return to us.

---

[219] Wilber, Ken, *Grace and Grit*, also quoted in *The Essential Ken Wilber, an Introductory Reader*. Boston, MA: Shambhala Publications, Inc. 1998.
[220] Spalding, Baird T. *Life and Teaching of the Masters of the Far East*, Santa Monica, CA: DeVorss, 1927.

Ancient Civilizations: New Light on Their Age and Sophistication

Introduction

To help us uncover our spiritual roots, let's look at what we know about ancient civilizations, not only how conventional academia views them—the prevailing view—but also alternative views of them, for greater understanding. Remember that our beliefs and level of consciousness dictate our views, so different levels cause people to see things quite differently. Alternative researchers view ancient human cultures and civilizations very differently than do orthodox academics, and have amassed considerable evidence showing not only greater antiquity of our earliest civilized ancestors but greater sophistication, knowledge, and spirituality than the orthodox can accept. Alternative researchers enable a broader, more holistic view, but generally, orthodox academics only ridicule them.

An example of different conclusions influenced by different approaches is the reading of ancient megaliths (cities, pyramids, rock circles such as Stonehenge, figures), hieroglyphs, and other symbolic art and scripts in determining their antiquity, purpose, and meaning.

Alternative researchers recognize highly advanced applications of complex mathematics, geometry, astronomy, and engineering in the configurations of megaliths all over the world. They see structures such as Stonehenge as astronomical/astrologic observatories or energy conductors. They read written and symbolic hieroglyphs, such as the Egyptian wall paintings, as historical record and meaningful mystical symbolism rather than merely decorative art, story-telling, or primitive doodling.

Unlike alternative scientists, orthodox scientists don't view the megaliths and their configurations as hard evidence. Confined and limited by their narrow view and adherence to established time lines, and believing sophisticated concepts and construction could not have been possible, they don't recognize signs of spirituality in ancient relics, and discount alternative possibilities. They have few answers for how the building blocks and figures of the world's thousands of megaliths were cut, transported, and erected, with huge stones weighing up to several hundred tons each, often put precisely in place and fit together like pieces of jigsaw puzzles. They ignore the fact that those structures attest to the use of exact astronomy and highly advanced mathematics with construction and transportation methods unknown to us. The orthodox mind-set won't let academic materialists accept such early knowledge and sophistication so they don't delve into these issues and they discredit or just ignore alternative claims. Their beliefs limit their reality.

Our First Civilizations

The Sumerian civilization in the Mesopotamian region is traditionally considered humanity's first urban empire. Orthodox researchers, however, don't have a clear explanation for the known sophistication of that culture from nearly 4000 BCE. Sumerians reportedly made beautiful pottery vases, bowls, dishes, and special jars for oils, sealed with clay; and they wove baskets of reeds or leather, and made beds, stools, and chairs with carved legs. They had fireplaces with chimneys and canals for irrigation and fresh water and sewage disposal. They created weapons and tools from metals with wooden handles, and worked copper into plates, and gold and silver into necklaces. Time was counted in lunar months, with sixty seconds to a minute and sixty minutes to an hour. They had a complex spoken language and, after inventing writing around 3500 BCE, wrote laws and scientific texts on subjects that included mathematics, astronomy, and medicine.

The Sumerians had stories of creation, a flood, and a dying and resurrecting god-man, that inspired later Mesopotamian mythology, religion, and astrology. They wrote of "spirit" and "life" manifesting as the power of motion, with all things that move, including water, possessing life or spirit.[221]

Primitive? And there's no evidence of the typical learning curve for this, humanity's "first civilization!"

Egyptian Megaliths

The pyramids of Egypt are described in textbooks and tourist guides as the tombs of pharaohs. Alternative researchers, however, say that no evidence of burial has been found in any of the Egyptian pyramids because they weren't tombs. The "king's chamber" of the Great Pyramid appears to have been built around a stone box, usually described as Pharaoh Khufu's sarcophagus, but found empty of any burial relics. Orthodox researchers say the lack of burial evidence is due to thefts by grave robbers.

Alternative researchers believe those pyramids were temples erected to help Mystery-school initiates celebrate spiritual life, use astrology through knowledge of astronomy, and transcend materiality. That lidless stone box, for example, may have been used during Mystery initiation to symbolically represent the initiate's death to the material world, rather than as a real burial sarcophagus. Some believe the Great Pyramid was a kind of energy machine.

The Great Pyramid and sphinx, orthodox Egyptologists believe, were erected in 2600 and 2500 BCE respectively by local farmers. Assuming the pyramid was commissioned by Pharaoh Khufu and then designed and built before his death, Egyptologists allow 20 years (within Khufu's 22-year reign) for its construction—during farmers' off seasons. Stone placement, they say, was at a rate of 200 to 300 blocks per hour by ropes and pulleys.[222]

Including its missing capstone, that pyramid rises up nearly fifty stories in height and each side of its base is over two football fields in length! It covers more than 13 acres, aligns perfectly (within .01 degree) with true north, and is level to the same degree of accuracy, despite thousands of years' settling! It has over 2,300,000 stone blocks and a mass of many million tons. Most blocks weigh about 2.5 tons, while some of the highest placed ones weigh over 70 tons. Other details of precision boggle the mind even with today's technology.

How could men possibly have moved and placed by ropes and pulleys 200 to 300 blocks per hour, and into such precise positioning? That's three to five blocks every daylight minute of their "off" season for 20 years! During those years farmers were also digging bedrock, creating rooms and connecting tunnels, while others were perfectly cutting the blocks and the façade stones and transporting them many hundreds of miles and floating them across the Nile River to Giza.

This would have required very sophisticated planning, and a huge number of farmers, at the least. None of this addresses the issues of architecture and engineering involved in planning and constructing the four-sided pyramid, with each side identical and all four meeting at the exact center point.

Alternative researchers had the Great Pyramid examined by modern construction experts, who said we couldn't erect such a structure today by our technology. Even lasers couldn't cut the faces as perfectly flat as the remaining facade stones, nor could they cut the building blocks so precisely, placed without gaps between them.

And, experiments have shown the facade stones too heavy for any known flotation method.[223] If we are to believe those experts, the designers and builders of at least the Great Pyramid were more advanced in construction methods than we are today.

And, if one considers the evidence without prejudice, there is no evidence that Egyptians even built that pyramid. According to Manly P. Hall, the distinctive mortuary art associated with Egyptian royalty in tombs where burials have been found is entirely lacking, as are the other elements of Egyptian architecture and decoration.[224]

Further Evidence of Ancient Sophistication

Not only the Great Pyramid but all of the ancient megaliths (some 500 known pyramids, and thousands of "stone circles") around the world display advanced knowledge and techniques we know little or nothing about today.

Some are more incomprehensible than the Giza Plateau structures. As presented in a 2003 NBC television special, Robert Schoch, a maverick academic geologist, and alternative researcher John Anthony West demonstrate their proof that the Sphinx is more than 10,000 years old[225], having existed when rain was prevalent in the area before water levels reached their highest after the last ice age. Because most the facade stones of the Great Pyramid were removed centuries ago to build the mosques of Cairo, any water damage they may have incurred cannot be assessed.[227]

Engineer Arlan Andrews, referring to Christopher Dunn's *Lost Technologies of Ancient Egypt*, points out that because Dunn was open to an alternative perspective, with "a trained eye for such details," he was able to "read" the tool marks on the Abu Roash stone near Giza as machine-cut and modern. Andrews says:

> To suggest that the primitive tools ascribed to the ancient Egyptians could have produced anything like these markings is ridiculous.... [T]his machined stone by itself demonstrates... that the ancient Egyptians possessed technologies not replicated until the twentieth century—if even then.[228]

Andrews says that Dunn shows many examples that indicate the genius of the ancient machinists, engineers, designers, and planners, which taken together refute traditional Egyptologists' conclusions. Ancient Egypt underwent numerous upheavals caused by droughts, floods, earthquakes, civil wars, religious strife, and foreign invasions; and, when civilization fails for any reason, says Andrews, metals of all kinds become knives, spear points, scrapers, fishhooks, and plows. During their times of collapse, the ancient Egyptians' advanced metal tools were probably recycled (disassembled or melted down), and what wasn't used would corrode and after thousands of years leave no trace evidence. He adds: "Other advanced technology may also have been employed, the remnants of which we might not recognize today."[229]

"Archaeologists," Andrews writes, may "one day uncover an untouched ancient factory or workshop under the sands or in the caves of Egypt, a place that was purposefully hidden away from destructive recycling,...."[230] But to recognize evidence of ancient technologies, he says, those future discoverers must have minds open to alternative possibilities, "otherwise, that advanced machine shop of the ancients could wind up stored in unnumbered boxes in the basement of the Egyptian Museum in Cairo," labeled "funerary objects," as sadly, too many remarkable finds have.[231]

Andrews also reports on Gobekli Tepe, a huge newly-discovered temple complex in Turkey dated to between 12 and 13tya. He writes of T-shaped monuments nearly 20 feet tall, weighing from ten to fifty tons, many of which have carvings of wildlife and human-shaped reliefs. He says that for unknown reasons, this site was deliberately buried about 10,000 years ago. He writes:

> Because this site can be dated as existing prior to previously established dates for the beginning of agriculture and urbanization, not to mention cooperative construction of stone monuments, we can readily believe that conventional chronology is at the least incomplete, if not wholly inaccurate. We see that every new archaeological discovery pushes back

civilized development further and further into the past, never in the opposite direction.[232]

Also, it's common practice, even today, to construct new temples over old ones. Michael Baigent, co-author of *Holy Blood, Holy Grail*, reports that excavation beneath the Egyptian ziggurat uncovered 23 such temple levels, the oldest dating back to at least 5000 BCE.[233]

Atlantis and Other Possibilities

While orthodox researchers reject the possibility of an ancient civilization predating Sumer, many alternative researchers consider that Plato's and other descriptions of Atlantis may have some basis in reality. They surmise that spiritually awake Atlanteans must have realized that both their land and their culture were degenerating and sought to preserve their history, scientific achievements, and spiritual wisdom passed down orally through the ages. Ancient texts may one day be read to contain such information.

While nearly all ancient aboriginal cultures recite legends of very ancient peoples who traveled by sea and air and performed magic, orthodox scientists believe advanced civilizations could not have preceded ours.

Most academics consider Atlantis fantasy, even though Plato was not, to all appearances, given to fantasy. Using information given him by Solon, possibly his grandfather. Plato described the Atlantean culture, its architecture, government, commerce, military, religion and spiritual practices, and general living in great detail. Solon, Plato reported, received the story of Atlantis in Egypt from a high priest translating what was recorded in hieroglyphic text on a monument pylon.[234]

Why would both Solon and Plato be so specific if not to give credence to the validity of their reports?

According to Edgar Cayce, an American clairvoyant who used intuitive methods to respond to a wide variety of questions, an older group that has been called Lemurians built the first great Earth civilization, possibly a few million years ago. He stated that they used

> levitation of otherwise immovable objects, psychokinesis, communal telepathy, remote viewing, metaphysical healing, the shifting of space and time, prophecy, interspecies communication, interdimensional travel, ...far more than we can guess.[235]

Some of those abilities and the understandings that went with them were possibly passed on to Atlanteans, who in turn passed some on to other civilizations.

Cayce also said that Atlanteans went to teach the people of the Nile valley and that tunnels between the sphinx and second Giza Plateau pyramid (the Khafre) connect archival rooms still buried very deep, to be found only when humanity is more spiritually responsible.

Talk of Atlantis was reportedly common in Plato's day, but since his description provides the greatest detail and is the best preserved it is the one most often used. He claimed about 350 BCE that thousands of years earlier the great civilization of Atlantis came to an end when the last remaining island of its once large continent was inundated with sea water. Since then, alternative researchers worldwide have speculated as to the location of Atlantis and have sought physical evidence of its existence. Bimini, Cuba, Crete, Cyprus, and Antarctica have been proposed, places where researchers report finding submerged remnants of a great culture.

If advanced Atlanteans were able to perform what to more simple cultures were miracles, they likely were considered gods, or at least demigods, and idolized by primitive cultures. It was common practice for ancient cultures to deify their heroes and create mythic stories about them. But, there's no reason not to take the basics as truth. Similarities are found in most cultures' myths, which could well be stories originating in Atlantean times. Many may have been based on fact, and most were likely symbolic or metaphoric, designed to inform the spiritual initiate and those in future generations able to decipher them and use them responsibly.

Why would ancient Egyptians be so precise in their art and texts and go to such great lengths to preserve them if they were mere fantasy? Do we, today?

With alternative thinkers seeing them from a more open view, those texts and symbols are beginning to be understood. And as the new understandings emerge, they may tell of an entirely different and considerably older ancestry than orthodox Egyptologists can accept.

All known ancient cultures worshiped deity(ies) and maintained some form of spiritual life. Aborigines worldwide have passed down such oral traditions, and evidence indicates that the least civilized peoples of prehistoric time had knowledge of the Mysteries. (We'll see the "Mysteries" shortly.) Although there may always have been nonbelievers, it can be fairly stated that until the 19th century (amazingly recent) the majority of people everywhere based their life on the worship of God: God, however described, was the center of life.

Where and how did such beliefs and lore originate? When we developed consciousness, did we also, without cause or higher purpose, become spiritual? Is it in our genes? Did we maybe learn from our elder cousins, Neanderthals? The earliest known example of a deliberate ceremonial burial was conducted by Neanderthals one hundred thousand years ago in central Asia. Were Neanderthals perhaps Atlanteans, who were displaced from their homeland when it began breaking up, immigrating into Europe, the Middle East, and Asia?

Considerable evidence, particularly in the Sanskrit language common to peoples across an enormous area from Asia Minor and Europe to India, seems to attest to an early "mother civilization." Could that civilization be of the beings science calls Neanderthals, once believed to be unable to speak or create, but now thought to have had language and religion? Hominids showing Neanderthal characteristics began appearing in Europe as early as 600 tya and were fully developed by 130 tya when they began migrating east, then suddenly disappeared not quite 25 tya. If Neanderthals were Lemurians or Atlanteans, surviving after the breakup of their land, they may have been far more sophisticated than science has believed them to be. As we observed earlier, the fact that they had larger brains than ours confuses orthodox scientists, because to them the larger the brain the more intelligent, and since they believe modern humans to be evolution's acme, in their minds it's impossible that any predecessor could have been more intelligent.

It seems obvious that previous civilizations were more advanced than our current one in many ways, though maybe not in modern technologies (but that's probably good). The hundreds of great mys-teries give us clues (and empirical evidence) of early advances we should not ignore.

Extraterrestrial Influence or Circular Evolution?

The advanced nature of megalithic configurations—not only their size but their polar and astronomical alignments—makes many people believers in extraterrestrial influence. Existence on Earth of highly evolved extraterrestrials early in our history could explain many mysteries of the world. Aliens could have moved the huge stones used to build the great megalithic structures by "beaming them up" to their new location on the Giza Plateau, in Turkey and Mexico, at Stonehenge, on Easter Island, in China, South America, and many other sites. ET involvement could also account for the advanced astronomical knowledge and the higher mathematics used in those impressive structures and in the Maya calendars. It could explain the huge "aerial runways" in Peru.

But to explain our early sophistication by saying it came from people of another planet, solar system, or galaxy is to beg the issue. It merely moves the location of the puzzle to another part of physical existence. We still would have to ask how life began, and how it got so advanced.

People believe the "ancient alien" notion often because they have bought into conventional science's evolution patterns, if not time lines. Without those limitations, the existence of advanced civilizations as earlier ordinary phases of circular human evolution could also explain these anomalies.

Many alternative researchers have catalogued ancient petroglyphs (rock drawings) and other symbolic art, worldwide, that depict what appear to be flying machines: airplanes, helicopters, rockets, and astronauts in spacesuits. Also, aboriginal stories tell of gods arriving by air or sea. Those who insist that our human origins, or at least our knowledge and technologies, are extraterrestrial point to these as supporting evidence. But one could also see them as further evidence of the sophistication of an earlier, advanced civilization, perhaps Atlantean with those abilities. Atlanteans may have interacted with extraterrestrials, an idea that doesn't deny the existence of ETs, but may open one's thinking to possibilities of a circular, rather than a linear development path for humanity.

Most Metas speak freely of Atlantis and Lemuria, because our views of human life on Earth indicate a circular evolutionary pattern rather than linear. We would say that humans began life on Earth as wholly spiritual beings using pure intelligence, then gradually became increasingly material. In this understanding, some of our human ancestors, once they became physical, deliberately devolved to almost base creatures, forgetting how to use their pure intelligence and extra-sensory abilities, before beginning a gradual evolution back. On this upward round of the circular, humanity is moving back toward those abilities and, with them, an ultimate reawakening to the spirituality of our true being. As a result, Metas' beliefs not only allow for such earlier advanced civilizations but direct us to them.

Continental Drift

One issue for science is that Atlantis is thought of as a continent in the Atlantic Ocean and current science's theory of plate tectonics does not allow for such a continent.

Plate tectonics is, however, a relatively new theory. Early in the 20th century, astronomer Alfred Wegener realized (as have many of us on looking at a globe) that the configuration of the coast lines of South America and Africa seemed to fit like pieces of a jigsaw puzzle. Building on the work of earlier theorists, but with more mathematical precision, Wegener developed a theory of continental drift, in which the continents we see today are the result of the splitting of a larger land mass and drifting apart. Wegner produced evidence of this theory with similarities in animals and plants—in particular the fossilized life—along and near the shores of South America and Africa. As might be expected, orthodox science, because it was married at the time to a static Earth, rejected Wegener's theory as coincidental fantasy. But in the 1960s, aerial photography disclosed a closer match than could be noted on previous maps, enabling scientists to see that not only the coastlines of South America and Africa matched remarkably, but so did other opposing coastlines.

Geologists then developed a "plate tectonics" model, in which the Earth's hard stone crust and upper mantle, or lithosphere, is made up of thirteen "relatively thin, rigid plates which include both continental and ocean crust and which move relative to one another." Current science says that movement of these plates has created mountains, earthquakes, and volcanic eruptions.[236]

With continental drift in mind, scientists of the Geological Survey in 2014 saw the configuration of land masses on Earth as originally far different from what it is today. They posit that roughly 225 mya, land on Earth was one large mass or supercontinent, which they call Pangaea, a Greek word meaning "all of Earth." They say that by 200 mya that single land mass had begun splitting horizontally, with water moving in from both sides at its midsection to nearly separate the north (Laurasia) from the south (Gondwanaland).

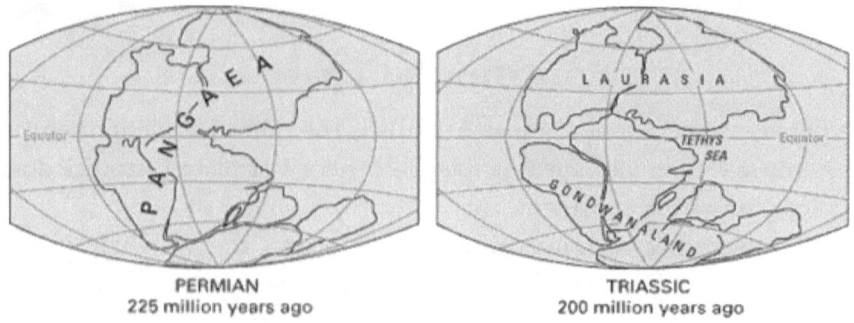

Figure 1

By 135mya, what is now India had separated from the southernmost area and was an island moving north, leaving what has become Antarctica and Australia/New Zealand together as a single land mass in the far southern hemisphere.

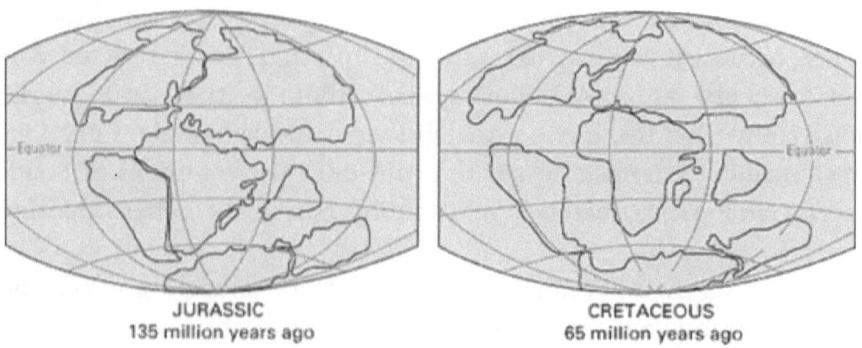

Figure 2

By 65 mya, Gondwanaland was split apart vertically, and the continents we identify today as South America and Africa were separated. As they spread apart, sea water filled in the space between, forming the Atlantic Ocean.

Though Africa was still attached to what eventually became Europe, the Middle East, and Asia, definition between them had begun, as well as between those portions of Laurasia that were destined to become Europe and North America. The northernmost part of Laurasia was still joined.

When India ran into Asia, sometime in the last 50 million years, the collision created the Himalayas. North America's land link with Europe was broken only about 2.5 mya.[237] (This accepted continental drift theory can also be recognized in the Genesis phrase "Let the waters part the land.")

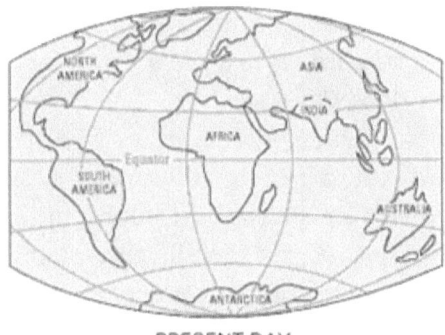

PRESENT DAY

Figure 3

Evidence of Very Ancient Civilizations

South Pacific natives tell of a great civilization that thrived in their area, spread over the lands of what Edgar Cayce and others called Mu. This culture (today called "Lemurian" after the many lemurs found across the area) predated and overlapped Atlanteans, reportedly inhabiting former archipelagos stretching continuously from Peru to the South China Sea and probably north to the East China Sea. Forced abandonment dispersed those Mu people east, west, and north.

After World War II, sunken remains of ancient structures were found in the shallow waters all around the Japanese islands, extending over 300 miles in length. Researchers who investigated them said they comprise paved roads, grand staircases, broad plazas, and huge altar-like structures.[238]

A submerged "monument" was found in 1987 off the coast of the southernmost Japanese island of Yanaguni-jima, just north of Taiwan, and is now said to be part of a huge complex that stretches for many hundred miles. Professor Masaaki Kimura of the University of the Ryukyus on Okinawa, Japan, has studied those ruins for more than ten years, leading teams of graduate students.

Kimura is convinced by the evidence that the area was once above sea level, so dates to at least 8000 BCE, and possibly up to 16 tya. Kimura's team has salvaged pieces of stone tools, typically adzes, dated to 10 tya. He says there are 15 formations involved, including a castle, linked by water channels, trenches, and roads.[239] One trench has two internal 90° angles, while twin megaliths with straight edges and square corners appear to have been placed where they sit. But, although the right angles, sharp edges and flat parallel faces indicate artificial formation to those researchers, other orthodox researchers consider them natural formations of cliffs and slabs.[240]

Numerous other submerged complexes have been located around the world. There are said to be over 200 sunken cities in the Mediterranean Sea alone, and two sites have been found in the Indian Ocean off northwest India, dating to 32 tya. Fossilized remains of some 2,000 humans have been found there and carbon dated to nearly 10 tya.

Most of these underwater formations, researchers believe, were submerged by rising sea levels as the ice of the last Glacial Age melted. Dating is thus based on that timing, and indicates the "cities" existed above water conservatively prior to 10 tya, and possibly closer to 16 tya. Was Sumeria truly our first civilization, only 5-6 tya?

Intuitive researchers say that in their observations Atlanteans built magnificent cities, temples for spiritual practices, and Stonehenge-type astronomical equipment out of megalithic rocks. As Atlanteans, they say, humanoids created land, sea, and air vehicles, computers, and household conveniences, and used natural crystals, electromagnetic forces, and solar power to run the computers, propel the vehicles, and perform other tasks.

Based on the results of regressions and other intuitive methods it appears that Atlanteans may have used teleportation, visualization, solar power, and natural gases in cooperation with the living, cognizant rocks and minerals to erect those wonderful structures. They likely left their disintegrating homeland before its final destruction, and probably aided other civilizations in many ways.

Many alternative thinkers believe Atlanteans built those Giza Plateau pyramids and sphinx and either built or influenced the construction of megalithic structures all over the world. If so, those structures may be considerably older than currently thought.

Evidence of Ancient Advancement: Modern Humans—When?

Orthodox scientists use the fact that no evidence of advanced technology has been found as proof it never existed. But alternative researchers recognize in the megalithic structures themselves different kinds of technology from what we use today, and maybe more advanced. Devices may have been environmentally friendly and biodegraded, and still other methods, based on energy, may have been used to accomplish what we now do through material technology. They may have used thought processes to create things and then dissolve them when through using them. Fossil evidence doesn't exist of a Lemurian civilization probably because we humans were not originally physical when we started experiencing this planet. Even as early Atlanteans, we may not have yet fully slowed our vibrations to maintain material forms and possibly still didn't die, so also wouldn't have left bones to fossilize—hard evidence the orthodox look for. At least, not until taking the form that is now called Neanderthal.

Much of the evidence indicating that modern humans lived on Earth a very long time ago has been ignored completely as not worth investigating, because given Darwinism it couldn't be valid; it must be misinterpretation of facts, or mistaken dating.

Investigating the documented discoveries of the last 150 years, Michael Cremo and Richard Thompson uncovered a picture of humanity's antiquity very different from that of conventional science. In their 1993 *Forbidden Archaeology, The Hidden History of The Human Race*, they offer evidence of modern humans and advanced civilizations dating back many million years, evidence in the form of both anatomically modern human fossils and artifacts of tools, art, and adornments. This large book (962 pages) contains virtually nothing but such evidence, and succinctly at that. Cremo is a research associate at and Thompson is a founding member of The Bhadtevedanta Institute, founded in 1975, "dedicated to the advanced study of the nature and origin of life and the universe in light of ancient India's Vedic literature."

Because of the length (and sometimes tedious) details of *Forbidden Archaeology*, Cremo and Thompson published an abridged version, entitled *The Hidden History of the Human Race.* In its introduction, Cremo writes that he and Thompson "look closely at the vast amount of controversial evidence that contradicts current ideas about human evolution." He says,

> We recount in detail how this evidence has been systematically suppressed, ignored, or forgotten, even though it is qualitatively (and quantitatively) equivalent to the evidence favoring currently accepted views on human origins. When we speak of suppression of evidence... we are talking about an ongoing social process of knowledge filtration that appears quite innocuous but has a substantial cumulative effect. Certain categories of evidence simply disappear from view....[241]

They give examples: a California State geologist published a review of stone tools found in California gold mine shafts beneath undisturbed lava rock that was formed from 8 mya to over 25 mya. A director of the Smithsonian Institution wrote that if the geologist

> ...had fully appreciated the story of human evolution as it is understood today, he would have hesitated to announce the conclusions formulated (that humans existed in very ancient times in North America), notwithstanding the imposing array of testimony with which he was confronted.[242]

In other words, says Cremo, "if the facts do not agree with the favored theory, then such facts, even an imposing array of them, must be discarded."[243]

Cremo says there are also what appear to be cases of direct suppression, and gives examples of those, too. One is about a staff member of the National Museum of Canada in the 1950s who found large numbers of advanced stone tools in glacial deposits that were known to have been laid between 65 tya and 125 tya. Since humans were then thought to have entered North America only about 12 tya, those datings were unacceptable to those in power:

> The discoverer was hounded from his Civil Service position into prolonged unemployment; publication outlets were cut off; the evidence was misrepresented by several prominent authors... the tons of artifacts vanished into storage bins of the National Museum of Canada; for refusing to fire the discoverer, the Director of the National Museum... was himself fired and driven into exile; and the site has been turned

into a tourist resort.... It would have forced the rewriting of almost every book in the business. It had to be killed, [and] was.[244]

In *Human Devolution*, Cremo summarizes the evidence, and then offers a Vedantic premise of circular evolution for science to use to replace its old, worn out one. He writes a column in *Atlantis Rising*, a (now defunct) magazine that covered alternative views on ancient mysteries, unexplained anomalies, future science, and new finds for several decades. Entitled "The Forbidden Archaeologist," the column shows the mounting evidence and covers new discoveries and alternative theories.

The majority of found objects (fossils and artifacts), Cremo and Thompson report, are dated to between 300 tya and 25 mya, but some have been dated to as long ago as 300 million years. A metal vase found in Massachusetts dates to 600 mya, and a grooved metallic sphere was found in South Africa and dated to 2.8 billion years![245] Such dates certainly must pose confusion to both orthodox and alternative scientists, but, as they suggest, the dating methods may be at least part of this problem. [246]

Nonetheless, Cremo's and Thompson's evidence pushes modern humans back many million years, and civilization back at least many hundred thousand years. Cremo says that while "standard Western accounts" put Mesopotamian civilization at about 7 tya, Babylonian king lists cover 432,000 years, and Egyptian, Chinese, and Indian civilizations "go back much further in time than the standard Western histories now tell us." He adds that the Mayan calendars "cover vast spans of time, millions of years."[247] Manly Hall says: "The human race is exceedingly old. Modern science counts its age in tens of thousands of years; occultism, in tens of millions."[248] And, of course, fundamentalist Christians limit it to only 6,000 years.

Comments & Questions: Ancient Lore

Why, if such evidence really does exist, don't we hear about it from the scientific community? It's really very simple: if the orthodoxy accepted the evidence as valid, they would have to rethink the whole premise on which they have based their work for 150 years, and most are not willing to do that. They would also have to develop a whole new premise and would be at a loss as to what that might be. So, instead, conventional science ridicules, rejects, refuses publication of, and "loses" authenticated evidence and forces people out of academia who try to publicize such discoveries.

Aborigines worldwide tell of very ancient, highly advanced ancestors. Can they all—rather than conventional science—be wrong?

Many of the discoverers of underwater megalithic "cities" are convinced that they have found the one, single Atlantis. That may be true, but there may be another way to think about them and I haven't yet seen anyone put all the discoveries together in their thinking.

Consider this possibility: the supercontinent called Pangaea by orthodox scientists could have been what alternative thinkers call Mu or Lemuria, with its east and west coasts fringing the ocean (now the Pacific), and seeming like island archipelagos. Edgar Cayce said the Lemurian "semi-human culture" began around 12mya, and lasted for millions of years, which would support this hypothesis.

It's possible that, before the Atlantic Ocean split Laurasia and Gondwanaland vertically up the middle, a more inland Atlantean humanoid culture occupied the region, and instead of disintegrating and submerging, it gradually split apart and is still in existence as parts of Greenland, North America, Central and South America, Europe, Africa, and Antarctica—those areas fringing the Atlantic Ocean. Sunken evidence of earlier civilizations may well support this idea, and the numerous megaliths worldwide, whether still on land or submerged, may have been parts of that Atlantean civilization.

Consider also, that what seems today to have been many hundred million years, may actually have been only a few hundred thousand years. Slowing vibrations created time and the materiality we see as Earth, and it's likely that our human vibrations were initially much faster than they are today. This would mean truly ancient time is not at all comparable with our current time and would make our current measurements irrelevant to the actuality.

My point is that it seems clear that highly sophisticated and hugely populated civilizations (with as many as a million people) existed far longer ago than fits the orthodox belief system. That the sunken ruins are likely far older than many excavated sites can be surmised from the mere fact that they are underwater and must have existed above water prior to rising sea levels at the *end* of the last Ice Age, nearly 12 tya. In fact, they must have been there well before the melting and rising began, and, of course, we have no idea how many thousands of years those cities stood before they were submerged.

The peak of the last Ice Age, scientists now tell us, was about 21 tya, so sea levels were at their lowest then. It seems logical that building of coastal cities may have been as far back as 23 tya, when the waters were receding. Then, when the waters began to rise, people would have moved to higher, drier ground—in places like Jericho and Catal Huyuk, where cities with populations of several thousand people have been excavated, dating as far back as about 11tya.

Clearly, I'm speculating here, but it seems to me to be just as plausible and more logical than dating sunken cities to only the *end* of the last Ice Age and the peak of the then-rising sea levels.

---

[221] "Sumer" Wikipedia.com, http://en.wikipedia.org, 2009

[222] Hart, Will, "Getting to the Bottom of the Human Origin: My Story," *Atlantis Rising*, May/June 2004. Livingston, MT: Atlantis Rising

[223] *Technologies of the Gods, The Case for Pre-Historic High Technology*, a video presentation by Atlantis Rising. New York, NY: Mystic Fire Video, Inc. 1998

[224] Hall, Manly P., *The Secret Teachings of All Ages*. New York, NY: Jeremy P. Tarcher/Penguin, 2003.

[225] West, John Anthony, "An Open Letter to the Editors of Archaeology," *Atlantis Rising*, July/August, 2003. Livingston, MT.

[227] Brier, Bob, *The History of Ancient Egypt*, an audio course. Chantilly, VA: The Teaching Company, 2006.

[228] Andrews, Arlan, "The Pursuit of Ancient Precision," *Atlantis Rising* September/October 2010. Livingston, MT.

[229] Ibid.

[230] Ibid.

[231] Ibid.

[232] Ibid.

[233] Baigent, Michael, *The Jesus Papers*. New York: HarperCollins Publishers, 2006.

[234] Joseph, Frank, *Atlantis and 2012*. Rochester, VT: Bear & Company, 2010.

[235] Joseph, Frank, *Edgar Cayce's Atlantis and Lemuria*. Virginia Beach, VA: Association for Research & Enlightenment 2001.

[236] "Plate Tectonics," *Webster's World Encyclopedia 2002*, Webster Publishing.

[237] Van Auken, John, "Science's Mythology," *Ancient Mysteries*, a newsletter. Virginia Beach, VA: Association for Research & Enlightenment, 2004

[238] Joseph, Frank, *Edgar Cayce's Atlantis and Lemuria*. Virginia Beach, VA: A.R.E. Press, 2001.

[239] Morien Institute, interview with Professor Masaaki Kimura on their websitewww.bibliotecapleyades.net/arqueologia/esp_ruinas_yonaguni, 11/25/2010.

[240] "Yonoguni" Wikipedia.com

[241] Cremo, Michael A. and Richard L. Thompson, *The Hidden History of The Human Race*. Los Angeles, CA: Bhaktivedanta Book Publishing, Inc., 1999.

[242] Ibid.

[243] Ibid.

[244] Ibid.

[245] Cremo, Michael A. and Richard L. Thompson, *Forbidden Archaeology, The Hidden History of The Human Race*. Los Angeles, CA: Bhaktivedanta Book Publishing, 1993.

[246] Ibid.

[247] Cremo, Michael A., "The Forbidden Archaeologist," *Atlantis Rising*, July/August 2003. Livingston, MT: Atlantis Rising.

[248] Hall, Manly P., *The Secret Teachings of All Ages*. New York, NY: Jeremy P. Tarcher/Penguin, 2003.

Our Long-Lost Spiritual Roots

Introduction

To discourage attraction to Pagan religion, Christianity taught us that Pagans and heathens were uncivilized, immoral idol-worshipers who used animal (and probably human) sacrifice to appease their many gods. The words "pagan" and "heathen" originally meant "country dweller," but as the urban Church of Rome grew, they were used derogatorily by Christians to imply that the spirituality previously in existence outside of Rome was evil superstition.

Yet, some of the greatest thinkers of the ancient world and maybe of all time, such as Pythagoras, Socrates, Plato, and Aristotle, were Pagans whose legacy is exceedingly spiritual and whose ideas were woven into Church doctrine. That spirituality inspired the Egyptian pyramids at Giza, the Parthenon's architecture in Athens, as well as Phideas' sculptures, and Euripides' and Sophocles' plays.

> Pagan civilizations built vast libraries to house hundreds of thousands of works of literary and scientific genius. Its natural philosophers speculated that human beings had evolved from animals. Its astronomers knew the Earth was a sphere, which along with the planets, revolves around the sun. They had even estimated Earth's circumference to within one degree of accuracy...[249]

Greek Pagans also gave us philosophy, democracy, geometry, and the alphabet, as well as the Olympic Games, theater, and public libraries. Ancient Sumerians and Egyptians, also Pagans, were also very sophisticated and developed beautiful art, philosophy, political systems, and architecture long before the Greeks. Egyptians may have been a source of Greek knowledge—given that most Greek scholars studied in Egypt at one point in their careers. Pythagoras, for example, developed his theories after a long-desired several-year sojourn in Alexandria, Egypt.

The Mysteries

Reportedly, esoteric philosophy has been taught through secret societies since the time of Atlantis. Many teachers of occult (meaning beyond ordinary knowledge or experience) wisdom and methods say that spiritual Atlanteans and Egyptians, afraid their degenerating culture would misuse the powers and knowledge of esoteric (meaning "inner" or "hidden within") wisdom, taught selected individuals through secret societies. They also taught the public through mythic stories, using the entertaining features of plays and poetry to make the ideas that the gods represented accessible to the illiterate populace. Since then, secret societies have existed throughout the world to preserve and teach the esoteric doctrines and methods to those willing to unselfishly devote themselves to God and humanity.

Nearly all the philosophers of antiquity were initiates of the "Mysteries," but only after thorough progressive preparation. Secret societies flourished in ancient times; some continued throughout the Middle Ages and into the present, not only in the Mediterranean region but worldwide. Freemasons and Rosicrucians are both counted as modern continuations of such ancient secret societies.

Those in antiquity—most likely Atlanteans—did everything they could to ensure preservation of their wisdom for future generations able to use it wisely. Manly Hall writes:

> ...They engraved it upon the face of mountains and concealed it within the measurements of colossal images.... Their knowledge of chemistry and mathematics they hid within mythologies which the ignorant would perpetuate, or in the spans and arches of their temples which time has not entirely obliterated. They wrote in characters that neither the vandalism of men nor the ruthlessness of the elements could completely efface... and concealed this wisdom must remain until this race has learned to read the universal language—Symbolism.[250]

Plato "was severely criticized," says Hall, for revealing "to the public many of the secret philosophic principles of the Mysteries." Apparently, he was fortunate to have been only criticized, for the Mysteries bound "their initiates to inviolable secrecy," and often avenged violations with death—Pythagoras was stoned to death.[251]

The Egyptians used a myth of the death and resurrection of the god Osiris to bring the idea of God into their world in their own terms, using allegories, aphorisms, and parables that people could resonate with. Their myth, "found in pyramid texts, was written over 4,500 years ago." That myth was also used to teach the Inner (esoteric) spirituality to literate individual initiates by providing a deeper understanding of its metaphors and symbolism.

Like the Egyptians, most ancient Mediterranean gardening cultures had their own Mysteries, using a myth of a similar "dying and resurrecting" god-man. By 2000 BCE, virtually all agrarian cultures had a similar myth, each creating its own stories to serve its particular customs and needs. At the heart of each was the dying and resurrecting god-man, which scholars have given the collective name Osiris-Dionysus. Although different communities and language groups used different names—Attis in Asia Minor, Adonis in Syria, Bacchus in Italy, Mithras in Persia—they were all essentially "the same mythical being," understood as symbolic and encoding "the mystical teachings of the Inner Mysteries." They were the seed of life, dying in the ground to be resurrected as the green and verdant plant, which, when harvested, is transformed again into the grain of life that feeds all.[252]

Hundreds of years later, Pythagoras, it is said, was initiated into Babylonian, Chaldean, and Egyptian Mysteries, and after his Egyptian initiation, he returned to urban Greece with an aim of creating similar Outer and Inner Mysteries for his Greek people. Since it was heretical to Greeks that a god could die, to gain acceptance Pythagoras chose a lesser Greek god Dionysus to be the Greek face of the Egyptian god-man Osiris, and created a Greek version of the Mysteries myth, with parables, allegories, and aphorisms appropriate for Outer teaching to the simple Greek public. It would also be used by the Pythagorean Brotherhood to lead individual Mystery initiates to their Inner depths. The Dionysian story and rituals remained a part of Greek culture for centuries and were adopted and adapted by the Romans in the Bacchanalia.

Through ritual and the retelling of myth, each culture's Outer Mysteries accomplished their intended social cohesion, while the Inner Mysteries helped individuals gain personal enlightenment in a way that served the community.

Through the initiation process, the student's state of consciousness was profoundly transformed. As Plato described it:

There was a time when with the rest of the happy band
they saw beauty shining in brightness,---

we philosophers following in the train of Zeus,
others in company with other gods;
and then we saw the beatific vision
and were initiated into a mystery
which may be truly called most blessed,
celebrated by us in our state of innocence,
before we had any experience of evils to come,
when we were admitted to the sight of apparitions
innocent and simple and calm and happy,
which we saw shining in pure light,
pure ourselves and not yet enshrined in that living tomb
which we carry about, now that we are imprisoned in the body,
like an oyster in his shell.[253]

The Mystery School form of spirituality prevailed well into the common era. The literate and cultural elite of Greece, Rome, and Egypt held their mysteries to be the heart and soul of their culture. As the Roman statesman Cicero put it:

For among the many excellent and indeed divine institutions
which your Athens has brought forth and contributed to human life,
none, in my opinion, is better than those mysteries.
For by their means we have been brought out
of our barbarous and savage mode of life
and educated and refined to a state of civilization;
and as the rites are called "initiations,"
so in very truth we have learned from them the beginnings of life,
and have gained the power not only to live happily,
but also to die with a better hope.[254]

Actual Pagan Beliefs

Over time and across cultures, many god-men were portrayed in legends "as saviors and Sons of God."[255] It was common practice to deify heroes: the first emperor of Sumer set the pattern, and when Alexander conquered Egypt for the Greeks, and Julius Caesar's nephew took the name Augustus Caesar, they too, were dubbed Son of God. The Egyptian version of the myth enabled a tradition in which each pharaoh was considered, Timothy Freke and Peter Gandy tell us, to be "an embodiment of the godman Osiris, and was praised in hymns as the Son of God."[256] As the Son of God with a human mother he could be the Incarnate God, the Giver of Fertility to his country and people.

Later, other contributors to a nation's greatness besides emperors were given the title. In the centuries following his death, Pythagoras was considered the son of Apollo and a mortal virgin mother. After his death, Plato, too, was said "to be the son of Apollo." Clearly, the term applied to their enlightening ideas more than their physical birth.

Actually, the Egyptian supreme God was not a person who could be killed. *Neter*, the ancient Egyptian word that is usually translated as God in English,

> ...refers to a spiritual essence or principle. The many *neters* of the Egyptians represented the many natures of the one all-embracing Being—the gods were different aspects or faces of the one supreme God.[257]

The god-man figure "symbolically represented each initiate," who would realize that they, too, were "'God made flesh,'" and that they

> ...were immortal Spirit trapped within a physical body. Through sharing in the death of Osiris-Dionysus initiates symbolically 'died' to their lower earthly nature. Through sharing in his resurrection they were spiritually reborn and experienced their eternal and divine essence.[258]

The core of Mystery teaching is that every person has two aspects, which show up in their thoughts, feelings, actions, and experiences. Each of us

> ...has a mortal lower self called the eidolon and an immortal Higher Self called the Daemon. The eidolon is the embodied self, the physical body, and personality. The Daemon is the Spirit, the true Self, which is each person's spiritual connection to God. The Mysteries were designed to help initiates realize the eidolon is a false self and that their true identity is the immortal Daemon.

> From the eidolon's point of view the Daemon appears to be an independent Guardian Angel.

> Initiates who still identify with the eidolon, therefore, do not experience the Daemon as their own true Self, but as a spirit guide whose job it is to lead them to their spiritual destination.

> Gnostic... Valentinus explains that a person receives Gnosis from their Guardian Angel, but that this angelic being is actually the seeker's own Higher Self....

The goal of Gnostic initiation was, likewise, to bring the lower self into union with the Higher Self, for it is when they are made one that enlightenment [awakening] occurs.

Although it appears as if each of us has our own Daemon or Higher Self, the enlightened initiate discovers that actually there is one Daemon shared by all—a universal Self, which inhabits every being. Each soul is a part of the one Soul of God. To know oneself therefore is to know God....[259]

Freke & Gandy add,

The supreme God of the Pagan Mysteries was an ineffable Oneness beyond all qualities... understood as the Mind of the Universe which expresses itself through all beings.[260]

Pythagoras, having gone through the full initiation process in several cultures, wrote:

God is the Universal Spirit
that diffuses itself over all Nature.
All Beings receive their Life from Him.

There is but One Only God, who is not
as some are apt to imagine
seated above the World
beyond the orb of the Universe;
but being Himself All-in-All,
He sees all the Beings
that fill His Immensity -
the Only Principle,
 the Light of Heaven,
the Father of All.
...the Reason
 the Life
and
Motion
of all things.[261]

Manly Hall goes on to say that Pythagoras taught that

both man and the universe were made in the image of God, ... [and] that the visible human form is but the encasing vehicle for an invisible spiritual organism which is, in reality, the conscious individual.[262]

"Socrates believed that invisible souls shape the physical realm," says philosophy professor Phillip Cary.[263] Plato taught the same "immortality of the soul" and also that the universe's features were intentionally designed as they are. Plato's ideas can be summarized as:

- God exists as "First Principle" and "Supreme Good";
- the Divine Mind contains the whole intelligible world;
- Forms of the intelligible [unmanifest spirit] world can be seen by the mind's eye;
- a divine craftsman (demiurge) shaped the material of that world into an ordered cosmos using these Forms as models;
- the sensible world, "the visible world is a living thing, animated by a divine World soul," which is the "highest part of the universe, and the highest part of Soul, the One;"
- our souls exist in an other-worldly home and are related to the one Soul;
- our individual soul ascends to heaven at its body's death and transmigrates, but there's a part of our soul which has never descended.[264]

Plato believed there was a "fall" through which individual souls became alienated from Soul. Motivated by a desire to have power over lower things, they descended into bodies. That fall resulted in those souls' imprisonment in physical bodies on Earth where evil and suffering are the rule. He taught that we must climb the "ladder of love leading us 'upward' from bodily things to souls to the Forms, the ultimate in mystical ascent [being] to go beyond the vision of the Divine Mind and experience unity with the One."[265]

The early Christian mystic Plotinus (204-270 CE) is regarded as one of the most influential ancient philosophers after Plato and Aristotle. Believing that Plato needed to be both interpreted and defended against those who had misunderstood and thus unfairly criticized him, he founded the intellectual school now called Neoplatonism.

Plotinus broke his metaphysics down to three principles: "the One," Intellect, and Soul. "The One" is the "absolute simple first principle of all," and is both "self-caused" and the "cause of being for everything else in the universe." To the question: "If the One is absolutely simple, how can it be the cause of the being of anything much less the cause of everything?" Plotinus answered: "The One is such a cause in the sense that it is virtually everything else."²⁶⁶ He stated that his second principle, Intellect, is the central source for the Platonic Forms, and accounts for the real uniqueness of all Forms, united in the One.

Each Form, though, still has an identity, he said, "maintained by being thought by an eternal intellect... an ... instrument of the One's causality."²⁶⁷ His third principle says that everything has a Soul, "from human beings to the most insignificant plant" and the sensible world consists of images of the intelligible world, which could not exist without matter. Matter, he said, "is to be identified with evil and privation of all form or intelligibility."²⁶⁸ But he also said:

> Matter is only evil... when it becomes an impediment to return to the One. It is evil when considered as a goal or end that is a polar opposite to the Good. To deny the necessity of evil is to deny the necessity of the Good. Matter is only evil for entities that can consider it as a goal of desire... the only entities that can be self-conscious of their goals. Specifically, human beings, by opting for attachments to the bodily, orient themselves in the direction of evil. ²⁶⁹

Plotinus believed a human is essentially a soul using a body as a temporary instrument in life.

> Having separated from God and descended into the material world, (the human soul) is now journeying back to God and passes through births in this ascent towards its Supreme Source. In the state of ecstasy, the soul is raised above all limitations and merges with the Soul of God.²⁷⁰

Freke and Gandy relate that Pagan understanding is that

> ...all things are One. The Mysteries aimed at awakening within the initiate a sublime experience of this Oneness. ... Plotinus describes the initiate transcending his limited sense of himself as a separate ego and experiencing mystical union with God.²⁷¹

European Philosopher-mystics

In the 1600s, around the time of Isaac Newton's alchemical and physical discoveries in England, Gottfried Leibniz, one of Germany's first scientists and mathematicians, developed a new mathematics. His goal was to set out a description of the universe as made up of countless conscious centers of spiritual energy. Using a series of algebraic equations in which unknown quantities were for the first time represented by Xs and

Ys, Leibniz described the behavior of these centers, which he, like Pythagoras and many others, called "monads." and said they each developed independently. The universe, he said

> ...is the harmonious result of a divine plan. Humans, however, with their limited vision, cannot accept such evils as disease and death as part of a universal harmony.[272]

According to professor Cary, Leibniz's thesis of pre-established harmony,

> ...is a very deep way to reconcile the sovereignty of God and the free will of his creatures...

> God creates the universe as a set of monads whose perceptions, feelings, desires and choices are coordinated with one another from the start. [So, the] whole history of each monad is already determined at creation--including every free choice it will make: [W]hat God creates is that whole life-span.... Thus God does not compel any monad to choose X rather than Y, but rather creates a monad who freely chooses X rather than Y.[273]

Finally, Baruch Spinoza, a contemporary of Leibniz, centered his Metaphysics around the pantheistic idea that the whole universe is God:

> God, the only substance in the universe, is outwardly visible as the physical world and inwardly present as divine intellect. Hence everything exists in God as a modification of his being.[274]

Recapturing and Reconstructing Ancient Wisdom

One of the Dead Sea scrolls says that ancient texts and secret Mystery traditions relate that "a long time ago the wisdom of the heavens was given to the family of man."[275] Those scrolls were found between 1946 and 1959 in eleven caves along the shores of the Dead Sea. Although most of the 930 scrolls had been reduced to bits and pieces and were illegible, modern technology helped a group of seven scholars piece them together and translate most of them into English. The effort began in the 1950s and was finally completed with the last pieces made public in 2002.

The scrolls are generally thought to be a library brought to Qumran by the ascetic sect of Jewish Essenes when they exiled themselves from Jerusalem around 100 BCE. Biblical Studies professor Gary Rendsburg says that scholars are unsure precisely who wrote the scrolls but believe they were written by a previously unknown brotherhood related to the Essenes.[276]

Some suggest the scrolls were the Jerusalem library, hidden before the Romans destroyed the temple in 70 CE. Although Rendsburg says most scholars reject this idea, it seems reasonable; the scrolls contain every book of Hebrew Scripture except Esther and many other texts thought to have been written around Jesus' time. [277]

Some people believe the scrolls could have been teachings of Atlanteans, preserved for future generations. Little is known about Essenes and Edgar Cayce suggested they were Atlanteans who immigrated to Israel when their land was breaking up. They are also said to have been Jesus' teachers in the Mysteries.

Other scriptural texts were found near Nag Hammadi, Egypt, in the 1940s. Translated and made public between 1977 and 1995, they are now a regular part of scholarly research. Most are thought to have been originally written in the century after Jesus' ministry, though copied and bound in the 300s, and a few may well be the only true eyewitness accounts by disciples of Jesus. We'll see more about these texts in the next chapter.

The Gospel of Judas, found in Egypt late in the twentieth century, reached its conservators' hands in only 2001; then it took five years for experts to piece its disintegrating fragments together and translate it into English. It was previously known of only through writings of second-century church leaders as part of the Gnostic heresy and from segments in Greek found earlier.

Only now are we beginning to understand ancient Egyptian teaching, and again we find perennial wisdom. John Van Auken tells that what's been called *The Egyptian Book of the Dead* "actually carries the hieroglyphic title, *The Book of the Masters of the Hidden Places.*"[278] It's not a death-ritual book, as Egyptologists say, but is an inner map, a guide to help evolving souls return home. In Egyptian mythology, he says: "[T]he created, the godlings in Ra's image... move away from the creator in order to know themselves, find themselves."[279]

Using Cayce's intuitive responses to questions, Van Auken says also that human souls "descended from higher realms and higher states of consciousness during an involution into matter." That descent caused us to lose consciousness of higher levels and focus on this physical dimension. Some of our soul group, understanding that we were descending into a more limited condition, wrote down "important stories and information that would later help us rise...." to our original glorious heights. A plan was devised, and the "way in and out of this realm was recorded, but cryptically, so that only those who sought it for the right reasons could find it."[280]

Comments & Questions: Ancient Wisdom

Much of what we know today about ancient beliefs has been reconstructed from fragments of information written in numerous obsolete languages. Nearly all of them conveyed information passed down earlier in a culture's oral tradition.

Few of the original documents have survived the ravages of time or Christian bonfires, so what we have now are often transcriptions and interpretations of lost originals. Also, most of the ancient books academicians study today were found in the late Middle Ages and have either been studied in an ancient language or, in most cases, translated into English or into German then English.

Those translations, as always, were subject to error and misinterpretation. Many languages have several different meanings for one word, so several different interpretations of single phrases in ancient texts may arise. This holds true for all ancient writings, including the canonical texts of Hebrew Scriptures, the New Testament, and the Qur'an, along with the non-canonical texts, scientific and medical texts, and historical records.

We must remember, too, that in ancient times books were "published" by hand from what others wrote, and each time a book was copied, undoubtedly the scribe made mistakes—but also, probably made some changes to make more sense to him or, in some cases, to change the sense to conform to other beliefs. Some of what we read is what an interpreter "thinks" the original writer must have meant.

Also, interpretation of symbolic languages is always informed by the interpreter's belief system and level of consciousness. A materialist, hindered by a limited belief system which precludes recognition of both a spiritual context and advanced intelligence in what they think of as a primitive culture, might see them as merely drawings, at most telling simple stories. Alternative researchers read them with greater depth, especially if they address them with a more spiritual mindset, often seeing them as historical accounts of events or instructions for higher consciousness.

It stands to reason that the various texts found in only the last few decades after millennia in hiding—without all the copying, interpreting, changing, and editing—would come closest to original intent, so would be the most reliable. The Nag Hammadi Library, the Dead Sea Scrolls, and the Gospels of Mary and of Judas, found elsewhere in Egypt over the past century, stand out in this way as texts worthy of serious consideration. And even interpretation of the more recent finds is subject to their interpreters' beliefs. For example: a well-known interpreter of the Nag Hammadi codices, Elaine Pagels, and Gnostic Steven Hoeller seem to read the Gospel of Thomas differently than do interpreters influenced by more fundamentalist Christian theology. It's human nature to see what we want to see, based on our personal beliefs.

The ancients left us their wisdom in symbols, so it could be read and understood by any culture ready for it. It may be that the ancients purposely gave us enigmatic messages to cause us to go within in search of our own understanding, or to learn different things to serve different purposes. More of it is being understood every day, and soon we may be able to read and understand all the ancient texts, and learn so much we don't yet know.

Academia, as well as Western religions, could greatly benefit humanity by exploring the texts of our spiritual roots to interpret and help us understand their symbolism. The ancients have so much to tell us of spirituality, natural technology, and of how to live in harmony with all life and our environment! We need a combination of orthodox methodology—within a holistic framework—and alternative openness and vision to understand our life on Earth, an integrative approach to understanding our life.

The new frontier for scientists, historians, philosophers, and theologians could be ancient civilizations and our lost spiritual and technological roots. Those seem far more important to our future than the current frontiers of space and of consciousness as a brain function. The ancients may have known more about both than we can ever know through modern orthodox science. As we learn more about them we may learn about sustainable, non-harmful energy and how to live in harmony with our environment and other life, as a global, even universal, civilization.

[249] Freke, Timothy and Peter Gandy *The Jesus Mysteries*. New York: Three Rivers Press, 1999.
[250] Hall, Manly P., *The Secret Teachings of All Ages*. New York, NY: Jeremy P. Tarcher/Penguin, 2003.
[251] Ibid.
[252] To explore this concept further, read one of Joseph Campbell's books or the classic *The Golden Bough* by Sir James George Frazer.
[253] Socrates speaking in Plato's *Phaedrus*
[254] Cicero, Marcus Tullius, *Laws* II, xiv, 36
[255] Freke, Timothy and Peter Gandy *The Jesus Mysteries*. New York: Three Rivers Press, 1999.
[256] Ibid
[257] Ibid. See also the work of both Isha Schwaller de Lubicz and her father for more insight into the deeper meaning of Egyptian religious practices.
[258] Ibid.
[259] Ibid.
[260] Ibid.
[261] Chavez, M. B. *Criticism On The Theological Idea Of Deity Contrasting The Views Entertained Of A Supreme Being By The Ancient Grecian Sages, With Those Of Moses And The Hebrew Writers; And Blending Ancient Judaism, Paganism, And Christianity Into A Common Original*. Philadelphia: Barclay & Co. 1871.
[262] Hall, Manly P., *The Secret Teachings of All Ages*. New York, NY: Jeremy P. Tarcher/Penguin, 2003.
[263] Cary, Phillip, *Philosophy & Religion in the West*, Chantilly, VA: The Teaching Company, 1999
[264] Ibid.
[265] Ibid.
[266] Gerson, Lloyd, "Plotinus," *Stanford Encyclopedia of Philosophy*, 2008.
[267] Ibid.
[268] Ibid.
[269] Ibid.
[270] Sharma, I. C., *Cayce, Karma, and Reincarnation*. New York, NY: Harper & Row, 1975.
[271] Freke, Timothy and Peter Gandy *The Jesus Mysteries*. New York: Three Rivers Press, 1999.

[272] "Liebniz, Gottfried Wilhelm," *Funk and Wagnals New Encyclopedia on Infopedia* CD-Rom, by SoftKey Multimedia, 1996.
[273] Cary, Phillip, *Philosophy & Religion in the West*, an audio course in the Great Courses series. Chantilly, VA: The Teaching Company, 1999.
[274] Ibid.
[275] Braden, Gregg, *Speaking the Lost Language of God*. IL: Injoi Corporation, 2004
[276] Rendsburg, Gary A. *The Dead Sea Scrolls*, an audio course in the Great Courses series. Chantilly, VA: The Teaching Company, 2010.
[277] Ibid.
[278] Van Auken, John, *Ancient Egyptian Mysticism And Its Relevance Today*. Virginia Beach, VA: A.R.E. Press, 1999
[279] Ibid.
[280] Ibid.

Gnosticism: What Christianity Could Have Been Had It Followed Its Own Mystery Tradition

Introduction

Ancient history and religion scholars say that during Jesus' ministry and the early years of the Christian religion, Jesus' followers formed essentially three groups. One group continued to consider themselves Jews, taught in the Jerusalem Temple, and followed the Mosaic laws; they were pretty much eradicated when Rome destroyed the Temple in 70 CE. Another group, lead by the apostle Paul, pursued a path similar to what we've seen as the Outer Pagan Mysteries and excluded the Inner mysteries. By late in the 2nd century this group considered itself orthodox; it consisted of household churches that conformed to the accepted tenets, dogma, and practices of ruling bishops, and eventually became the Roman Catholic Church. Another group, of several slightly differing sects, was more involved with the Inner Mysteries. One of these, called "Gnostics," from the Greek word *gnosis*, meaning "revealed knowledge," claimed that Jesus privately gave selected disciples a true, Gnostic interpretation of his teachings.

Gnostic beliefs differed widely from those of early orthodox Christians; for example, for the Gnostics it was a defective being who created Earth and our forms and personalities in its own image: flawed, and subject to suffering, impermanence, and evil. Stephan Hoeller, Director of Studies at the Gnostic Society, explains that Earth's creator, or architect, was called the "Demiurge" (a Greek word meaning "halfmaker,") because he created only the form, not the inner life. While "the human body originates on Earth," Hoeller says, the spirit comes from and returns to the "realms of the Fullness, where the true Godhead dwells."[281]

Identifying the demiurge with the demanding, jealous, vengeful god of Hebrew Scripture, Gnostics viewed Genesis as an account of the Demiurge's efforts to keep humans in ignorance in the material world and to punish their attempts to acquire spiritual knowledge. They rejected the moral commandments of the Hebrew Torah as the Demiurge's efforts to control us. To Gnostics, says Hoeller, "evil is part of the fabric of the world we live in. If there is a Creator of this reality, then surely this Creator is responsible for the evil in it." Gnostics believed there had to be another higher, wholly good God, and identified Jesus' "Father" God as the authentic God.[282]

Gnostics saw nothing special in Jesus' death: "Christ, the divine spirit, inhabited the body of the man Jesus and did not die on the cross but ascended to the divine realm from which it had come."[283] Gnostics also didn't see Jesus' mission as starting a new religion, but believed it was to bring to humanity knowledge of the individual's own divinity. His mission had nothing to do with sin and saving humanity; *gnosis* alone would bring salvation—meaning awakening from the illusions of Earthly existence.[284] Believing in the reality of those illusions was seen by Gnostics as ignorance and the cause of sin. But, says Hoeller,

> Ignorance of spiritual realities is dispelled by gnosis, interior knowing that liberates one from unconsciousness.... Those who know the Divine through gnosis shed all sin, while those without gnosis cannot help but persist in transgressions.[285]

So it is knowledge, not faith (which orthodox Christians focus on) that is important to Gnostics.

Gnosis/Knowledge vs. Belief/Faith

Knowledge of "the eternal realm where souls originate," writes Hoeller,

> ...makes all issues of life and death self-evident and takes away all fear of what the world calls death. When we are in contact with the ineffable, divine reality that is our source, we also know what state we shall return to.[286]

To Gnostics: "Gnosis is not an idea that is open to doubt, but a mystical experience of the Truth...."[287] This is in alignment with the teachings of Plato, who "argued that belief is concerned only with appearances of things, while knowledge penetrates to the underlying reality."[288]

The Gnostic Gospels

Anti-Gnostic writings of second-century bishops were for centuries our primary indicator that the Gnostics existed. These texts say that Gnostics had their own gospels, which the orthodox tried hard to destroy. Some of those Gnostic gospels, most of which had been written in Greek, were translated into the Coptic language (a blend of Greek and ancient Egyptian).

While the New Testament was being formulated by the orthodox, many of the Gnostic gospels were excluded and banned as heresy. When ordered by the Church to burn them, someone at a desert monastery that had copied and bound them stored them instead, in a heavy, six-foot clay jar, and hid it in a nearby cave at Nag Hammadi, Egypt.

In 1945, an Arab peasant happened upon that earthenware jar containing leather-bound papyrus books, or codices. Treated as kindling by the goatherd's family, the books were scattered and some were lost, but twelve of them and pages of another were gathered together in 1955 by Dutch religious historian Gilles Quispel.

Deciphering a first line, Quispel read: "These are the secret words which the living Jesus spoke, and which the twin, Judas Thomas, wrote down." This was the Gospel of Thomas, one of 52 texts of the "Nag Hammadi Library." In 1977, an English translation of some of the texts was completed and made public. Two years later, Elaine Pagels, one of the translators, published *The Gnostic Gospels*, and for the first time we had direct knowledge of early Gnostic beliefs. Gnostics, she says, saw their gospels as advanced-level teaching for those who had already received Jesus' basic message. Many of those texts say they offer secret teaching given them by Jesus in private. The Gospel of Mark in the New Testament, Pagels points out, supports that claim, relating that Jesus explained things to certain disciples in private.

"The 'living Jesus' of these texts," Pagels says, "speaks of illusion and enlightenment, not of sin and repentance" like the New Testament Jesus. He "comes as a guide who opens access to spiritual understanding." Gnostics taught that we can overcome evil and suffering through communion with God, which involves

> an intuitive process of knowing oneself. And to know oneself... is to know human nature and human destiny.... [T]o know oneself, at the

deepest level, is simultaneously to know God; this is the secret of gnosis.... [S]elf-knowledge is knowledge of God; the self and the divine are identical."[289]

This may be why Gnostics have always referred to themselves as twins.

The Light in Human Form

While the accepted, canonical gospels of Mark, Matthew, and Luke "identify Jesus as God's human agent," writes Pagels in *Beyond Belief*, the gospels of John (biblical) and Thomas (Gnostic) "characterize him instead as God's own light in human form."

Although this makes them seem in agreement, they actually "take Jesus' private teaching in sharply different directions." Pagels explains that John, calling Jesus the "only begotten son" and the "light of all humanity," identifies Jesus as the light that came into being "in the beginning," making him unique. John insists that "Jesus alone" brings that light and only through him can we "experience God."[290] She says that Thomas, on the other hand, says "the divine light Jesus embodied is shared by humanity, since we are all made 'in the image of God.'" It is this light of the self and the divine that makes twins of all who learn of it through gnosis.

Thomas's gospel, Pagels says, "encourages the hearer not so much to believe in Jesus, as John requires, as to seek to know God through one's own, divinely given capacity, since all are created in the image of God." Pagels is convinced that the author of the gospel of John wrote his gospel well after Thomas wrote his, as a way to support the orthodox line by refuting Thomas.[291]

Reincarnation and the Kingdom of God

A spirit is reborn over and over, says Hoeller, until it has experienced all that Earth life "has to offer... every kind of activity and condition." Eventually, the spirit's "consciousness becomes disenchanted with the attractions of this lower world... [which is a] necessary precondition for liberation."[292] Edgar Cayce's Akashic research adds that "each lifetime provides an opportunity to raise the spiritual consciousness and to make contact with the God-force within."[293]

In the Gospel of Thomas, Pagels says, Jesus rebukes those who "seek access to God elsewhere"—especially those who do so by trying to 'follow Jesus' himself."[294] He also dismisses "those who expect the future coming of the kingdom of God," and declares:

> The Kingdom is inside you and outside you... examine yourself and learn who you are.... [A]lthough you do not understand it yet... you will be called 'the one who knows himself.' For whoever has not known himself knows nothing, but whoever has known himself has simultaneously come to know the depth of all things.[295]

Who Were the Gnostics?

Until discovery of their gospels, what we knew about Gnostics was from anti-Gnostic Christian writings of the 2nd and 3rd centuries reporting on heresies. Scattered document fragments found in the 19th and early 20th centuries and oral teachings from within small bands of existing Gnostics added to our knowledge.

The Church has always wanted Gnosticism to appear as a heretical offshoot of Christianity that appeared in the 2nd century. But scholars weren't convinced that was true, and sought evidence to the contrary. A form of gnosticism was a known movement within Greek philosophy long before Jesus was born. Pagels reports that early in the 20th century, Wilhelm Bousset concluded: "Gnosticism is first of all a pre-Christian movement which had its roots in itself. It is therefore to be understood ... in its own terms, and not as an offshoot or byproduct of the Christian religion."[296]

Mark Gaffney says that "The Gnostic element was present in Christianity from the beginning, and was, in fact, the very heart of the teachings of Jesus." He explains that the controversy

> occurred not because pristine Christianity became polluted by Gnostic heresy, as the Church argued..., but because the bishops of the fledgling Church so rearranged their priorities in their attempts to consolidate institutional Christianity that they lost contact with their own spiritual roots.[297]

He tells us that Gnosticism, therefore, was "not a heretical derivative of Christianity but the authentic foundation and purveyor of Christ's message."[298]

Orthodox Christianity reflected the views of powerful, educated, politically savvy bishops, and never represented most Christians. While seen by the bishops as threatening to the universality of their version of Christian doctrine, Gnostics, concerned as they were with only "personal enlightenment," had no wish to start an institutionalized church or missionary movement.[299]

Relation to the Hindu Vedas

Gnosticism could have derived from Brahmanism. Gnostic teaching, Gaffney says, is similar to those of the Hindu Vedas—"so ancient that no one knows when they were first written down." And scholars have long known that Hindu and Buddhist teachers traveled the Silk Road between China, India, and Greece.

The root word for Veda is *vid* meaning "to know," so is synonymous with gnosis. He says that, although we have been cut off from our own roots, those teachings survive today in the Hindu and Buddhist yoga traditions of India. He writes of a Vedic concept which helped me understand the Eastern concept of emptiness, called Fullness (*Pleroma*) by Gnostics. He tells of the *hrit* or heart center as a chakra (energy center) located above the diaphragm and back toward the spine:

> The Vedas say that in relation to this subtle *hrit* center there lies an infinitesimal void 'wherein is situated the whole.' The scripture's meaning is not metaphorical. 'The whole' means just that—the direct experience of a non-dual, unitive state. This infinitesimal void is known in the yoga traditions as *hridaya*, the heart space, where inside and outside merge and become one... in Gnostic parlance, the all, or *Pleroma*. Sometimes it is described as a fertile void because, though it is a condition of nothingness with no material substance, it contains the entire universe.[300]

Comments & Questions: Gnosticism

Although the Gnostic people, texts, and beliefs discussed here relate to Jesus' followers, Gnosticism almost certainly pre-dated those first centuries of the common era. Some Gnostics were in fact followers, maybe even disciples, of Jesus, who enjoyed his teachings, which they wrote down as what are called today "Gnostic gospels." Other Gnostics—who may not even have known of Jesus—likely lived in other places and followed other teachers.

The people lumped together under the term Gnostics were diverse groups with little connection, scattered throughout the area we know today as the Middle East and southern Europe. They may have existed also in India and the Far East. Do the Vedic *hridaya* and the Gnostic *Pleroma* equate to the quantum physics' "hologram" in which everything is at once both the whole and a part? Is it possible that "Gnostics" was merely a descriptive name for the early common era's Inner Mystery schools, as seen from a Christian perspective?

If the world's religions were to seriously search out the wisdom of the ancients, we would be living in a different world. If Christian churches were to focus on the wisdom of Jesus and teach it openly now, they would surely help humanity transform from its current materialism back to its nearly lost spirituality. A spiritual renaissance would be fact.

---

[281] Hoeller, Steven, *Gnosticism, New Light on the Ancient Tradition of Inner Knowing*. Wheaton, IL: Quest Books, Theosophical Publishing House, 2002.

[282] Hoeller, Steven, Gnosticism. Wheaton, IL: Quest Books, Theosophical Publishing House, 2002.

[283] "Gnostic," *Funk and Wagnalls New Encyclopedia*, on Infopedia, CD-Rom by SoftKey Multimedia, Inc. Funk and Wagnalls, 1996.

[284] Freke, Timothy and Gandy, Peter, *The Jesus Mysteries, was the Original Jesus a Pagan God?* New York: Three Rivers Press, 1999.

[285] Hoeller, Steven, *Gnosticism*. Wheaton, IL: Quest Books, Theosophical Publishing House, 2002.

[286] Ibid.

[287] Ibid.

[288] Freke, Timothy and Gandy, Peter, *The Jesus Mysteries, was the Original Jesus a Pagan God?* New York: Three Rivers Press, 1999.

[289] Pagels, Elaine, *The Gnostic Gospels*. New York, NY: Random House, 1979.

[290] Ibid.

[291] Pagels, Elaine, *Beyond Belief.* New York, NY: Random House, 2003.

[292] Hoeller, Steven, *Gnosticism*. Wheaton, IL: Quest Books, Theosophical Publishing House, 2002.

[293] Robinson, Barbara, "Reconsidering Judas Iscariot," *Venture Inward*, November/December 2006, Virginia Beach, VA: Association for Research & Enlightenment.

[294] Pagels, Elaine, *Beyond Belief.* New York, NY: Random House, 2003
[295] Ibid.
[296] Pagels, Elaine, *The Gnostic Gospels.* New York, NY: Random House, 1979.
[297] Gaffney, Mark H., *Gnostic Secrets of the Naassenes.* Rochester, VT: Inner Traditions, 2004.
[298] Ibid.
[299] Freke, Timothy and Peter Gandy *The Jesus Mysteries.* New York: Three Rivers Press, 1999.
[300] Ibid.

The Jesus Story: A Mysteries Myth?

Introduction

"[S]tunned" when they uncovered extraordinary similarities between the New Testament gospel stories of Jesus and myths of the Pagan Mystery tradition, Timothy Freke and Peter Gandy asked themselves if the Jesus story could also be a myth encoding the same perennial spiritual teaching as the Mysteries. Convinced by extensive follow-up research that the story of Jesus is a "myth based on perennial Pagan" tales rather than a "biography of a historical Messiah," they conclude that Jesus was not a historical figure but a myth, one like those of every other culture in that region, "a Jewish adaptation of the ancient Pagan Mystery religion."[301]

The Jesus Mysteries

Freke and Gandy surmise that a group of Jews wanted a god-man myth for their culture. They had a problem, though, because the Jewish religion had become strictly monotheistic; they didn't have a lesser god about whom they could create such a myth. The only hero figure they had besides Yahweh was their Messiah. So they created their own myth and assigned to Jeshuah (the expected name of the Messiah, meaning "savior" in Hebrew) the functions of the Messiah along with the godly attributes of Osiris-Dionysus. Their myth also had to be available to everyone, not just for the intellectually elite.

A revolt of Judean Jews against their captors had led to the Jewish-Roman war of 66-73 CE and terrible retaliations by the Romans. Reportedly, out of three million Jews, one million died and another "100,000 were sold into slavery." By the year 70, the center of Jewish religion, the Jerusalem Temple, had been destroyed, and when Jerusalem fell it was in smoldering ruins. After the war, Jews were scattered throughout the Roman empire, and were in desperate need of their Messiah. As reported by several authors of that time, many Jews felt that their God had betrayed them, having failed to protect them from their enemies.

Shortly after the temple was destroyed, the Gospel of Mark was written, possibly initially to offer Jews a messiah, come to save them from Roman rule. But a Messiah who had been crucified as a common criminal wasn't the savior they awaited.

Freke and Gandy postulate that Jews who had been Hellenized to only the Outer Mysteries, would have been scattered around the ancient world, taking with them only the "biography" of Jesus the Messiah. Those relocated to the western areas of the Empire were cut off from the Gnostic Jesus Mysteries centers in eastern areas of the Empire, so never became immersed in the Inner Mysteries.

The Jesus Inner Mysteries flourished where they originated, in Alexandria and in other eastern areas and, called Gnosticism, produced many second- and third-century Gnostic masters. Literalism, however, developed in areas of the Empire cut off from those eastern masters.

Western Christians created a religion based on Jesus' death and bodily resurrection as the Son of God. They viewed the gospels as actual historical accounts of real events, and taught that salvation would be guaranteed only to believers of the Jesus story as completely true and factual. Literalist bishops then deduced the continuous apostolic succession from Peter by piecing together available texts, which lent them authority and justified their interpreting the Jesus stories as historical fact. This limited form of Christianity, being all that the bishops who came to Constantine's Council at Nicea knew and trusted, would thus become the doctrine of the Roman church and would determine the course of Western culture and our worldviews.

Freke & Gandy enumerate at length the similarities between the biography of Jesus and the god-men of other traditions. "Event by event, we found we were able to construct Jesus' supposed biography from mythic motifs previously relating to Osiris-Dionysus." Here are only ten of them. Collectively, and by whatever name, Osiris-Dionysus:

- Is God made flesh, the savior and "Son of God"
- His father is God and his mother is a mortal virgin
- He is born in a cave or humble cowshed on December 25 before three shepherds
- He offers his followers the chance to be born again through the rites of baptism
- He miraculously turns water into wine at a marriage ceremony

- He rides triumphantly into town on a donkey while people wave palm leaves to honor him
- He dies at Easter time as a sacrifice for the sins of the world
- After his death he descends to hell, then on the third day he rises from the dead and ascends to heaven in glory
- His followers await his return as the judge during the Last Days
- His death and resurrection are celebrated by a ritual meal of bread and wine, which symbolizes his body and blood.[302]

To Pagan writers of the first few centuries, similarities between the new religion and the ancient Mysteries were obvious. It's clear from currently available texts that they considered the new religion "a pale reflection of their own ancient teachings." In one such writing, the 2nd-century Greek philosopher Celsus was upset with Christians for claiming that their Jesus story was somehow a "new revelation" and factual historical accounts. He asked:

> [H]ow are they unique? Are ours to be accounted myths and theirs believed? What reasons do the Christians give for the distinctiveness of their beliefs? In truth there is nothing at all unusual about what the Christians believe, except that they believe it to the exclusion of more comprehensive truths about God.[303]

Christians borrowed both the Son of God motif and Jesus' embodiment of the Logos (Christ) from Pagans, but used them quite differently. In one document explaining mystic Christian doctrine at the time of Constantine, Clement, Bishop of Alexandria, said: "The Son is the consciousness of God. The father only sees the world as reflected in the Son." Freke and Gandy add: "The Logos is God conscious of Himself. It is the One Soul of the Universe, which is conscious through all beings."

The church fathers were upset by Pagan denial of their claim that the Jesus biography was the only truth, and, "using one of the most absurd arguments ever advanced, they accused the 'Devil of plagiarism by anticipation,' of deviously copying the true story of Jesus before it had actually happened [and spreading it around to other religions] in an attempt to mislead the gullible!"[304]

No historical document outside the various gospels relates anything about the person we know as Jesus Christ. The Jewish historian Josephus wrote in the first century that people spoke about a teacher by that name, but provides no direct description—and, in fact, gives far more detail about John the Baptist. The Greek and Roman statesmen of the time who wrote of the unrest in Palestine and the developing problems associated with Christianity didn't mention Jesus, either. These glaring omissions have caused many scholars to question if Jesus was an actual person or merely one created by Paul and the author of the Gospel of Mark to serve their purposes in starting a new religion.

Comments & Questions: The Jesus Story

Was Jesus invented by Paul? Did Paul initiate the Christ myth as a Jesus Mystery myth? If so, he may have been the originator of what not only became Christianity as the Outer religion of the west but also of what became Gnostic Christianity, the Inner religion of the Middle East, and still in existence and possibly growing today in that area, Europe, and America.

Also, if Christianity truly was a Mysteries myth, then Christians deliberately excluded the Osiris-Dionysus god-man's goddess partner present in all other versions of the myth.

---

[301] Freke, Timothy and Gandy, Peter, *The Jesus Mysteries, was the Original Jesus a Pagan God?* New York: Three Rivers Press, 1999.
[302] Ibid.
[303] Celsus, quoted in Freke and Gandy.
[304] Freke, Timothy and Peter Gandy *The Jesus Mysteries*. New York: Three Rivers Press, 1999.

PART FOUR:

MORE PERENNIAL WISDOM - TODAY'S NON-ORTHODOX METAPHYSICS

Reality is merely an illusion, albeit a very persistent one.
~ Albert Einstein

Spiritual Metaphysical Philosophies (Metas)

Introduction

We've examined the materialist belief systems to see what we need to move away from. Then, in Part Three we looked at our roots, the belief systems of our ancient ancestors, to consider some beliefs we might want to move toward. Continuing with perennial wisdom, let's look now at the spiritual teachings of some of our contemporary Western spiritual metaphysical philosophers (whom I call Metas) including some of the more mystical sides of science, again as belief systems we might want to move toward. Remember, all of this is to help us know who we truly are so we can raise our consciousness to higher levels. Then, living as higher level beings, we will effectively address our world conditions with our heart and reason in balance, with feminine and masculine energy in balance, and from an integral, holistic, compassionate world-view.

The Metaphysical Perspective

In academia, metaphysics is a branch of philosophy concerned with the nature of existence, reality, truth, or knowledge that also examines the relationship between mind and matter. As we've seen, metaphysics was a major interest to those classical Greek philosophers, with Aristotle formalizing it as the intellectual investigation of the nature of reality or being, and popularizing the term when he titled one of his treatises "Metaphysics." As the name suggests—"Meta" meaning beyond or above and "physics" implying the physical, material world—taking a metaphysical perspective involves our changing physical reality and can be interpreted to mean "development," "transformation," or even "evolution."

But keep in mind, evolution does not necessarily equate with Darwinian science.

As 18th-century scientists were beginning to break away from Christianity's rule, two basic metaphysical philosophies surfaced: Dualism and idealism. Dualism, as originally posited by Plato 2,000 years earlier, is that there are two substances, kinds, categories, or principles, usually considered in terms of matter and spirit or mind and body. Plato believed we have immortal souls imprisoned in earthly physical bodies. Extending Plato's teachings, Plotinus taught a form of idealism that says "the Soul has made the world by stepping from eternity into time...."[305]

The metaphysical stance called monistic idealism, as put forth by early 18th-century bishop George Berkeley, is that there is only one substance: mind—what we might today call consciousness. His "immaterialism" denied the existence of the material as only ideas in the minds of perceivers, saying things exist only while being perceived. He famously remarked: "To be is to be perceived."[306]

Today, idealism includes

> ...any philosophy that places importance on the ideal or spiritual realm in its account of human existence. Metaphysical idealism holds that reality itself is essentially spirit or consciousness or, at least, that abstractions and laws are more basic to reality than the things we perceive.[307]

"I think, therefore I am" was René Descartes metaphysical philosophy. He says: "I knew I was a substance whose whole essence or nature is simply to think, and which does not require any place, or depend on any material thing, in order to exist."[308] Later philosophers, including Baruch Spinoza and Gottfried von Leibniz, were influenced by Descartes and Berkeley but developed their own systems: Spinoza defined monism and Leibniz the above-described pre-established harmony. The concept has been brought into modern popular culture by quantum physicist Amit Goswami, who proposes in *The Self-Aware Universe* that the only way to resolve the fundamental issues of quantum mechanics is by taking the monistic idealist view.

When we come from a strictly scientific perspective, whether mainstream or the more materialist of the new sciences, we are forced to consider what might otherwise be considered inessential. That is, we have to wonder whether, as in dualism, mind and body are separate from one another and, if so, how they can interact.

Looking at these same things from a metaphysical perspective we don't have to wonder either if they are separate or whether they can interact, because both are of the same substance: consciousness.

From this perspective the body is a manifestation of the unmani-fest mind. We might have to wonder which controls and/or influences which, but the answer seems obvious when we consider that the body dies and the mind, or consciousness, does not (evidenced by "past-life" regressions and near-death experiences). The question of whether mind is of the brain or separate from it is likewise answered by that same perspective, and has been empirically proven in numerous experiments by the new sciences.

Monistic Idealism as a Scientific Spiritual Philosophy

When writing of metaphysics, I mean specifically the spiritual metaphysical philosophies expressed as monistic idealism, not constrained by academic biases and protocols. Although the study of the nature of reality or being is abstract, since the academic mind set is almost exclusively materialist, most academic metaphysical philosophers are reluctant to delve very far into the supernatural, or spiritual aspects of that reality. So, since I wanted to present some prevailing spiritual beliefs of our Western world, I had to look outside academia. What follows, then, are non-orthodox views—the world of the people and ideas I call "Metas."

Metas, possibly more than people of most other philosophies, religions, or traditions, "live" their beliefs. Meta beliefs are not tied to a location like a church or other sacred place, but are personal and go with us wherever we go (I am most certainly a Meta). Ours is a dedication and lifetime commitment. We Metas often incorporate our beliefs into our work or career, and as a result usually love what we do. More often than not, Metas' commitment is to humanity as a whole, often through helping one person at a time. Most of us believe we have been given a "gift" and/or certain insight we feel we have to share with others; it's our life mission to help humanity to evolve to higher levels of consciousness.

Eastern and aboriginal traditions are all metaphysical in that they deal with the nature of reality and aren't constrained by the limits of physicality. Similarities abound in them.

Metas often address issues that religions don't touch and they offer explanations for many things religions ask us to take on faith. Metas want to know the whys of our existence that neither fundamentalist religion nor orthodox science addresses. Also, to most Metas, generally no one is more special than all others—we aren't deity or hero based—and recognize that we are each following a path that's appropriate for us individually and at our own pace.

Metas are not religions; they are philosophies, or in the case of Eastern and aboriginal beliefs and practices, they are "tradition." While certain tenets are common to most Metas and certain rituals are practiced by some, Metas are not organized. Unlike the institutions of religion and science, Metas as a whole don't offer a single, well-defined view.

Common Meta Beliefs

Beliefs common to most Metas are:
- We are first and foremost eternal spirit beings;
- Everything, seen and unseen, is One, spirit, entangled, without separation;
- The physical universe and all life are emanations of and within the One: God.

In addition, many Metas see our human life on Earth as circular, with us beginning as spiritual, devolving into the material, then evolving through reincarnation back to the spiritual, with greatly expanded, higher level consciousness. Metas instruct us to go within to realize God, and to allow our inner intuitive wisdom to enlighten us to who we are. Most Metas practice meditation, often for communion or gnosis. And most see consciousness as the One that is everything, and realize that matter and this life are not real.

A principal problem that conventional scientists have in considering the existence of higher intelligence as a first cause and continuing influence in evolution is that our Western religions posit their creator God as a person, human-like in nature, and separate from us as a Supreme Being. Because, according to the Bible, we humans were created in God's image and likeness, biblically literal religions see God as a bigger, grander, human-like being. They have created God in our exterior human image and view him as a supreme male person who is creator, controller, and destroyer. Because they impose human limitations on God, and since anything we create is external to us, they believe anything God has created must be outside him. To many biblical Christians, anyone who doesn't believe in this creator God as a person—which includes most Eastern traditions, aborigines worldwide, and Western Metas—is an atheist and an enemy.

In *Designer Universe*, Jimmy Davis and Harry Poe give a beautiful explanation of these two differing perspectives that speaks volumes (Hinduism here can represent all Metas):

> We may think of the artistic expression of the potter who fashions a lump of clay into a beautiful vessel in which the mind of the artist skillfully takes shape in physical form. We may also think of the creative expression of the dancer whose body moves gracefully into a thousand different shapes before the dance is done. The monotheism of Judaism, Islam, and Christianity involves faith in the potter, while the monism of Hinduism involves faith in the dancer. The pot and the potter are separate, but the dance and the dancer are inseparable.[309]

Eastern Influences

The Eastern traditions of Hinduism and Buddhism have greatly influenced Western Meta perspectives. These traditions, based on the ancient scriptures called Vedas, view what we call God as the "ground of being," the All-of-Everything: all dimensions, energy, and thought, everything seen and unseen. They, like ancient Pagans and Gnostics, view their many deities as other-world expressions or faces of the One.

Hinduism, the oldest known religion, is usually called a tradition because it is really more a set of metaphysical practices than a religion. It doesn't have a creed or dogma, nor a bible as such. The Hindu sacred texts, the Vedas, supply great wisdom through hymns, aphorisms, profound dissertations, and adages; the Upanishads are commentaries on the Vedas; while the Bhagavad Gita, the most commonly read text in India, and a part of one of the Vedas, offers insight through a mythic story. None are held as "God's Word" in the sense of the Bible or Qur'an.

Professor of religion Kathleen Higgins says the Hindu Vedas, the oldest scriptures in existence, relate that "a single principle underlies and animates everything (that is, it's both transcendent and immanent)."[310] The power of that supreme principle is *Brahman*. In its purest form Hinduism and its offspring, Buddhism, Sikkhism, and Jainism, view everything as *Brahman* and eternal. Brahman means "Absolute Reality," and takes in everything physical and immaterial, as differing expressions of the One.

Although supporting this monistic tradition, the Vedas feature "a pantheon of gods that came to be regarded as manifestations of the supreme power."[311] Referring to *Jiva* (the reincarnating soul) and *Atman* (the unmanifest Self of everyone and the impetus of evolution), Higgins says this tradition sees *Jiva* as *Atman* and *Atman* as *Brahman*. The Vedic supreme goal, as in Gnosticism, is to mystically discover *Brahman* inside *Jiva*.[312]

Spiritual Paths

Eastern traditions have also influenced Metas with the related concepts of reincarnation and karma. They see our Earthly life as one incarnation after another, with our bodily and environmental conditions and experiences determined by karma from our previous actions in both this lifetime and previous incarnations. To Metas, good deeds return as good conditions and experiences, and selfish, harmful acts come back to us as difficult and challenging experiences. Reincarnation is a burden to overcome, if at all possible.

Hindu belief in reincarnation seems to have no beginning, no source. Most ancient civilizations believed in it, including Egyptian and Greek and Gnostics throughout the ancient world. It was deliberately dropped by both Jews and Christians, with Islam following their lead.

Hindus and Buddhists both believe there are basically two paths to rising above reincarnation and achieving union in the One, called *Nirvana* (Buddhist) or *Moksha* (Hindu).

The first and most common path, *karma yoga,* is that of experiencing one's karma from this and previous lives and using it to achieve progressively greater goodness and tranquility in each new act and incarnation. The aim is to express only love and create only good karma for the future.

The second path is one of absolute non-action. By stopping all action one can stop amassing karma to experience its consequences in another life; when there is nothing to experience, reincarnation is no longer necessary. A person on this path must allow him/herself no desires, must see the self and everything else as nonexistent, and lead a completely ascetic life. Hindus say this path is the only sure way to achieve permanent termination of repeated lives on Earth and return to the emptiness of the One.

This reportedly was a path Siddhartha Gautama unsuccessfully tried before achieving awakening and becoming the Buddha. He gained enlightenment through contemplation (gnosis, or communion), and realized that nothing ever fully satisfies until one achieves enlightenment and awakens. Enlightenment then is also a path, and once we become enlightened and know our Self, we will automatically do little which would lead to negative karma.

There are many other specific paths, or yogas, designed to accomplish the same result, including, among others, what the Hindus call *hatha yoga,* using physical postures to clear and cleanse the body-mind, *prana yoga,* using the breath, and *bhakti yoga,* involving loving devotion to God and humankind.

Comments & Questions: The Spiritual Path

I find it unfortunate that so many people with many differing belief systems spend their life preparing for some "heavenly" future life (Western religions) or a moment when reincarnation is no longer necessary (Eastern traditions and most Metas) rather than making the most of and enjoying this life to its fullest. What a waste of this wonderful, glorious experience! There's no good reason to concern ourselves with transcending this life, achieving Nirvana/Moksha, and escaping effects of returning negative karma. We could be living every day of this life with verve and joy.

Rather than trying by ourselves to cope with the trials of this life, we would be better off going within and getting help as we delve deeply into the spirituality of our existence. The spiritual path of enlightenment, in which we learn—or rather remember—who we are helps us better cope with the trials and tribulations of this life, lessening them. While interesting, it's immaterial who we might have been in previous lives. It's more important to see who we truly are and to realize our Oneness, our entanglement with everyone and everything.

It's imperative that we raise our consciousness to a higher level, one of compassion and concern more for the wellbeing of all Earthly life than for ourselves individually. We must each commit to furthering humanity's evolution through the shift in humanity's consciousness. We are all One, and must make it real for us in Earthly life, as it is in spirit: "As above so below."

Let's see now what today's metaphysical perspectives can offer us to help us replace materialist beliefs with spiritual ones. I have selected the following because they not only seem to hold views popular today in the spiritual teacher/Meta milieu but also have similarities with my own philosophy. While I don't agree with everything they each say, there is enough agreement between us that I consider that all Metas espouse essentially the same general philosophy. Our ways of expressing the details of that philosophy may differ, but not enough to make them different philosophies.

---

[305] Boll, Nathaniel Alfred, and the Enneads quoted in "Idealism" Wikipedia.com
[306] "George Berkeley," Wikipedia.com
[307] "Idealism," Wikipedia.com
[308] Hatfield, Gary. "Rene Descartes," *The* Stanford Encyclopedia of *Philosophy*, stanford.edu, 2008.
[309] Davis, Jimmy and Poe, Harry, *Designer Universe*. Nashville, TN: Broadman & Holman Publishers, 2002.
[310] Higgins, Kathleen, *World Philosophy*. Chantilly, VA: The Teaching Company, 2005.
[311] Ibid.
[312] Ibid.

Metaphysics in the New Sciences: Proposals to "Save The World"

Introduction

The new quantum and noetic sciences offer so much to not just the sciences but all of Western humanity, and by extension, all life on Earth. They look at life on Earth from a holistic view, integrating spirituality with science, and give us new ways of viewing life. Our worldviews could benefit considerably from paying particular attention to the texts that follow from this point.

We'll look first at some remarkable scientific views which are expanding science into the spiritual and which could well provide a belief system that will take us to where we want to go. Then we'll see what four of today's Metas have to offer about ways we can live our life, for the most part also using ancient perennial wisdom as their base. We'll close this section with an extraterrestrial report on our beginnings and destiny.

A Quantum Proposal for Intelligent Design

Quantum physicist Amit Goswami says the debate between science and Christianity over evolution is really a struggle for worldview control between two "faulty" worldviews. In his book *Creative Evolution*, he explains that the current biological belief system is an "old paradigm," which is constructed on two implausible principles which are commonly known as "*upward causation*" and "*chance necessity*."[313]

The doctrine of upward causation says that matter is built up "bit by bit" from elementary particles to atoms to molecules to cells with genes, and then "genes determine all biological form and function."[314] Summarizing the materialist view, he says that, "guided by the genes," some cells
> make the brain, and the brain makes all subjective experiences, such as consciousness, thoughts, feelings, and so on. Cause rises upward from the elementary particles, and all causation is upward.[315]

This principle is also called "genetic determinism" when applied to biological systems.

The principle of "chance necessity" says that, to ensure the species' survival, changes in environment cause variations in the genes to be chosen through natural selection or "survival of the fittest." Although beneficial genetic mutations occur rarely, most biologists believe that this process, over time, is responsible for all facets of evolution.

Goswami begs to differ. He sees Intelligent Design evident everywhere, and seriously doubts it could "come from linear, step-by-incremental-step chance and necessity."[316]

He gives as an example the changes necessary in creating the giraffe's long neck. According to Darwinists, the giraffe's form was created as we see it today through slow, accumulated gene mutation variations and their selection and switching, gradually leading to longer and longer necks that enabled giraffes to reach higher and higher branches of trees where food is more abundant.

Francis Hitchings' *The Neck of the Giraffe* offers a very effective explanation of how that can't be the case. To get to a longer neck, numerous other harmonious modifications are needed, concurrently and with incredible coordination (not to mention planning, and that it all would also have to occur simultaneously in two giraffes of opposite sexes if the mutations weren't in the dominant genomes). Specific changes required include:

- a smaller head;
- expanded circulatory system for blood to reach the more remote head;
- increased lung capacity to supply the larger quantity of blood;
- lengthened forelegs, with associated changes in muscles, tendons, and the entire skeletal frame.[317]

Goswami writes: "All this through cumulative step-by-step chance and necessity? It's simply not credible."[318]

Besides, the gradual evolutionary process is not borne out by the fossil record.

At the same time, Goswami refers to "*creationism*" as "an old philosophy," which completely denies any fact of evolution. People of the Intelligent Design movement, he feels, incorrectly follow the Christian idea that "God's design, like God, must be perfect" at the outset, and proposes we instead see that design "evolves toward perfection."[319]

One reason orthodox scientists can't accept either creationism or ID theories is that they seem to them to imply the dualism that their science opposes: "Two entirely different substances with nothing in common cannot interact," one cannot cause something in another. So how can "a nonmaterial designer interact with matter to design something?"[320] To avoid this problem, orthodox scientists force themselves into "*material monism*," in which matter is the only substance in existence: the ground of being.

Goswami says, though, that dualism is resolved also with the idea that "everything is made of consciousness." Matter, he says, is created from "possibilities of consciousness itself."[321] And consciousness, choosing from "its own possibilities," causes the quantum possibility wave to collapse into what we see as matter.[322]

Goswami therefore proposes a form of Intelligent Design that he calls "Creative Evolution." He agrees with Christians that creation is "an aspect of God's downward causation," but not with the specifics. He proposes that, instead of seeing God as a person apart from us, we view God as all-pervading consciousness, "as a new, objective organizing principle capable of causation...." He suggests that we interpret Genesis' six-day creation process as "a metaphor for all the fast-evolution epochs that... explain the fossil gaps," and accept the empirical evidence (described above in Gould and Eldredge's "punctuated equilibrium" and in modern physics' "quantum leaps") that says that "creativity is sudden, instantaneous." Then he adds that we might then see that God's "downward causation is the organizing principle for species creation during the epochs of fast tempo... and creates new species out of existing manifestations."[323]

Evolution, he says, is a process of "consciousness choosing the actuality from possibility," leading to purposeful downward causation, not random and chance mutations and selection. Through what he calls "macroevolution" of forms, "consciousness creates new species by creatively choosing from genetic variations that exist as quantum possibilities." Then, during the fast evolution epochs, complexity is increased, and "consciousness gains the ability to experience itself with ever-greater sophistication."[324] After all,

> ...Evolution is needed for experiencing the possibilities of consciousness in manifestation. When consciousness is inseparable from its possibilities, there is only one thing, and no experience is possible.[325]

"Awareness," Goswami says, "is needed for experience." And evolution is needed "to make the unconscious... conscious... aware and capable of experiencing" what our senses tell us, or physicality.[326]

In all his work, Goswami proposes we integrate monistic idealism into quantum physics and that we recognize consciousness as the ground of being and matter as waves of possibility within that consciousness. Quantum physics, he says, is reclaiming the truths known by our forebears, reassuring us that "there is nothing unscientific about God." This new way of looking at God as consciousness, while emerging from an understanding of quantum physics, is, he says, "common to all spiritual traditions at their esoteric core. It just gets lost in popular translation."[327]

Applying the idea to other sciences is what *Creative Evolution* is all about. By incorporating God's creativity into an objective new biology, Goswami tells us, both "we and biology will be better for it."

He refers to Rupert Sheldrake's theory of morphic resonance based on a biological concept of nonmaterial and nonlocal "morphogenetic fields" that encourage a particular form to appear in multiple places, saying,

> ...consciousness uses the morphogenetic fields as blueprints to direct the choice of a particular form from among the myriad quantum possibilities of matter.... Consciousness does not just 'breathe' life into matter.... Quantum waves of possibility... are not separate from consciousness; they are possibilities of consciousness itself... because everything, including matter, is made of consciousness.... The physical body is thus a representation of the morphogenetic blueprints....[328]

Goswami says that in 1939 both Hindu philosopher Sri Aurobindo and Jesuit priest/paleontologist Pierre Teilhard de Chardin realized how evolution proceeds as a process of extension of consciousness as the ground of being, and more recently both he and philosopher Ken Wilber have done the same. Individually and independently, each of these scholars realized that "in the beginning, consciousness includes all possibilities." Goswami suggests we think about that:

> "all possibilities" must include literally *all* possibilities, past, present, and future. In other words, when every possibility is included, there is no scope for the passage of time [or for knowing and experiencing either the whole as the One or any of its individual possibilities] To bring time into the equation of the manifest universe, consciousness must limit what is possible. The imposition of progressive limitation

on what is possible is seen as an involution of consciousness. In this way, when evolution is viewed from the context of the primacy of consciousness, involution [slowing of consciousness energy vibrations] must precede it [for manifestation to occur].[329]

In his classic text *Laws of Form,* mathematician G. Spencer Brown said,

> We cannot escape the fact that the world we know is constructed in order (and in such a way as to be able) to see itself, but in order to do so, evidently it must first cut itself up into at least one state which sees, and at least one other state that is seen.[330]

Cooperation in Evolution

Bruce Lipton and Steve Bhaerman, describing the evolution of life on this planet in *Spontaneous Evolution*, write that the fundamental life forms "gave rise to individuated, membrane-bound communities" of multi-celled organisms called eukaryotes. Those communities then "provided for multi-cellular species" of animals and plants. And, those plant and animal species "subsequently assembled into higher order [social] communities." That is, societies, cultures, civilizations.[331]

In 1967 microbiologist Lynn Margulis, one of the formulators of "the Gaia Hypothesis," a breakthrough in planetary evolutionary models, published a paper in which she argued for something she called symbiogenesis to describe this process. She has since summarized it as:

> ...billions of years ago, protozoans symbiotically acquired photos-ynthetic plant cells and, working together, they eventually developed into an entirely new life form—the eukaryote or multicelled organism.[332]

In Margulis' model, symbiosis, the coming-together of individuals "based on mutually beneficial relationships, is a major driving force behind evolution." She argued against competition-driven Darwinism with the novel idea that "cooperation, interaction, and mutual dependence among life forms, allowed for the global expression of life." Later she asserted: "Life did not take over the globe by combat, but by networking,"[333] However, since evidence of cooperation in biology directly contradicted their "selfish genes" and "survival by competition" assumptions, Darwinists scoffed at Margulis' theory for two decades, before the evidence required that they finally accept it—another example of how scientific revolutions work.

More recently journalist Carter Phipps, a Meta, says that biologist David Sloan Wilson saw proof of cooperation in nature and expanded Neo-Darwinism to include the theory of

> group selection—the idea that individuals can cooperate rather than compete with one another and become social groups that are so functionally integrated they become higher-level organisms in their own right.[334]

Phipps also says that "directionalists," believe "the process of evolution is progressing toward broader and deeper cooperation and complexity." According to Phipps, directionalists say that, far from being random and aimless, evolution is unmistakably directional, with "more cooperative interaction, richer and richer complexity, and ever-vaster webs of interdependence at all levels, from gene to cell to organism to society."[335]

Purposeful Evolution

Denying the separation, competition, and conflict of Darwinian selection theories, Lipton and Bhaerman see all life but human life as cooperative and harmonious, and want to see the human mode change.

With this goal in mind, they offer a scientific approach to a sustainable future.[336] They start with the realization that our bodily cells are conscious and highly intelligent, each taking on a specific mission in life while working together harmoniously for the good of the whole; while they all have the same DNA, each cell knows its purpose and assignment. Some join to form the heart, others lungs, kidneys, the brain—with specific jobs within the brain—while others work together to fight infection or to transport oxygen throughout their world, all for the survival of their body. If the cells hadn't been conscious, known their individual assignment, and worked cooperatively with other cells to carry out their mission, they would have been in utter chaos and incapable of creating our bodies. We would not exist. No form would exist.[337]

Lipton and Bhaerman explain that the success of cells "is not based on competitiveness with other organs and tissues, [but] is measured by how well each organ fulfills its job of cooperating with other systems."[338] They say that individual cells, knowing their biological imperative was to survive, learned a very long time ago that their survival chances would be better if they joined forces, became eukaryotes, and lived harmoniously. Since the cell membrane is what is aware of its environment and causes the cell to adapt, in joining with other cells they formed a larger membrane enabling greater awareness and a better chance of survival.

Comparing the many trillion cells in a human body with the individuals who constitute humanity, they say that if we were to follow the example of our cells, we could not only survive as a species but truly thrive. They suggest we take a lesson from our cells, and hope to persuade us, the nearly seven billion individual cells of humanity, to join together symbiotically in harmony and cooperation, creating what amounts to a higher-level organism out of a higher order, holistic community, thereby enlarging its collective membrane for greater awareness and ultimately the good and survival of the whole.[339]

Comments & Questions: The New Sciences

Orthodox scientists say that two different substances can't interact and impose causation one on another. But that statement seems absurd. Since they have no idea what God's substance is or how God interacts, those scientists are imposing their view of the physical world and its laws on God. If God is truly omniscient and omnipotent and creator of all that's physical, it seems to me He/She/It can do anything it wants to with its creation. God not only created the physical but the laws governing it. And it's evident that science doesn't understand God, the physical, or the laws.

This is hard stuff to fathom (at least for this nonscientist). But I think that if Western science and religion were to understand what writers like Goswami and Lipton and Bhaerman propose well enough to adopt consciousness as the ground of being, Goswami's creative evolution theory, and Lipton and Bhaerman's cooperation of a higher order community as an operational paradigm, humanity could move from materialism to spirituality and pursue sciences and religions that are not only compatible, but are in line with ancient wisdom.

Much of Goswami's "creative evolution" is similar to my own understanding; we just come from different directions to express our beliefs. I'm grateful to Goswami for putting these ideas into scientific context, so they can be pursued in science and religion and our culture more generally. Lipton and Bhaerman also express ideas very compatible and similar to my own.

One question does come to mind, though, as I read these texts: Are Plato's "Forms of the intelligible world" and Sheldrake's morphogenetic fields, the blueprints, the same thing? It seems a useful avenue of research to explore.

There's absolutely no reason why we can't accomplish the shift in consciousness that will create an all-inclusive membrane of humanity and result in a higher-level organism (a new culture) needed for a better future for all life on Earth. To do so, I believe we each individually have to become enlightened through a spiritual belief system that will help us integrate our own spirituality and our Oneness into our worldview and basis of living. And, we have to each commit to helping the whole of humanity evolve into that higher-level organism.

---

[313] Goswami, Amit, *Creative Evolution, a Physicist's Resolution between Darwinism and Intelligent Design*. Wheaton, IL: Quest Books, Theosophical Publishing House, 2008.

[314] Ibid.

[315] Ibid.

[316] Ibid.

[317] Hitching, Francis, *The Neck of the Giraffe*, New American Library, 1982, quoted by Amit Goswami in *Creative Evolution, a Physicist's Resolution between Darwinism and Intelligent Design*. Wheaton, IL: Quest Books, Theosophical Publishing House, 2008

[318] Goswami, Amit, Creative Evolution, a Physicist's Resolution between Darwinism and Intelligent Design. Wheaton, IL: Quest Books, Theosophical Publishing House, 2008

[319] Ibid.

[320] Ibid.

[321] Ibid.

[322] Goswami, Amit, *The Self-Aware Universe,* New York: Tarcher, 1995.

[323] Goswami, Amit, *Creative Evolution, a Physicist's Resolution between Darwinism and Intelligent Design*. Wheaton, IL: Quest Books, Theosophical Publishing House, 2008.

[324] Ibid.

[325] Ibid.

[326] Ibid.
[327] Ibid.
[328] Ibid.
[329] Ibid.
[330] Brown, George Spencer, *The Laws of Form,* London: Houghton-Miffler, 1969.
[331] Lipton, Bruce and Steve Bhaerman, *Spontaneous Evolution, Our Positive Future.* Carlsbad, CA: Hay House, Inc., 2009
[332] Margulis, Lynn, *"Symbiosis," in Cell Evolution: Microbial Communities in the Archean and Protozoan Eras.* New York: Freeman, 1993.
[333] Margulis, Lynn, quoted in Lipton, Bruce and Steve Bhaerman, *Spontaneous Evolution, Our Positive Future.* Carlsbad, CA: Hay House, Inc., 2009
[334] Phipps, Carter, "The Real Evolution Debate," *EnlightenNext* e-zine, November/December 2009.
[335] Ibid.
[336] Lipton, Bruce and Steve Bhaerman, *Spontaneous Evolution, Our Positive Future.* Carlsbad, CA: Hay House, Inc., 2009
[337] Ibid.
[338] Ibid
[339] Ibid.

Evolutionary Spirituality and Enlightenment: Andrew Cohen and Ken Wilber

Introduction

Ken Wilber is an American philosopher and writer who, as editor of Shambhala Press, has had the opportunity to integrate many ways of thinking about science, society, evolution, and enlightenment. Andrew Cohen integrates Hindu ideas about the nature of consciousness with distinctly Western notions of progressive development. Together, they provide a fascinating integrated view of our potential—and what it takes to get there.

Andrew Cohen's Teaching

After living in India studying and teaching Hindu wisdom, Andrew Cohen returned to America to teach his own brand of wisdom. Evolutionary Spirituality, taught by Cohen since 1986, has been likened to the philosophy of the late 18th-century German idealists Hegel, Fichte, and Schelling, who spoke of human history as the "ever-greater unfolding of spirit in our world."[340] His work suggests the early 20th-century teachings of Sri Aurobindo and Pierre Teilhard de Chardin, who perceived a "spiritual unfolding in the natural processes of cosmic evolution, a powerful evolutionary impulse at work in nature that was... the God principle itself.., urging us to ever-greater heights of consciousness."[341] With them, he sees the "true purpose of spiritual life... as further evolution of consciousness on earth."[342]

The above ideas are basic to Cohen's teaching, along with the following description:

> From absolutely nothing, suddenly Something emerged, and that Something has remained ever since in a constant state of becoming.... [A]ll of life is One—the whole universe and everything that exists within it, seen and unseen, known and unknown, is one conscious,

glorious, intelligent Being that is self-aware. Its nature is Love...
[T]here is no such thing as death; life has no beginning and no end.[343]

Before the universe existed, Cohen says, there was a void which was peaceful because nothing had yet occurred; then an impulse to become emerged and exploded as the big bang, giving birth to a powerful creative process. To him, that quantum leap could only have been made by a God-like force, so for him the word God means

> not only the empty Ground of all Being but also the creative principle—the evolutionary impulse... the First Cause, the elemental driving force behind the evolving universe... your very own consciousness.[344]

Matter, time, and space were a great singularity, compressed into one fine point, and everything was there as the One. He adds: that

> The One had not yet become the many. So there was only You, and You were alone.... As God, or the creative principle, you/we/I chose to take form...; we made a decision to create the Kosmos. We chose to manifest a material universe from our own un-manifest body.... to manifest our own Self in and through form.[345]

But, he adds,

> ...we forgot who we were, forgot our roots,... We forgot that we were always already free, perfect, whole, and complete. We got lost in the show... seemed to forget that we were never separate from the universe.... And so then we began the search for our Self.[346]

If we were able to get passed all "sense of being separate, individual, or unique" we would find ourselves in an "identical state of consciousness" and would realize we are "the same One Self."[347]

This realization is our goal through enlightenment.

Conscious Evolution through Enlightenment

Cohen tells us, "we are all desperately needed" by our very own Self, to become enlightened.

> The energy and intelligence that initiated the big bang is compelling you, as its own creation, to evolve. Why? Because to whatever degree you evolve, that very energy and intelligence evolves also. God evolves through you—through each and every one of us, as we evolve. Then we can consciously participate in and give ourselves *whole-heartedly* to conscious evolution.[348]

As part of the One, in which creative evolution is the driving impulse, our job is to accept our individual responsibility by actively helping all sentient beings to evolve. Our aim is "to transform the world, becoming an agent of the evolutionary impulse itself."[349]

Cohen says this is a two-fold process: first, to realize our Self as the Ground of Being; and second, to "become a radically and profoundly transformed human being who is going to be able to manifest our higher evolutionary potential in the world."[350]

Once we understand our role in evolution, we have to do everything in our power to become enlightened. God's purpose becomes our purpose. God's purpose, Cohen says, is to

> ...create the universe in [its] own image, which is consciousness. Now that highly evolved humans are awakening to the evolutionary impulse, God is able to experience through us what it is to be physically alive with human senses.
>
> God is completely dependent upon us.... [T]he evolution of consciousness... is entirely dependent upon the conscious evolution of human beings... There is no other way for God to evolve [than] in and through matter.[351]

Cohen explains that in becoming aware of consciousness, we humans began an evolutionary process that is awakening the One in its entirety to ever greater self-awareness. As each of us is enlightened and awaken, the One becomes more conscious. All humans eventually will awaken, awakening all sentient beings, and then the One will be fully self-aware. We each have that responsibility to all life in the cosmos. The process of "Evolutionary Enlightenment," as he calls it, is not merely to transcend and be free of the world, but is "to embrace the entire process as our own Self, knowing [we each] are the creative principle incarnate...." God is emerging as the creative impulse, which is our own Authentic Self, longing to consciously evolve, in, through, and as us. This impulse, he says, is a "force of nature, a function in consciousness," and it is to be found within each of us.[352]

He goes on to say that when we are flooded with evolutionary energy, we are "spontaneously liberated from fear and self-concern," because our "attention is focused primarily on the power and the purpose of that creative principle."[353]

Enlightenment is the direct realization of ... the inherent perfection of all things at all times, in all places, through all circumstances. Even earthquakes, disease and bloody warfare, ... heaven and hell, good and evil, everything known and unknown, seen and unseen are all recognized only to be different expressions of that one inconceivable mystery beyond name and form.[354]

Ken Wilber & Levels of Consciousness

From 2002 to 2011, Andrew Cohen and Ken Wilber carried on a dialogue about evolutionary spirituality and enlightenment in Cohen's *EnlightenNext* magazine (formerly called *What Is Enlightenment?* and now defunct*)*. Among other things, they talk about levels of consciousness in which our normal waking self evolves into the "Self Absolute."

The "Self Absolute" is the "unmanifest ground of being" called "emptiness" in Eastern traditions because it is unmanifest, timeless, transcendent, unseeable, and unknowable.

Cohen and Wilber both veer from their Eastern view by inserting a level between Self Absolute and ego—which exists only in this world.[355] Cohen calls his new level the "Authentic Self" and Wilber calls it the "deeper psychic," or "soul," and they both say we must become "grounded in this authentic self, or psychic being—which is the true self, beyond ego, or the awakened spiritual conscience."[356] I call it the Self or soul-Self.

Cohen says this level is a part of our consciousness that has never manifested physically, a dimension of the self that is completely different from either the Self Absolute or the ego. It's that part of ourselves that is always whole and complete, that has "never been hurt, wounded, traumatized or victimized," yet evolves. This part of us is our internal summoner to the evolutionary imperative. That Authentic Self dwells in the spirit realm, yet is aware of and cares passionately about everything going on in the physical world.[357]

In several of his books, articles, and audio presentations, Wilber says we develop in stages of consciousness, which represent our identity as we become ever more enlightened. We are moving from identifying with me (egocentric), to identifying with us (ethnocentric), to all of us (worldcentric), and finally to identifying with the all (which he calls "Kosmocentric," being beyond the limitations of the measurable cosmos). These stages unfold as levels, occurring sequentially. They create our worldviews as our belief systems evolve, moving us from self-centered, to ethnic identification and patriotism, to holistic in our approach to the world and its inhabitants as our compassion increases, and to identifying with all life in the Kosmos as One.

Wilber and Cohen agree that as we each rise to a higher stage, we are better able to understand life through that higher level. When we have a higher-stage spiritual experience from a lower stage, then go back to our old level—as will always happen at first—we interpret that experience from the lower level, and don't fully understand it. But as we continue to have higher-level spiritual experiences, life becomes easier to understand from the higher level. Suddenly we find ourselves at the higher level reaching for the next, and can understand all levels lower than our current one.

According to their model, when we've had an experience somewhere between the world-centric and Kosmocentric, the soul, the Authentic Self, is able to express itself. Once we've gotten the initial glimmer to awaken, the Authentic Self eagerly calls us and helps us more fully awaken; it pulls us up to its Self level, and raises us to our higher potential. The more dedicated and single-minded we are to this enlightenment process, the easier it is to climb to higher levels; and as each person climbs higher, it gets ever easier for others to climb higher as well.

Wilber and Cohen also agree that when people awaken to their Authentic Self, they "begin to see the world in a completely new way."[358] Wilber says we respond to the evolutionary impulse, because it is increasing wholeness, compassion, consciousness, and care. "And the Authentic Self, the deeper psychic, is the one that is relaying that to us." Cohen says it's exciting to awaken to the evolutionary potential and realize it's actually up to us to create a new stage of development.[359] Wilber adds, though, that "Those who are allowed to see are saddled with the obligation to... speak out," not merely to whisper, but to shout in whatever way we can. [360]

Stepping Away from Ego

Most seekers look for peace and bliss, in hopes of alleviating their own suffering and becoming happy in this life. But, says Cohen, that's self-centered, and we can succeed only when we make our enlightenment an instrument to awaken the whole of sentient beings. We must decide to become enlightened and then step away from ego, not the persona ego, but "the sense of one's self as being separate." As he puts it, "Ego is the need to personalize, and the only obstacle to enlightenment." He calls on us to liberate ourselves from ego, and says that, once we do, we will see that only we are responsible for whatever happens in our life. When we no longer need to personalize our experiences, our true Self can freely express as us.[361]

Wilber clarifies: "[E]golessness does not mean the absence of a functional self...it means that one is no longer exclusively identified with that self." While there's truth to the notion of transcending ego, "it doesn't mean destroy the ego," he writes,

> ...it means plug it into something bigger.... The small ego does not evaporate; it remains as the functional center of activity in the conventional realm.... to lose the ego is to become a psychotic, not a sage. 'Transcending the ego' thus actually means to transcend but include the ego in a deeper and higher embrace, first in the soul or deeper psychic... And that means we do not 'get rid' of the small ego, but rather, we inhabit it fully, live it with verve, use it as the necessary vehicle through which higher truths are communicated.[362]

He further clarifies, "We assume the [ego] hides or obstructs Spirit, whereas in fact it is simply a radiant manifestation of Spirit itself, like absolutely every other Form in the universe."[363]

Karma

Cohen says we create karma when we "act out of ignorance and selfishness in ways that cause suffering to others...."[364] He says we constantly are exposed to possibilities that present us with choice, and the choices we make define who we are, which therefore can radically change moment to moment.

To be ignorant, he says, means "we are compulsively making the wrong choices in a blind and deeply conditioned way." To be awake means "we are constantly making the right choices."[365]

Pierre Teilhard de Chardin

As mentioned earlier, the philosophers Pierre Teilhard de Chardin and Sri Aurobindo both saw a "spiritual unfolding in the natural processes of cosmic evolution" in the 1930s. Teilhard (1881-1955) was a French Jesuit priest and paleontologist. Although completely devoted to the Christianity of the Roman church, he had a very different view of God, Christ, and the world from that taught by orthodox Catholicism and much of Christianity.

At the same time, his view of evolution is very different from what is taught by orthodox science. He sees God in all matter, Christ Consciousness as spirit unfolding in the world through humans, and creation as an ongoing activity in which humans play a major role. He explains:

> What... we have to do is... in some way... bring Christ to completion; we must, therefore, devote ourselves with still more ardor, even in the natural domain, to the cultivation of the world.... Since immanent progress is the natural soul of the cosmos, and since the cosmos is centered on Christ [consciousness], it must be accepted as proved that, in one way or another, collaboration with the development of the cosmos holds an essential and prime position among the duties of the Christian [or anyone]. To live the cosmic life is to live dominated by the consciousness that one is an atom of the body of the mystical and cosmic Christ.[366]

Teilhard was allowed to freely pursue paleontology and became famous for his work in that field, especially with early hominid fossils, but his unorthodox Christianity was objected to by the Vatican, and he was forbidden to publish anything of a religious nature. Like so many of his predecessors who were subject to the church's law, his most important writings were published after his death.

In those writings, he posed as a statement the same idea that Edgar Mitchell later put as a question, saying "We are not human beings having a spiritual experience. We are spiritual beings having a human experience."

Sri Aurobindo

Sri Aurobindo (1872 -1950) was a Hindu yogi, a philosopher, and spiritual teacher. His work forming a global community based on evolutionary spirituality continues to unfold today in Auroville in southern India. Regarding evolution and spirituality, he says in *The Human Aspiration*:

> We speak of the evolution of Life in Matter, the evolution of Mind in Matter; but evolution is a word which merely states the phenomenon without explaining it. For there seems to be no reason why Life should evolve out of material elements or Mind out of living form,

unless we accept the Vedantic solution that Life is already involved in Matter and Mind in Life because in essence Matter is a form of veiled Life, Life a form of veiled Consciousness....

If it be true that Spirit is involved in Matter and apparent Nature is secret God, then the manifestation of the divine in himself and the realization of God within and without are the highest and most legitimate aims possible to man upon earth.[367]

Comments & Questions: Evolutionary Spirituality

It seems clear to me that Cohen believes in "evolutionary science," its big bang and creation of the physical and its evolution. Then he adds his own brand of spirituality to that basic assumption. He says the big bang was God—as you and I—creating the physical universe from nothing except the unmanifest multiplicity as possibilities within us as a singularity. We made a decision to experience form; we were the evolutionary imperative, God.[368]

Cohen also says that although Eastern traditions and most Metas say this world is all illusion, he believes the world is very real, and in fact, is "an inherent and all-important dimension of what God always is." He counters those who say it isn't real by saying: "then nothing needs to be done about the way things are."[369]

I believe the world isn't real in a physical sense—it is a materialized emanation of the One consciousness that is God, just as everything is. But it is real in the sense of providing interactive experience through which we expand our awareness of who and what we are, and evolve as spirit beings, which is our purpose for being here.

That means that, in a sense it's true that nothing needs to be done. We could sit back and watch as humanity destroys all life on Earth including us and possibly the planet itself.

But then we wouldn't gain the benefits of the experiences through which we came into this life to learn. There would be no point in our being here. We want to develop, we want to evolve, we want Earthly, interactive experience. So what if it isn't real?

Cohen also says, "Enlightenment is not the end of the path [as Eastern traditions teach]. It is the beginning."[370] I agree that the experience of the light which we call en*light*enment is the beginning of our conscious evolution into greater spirituality and helping our fellow humans awaken. However, I feel that the process of enlightenment itself is just as important to our evolution and our enjoyment of our Earthly experiences as what follows, so achieving it is not really the beginning. I would say the beginning of our evolution into conscious spirituality is when we commit to our individual evolution through the enlightenment process.

Clearly, Teilhard de Chardin, Aurobindo, Cohen, and Wilber are expressing essentially the same philosophy regarding the emergence of spirituality in this world through evolution and humanity's role in it. This belief system seems almost an elaborative sequel or prequel to Amit Goswami's "creative evolution."

---

[340] Phipps, Carter, "From the Editors," *What Is Enlightenment?*, Spring/Summer 2003. Lenox MA: EnlightenNext Media.
[341] Ibid.
[342] Ibid.
[343] Cohen, Andrew, *Living Enlightenment, a call for evolution beyond ego*. Lenox, MA: EnlightenNext Media, 2002
[344] Cohen, Andrew, "Being & Becoming: the philosophy of Evolutionary Enlightenment," and online article attached to Quote of the Week e-mailed 6/02/08.
[345] Ibid.
[346] Cohen, Andrew, "Introduction," *What Is Enlightenment?*, Spring/Summer 2002. Lenox, MA: EnlightenNext Media.
[347] Cohen, Andrew, *Living Enlightenment*. Lenox, MA: EnlightenNext Media, 2002
[348] Ibid.
[349] Cohen, Andrew and Ken Wilber in dialogue, "The Evolution of Enlightenment," *EnlightenNext*, Spring/summer 2002. Lenox, MA: EnlightenNext Media
[350] Cohen, Andrew, "Being & Becoming: the philosophy of Evolutionary Enlightenment," an online article attached to Quote of the Week e-mailed 6/02/08. Lenox, MA: EnlightenNext Media.
[351] Ibid.
[352] Ibid.
[353] Ibid.

354 Cohen, Andrew, *Embracing Heaven & Earth*. Lenox, MA: EnlightenNext Media, 2000.

355 Cohen, Andrew and Ken Wilber in dialogue, "Following the Grain of the Kosmos," *What Is Enlightenment?*, May-July 2004. Lenox, MA: EnlightenNext Media

356 Cohen, Andrew and Ken Wilber in dialogue, "Breaking the Rules," *What Is Enlightenment?*, Fall/Winter 2002. Lenox, MA: EnlightenNext Media.

357 Cohen, Andrew, "Being & Becoming" an online article attached to Quote of the Week e-mailed 6/02/08. Lenox, MA: EnlightenNext Media

358 Cohen, Andrew and Ken Wilber in dialogue, "Following the Grain of the Kosmos," *What Is Enlightenment?*, May-July 2004. Lenox, MA: EnlightenNext Media.

359 Ibid.

360 Wilber, Ken, "A Spirituality that Transforms," *What Is Enlightenment?*, Fall/Winter 2001. Lenox, MA: EnlightenNext Media.

361 Cohen, Andrew. *Embracing Heaven & Earth*, Lenox, MA: EnlightenNext Media, 2000

362 Wilber, Ken, *One Taste: Daily Reflections on Integral Spirituality* Boston, MA: Shambhala Publications, Inc., 2001.

363 Wilber, Ken, Grace and Grit: Spirituality and Healing in the Life and Death of Treya Killam Wilber, Boston, MA: Shambhala, 2000.

364 Cohen, Andrew, *Living Enlightenment*. Lenox, MA: EnlightenNext Media, 2002.

365 Cohen, Andrew, *Embracing Heaven & Earth*. Lenox, MA: EnlightenNext Media, 2000

366 Teilhard De Chardin, Pierre, "Cosmic Life," from *Writing in Time of War*, cited by Ursula King in *Pierre Teilhard De Chardin*. Maryknoll, NY: Orbis Books, 1999

367 Aurobindo, Sri, *The Essential Aurobindo, the Writings of Sri Aurobindo* compiled and edited with Introduction and Afterword by Robert McDermott, Lindisfarne Books, 1987, 2001.

368 Cohen, Andrew, *Evolutionary Enlightenment, A New Path to Spiritual Awakening*. New York: Select Books, Inc., 2011.

369 Cohen, Andrew, "The Evolution of Enlightenment. An introduction to the philosophy and vision of Andrew Cohen," article on Cohen's website: www.andrewcohen.org. Lenox, MA: EnlightenNext Media, 2010.

370 ibid.

Edgar Cayce's Christian Mysticism

Introduction

Called the "Sleeping Prophet," Edgar Cayce (1877-1945) went into trance to give over 14,000 health and life "readings." That is, he closed his eyes, breathed deeply, and responded to whatever questions he was asked with a knowledge and understanding that are normally impossible for someone of his experience. In trance, Cayce tapped the energy field that surrounds and permeates all existence, what he, like Hindus, called the *Akasha*, which contains a complete record of every event and thought that has ever occurred. John Van Auken explains that

> Cayce was able to perceive the *Akasha* during his deep, meditative-like states by shifting his consciousness in such a way as to totally subdue the predominant three-dimensional mind, allowing his fourth-dimensional (and higher) mind to awaken and speak through his receptive body.[371]

Cayce said anyone can read the Akasha, but properly interpreting what one perceives is challenging, because the "language of the deeper consciousness" contains "more imagery and metaphor and is holistic," unlike the "language of the outer self."[372] Time lines especially are hard; everything seems to be happening at once, as clusters of actions rather than linear sequences of events.

The Association for Research & Enlightenment (A.R.E.) was formed to organize and disseminate Cayce's work. The many books expressing Cayce's message were written by others, interpreting and quoting from the mountain of material recorded during his readings. Cayce's readings were for individuals, so much of the material is difficult to put into general context, leaving room for interpretation.

Since Cayce was a biblical Christian, his teaching is thought of as mystical Christian, and many writers of his teaching are themselves Christian, so they often interpret his material to deny Darwinian evolution in favor of biblical creationism.

Evolution/Involution

Mark Thurston, though, writes that evolution was not a principle Cayce disputed in its entirety. Rather it was a matter of defining 'what' evolves and how the invisible, non-material world of spirit is also involved in the process." Thurston, Director of Academic Affairs at A.R.E.'s Atlantic University, says Cayce emphasized involution over evolution: to be involved "with or entangled within." He says that "man's origin is a spiritual creation… man did not evolve from apes" because each of us was initially a being of the spiritual world.

> But the divine plan was for us to grow beyond what we were at the beginning… to "evolve" in consciousness. The plan was for us to know our oneness with God and to know fully our own individuality…. That plan required involution—the coming of spiritual beings into the three-dimensional, material world. Through involution we were given the opportunity to experience ourselves in a focused, individual way. A new kind of awareness… was being made possible.[373]

Thurston says that following the physical laws of mutation and natural selection, a new species slowly evolved as Homo sapiens. He elaborates through a quote from Cayce's biography, *There is a River,* by Thomas Sugrue:

> Souls descended on these apes—hovering above and about them rather than inhabiting them—and influenced them to move toward a different goal from the simple one they had been pursuing.[374]

Cayce's Story of Our Beginnings

Cayce made it clear that we are first and foremost spirit beings:

[A]ll life begins in the spirit, gains a pattern in the mind, and then becomes manifest in the physical. The physical is the result of activity in the spirit and mind, not the other way around.[375]

Lytle Robinson begins *Edgar Cayce's Story of the Origin and Destiny of Man* with a parallel to the opening chapters of Genesis:

> In the beginning was the Spirit; a vast sea of mind-force, of discerning energy…. Omniscient, Omnipotent, Omnipresent, this was the source of all; the First Cause… the eternal God…. The second cause was desire: desire for self-expression, desire to create, desire for companionship…. [A]ll souls were created in the beginning… a part of the Whole yet aware of being separate and independent entities….[376]

Cayce said that some souls, fascinated with the power of their own creative individuality, turned away from God's will, "giving in to desire and self-aggrandizement...." Egoic selfishness came into being, bringing about "the downfall, the separation, and end of the state of perfection." The universe, Earth, and the basic life forms were created, he said, with minerals, plants, and animals thriving long before humans.[377]

The lost souls, Cayce said, became absorbed in using their creative powers to mimic beasts and fowl, and dreaming up bodies to inhabit, "congealed into matter," and propagated "a race of monstrosities." Driven by sexual desire and trapped in matter, souls drifted ever farther from their Source. Cayce claimed it was this willful disregard in favor of "selfish gratification of the carnal... the spiritually destructive use of creative powers for self," that was the "Original Sin of man." This was what's been called "the revolt of the angels."[378]

A rescue plan was devised to create matter in which to demonstrate physically to those lost souls their separation from spirit. To save those souls, the "sons of the Most High" asserted their influence. "From among the various physical forms on earth a body was patterned" to fit "the needs of man.... Adam [was] the first of the perfect race, the first of the Sons of God." Occurring 10½ million years ago, this began human evolution. Then genders were created, which Cayce called "the division of the nature of 'man' into positive and negative forces."[379]

Reason for Being

To Cayce, the reason for experiencing life in physical bodies, writes I. C. Sharma, is for "the entity to know itself as a part of the Whole, ...retaining its individuality... yet one with the purpose of the First Cause that called it into being, into the awareness... of itself."[380]

Cayce said that when we come to realize that our true soul-Self is not our body, mind, rationality, or ego but something so much greater, "a flash of inner light expands... [our] attitude." We are no longer "disturbed by the relativities and the distracting disabilities of ordinary existence." We see "the unity in diversity and the harmony in discord." We recognize the "light of God" in everyone, and understand the commandment, Love thy neighbor as thyself. Only then can we achieve a "stage of self-realization, knowing the soul—an emanation of God—is in constant connection with God."[381]

The Cayce readings, Barbara Robinson says,

> ...explain that each soul comes into the earth plane with a plan for their lives. Though the veil of forgetfulness drops over that memory soon after birth, that life goal is imbedded in the consciousness.[382]

Karma: Meeting Self

Cayce said that each of us is responsible for the circumstances in which we find ourselves; we are simply "meeting self," which to him meant "meeting the consequences of our own actions or attitudes."[383] He claimed we each must meet our self in our journey toward God by experiencing, in one life or another, the exact effect of whatever karma we bring from past lives.

Reincarnation and the suffering of returning karma, says Mary Ann Woodward, is what Cayce says is the only way we can meet ourselves. And only in this way can we learn love and compassion, and thereby achieve liberation from reincarnation.

We think of our karma as with other people, Woodward says, but we've misunderstood its true nature. Karma is unerring justice and a personal thing, not between individuals, but with "God or the Creative Forces." She explains that our interactions provide the situations through which we learn and gain self mastery and "become companions and co-creators with God the Father."[384]

Cayce made a distinction between karma and cause and effect, saying we bring karma with us from past lives, but cause and effect take place in the present life. He said that every contact

> ...is the opportunity for an entity to fulfill or meet itself. For it is not by chance that each entity enters, but that the entity... may fill that place which no other soul may fill so well. Each entity, each soul, enters the material experience for purposes.[386]

He spoke of group karma, saying we travel on our journey in groups from which we choose our family members and friends. In some cases we may inherit karma from past-life experiences of our family or of our culture. Cayce viewed returning karma as opportunity, with transcendence our goal. Experiencing trials and misery enables soul growth; we eventually achieve love and compassion for others, as we recognize our Oneness with God and each other, and finally escape reincarnation. This is confirmed by the A.R.E.'s Executive Director & CEO Keven Todeschi, who says Cayce didn't think of karma as a debt requiring atonement but as something to remember and benefit from.[387]

Cayce spoke of seven "root races," saying the first three were spiritual in descending levels toward the physical. To this model P. M. H. Atwater adds that the Adam man was the first of the fourth root race. She says we are going into the fifth now, when we will realize our Oneness with God. As that happens, those who incarnate will be more enlightened, more awake and through that process, we will continue into two more spiritual root races, in our circular spiritual evolution.[388]

Levels of Consciousness

Cayce distinguished "spirit" from "soul," saying spirit "is the spark, a portion of the Divine that is in every entity, while soul is the developing portion of our whole nature. ...." Van Auken, a director of the A.R.E., tells us that to Cayce:

> ...spirit is the life force... that animates.... It is a consciousness with individualness, though not nearly as individual as we are in our physical condition.... Within the one universal collective mind of God are infinite points of consciousness.... [T]he soul is uniquely able to bridge the gulf between the spirit realms and the physical realms, between our divine, godly self and our Earthly self.[389]

Soul is on a journey on the road of life, but spirit is high above the road, overarching it from beginning to end.

Comments & Questions: Edgar Cayce

Is what's called the *Akasha* simply a record of what has occurred, or is it perhaps a repository of all "possibilities" or "intelligences" from which consciousness chooses evolutionary steps or we choose thoughts, actions, and events? Or maybe both?

Cayce's "fall"—that we are here in this separate, material existence because we did something wrong—is a popular view, although in Cayce's, as in Pagan and Gnostic views, we erred while still spirit beings. Evil and suffering are thus explained

Speaking often of both Lemuria and Atlantis, Cayce said many of us living today have returned to conditions similar to those we lived under in Atlantis to settle group karma left over from that period. He cited the current emphasis on material possessions, moral degradation, selfishness, and greed as similar to the last days of Atlantis. Are we then entering the first days of the restoration of our greatness, the reverse image of the Atlantean civilization before its degeneration? Are we now in the upward arc, returning to the full spirituality of Lemurians in our circular evolutionary process?

---

[371] Van Auken, John, "The Akasha, Ancient & Modern," *Ancient Mysteries*, Nov./Dec. 2004Virginia Beach, VA: A.R.E. Press.

[372] Ibid.

[373] Thurston, "From Darwin to Cayce: The meeting of evolution and involution," *Venture Inward*, March/April 2004. Virginia Beach, VA: Association for Research & Enlightenment.

[374] Sugrue, Thomas, *There is a River: the Life of Edgar Cayce*, Virginia Beach, VA: A.R.E. Press, 1958.

[375] Van Auken, John, "The Akasha, Ancient & Modern," *Ancient Mysteries*, Nov./Dec. 2004. Virginia Beach, VA: A.R.E. Press.

[376] Robinson, Lytle, *Edgar Cayce's Story of the Origin and Destiny of Man*. New York: Berkley Publishing, 1972

[377] Ibid.

[378] Ibid.

[379] Ibid.

[380] Sharma, I. C., *Cayce, Karma, and Reincarnation*. New York, NY: Harper & Row, 1975.

[381] Ibid.

[382] Robinson, Barbara, "Reconsidering Judas Iscariot," *Venture Inward,*. November/December 2006. Virginia Beach, VA: A.R.E. Press.

[383] Woodward, Mary Ann, *Edgar Cayce's Story of Karma*. New York, NY: Berkley Publishing, 1971.

[384] Ibid.

[386] Cayce, Edgar, quoted by Mary Ann Woodward in, *Edgar Cayce's Story of Karma*. New York, NY: Berkley Publishing, 1971.

[387] Todeschi, Keven, "Are Intuition and Psychic Ability the Same?" *Venture Inward*, summer 2012. Virginia Beach, VA: A.R.E. Press

[388] Atwater, P. M. H., *Beyond the Indigo Children*. Rochester, VT: Bear & Company, 2005.

[389] Van Auken, John, "Understanding Spirit & Soul," *Personal Spirituality*, February 2003. Virginia Beach, VA: A.R.E. Press.

Helena Blavatsky's Theosophy

Introduction

Russian-born Helena Petrovna Blavatsky (1831-1891) called her teaching "Theosophy," a term originally coined by 3rd century Neo-platonists, meaning "Divine Wisdom." It denotes direct knowledge of God and the universe, with direct meaning (like noetic and mystic) through intuition and/or philosophical musing. It has elements in common with Gnosis and communion (the process of going within to know God).

Blavatsky, with others, established The Theosophical Society in 1875 "to collect and define a knowledge" of laws governing the universe, other than the known laws of physics. Her mission was to challenge both the "entrenched beliefs and dogmas of... Christianity" and the "equally dogmatic views" of the new Darwinian science.[390] She believed that humans came first, not last, and writes: "Darwin begins his evolution of species at the lowest point and traces upward. His only mistake may be that he applies his system at the wrong end."[391]

Blavatsky spent several years in Tibet, India, and other nearby countries studying Eastern philosophy, and had a "Master" teacher who lived in Tibet. She refers to the information she is passing on as "The Secret Doctrine," and says it reflects "universally diffused religion of the ancient and prehistoric world," antedating the Vedas. She claims no authorship of those teachings, saying they were passed down from Atlanteans before the final submersion of their land, 12 tya. She says she is recording ancient wisdom obscured for many thousand years by an "impenetrable veil of secrecy, [lest it] should be shared by the unworthy, and so desecrated."[392]

Blavatsky's Teaching

Blavatsky is difficult reading, but the Theosophical Society has published many small books, each focusing on a single issue or concept in the teaching. Henry Travers Edge addresses evolution, writing that its true cause is:

...spirit seeking to express itself in matter... a process of self-realization or manifestation carried on by the Cosmic Life or Spirit or Intelligence; God unfolding and revealing himself.... [E]volution is inconceivable except as a result of intelligence at work behind the scenes.... [It] must be considered as a twofold process—Spirit involving into matter, and matter evolving after the pattern of Spirit.... [393]

Theosophical teaching, like that of Edgar Cayce, sees a natural evolution proceeding below and producing ever more complex forms, and a spiritual involution descending from above, creating "the whole manifest universe...."[394]

Edge says, "It is spirit which causes the organisms to evolve; the form changes and adapts itself to the growing capacities of the indwelling Monad." It isn't true that animals become human by gradual transformation, he says; the gap is too great for spirit beings to directly incarnate into animal organisms. "Self-conscious mind" (*Manas*), acquired by humans at a certain point in their evolution, "bridges that gap." To help humans in the process the "Sons of Mind" awakened in "mindless man the latent seed [spark] of self-conscious mind which was already in him... bringing the Spiritual into union with the physical, and thus making the complete man."[395]

Edge writes "[M]atter itself evolves, and... the earth was not always physical...."

> There is one universal Life, which manifests itself under the two aspects which we call spirit and matter, but these two aspects exist only in contrast with each other... and spirit and matter, instead of being two distinct things, are merely different grades of one thing....
>
> [T]he one essence becomes gradually more material, and then again becomes more and more spiritual, until the cycle of evolution is accomplished.[396]

Monads, Mind, and Levels of Consciousness

According to Edge, Theosophists believe that evolution is bringing the invisible (unmanifest) into visibility (manifestation). This isn't creation, because the unmanifest already exists as a potentiality within the living spirit entity.

Evolution means the unfolding of what is latent, [it] does not mean a putting together of separate parts so as to make a composite; it is not an additive process. ³⁹⁷

"Periods of life on Earth alternate with periods of life elsewhere, in other states," Edge writes. "Death is the termination of one state and the beginning of another."

A human being in this model "is a fivefold entity":

1) Divine Monad - a self-conscious god, a spark of the Universal life
2) Spiritual soul, through which the Divine Monad manifests itself
3) Human soul, through which the spiritual soul, with its divinity, the Monad, works
4) Animal soul, which enables the human soul to work on the lower planes
5) Physical body, a vehicle for the above to work in physical matter.³⁹⁸

Blavatsky writes of the "One Absolute," "Over-Soul," God as eternal, without beginning or end, and invisible, yet everywhere. She says that its manifestations are periodic and, when in non-Being state, it is still absolute Consciousness. Its one attribute is "ceaseless Motion, called… the 'Great Breath,' which is the perpetual motion of the universe; there is nothing absolutely motionless."³⁹⁹

To become active, she says, God exhales the Great Breath and manifests the universe and ultimately materiality. To become inactive, God inhales and dissolves the universe.

She calls an active period a "manvantara," and says the current one comprises seven "Root-Races." Counting slightly differently than Cayce, she says the first two root races are purely spiritual, the third race is astral (still spiritual but slightly materialized); and the fourth is the ethereal semi-material Adamic race, at first androgynous then, mid-way in its evolution, split into male and female. These are the progenitors of the fifth race (ours, Cayce's fourth), which is fully material in human form, but now becoming ever more spiritual.⁴⁰⁰ The sixth and seventh races are once again fully spiritual, first ethereal, then astral. (Like Cayce, evolution is circular in her model, too.) Blavatsky says humans first became physical while Lemurians scattered throughout the world 18 mya in seven locations.⁴⁰¹

As spirit beings, Blavatsky says, we are "mindless," and experience physical life to gain mind (intellect and self-consciousness). As we have grown more material, we have developed more of the faculties of mind.

Once we reach "the limit of materiality, [we] then proceed on a gradually sublimating cycle towards spirituality." In materiality, the Monad has to temporarily forget its divinity and cover itself with "veils that hide" upper levels and powers from it. This helps the Monad focus on the "special work" to be done in the "lower worlds of matter."[402]

Edge explains that, in our individual consciousness that is the Monad, which is part of the ocean of consciousness, we are each a self-conscious, thinking being. Our bodies are instruments we have built to express ourselves in the outer world.[403]

Blavatsky continues the evolutionary story, saying that humans then went through physical evolution in many different incarnations on Earth (as its minerals, plants, the many animals to pre-human primates, and then modern humans); then spiritual devolution—or involution into matter—through various spirit essences (from astral, to etheric bodies, and finally into those modern humans). Through that process, she explains, the Monad develops self-conscious mind. It can then enjoy the third stage, of awakening, or ascension, to ever more of its spirituality—which is where we are now. It will then go through extensive evolutionary stages in spirit.[404]

Karma, Good, and Evil

Each monad gains mind by having its "spark" activated by one of the Sons of Mind. But, says Blavatsky, some of those gods didn't activate their assigned sparks (possibly deliberately), and set up conditions under which (again, like Cayce) monstrosities were born. This created karmic conditions that would have to be worked through. She explains that only by working through karma do we get the necessary experiences of contrasting states and conditions which ultimately enable us to know ourselves and awaken[405]

The Sanskrit term *Karma* expresses "the principle of action and reaction," forming a "law of unerring, never failing justice...." writes Gertrude Van Pelt. She says that the existence of karma necessitates repeated reincarnation of "the spiritual part of man" in Earth life. With each incarnation, she says, we have a new body, environment, and life circumstances resulting from our karma of past lives.[406]

Blavatsky elaborates:

No Entity can reach the state of Nirvana, or of absolute purity, except through aeons of suffering and the knowledge of EVIL as well as of good, as otherwise the latter remains incomprehensible.... Perfection, to be fully such, must be born out of imperfection... having the latter as its vehicle and basis and contrast.... Good and Evil are twins.... Neither exists per se, since each has to be generated and created out of the other, in order to come into being... hence, in mortal mind, they must be divided.[407]

Blavatsky says that everything that is manifest into the physical "has only a relative, not an absolute, reality." She explains, though, that everything is "relatively real, for the cognizer is also a reflection, and the things cognized are therefore as real to him as himself." When we eventually awaken and reach and blend with "absolute consciousness," we will "be free from the delusions produced by maya," the illusions of this world experience.[408]

Comments & Questions: Theosophy

Blavatsky and Gowsami agree that Darwin, by beginning his evolution at the lowest level and building upward, "applies his system at the wrong end." Shadows of Blavatsky's ideas can also be seen in Andrew Cohen's evolutionary spirituality, and her view and Edgar Cayce's are so similar they seem to express a single philosophy. This leads me to think that Blavatsky and Cayce, and maybe Plato and a few others, tapped the same source, known as the Akashic record, perhaps each reading it through their own personal filter and coming up with a slightly different story. Maybe we all do that, without realizing it.

---

[390] Preston, Elizabeth & Christmas Humphreys, editors, in "A Brief Biography" at the start of an abridgement of Blavatsky's *The Secret Doctrine*. Wheaton, Ill.: The Theosophical Publishing House, 1967

[391] Blavatsky, H. P., *Isis Unveiled*, quoted by W. H. Church in *Edgar Cayce's Story of the Soul*. Virginia Beach, VA: Association for Research and Enlightenment, 1989.

[392] *Blavatsky, an Abridgement of The Secret Doctrine*, edited by Elizabeth Preston & Christmas Humphreys. Wheaton, Ill.: The Theosophical Publishing House, 1967.

[393] Edge, Henry Travers, *Evolution, Who and What is Man*. San Diego, CA: Point Loma Publications, Inc., 1979.
[394] Ibid.
[395] Ibid.
[396] Ibid.
[397] Ibid.
[398] Edge, Henry Travers, *Design and Purpose, a Study in the Drama of Evolution*. San Diego, CA: Point Loma Publications, Inc., 1979.
[399] Blavatsky, H. P., *An Abridgement of The Secret Doctrine*, edited by Elizabeth Preston & Christmas Humphreys. Wheaton, Ill.: The Theosophical Publishing House, 1967.
[400] Ibid.
[401] Ibid.
[402] Edge, Henry Travers, *Design and Purpose, a Study in the Drama of Evolution*. San Diego, CA: Point Loma Publications, Inc., 1979.
[403] Edge, Henry Travers, *Evolution, Who and What is Man*. San Diego, CA: Point Loma Publications, Inc., 1979.
[404] Blavatsky, H. P., *An Abridgement of The Secret Doctrine*, edited by Elizabeth Preston & Christmas Humphreys. Wheaton, Ill.: The Theosophical Publishing House, 1967.
[405] Ibid.
[406] Van Pelt, Gertrude, *The Doctrine of Karma, Chance or Justice?* San Diego, CA: Point Loma Pubolications, 1974.
[407] Blavatsky, H. P., *An Abridgement of The Secret Doctrine*, edited by Elizabeth Preston & Christmas Humphreys. Wheaton, Ill.: The Theosophical Publishing House, 1967.
[407] Ibid.

Kabbalah: Jewish Mysticism

Introduction

Rabbi David A. Cooper's *God is a Verb* introduced me to Kabbalah fairly recently. I had listened to an audio course on Judaism, and was left with the impression that Jewish religion had little relation to spirituality. But Cooper's book showed me a whole mystical arm of Jewish religion which was almost exclusively spiritual. Thrilled, I determined to include a chapter on Kabbalah in the metaphysical part of this book to share with readers this exciting information.

Kabbalah (QBLH in Hebrew "to receive") is very much a Meta in its own right and, spiritual to its core, has never been a part of traditional Judaism. Kabbalah is a collection of ancient manuscripts and over a hundred elaborations and commentaries. Manly Hall says:

> "Qabbalah" is the secret or hidden tradition, the unwritten law, and according to an early Rabbi, it was delivered to man in order that through the aid of its abstruse principles he might learn to understand the mystery of both the universe about him and the universe within him.[409]

"Kabbalah is not a system, as some suppose," says Cooper, "... it is an outlook, a way of perceiving the nature of reality. It teaches us about the mysteries of life, how the creation works, where we are going, and how we get there."[410]

Although leaning heavily on the Torah, it has elements of Vedic wisdom, Gnosticism, Hermeticism (teachings of Egyptian prophet-God Thoth, Hermes in Greek), and Neoplatonism. Some say Kabbalah preceded those traditions and was their source of wisdom. Others say it developed in the early Middle Ages, maybe the 7th century. In his book *Edgar Cayce and the Kabbalah*, John Van Auken says that "The Book of Creation" is usually ascribed to Abraham, and believed to be at least 2,500 years old. Parts of the *Zohar* (a major book of elaboration and explanation) are known to have been written in the 100s CE.[411]

Until the 20th-century the "mystical wisdom" of Kabbalah had been "cast as a secret knowledge to be kept from the mundane public and from the ruling authorities who opposed anything alien to the establishment," writes Van Auken.[412] Many rabbis still believe that Kabbalah is only for select initiates, and some teachers regard Kabbalah as "too ethereal, too otherworldly, not practical enough to be useful in normal people's lives...."[413] There's even a popular saying: "a man is not ready for Kabbalah until his home is built and his belly is full," making it clear that one needs to have completed one's worldly work before beginning to explore the unworldly. Cooper says: "many Jewish teachers today believe that contemplative practices are not acceptable in the Jewish world... [The focus is] on the study of Torah, meeting the requirements of Jewish law, and celebrating the holy days."[414]

Kabbalistic Teaching

Kabbalists, Cooper says, are "interested in the esoteric nature of creation." They ask questions like, "What is God?" "How did creation occur?" "What is ultimate truth?" They look for hidden meanings in the symbolic teachings of the Torah. He gives the example that, rather than seeing Adam and Eve as representing genders, "the mystics treat those and all other major biblical characters as divine principles." He tells us that "Adam and Eve represent the principle of duality ..." and adds:

> ... Each event that we experience has a deeper message if we have the eyes to see and the ears to hear. Everything has mystical meaning and significance. Life is enormously rich and purposeful once we are able to penetrate its mysteries. ... The secrets are hidden behind veils within veils, so that those who are ignorant of the power of truth cannot misuse these teachings.[415]

A fundamental teaching of Kabbalah is that "everything and every 'non-thing,' or quality, that ever was or will be in creation are all interconnected." Cooper says that the common idea of "As above, so below" shouldn't be taken literally. "Higher and lower realms of consciousness are not separated by space, rather, they are different dimensions that represent a proximity of relationship to ultimate truth. The higher the consciousness, the less there is an illusion of separateness."[416]

Mystical interpretation of Genesis led Kabbalists to their own account of the creation, differing greatly from the more literal traditional understanding. Although still beginning with God, the kabbalistic version covers the journey of the soul, integrating the outer life with its inner source. Van Auken says, "Behind the visible life, is a vast, invisible reality from which the visible came into being and in which the visible exists.... [T]he seen is actually an expression or emanation of the unseen."[417] As Van Auken describes it:

> Before anything existed, there was... absolutely nothing. Only infinite emptiness and stillness existed. This was the condition of the Creator before the Creation.... If we think of this pre-Creation condition as... an infinite, universal consciousness, that was perfect, still with no thoughts, then we can see how it could be empty and yet possess the power to conceive. The unseen gave birth to the seen. In this process, the initial expressions or emanations reflect the nature of the Unseen God.... the seen universe is within the unseen and was given life from the unseen, original essence that is pre-Creation God.[418]

He goes on to say, "Kabbalah helps us perceive the oneness of infinite life that runs through the maze of multiplicity of the Creation and this temporary incarnation.... God creates through emanations, or projections of its being..."[419] Everything is an emanation of what the *Zohar* calls *Ein Sof*—meaning "Infinite Eternal"—"the emanator of the emanations, God's energy and consciousness emanating throughout creation."[420]

The creation is nothing more than a thought in the "mind" of *Ein Sof*. Cooper says that the instant "the infinite source of giving... has the will to give, this will initiates a 'thought'... instantly creates a will to receive."[421]

Shattering the Vessel

Clearly Kabbalah describes the nature of the Life Force we call God as sharing, giving. But before anything existed, there was nothing, no one with whom to share. In one teaching story, it is said that God created one thing: a vessel to receive the energy of the Life Force. The energy of both is the same thing, just in different states: the state of giving, the state of receiving. Into this vessel, God poured its benevolence, filling it to overflowing with God's complete nature, fulfillment, and joy, including the attribute to share, so the vessel had that desire, too.

But as a singularity also, the vessel, too, had no one with whom to share. Finally, the vessel told God, the Life Force, that it would accept

Light only if given the opportunity to earn it by sharing what it received. So God stopped sharing Light (*tzimtzum*), and all became dark. Instantly, the vessel shattered (*sheviroh*), creating an infinite number of smaller vessels (*sephirot*)—the souls of the universe—along with time, space, and all matter. In later traditions, these fragments were described as sparks of light in the physical realm. Through this process the illusion of lack came into existence to give all beings the opportunity to share and thereby experience the Light of the Originating Life Force (*Ein Sof*).

Because human beings are souls incarnate in bodies, we are therefore aspects of this original vessel; we are of God's nature and so we enjoy the experiences of human life only when we share the Light through our loving actions—which leads to the repairing of the vessel (*tikkun olam*). When we are selfish or unkind, we are not sharing, not loving, and that nonsharing must be corrected for the "vessel" of our soul's life to be whole with God.

In the Hebrew tradition overall, all actions are kept in a great record book and must be corrected or repaired if we are to stay in God's good graces—which is one of the functions of *Yom Kippur*, also called a Day of Atonement. All our actions are recorded into our life record as *tikkun*, a word that means "work" or "action" (similar to the Hindu concept of *karma*, both individual action and accumulated consequences of those actions) and on *Yom Kippur*, God finalizes the previous year's record for all eternity—so every effort is taken to correct the past.

Reincarnation, Resurrection, and Awakening

There's some evidence that the ancient Hebrew tradition included the idea of reincarnation. Even in the New Testament, Jesus and the disciples, as Jews, talk of people being reborn into new bodies. And some Kabbalists (those who follow Luria instead of The *Zohar*) include reincarnation as a means of *tikkun olam*. This form of Kabbalah teaches that the destiny of every soul is to return to its source. But, those who haven't sufficiently cleansed their *tikkun* and thereby gained access to their source are given the grace to reincarnate in a new body and, if necessary, repeat their experiences until they are completely cleansed.

In this understanding we choose our family, friends, and all the people of importance in our life to help us in this correction process. We choose the locale and socio-economic conditions that provide us the most opportunities to experience and correct our past-life *tikkun*. It's rarely the happy, pleasant events and people that provide an opportunity for correction. Instead, those who push our buttons are providing mirrors to show us what in ourselves we need to change to effect the necessary correction. When we react to what someone does or says, that's what we need to look at and change in ourselves. So, for this correction process, we should not avoid such people and encounters, but go to them if we are to shorten the reincarnation process.

Van Auken writes of another type of reincarnation:

> It involves receiving a new... soul... while... still incarnate.... This is an explanation of how some people go through dynamic changes in their perception and character. They undergo a change of mind, a change of lifestyle, and thereby ascend to the next spiritual level. They are now hosting a "new" soul—or, more accurately, a higher part of their own soul. This is what occurs when a person is ready to advance in soul evolution.... This is not possession by a different soul, not a "walk-in"... It is more aligned with being "born anew."[422]

Cooper refers to this as "resurrection," the "heralding of a new era, a transformation into a consciousness previously unknown in which reality undergoes a profound change." He writes,

> Resurrection represents a new level of consciousness well outside the boundaries of [previous] human experience. In it, humans will not sense an ego barrier of separation, but will be united in the totality of the universe. In this realm, we do not live and die as disconnected entities, but expand and contract as an extension of God, each of us representing an eternal pulse-beat of the Divine.[423]

He explains that since resurrection is beyond time and space, the possibility of it is always with us. Regardless of where we are in life, or the afterlife, we can "move from ego consciousness to God consciousness" whenever we choose, for we are still and always part of the Divine. That reality assures our resurrection. In fact, Cooper says:

> Each moment we are sustained in life as we know it, it is as if we are being raised from the dead. Our entire life is a perpetual experience of resurrection, if only we were able to perceive it in this way.[424]

Satan and Evil—Duality Within the Singularity

According to Cooper, Kabbalists believe that "Satan" is not a force for evil, but is "the force of fragmentation," and as such is crucial to the forms of creation. Without Satan "everything would unite with God—everything would become one." The unity of God includes everything; Satan allows for the individualization of the multitude within the divine singularity.[425]

Cooper adds about evil:

> Kabbalah teaches that in reality, evil as we know it can never be eradicated, even if we wanted, for it fulfills a primary function in creation. Without something pulling us away from the Divine, we would be overwhelmed by God, we would lose our free will, and creation could not exist as it does now.[426]

Levels of Consciousness

Philosophies and religions, both ancient and modern, say there are various components to our whole being. Kabbalah identifies five distinguishable parts, as do many others. Van Auken reminds us these are temporary delineations of the Oneness for our benefit in under-standing, not fixed conditions.

According to Cooper, Kabbalah's five levels of consciousness or dimensions of awareness are:

1) NEFESH: The level of the soul most connected with physicality.
2) RUACH: associated with elementary consciousness and information that moves through the senses.... [We realize] our spirituality.... Love is more real to us and longer lasting.
3) NESHAMA: associated with higher awareness....
4) CHAYAH: Etheric... dwells mostly in other realms.... [W]e gain awareness of this level only when we enter altered states... it is the realm of wisdom... the source of all understanding.
5) YEHIDAH: [C]onnected with the source of awareness... the center point of the soul... It is not 'with' us, but we are never apart from it. This is where duality dissolves. It is far too subtle for human consciousness.[427]

Appendix A is a chart comparing these with other levels of human consciousness from various views.

Go Within; Awaken!

Each moment in everyday life our consciousness is raised a little higher, without our conscious awareness. With intention and enlightenment it is raised significantly higher, especially when we consciously commune with the Divine, and are awakening.

Direct communion with God is central to Kabbalist teaching, as it is in Gnosticism. We gain wisdom, or inner *knowing*, when we expand "our consciousness into the infinite mind of God," says Van Auken.[428] As we each empty our self of our own desires and interests, we make room for God to flow in and that is our destiny, to return to our source fully consciously awake. [429]

> The *Zohar* cries out to humankind, saying, 'You beings on earth who are in deep slumber, awaken!' It pleads with us, 'Stop sleeping! Wake up! What are you waiting for?'[430]

Comments & Questions: Kabbalah

What Cooper calls "resurrection" and Van Auken refers to as a form of "reincarnation," seems to be what I call a shift in consciousness and what others might call "ascension." And, it is occurring right now within the multitude, an essential step in the process of awakening.

The Jewish religion seems to me a Mystery tradition, with Judaism essentially the non-spiritual outer religion for the general populace and Kabbalah the mystical, inner spirituality for those who want to go deeper. The TaNaKH contains mythic stories for traditional outer teaching, while the *Zohar* contains the mystical teaching of Kabbalah, a deeper understanding of the symbolism of the TaNaKH.

Similarities abound among Kabbalah, the ancient wisdom traditions, and the many spiritual metaphysical philosophies, of which we've seen only a sampling. It's all perennial wisdom. We merely need to wake up to it.

---

[409] Hall, Manly P., *The Secret Teachings of the Ages*. New York: Penguin Group, Jeremy P. Tarcher, 2003.
[410] Cooper, David A., *God is a Verb*. New York, NY: Riverhead Books, 1997.

[411] Van Auken, John, *Edgar Cayce and the Kabbalah*. Virginia Beach, VA: A.R.E. Press, 2010.
[412] Ibid.
[413] Ibid.
[414] Cooper, David A., *God is a Verb*. New York, NY: Riverhead Books, 1997.
[415] Ibid.
[416] Ibid.
[417] Van Auken, John, *Edgar Cayce and the Kabbalah*. Virginia Beach, VA: A.R.E. Press, 2010.
[418] ibid.
[419] Ibid.
[420] Ibid.
[421] Cooper, David A., *God is a Verb*. New York, NY: Riverhead Books, 1997.
[422] Van Auken, John, *Edgar Cayce and the Kabbalah*. Virginia Beach, VA: A.R.E. Press, 2010.
[423] Cooper, David A., *God is a Verb*. New York, NY: Riverhead Books, 1997.
[424] Ibid.
[425] Ibid.
[426] Ibid.
[427] Ibid.
[428] Van Auken, John, *Edgar Cayce and the Kabbalah*. Virginia Beach, VA: A.R.E. Press, 2010.
[429] ibid.
[430] Cooper, David A., *God is a Verb*. New York, NY: Riverhead Books, 1997.

The Starseed Perspective: An Extraterrestrial Report

Introduction

In 1982, Ken Carey issued *The Starseed Transmissions—an Extraterrestrial Report*, expressing yet another Meta perspective, again with similarities to the others. Carey experienced what felt to him like beings from another planet, "Extraterrestrials" (ETs), speaking to him and encouraging him to share their message. It's by no means the only such offering, but since it has an interesting twist, let's consider it.

The ET Message

The extraterrestrials reporting to Carey say that, as the One, we had been roaming around inside of Creation for billions of years, expanding and contracting, drifting in and out" of galaxies. We decided to form "a physical body" in which to "travel around, perceiving matter from the same perspective with which matter perceives herself... Until then, there was no biological life in the universe." We searched out a planet to suit what we wanted to do; then "focused... attention and... vibrational body in an entirely new...loving way..."[431]

They say:

> As the outermost edges of your vibrational field touched the waters of the planet, particles of previously inert matter began gently vibrating to the rhythms of your being.... There, on the Precambrian ocean floors, they began combining to form the first cells, the first minute containers for your consciousness.... As you drew ever nearer to the planet, the life forms that were taking shape began to contain more and more of your awareness....[432]

They tell us that throughout the normal course of our existence, we occasionally take on "missions," during which we experience an identity and linear time, but are also on some level still aware of our identity with the Creator, the Oneness. And through Carey's writing they provide another perspective on human development:

> Before incarnation you were single. You drew identity from the totality of the relationship between Creator and Creation. You were the Christ, fully conscious and alert, aware of yourself, unified, integrated. You realized that to accomplish incarnation you would have to allow at least a portion of your identity to come to rest among the creatures you were bringing to life. Each of these would possess a type of hologramatic consciousness that rightly thought of itself as both part and whole simultaneously.[433]

Carey's sources say that we humans constantly change states of being, that we "oscillate... in and out of focus, in and out of definition... into a finite expression of God's infinite potential, and then back into unity once more."[434]

For some reason we lost "confidence in the absolute perfection of the universal design" and, succumbing to fear, were tempted into what is called "Original Sin." The resulting "fall" into the illusion of separation was, they tell us, through a "simple lack of faith." We shifted our awareness from God-centered toward more and more self-centered, and identified more with our form than with God. This shift spiraled us down into ever "denser levels of energy-bondage," physical expression, and ego structure.

> Before the Fall, you had the ability to shift the center of your awareness from deity to identity, from form to Meta-form at will... functioning in two realities at once.... In the fallen state of consciousness, you find yourself trapped with your awareness on one side only, while the actual substance of your being continues in that other reality, but you are asleep.[435]

We are, they tell us, now "sleeping under... a spell, an illusion..." from which we must and will awaken. To help us do so, we decided to have some part of our self remain wholly spiritual to observe this process and regulate it from without. So, we "created beings to represent" our original unified state of awareness: the reporting ETs. We assigned them the task of communing with us as humans, preparing us for our awakening back to "unified consciousness."[436]

According to Carey these ETs have been working with us for nearly two thousand years. They say their mission is to assist us in shifting from our current condition to our true Self, helping those of us who are ready to remember all we once knew and to awaken to full awareness. That is now occurring for increasing numbers of us.

They say that "outside of time and space" we are the "All that is." But, when our consciousness nears the physical universe, we "...become the Son, the Christ. In essence... the relationship between Spirit and Matter... the bridge, the means through which the Creator relates to Creation." They insist that although we now see ourselves as "separate and fragmented," we are actually "a single unified being, sharing the full consciousness of the Creator." We are "the Christ, as the only begotten consciousness of the... Father Creator," who is relying on us for his "focus."[437] (This is also an essential part of the message of *A Course in Miracles.*)

What Blavatsky, the Buddhists, and the Hindus refer to as Brahma breathing in and breathing out is the process through which God creates a universe and then eventually dissolves it.[438] The ETs speaking through Carey say it's planned that the manifest universe will soon "stop expanding and begin to contract," and when that happens, there will be an instant of "absolute rest" when "the Creator will slip inside Creation" as the "Planetary Being." They add that this event is "the much misunderstood Second Coming of Christianity... 'the return of the gods,'" and it is fast approaching (around the time when the Mayan calendar completes its cycle.) The period of written human history has been a "gestation" period, setting the stage for our emergence as that Planetary Being.[439]

What we perceive as the process of evolution, which we see as increasingly complex life-forms evolving toward ever higher levels of consciousness, they say, is not that at all. Instead, our "vibrational body" is influencing the "matter of Earth" as we "draw nearer."[440]

Writing in the early 1980s, Carey said that the ETs told him that in "thirty years" the world will be polarized into essentially two levels of consciousness: one of "Love and Life," and the other of "fear and death." But there will be a sufficient number... of individual awakenings to the reality of Christ consciousness... to consciously undertake the final cycle of Creation." Then we "will recognize the Unified Collective Consciousness of all Humankind as... [our] own true identity."[441]

They say they aren't bringing what they call the "Presence of God" to us—they tell us that is already everywhere—but they are removing "conceptual and emotional blocks that prevent the full experience of that

Presence." They say they do this work with those of us "who are vibrationally sympathetic." Then, once we've made our choice of love over fear and are committed to following it, we suddenly just know who we really are.[442]

When we're ready, they say, we'll know beyond any doubt. The ETs Carey writes for explain that a "fundamental identity shift" takes place: Each of us will begin to see him or herself not as our body, our thoughts, what we feel, or our role in our community, but to realize we "are the Spirit of Life itself... delighting in the glorious opportunity of incarnation, exploring the realms of matter..."[443]

Then, they add, we will get direction through intuition, which they call our "direct link with the totality of... being." They say to trust our intuition, which arises "involuntarily from the depths of... your being like the breath... you breathe, [and] inform... yourself instantly of all... you need to know in any situation."[444]

The coming age, they say, will be one of "restored ecological balance, international cooperation, and universal harmony." All humans will be fulfilled, consciously creating whatever we want in our world. We will recognize how creative our thoughts are as "the energizing force of the material plane." They say that through us, "God is revealed in material form."[445]

And how will all this happen? The reporting ET commands: "Wake up! Let me express through you. Put on my awareness. We are one. We have always been one.... There is only one of us here in consciousness."[446]

Comments & Questions: The Starseed Transmissions

Is Carey's ETs perhaps his "still small voice within"? Is it what others (myself included) call our "higher Self" or soul, a part of our own consciousness, with whom we commune and gain wisdom through intuition? Are we each awakening to our Self?

Today's Metaphysics

The "fall" story certainly has been influential to not only Western religions but in the thinking of many Metas, including Cayce and Carey, and also to Pagans and Gnostics.

Still, I have to ask how an omnipotent God (however we perceive it) could create beings who could err, or through "desire and self-aggrandizement," or "lack of faith," choose separation, especially as spirit beings, as fully conscious expressions of God. If we are all one consciousness, how could we have become separated from God and each other, unless it was part of our plan, and to believe we erred? Was it all only seemingly error, intentionally done perhaps to cause us to meet ourselves, as parts of our human experience—as Cayce explains it?

But then, Carey's ETs say they are working with each of us within the context of our current belief system, so, once again, our beliefs determine our reality, even in how we perceive what we get through intuition.

It's clear to me that no matter what their source, whether ancient or modern or even extraterrestrial, and no matter how they're stated, all spiritual teachings express essentially the same perennial wisdom. They may use different terms, but the sense is the same.

It's obvious that outside of fundamentalist religion and materialist science, the message is that we all, everything, are first and foremost spiritual. We are One, consciousness. We humans are evolving back to the full consciousness of our original spirituality and our Oneness, awakening, remembering. And, we can remember it all by going within—in gnosis, theosophy, communion, mysticism—to *know* ourselves as God.

Our higher Selves—ETs or whoever—are helping us in every way possible to become enlightened, to know ourselves and our Oneness with all. We are waking up.

There are many other teachings today that express essentially this same perennial wisdom, but I must leave those for you to pursue on your own. Those interested might examine the Islamic Sufi beliefs, those of Native Americans, aborigines in Africa and Australia, and mysticism wherever found. But, above all, enjoy your journey.

---

[431] Carey, Ken, *The Starseed Transmissions, an Extraterrestrial Report*. Kansas City, MO: Uni*Sun 1982; HarperOne edition, 1991.
[432] Ibid.
[433] Ibid.

[434] Ibid.
[435] Ibid.
[436] Ibid.
[437] Ibid.
[438] Edge, Henry Travers, *Evolution, Who and What is Man*. San Diego, CA: Point Loma Publications, 1979
[439] Carey, Ken, *The Starseed Transmissions, an Extraterrestrial Report*. Kansas City, MO: Uni*Sun 1982; HarperOne edition, 1991
[440] Ibid.
[441] Ibid.
[442] Ibid.
[443] Ibid.
[444] Ibid.
[445] Ibid.
[446] Ibid.

PART FIVE: WHAT IT'S ALL ABOUT—MY PERSONAL PHILOSOPHY OF LIFE

All the world's a stage, and all the men and women merely players: They have their exits and their entrances; and one man in his time plays many parts.
~ William Shakespeare

My Personal Belief System

Introduction

Many of us can't help wondering if there isn't a lot more to our existence than what we experience. But, can we ever know?

Yes, we can *know*, but we will probably never be able to prove the spiritual with materialist methods.

Those of us who are firmly committed to spirituality have no doubts whatever as to the authenticity of our beliefs for us individually. Most of us have had spiritual experiences that confirm our truths, and many of us commune regularly with what's been called "the other side," or "the voice within."

I offer this wholly spiritual perspective to put into words what many people seem to believe but maybe haven't congealed into a whole philosophy, and to show how those beliefs fit into the overall scheme of things. I offer a possibly different way of viewing yourself, the world we live in, and what might be called God. I offer my belief system to further our shift toward the spiritual.

My belief system is philosophic, not scientific or religious, so I don't support it with dogma or empirical evidence. I can say, however, that it conforms with the perennial wisdom of many traditions and the ideas presented by contemporary spiritual teachers.

Remember that a great deal of our thought today began in the musings of classical Greek philosophers, so any philosophical musings, possibly backed by intuitive wisdom, may someday prove to be more true than today's materialist scientists' reading of empirical evidence.

What follows is my own view of God, our personal spirituality, and our human experience: my answer to Edgar Mitchell's question. I came to know these "truths" through communion with my inner soul-Self over the course of a few years, and then refined them over many more years. They are still evolving, and always will. I express them as positive statements of fact, because that's how they are for me.

I see two journeys on Earth: one for us as humans and one for us spirit beings. The human one is circular. Although in a sense we are growing spiritually, this Earthly experience isn't real and is only for one lifetime at a time, so I prefer to think of it as circular. The spiritual one is a spiral or helix, since, due to our Earthly experience, we rise to higher levels of consciousness than from where we started.

This philosophy satisfies my needs perfectly, but I don't intend for it to do the same for others. If it works for you, fine; but that's a personal choice.

I offer it to provide a completely spiritual view of our existence to contrast with the prevailing materialist views, and to give a more cohesive and comprehensive spiritual metaphysical picture than I could form from either the ancient philosophers or the other Metas. I seek to give the reader food for thought in forming or expanding their personal belief system. I intend to encourage our culture to be more aware of our spirituality, our Oneness, and to allow that awareness to help us all see the world and everyone and everything in it differently than our current worldview allows.

I ask only that you read it with an open mind and allow your heart, not your head, to assess it and consider what to accept and what to deny.

Early in my search for truth, I met people who were further along in their own quests for enlightenment and willing to share their wisdom with me. They taught me the single most important step in my pursuit of enlightenment: communion, or gnosis, with my all-knowing inner voice. Whether one experiences the voice as that of God, a spirit guide, Jesus, an archangel, one's own soul, an ET, or one's imagination isn't important. Consciously communing with it and receiving its wisdom is, I believe, the most important and most thrilling thing anyone can do in this life.

In communion with what I came to see as my own higher-vibrating soul-Self—that part of me that has never manifested into the physical—I received infusions of *knowing* into my consciousness as my own truths. Those who have had the experience will know what I mean when I say my consciousness was flooded with insight, concepts, and answers, often simultaneously with the questions. I feel I was given questions when I was ready for answers. I gained answers to all my questions, both lofty and mundane, through this intuition, from which I formulated an overall philosophy.

My truths explain to my satisfaction, not only the suffering that plagues humankind, but evil in its many forms, and in wholly positive terms.

Except for the primary beliefs of most Metas, most other views of our origin and beginnings are not my "truths." Although I listed the basic Meta beliefs earlier, I'll restate them here to clarify what follows; they are:

(1) We are first and foremost eternal spirit beings;
(2) Everything, seen and unseen, is One, entangled, without separation;
(3) The physical universe and all life are emanations of and within the One, God; we are all God.

Like many Metas I also believe that consciousness is the "ground of being," that One, God; and I more than most say that human life on Earth is circular. And, like Gnostics and teachers of the Inner Mysteries as well as many Metas, I make my instruction going within to find God, to allow inner intuitive wisdom to enlighten us.

What Is God?

The most important and most thrilling breakthrough I made in my search for enlightenment had to do with God. I was pondering a phrase in a lesson I'd just been given by a spiritual teacher friend. Strolling along a creek with another spiritual teacher, I wondered aloud: "What does it mean to be One *with* God?"

Immediately, the answer came to me, and with total clarity. I was stunned. I looked at my friend; I looked at the colorful trout swimming at our feet; I looked up at the mountain towering above us; I looked around at the deep green myrtle trees, and I saw God!

In awe, I almost shouted, "God is everything!!! Everything is God!!!"

I knew this with unquestionable certainty. I also knew as an experience of truth that God is the energy that is, surrounds, and permeates everything in existence and maintains the life movement of everything in the universe. God is the principles of love and creativity in and behind everything that goes on. God is pure intelligence. God is the radiant light energy in existence throughout the universe. Our Real existence is that light.

I could feel, in every aspect of my being:

Our Old Beliefs Don't Work Anymore

- There is only an all-encompassing One, without bounds.
- Everything, whether known or unknown, physical or immaterial, is part of the One, which, because of my "aha," I think of as "God."
- Everything is interconnected; nothing can happen in one part of the Oneness without it affecting all parts of the One in some way.
- Nothing can break away and be separated; separation is impossible; there is only God. There's nowhere else to go, nothing else to be.

We are each individualized expressions of God. Everything physical is a manifestation of God, an emanation of God. You are God. I am God. Our mothers, fathers, friends, neighbors, and enemies are God incarnate. Trees, plants, fishes, animals, and rocks, too, are all faces of God. Our feelings, thoughts, words, and actions express God.

People wonder how we can truly all be One when we seem so clearly individual. It's true, we are individual in this physical life in order to experience life in our own unique way, different from how anyone else might experience it. But this life isn't real; it isn't our home, our true Reality (my word for our unmanifest spirit life).

In that Reality, in Real Life, we are individualized expressions of the One, but not as completely individual as everything seems in Earth life in which we identify our individual bodies and egos as unique and separate from everyone else. Everything we see only seems separate because we have wanted it to. We, individually and collectively, created Earth and our life here to make it all appear separate, to provide definition and focus.

If we were to put ourselves in the place of one of our bodily cells we would undoubtedly think of ourselves and all other cells around us as separate. We would have no way of knowing about the larger body of which we all are integral parts. Our physical body is a microcosm of the cosmos. The individual organs are like our sun, moon, and planets. The cells, each with its own consciousness, its own pure intelligence, work together and separately, just as all beings do in Earth life. Each cell is its own universe, and each particle is a universe. The physical body is finely tuned to support its life just as our Earth is finely tuned to support its life, and the universe likewise, all quantum holograms.

In fact, the term "cosmos" is insufficient, so I have borrowed from Helena Blavatsky and Ken Wilber the term "Kosmos" to indicate the entirety of the seen and unseen, much more than the materialist word "cosmos" suggests.

Some people are agnostic. That is, they are "without knowledge" on the subject of God, due to our inability to define God in finite words. Eastern traditions don't like to speculate on the nature of God, saying it can't be done. The personal God of Jews in Hebrew is a set of un-pronounceable consonants called the tetragrammaton: "YHWH." I find it meaningful that both "YHWH" and the Babylonian word for God, "Ah-Yah," are usually translated simply as "I Am."

While biblical Christians see God as a trinity of persons, to me, God is not a Being and certainly not a person. Nor is God empty—as can be mistakenly interpreted from Eastern traditions' use of the word "emptiness" to define the state of union with God—except in the sense of being unmanifest. God is fullness, as in Gnosticism, the All of everything: manifest and unmanifest, seen and unseen, material and spiritual.

God is all possibilities. God is an unbound sea of love. When we try to describe God, we use the finite terms available to us in our language as human beings, clearly associated with what is physical and limited. But it's not that we can't adequately describe God; it's that *everything defines and describes God.* God is everything.

What Are We?

It's important for us to know that since everything is God, we each are God in manifestation. We are spirit beings, emanations of God, expressing God in materiality. We always have existed and always will; each of us as a soul, our real, true Self. But only a part of us enters Earthly human life to experience the physical. That part dons a physical persona, ego, intellect, and body through which to experience. When we as humans die, the little-self aspect of our soul awakens to its true Self, its larger part. That part is eternal, remains always at a high vibrating level, is never hurt, limited, victimized, or traumatized, yet evolves through our experiences, expanding its awareness to know itself and Reality through the contrasts of physical existence. To summarize:

We are eternal spirit beings co-creating physical experience and expanding our awareness, evolving.

There is no death; only life, without beginning or end, everywhere, either unmanifest or slowed in energy vibration to create material form. What we think of as death is merely a change in environment: the material decomposes to its elements and the spiritual returns to its unmanifest dimension of being.

Although I know that all of me is God, still, having been thoroughly indoctrinated in the world, I often think of the part of me that is my soul-Self as my personal God, my companion and advisor, my intimate conscious connection to the One. I am an extension of that God.

My soul-Self is the I-Am of me, my primary spirit guide. I receive my innermost thoughts and feelings, and wisdom and truth through intuition, from my God within. While I identify my soul almost as an entity unto itself, it's not separate from either me or the whole of the Kosmos. There is no real separation, merely individualized expressions of it all.

Did We Err?

Why we came into Earth life in the first place is very important to our understanding of life on Earth. It defines us and our experiences, and influences our take on suffering and evil and on salvation. The why determines our individual view of all life, our belief system, and our worldview.

A problem I have with many other Meta belief systems is that they either don't address why or, if they do, they say we erred in some way, or need to perfect ourselves. It seems to me that if God, no matter how defined, created the universe, then there had to have been a reason, a purpose to be served in doing so. It also had to have been based in love.

Believing we came into this Earthly life because of some error we made in the remote past, whether as humans or spirit beings, is very different in its influence on our understanding of life and our worldviews from believing we came into life voluntarily for loving purposes. I *know* the latter is true and that there are no accidents.

Love and Perfection

Love is the only sustaining force, the only true purpose, and the only grand rule in the universe, giving purpose to everything that exists and occurs. No matter how minuscule, everything has its place in the loving design of things, and is perfect, just as it is.

There is no order for some and lack of order for others. Everything is in harmony, One with all, in a coordinated pattern and flow of life. G. W. Leibniz determined this to be the case for the stars and planets back in the 1600s, but of course, I'm thinking spiritually here. Love enables all life in this Kosmos to do and be anything we want.

At the same time Love is controlling in that we are unable to do or be anything that is not based in love. In a sense this path is narrow, but we don't feel constrained by it because we cannot by our nature be anything but expressions of love. Therefore, nothing can occur that is not founded in love. No matter its appearance, everything happens just as it does because to do so serves a loving purpose.

As such it is perfect, and there is no evil except in our judgmental human minds; and that, too, is purposeful, to help us discover and define the perfection of all.

Friends have questioned my use of the word "perfect" so I'll explain. I use it the same as Webster's definition, but from a spiritual, rather than material, standpoint.

I believe that everyone has all the requisite qualities of our kind, that all are complete and without defect—from a spiritual perspective. From that view we are never incomplete, never flawed. God expresses through us, so we can't be less than perfect. Who we are, where we are, and what we do in every moment, is all correct for us and is all we can do and be in that moment.

It will all change. Then it too will be perfect as we move into future moments.

We have evolved to where we each are in complete perfection, regardless of appearances to our human perceptions. We may not seem perfect to those human perceptions, because we equate "perfect" with our concept of "ideal" and know we're not there—that's something to strive toward and likely never achieve.

"Ideal" is determined by human judgment, and can mean something different for each judging human. We observe the actions of others, and if we judge them to be wrong, mean, harmful, sinful, we see no perfection there. We see others' actions as bad because we are unaware of their true purposes and because we've been told it's natural for us to judge.

But no judgment is involved in perfection. It isn't comparative, isn't limited. It, like God, just *is*.

Without the contrast of negative expressions, experiences, and conditions, we could not know or enjoy the positives, and our life here on Earth would be of little value. The contrast, the continuum, is love.

To What Extent Are We Divine?

Everything and everyone we think of as bad or harmful is also God. They are parts of the continuum of the seeming duality of good and evil that makes experiences of ourselves possible. They are just as perfect as everything we think of as good and beautiful.

How we view ourselves in relation to God is very important.

Many people qualify the Oneness, believing it's made up of hierarchical levels. They claim that some levels of beings have more of the stuff of divinity than others: Angels are more divine than we; we are more divine than animals, animals have greater divinity than rocks.

I say that's impossible. If God is truly omnipresent and everything is God, then everything and every being is equally God. There cannot be any greater or lesser in content or in perfection. Again, I'm thinking spiritually not physically; although, since everything is God, everything physical is also God manifesting physically.

Granted, we don't all know this. Our experience of our divinity is determined by our purposes in this Earthly life and our level of consciousness. Still, before any being (whether human, animal, plant, or rock) came into this physical existence, it was consciously wholly spiritual and wholly God. Its physical expression and enjoyment of physicality was made possible by slowing its vibrations to create form and, in the case of humans, by hiding our Reality. But still, no being has lost its spiritual beingness, its divinity.

And in all cases, when a being—let's say a tree—"dies," its inner real self returns to its spirit essence as Godliness. In the case of humans, we each return to wholeness as our higher soul-Self, in and as the One.

Only we humans have hidden our true Oneness, intelligence, and spirituality from ourselves while in physical form. All other beings remain spiritually conscious. It is we humans who have been asleep, and who are now shifting our awareness into more enlightened consciousness, coming full circle to awakened spirituality. Awakening is our ultimate goal of realizing our wholeness with our soul-Self and being aware of *knowing* we are God.

In *knowing* and being God, we experience ourselves as the One—what we've been all along, only now we're consciously aware of it.

The Why of It All

What is my answer to the big why question? We'll see it in detail next, but briefly it is that as the One we wanted to know both our self and our many aspects, and through them to experience dualistic contrasts that help us define Reality.

As I see it, so long as we were in that Oneness state, the whole had no way of seeing itself, no contrast to define it. We also were wholly spiritual, so had no way of understanding the nature of our spirituality and the general Reality of our being.

To know our self and our spiritual Reality, we, the unmanifest One, decided to experience our Self as the manifest many. We had to shatter our Self, the quantum hologram, into aspects, the multitude—to experience the possibilities inherent in dualistic contrasts—in order to be aware of and define the relationship between ourselves and Reality.

Much of what follows as my philosophy was first expressed in my 1995 book, *AWAKENING, A Journey of Enlightenment*.[447] It has been refined, added to, and clarified in the years since I wrote that book.

---

[447] *Awakening* has since been republished by Portal Center Press.

A Story of Our "Creation" and Evolution

Introduction

Since a new "creation" story hasn't been presented in a very long time, I thought I would share mine to maybe put all this spirituality I've been talking about into perspective for both the novice and the advanced Meta, and maybe even the new scientist. The following story was constructed from insights I gleaned over several years from my soul-Self. Those truths formed a complete picture of our origin, beginnings, our evolution, and our destiny.

Here is that story, as told by my higher soul-Self.

The Story

The unmanifest (unseen Reality, the Kosmos,) is an unbound sea of consciousness, which is pure intelligence, energy, and light; it is the Mind of God. Love, alone, directs this sea. We are love. We, what one might call spirit entities, are the multitude, individualized expressions of that consciousness. We are like droplets that make up an ocean; the droplets are the ocean, which doesn't exist without them. Our sea of consciousness is the hologram of which quantum physicists speak, and each of us, each droplet, is also the whole. There are an infinite number of us, without beginning or end, yet we are not separate; we are the One, or All-Of-Everything. We are quantum physics' "possibilities," Plato's "Intelligences," or "Forms of the intelligible world." As intelligence we imagine. By imagining we create, and we create what we want to experience. And since love is what we are, whatever we create has love behind it. Here is our story.

Initially, before there was time and material form, we couldn't fully know what we were because we were One consciousness, a singularity, with nothing to help us define individuality. Since we couldn't realize our individuality, we also couldn't appreciate our Oneness. With nothing physical, there was no contrast to define what we were, our spirituality.

In playful experimentation, we found we could create ethereal forms by thinking them into existence then slightly slowing their vibrations. By minimally slowing our own vibrations, we could see and interact with those forms on their level. When we returned to our normal vibrations, we got a suggestion of the beauty of Reality. That minimal slowing had made our view of Reality slightly hazy, giving us a hint of contrast that enabled us to see Reality differently upon return. We were thrilled.

Wanting to know ourselves and our Oneness, we decided to create an existence through which we could experience something different in contrast to what we were. Experience would define—like in human art, where negative space is used to define form—and help us know and appreciate us and our life as spirit beings, what we'll call "Reality."

Without contrast and comparison, no matter how knowing we are, we can't fully know ourselves. Also, no matter how intelligent we are and how much we learn about ourselves from what we imaginatively create, we can't truly know without experiencing. We wanted to experience ourselves to the fullest, and realized we would have to focus on our multiplicity, defining it and making it seem real, to know our singularity, our Oneness. We didn't change our self, or even ourselves; we chose to look at us differently, to see the many in the One. We wanted the many to make possible observation of the One.

We emanated from our consciousness, each part of the universe a spiritual replica, and a living, intelligent entity that would participate fully in whatever was to go on there. We gradually slowed the vibrations of what we had created to give it substance, initially in etheric form, then ever more solid. It would never be truly solid, but in constant vibration. Nor was it separate from us; as an emanation of us, it was us in manifestation.

Contrary to appearances, there is neither solid matter nor space in the universe. All of it is energy, love-filled consciousness, an un-bound sea of spiritual intelligence: us. It has the appearance of either matter or emptiness because of vibrations: either slowed to manifest form or so rapid as to not be seen from slower vibration levels. Our sea surrounds, permeates, and interlinks everything material, which is still and always consciousness, always spirit. Since the universe was manifested of our collective consciousness, we didn't really "create" it. Everything exists in us, in our imagination, as possibilities.

We imagined what we wanted to experience, and thought it all into being as emanations of us. We considered how best to use and enjoy our universe, and evolved a plan to create theaters and enact plays.

We then designed this universe as it is, to support the kinds of life we wanted to experience on Earth and on other globes, materializing a universe in which everything is interdependent, nothing isolated, nothing independent, nothing separate. We watched our universe form. Then we chose certain globes to develop in great detail, each to differently serve specific needs in our quest for self-knowledge and expanded awareness. We designed those globes to be theaters through which we could enact plays to help us experience both what we were and what we were not.

Gradually, we slowed the vibrations of the universe even more until it became the combination of seemingly dense matter and gases and energy appearing as space. This creative thinking and vibrational slowing, like observation in quantum physics, actuated what scientists call the "big bang." We spirit entities, or souls of the Kosmos, were the First Cause. We are the observers. We are the infinite possibilities, the blueprints.

Those of us who chose Earth did so because in the planning process we shared an interest in the nature of the plays we wanted to enact. We desired a certain sort of function and beauty for our theater, so we set it in revolving motion, put it in a specific orbit around a particular sun, and gave it its own orbiting moon. We gave it gravity, a certain mineral composition—to protect it from hurtling debris of universal matter—oxygen atmosphere, and an ozone layer to protect it from too much of its sun's radiation. We gave it both land masses and oceans. We added flora to provide oxygen and food, and to help Earth create fresh water to gather into ponds, lakes, and rivers to flow back to the seas. With each step we were thrilled by its beauty.

To set our stage, we created—thought into being, usually in clusters—invertebrate marine life, then fish, reptiles, insects, animals, and birds, and we added trees and nut-, berry-, vegetable-and-flower-producing plants to those already thriving in Earth's glory. These were emanations of our consciousness, formed from our possibilities.

We experimented with various forms for our self-expression, each, an emanation of our consciousness, fully aware, intelligent, and loving. We minimally slowed our vibrations, so we were still consciously connected. We didn't have material form; we were individualized energy, or light beings, with astral bodies that bore some resemblance to various forms of species. Some of us chose what would become human forms, but were initially androgynous, or asexual, more complete than the combination of male and female genders.

Those of us who chose human form through which to experience physicality coexisted with our more material emanations—rocks, minerals, vegetation, and animals—for what would be in much slower vibrations many hundred million human years. This early stage of existence on Earth was what ancient wisdom accounts called the "Motherland," later called Lemuria. It was a time on Earth, lasting until about 30 mya in human time. We didn't have language, didn't need it; our communication was far deeper through thought and feelings. We had music, the beauty, lilt, and harmony of which today's humans would enjoy beyond description. Music is in our consciousness and part of our Reality, so we had no need or desire for limited physical instruments.

Because there was no disease or decay, there was also no death and no birth. We interacted with all life on Earth and Earth itself, in complete cooperation, harmony, and love, designing our theater.

We finally realized that, although we were enjoying our experiences and were beginning to know ourselves, we would benefit from conditions still more foreign to us. We decided the contrast of more solidly physical existence would help us better define us and our Reality as spirit. How could we appreciate what we were and what we had unless we knew an entirely different life? To create such conditions, we would have to slow our vibrations considerably more and create physical forms to inhabit and through which we could enact Earthly plays. In slowing our vibrations, though, we might weaken our contact with higher vibrating Reality. In one sense this would be good, because then we could truly experience a foreign existence, but we didn't want to be cut off from Reality.

We solved this dilemma by creating a new type of emanations of ourselves: extensions of us, to be actors who would enact plays which we would experience through them. These actors, or inner human beings, were us in every spiritual way: intelligent, loving, kind, and creative. They, like our other expressions, were beautiful inside and out, created in our spiritual "image and likeness," replicas of us, not merely copies of us but small parts of us, and not really created but extended into etheric form—rather like a cell splitting itself into two cells, with one considerably smaller than the other and still connected.

This period covered the later years of Lemuria and the early years of what is called Atlantis, which was a time period as well as a place.

Those of us who created such extensions are called their souls; other spirit entities are souls manifesting as animals, other land and sea creatures, plants and trees. Other souls are Earth and its makeup and elements. Still others are often called angels and spirit guides.

We experimented with different levels of vibration and their resulting denseness, learning that the greater the contrast created by slowed vibrations and the longer our extensions were in that slower state, the more gloriously beautiful Reality appeared to us. Our actors began to focus their attention on plants and animals as separate things in their illusion world; and we found that by applying that focus to Reality we could see and appreciate so much more of it. From this experience, we realized the benefit of using truly dense, material form and conditions to provide extreme contrasts to Reality. As we gained awareness, we learned how to create a greater variety of experience.

We were becoming more aware of ourselves and Reality.

We decided our human extensions should forget the Reality of spirit life, set aside their spiritual senses, and be restricted to the use of limited physical senses. They would need a new thinking process, a self-awareness, with which to perceive the events and people in their life in relationships, one that would be reactionary, yet logical and analytical. It would be good for them to judge and make choices, so a system of duality (positive and negative) would be useful. Emotions with which to spontaneously react to each other, events, and conditions would create interactive experiences.

We realized it would be especially effective to have our human extensions go through a process of de-evolution, to slowly lose their spiritual senses and capabilities before gaining and beginning to use their new attributes. We split up into groups with common interests so that, through a gradual decreasing of our extensions' vibrations, they would devolve at slightly different rates, letting awareness of spiritual Reality slowly and completely slip away. Some would become less and less creative, eventually living almost by instinct rather than by pure intelligence. Once fully devolved, our human extensions would begin to slowly evolve through growth experiences, developing their new physical capabilities. No longer able to communicate telepathically, they would develop language. Their growth would come through relationships and interactive experiences.

As the first wave of humans began to devolve, we realized we would derive great benefits from humans entering physical life with only part of their energy, making them either female or male. Leaving some energy home would create a void in each human self that would need filling. This would cause them to yearn for their missing energy, prodding them to seek fulfillment, and adding to their plot possibilities. We added sexual attraction and procreation, then growth and maturing of human bodies and development of personalities, followed by an aging process, which would lead to death of the body and its persona, the role played by the actor. We first tested these processes in plants and animals then, finally, we put them into effect in our human extensions.

Meanwhile, many of our emanations (deciduous plants and trees and hibernating animals) were enjoying cycles of active life and physical dormancy, when their inner self returned to Reality. To effect human evolution, we created reincarnation, or cycles of Earth and non-Earth life (Reality). With each generation, human vibrations slowed a little more, until the first group's descent into relatively dense matter was complete. Each step cut off human actors from higher vibration levels. They were now relatively primitive, seeming little different from their animal cousins, only less aware and naturally intelligent.

By truly slowing vibrations, we created time as it is now used, and we established duality in which everything would have an opposite.

This would enable suffering and help define everything, since without one we wouldn't know the other, so wouldn't appreciate the one we had. One of our globes has multiple suns that always shine all over its theater, so beings living there know nothing of darkness or cold, and have no way of appreciating natural light and warmth. They never see the glory of a starlit sky or the beauty of a sunrise or sunset. They are enjoying other things. We also limited human senses to the five now familiar ones. Sounds, gestures, words, and drawings would become the primary and greatly limited forms of communication. We endowed each devolved human with intellect and assigned it the functions of perception, reasoning, judgment, and choice.

Not all of our human extensions went through the devolution process, and not all who devolved did so at the same time. We wanted some to remain more aware and naturally intelligent longer, to oversee and aid the fully devolved "children" as they began their return evolution. Those higher vibrating beings helped the "children" learn to fend for themselves and develop written language. To prepare the children for their eventual conscious return to spirituality, they built megalithic structures that would withstand the ravages of time to serve special spiritual purposes and in which to leave symbolic wisdom for future use. The higher-level beings were often held in awe by the less sophisticated, and were the original deified human beings on which stories and myths were based. Most of them finally began minimally devolving about a million human years ago, so they, too, could experience the contrasts of physical life.

In devolving our human extensions, we effectively cut them off from higher vibration levels, so we needed a means by which we, their higher-vibrating souls, could communicate with them. We endowed each human with intuition through which we would provide guidance.

With gentle nudges, including feelings, desires, ideas, and thoughts of invention, insight, and creativity, we direct our human actors through the plays of life, one interaction and experience after another. In this way, they continually advance and unfold, seemingly naturally, making a complete circle in their evolution, and greatly expanding their awareness. Since they are extensions of us, we are able to experience everything they do, just not quite as directly, yet; but we, too, expand our awareness.

Since in our spirit life we use only feelings, not emotions, we decided that, through the use of both, we would gain greater experience and awareness-expansion. Feelings are heart based, and include love, joy, harmony, inner peace, and bliss, inherent in our very existence in Reality. Although humans could never physically stand to experience the depth of feelings natural to us, they could enjoy limited versions of them. We would sprinkle these "spiritual feelings" into their lives for their use in responding to the interactions of their life.

Emotions are reactions to outside stimuli—interactions with people and events in their lives. Humans also get feelings every day as they go about their life, which we'll call "worldly" feelings, to distinguish them from the feelings we give them that we're calling "spiritual." Worldly feelings are responses to outside stimuli, but are more subtle; they're not as reactive as regular emotions.

Feelings and emotions are just parts of a continuum, with high vibration love at one end and low vibration fear at the other end. In between are all the other feelings, worldly feelings, and emotions vibrating at different frequencies. There is no difference in value between the higher emotions and the lower ones; they serve different loving purposes in human life at different times, helping our humans and us to better know ourselves. In using emotions, our actors have wonderful experiences in contrast to Reality, enabling them, and us, to realize and appreciate all we truly are and have in Reality.

Once all the new functions were learned, each human intellect would judge everything in dualistic terms, making choices and stimulating emotions, creating experiences and expanding our joint awareness. Through numerous reincarnations, together we souls and our extensions jointly experience all the conditions and emotions available on Earth that are unfamiliar to us in Reality.

In the beginning of material existence, we created an overall plan of what we wanted to accomplish for each race or kingdom and how we would go about it. The plan for humans calls for conditions and events in clusters of astrological ages, each consuming a little more than 2,000 human years. It also set in motion a law of cause and effect, which allows our human actors to experience results of their choices and actions. It helps them to interact with each other. It enables them to experience those seeming negative emotions through their own intellectual process of judgment and choice.

Together in groups (souls and our human actor extensions), we plan play scenarios and decide what we want to generally accomplish through each enacted Earth play. Glorious are the scenarios available to us through male and female interaction, same-sex interaction, physical and emotional attraction, mating, friendship, birth, illness, injury, deformity, challenge, abuse, imagined success and failure, death, and through application of intellectual reasoning and judgment on the opposites of duality.

By mutual agreement in Reality before each play of life begins, in soul groups we decide what specific emotions we each want to have an opportunity to experience in an upcoming play. We outline conditions, experiences, and interchanges between actors that could provide those opportunities. We decide on the principal locale and the general ethnic, racial, and economic condition in which our play will mainly take place. We, in a sense, write our scenario, then cast an actor for each role. We outline the nature, purpose, and general aims of each relationship. Every interaction each person has with another human being, whether seemingly positive or negative, is of mutual benefit and adds to the growth of both parties. Varied interactions offer humans and their souls great opportunity to experience new reactions. Of course, we didn't know to plan all this originally but learned as our actors experienced. Our creativity evolved.

Having set up our theater with all our humans acting, almost 2,500 human years ago, we realized their interactions would benefit more if their energy was over-balanced toward its masculine expression. This would enable some humans to be aggressive, defensive, and competitive, greatly enhancing their scenarios, and affecting others' scenarios as well.

Following the vibration pattern we had put in motion, we set the Age of Pisces, with its particular energetic vibrations, as the time frame for this behavior to dominate, and the early years of the Age of Aquarius to gradually restore balance. Since our plan had already set the Aquarian Age as the time for great human awakening, the rebalancing of human energy would help in the planned shift in human consciousness.

Once we have experienced all we want to at the lower levels, we help our human extensions expand their conscious awareness to work their way back through each higher level of consciousness. As our human extensions rise higher through eons of experience, more frequent and deeper spiritual feelings reduce their use of emotions.

For example, the more love and compassion they feel, the less fear and other negativity they experience.

As our human actors evolve spiritually and their awareness rises to ever higher levels of consciousness, their physical vibration rate increases. As they gradually re-attune their inner human consciousness with their higher-vibrational Selves, they raise their overall vibrations.

They begin to awaken, gradually diminishing the veil created by lower vibration energy amassed into their collective unconscious. Their energy becomes increasingly more balanced. They begin to recognize their interconnectedness and the Oneness of all, and begin to exercise their divinity. Their consciousness shifts from strictly worldly to more and more spiritual, exhibiting greater love.

Beyond the Story

My higher soul-Self went beyond the story of our past to begin to explain what we, humanity as a whole, are going through now:

Humans are nearing a great shift in consciousness, the first of its kind since their devolution ended and their evolution began. That shift will make possible a new way of enjoying Earth life for all its forms. As our human extensions rise in levels of consciousness, we souls are better able to express through them. The more they attune to us the more directly we can express, the more directly we enjoy Earth life.

Once each human extension awakens and reunites with their soul, we—the unmanifest part of our whole being—are finally able to directly experience in physicality. We eagerly await that event, although we are already beginning to enjoy our own true nature in experiences of human life. All along, however, the journey has been the important thing, and immensely enjoyable. Our journey will never end.

Participation is always voluntary and for everyone's benefit. While suffering in human life seems like something a sane, loving being wouldn't choose to do or to inflict on another, we gain so much awareness from it that it's worth every pain. Also, understand that Earth life is illusion, and that suffering is only physical and temporary.

Time, too, is an illusion, created by slowed vibrations. A lifetime on Earth spans a much briefer time in Reality, some are almost instantaneous.

Enacting plays of human life is not much different from starring in a human movie or stage play. In the latter, there are breaks between scenes or acts when actors return to their real life. In our plays, actors often return home to Reality at the end of a day's act when their role is asleep.

Actors are never far from Real life. Reality is not a remote spot in the Kosmos, but is all around, in interpenetrating consciousness, not a separate place from Earth and its universe, but a different dimension, one of many.

We enjoy the same physical universe that our physical extensions do, only to us it is visibly more vibrant and beautiful, since we don't have the haze of the veiled physical human condition to obscure its glory.

My higher soul-Self concluded:

It's impossible to express in human language our joy in enacting these plays. Our consciousness has expanded so greatly over the many lives of our extensions. Our greatest joy is in helping and witnessing our extensions enlighten and ultimately awaken.

When speaking of a plan or scenario, we don't mean a detailed dialogue, but more a plot outline, generally defining the purposes, intents, and aims of major events and interactions. Flexible, it allows a variety of ways for each soul to get the experiences it wants. No one tells an actor it has to enter an Earthly play. Every life is voluntary, intended to provide opportunities for awareness expansion, with specifics chosen by the participants. As actors and audiences participate voluntarily and enjoy human stage plays and movies, we enjoy our plays. We enjoy it all, together.

Why Go Through It?

Why would we want to go through all the suffering of Earth life only to return to a Reality in which little happens, which probably seems pretty dull? My higher soul-Self had an answer:

In contrast to what we now know, it was rather dull initially, but we didn't know it, because we hadn't yet had the contrasting experience. We have learned so much since we set all this in motion and enjoy our power of creation so much more. We see more of Reality now and are able to focus on details we hadn't before realized existed. We can now appreciate both our singularity and our multiplicity. We will continue to use Earth and other globes for semi-physical and spiritual experiences any time we want, for much goes on in dimensions above what is familiar to humans.

We also have more to experience in other, different, theaters.

Our life is truly anything but dull; it's just not anxiety-ridden and exciting in the fearful ways of human life on Earth. But we have far deeper feelings than humans can possibly experience, or even imagine; our music is glorious and colors are so much more varied, vibrant, and vivid. More precious than any other advantage we have over humans is the love we feel for all life. In human words, it's incredible. And now we know it.

How It All Plays Out

Introduction

As is probably obvious from my story, I believe our life on Earth is all illusion, nothing more than a seemingly random jumble of overlapping plays. None of it is real. We humans are not real; we're only actors enacting roles in plays. It all seems real to us because we've designed it that way.

When you watch a well-enacted movie, don't you live the experiences of the actors? Don't you feel the emotions as if they were your own? You cry with the actors, laugh, love, hate, worry, hurt, and experience fear. That's what your life is: you're in the middle of your own movie.

We are not our bodies. Our body, our intellect, and our personality are tools we humans use to experience physical life. We hid our spiritual nature so we could experience this material existence as part of it. We are eternal spirit beings, co-creating this physical experience, manifesting the unmanifest.

We've purposely forgotten Reality and have greatly slowed our vibrations to experience time and materiality. Our entering this life was our own personal choice and so are all of our experiences. Every event and interaction in our lives is for our benefit in some way, and everything and everyone is spiritually perfect as is, at all times. Each of us is uniquely important in the role we play for each of the many others in our life and to the whole. There are no deaths, no accidents, no coincidences, or errors, no victims, and no real villains, so there is no need to fight to survive. There is no judgment, no need for salvation, and no need for karmic justice, or for perfecting ourselves or correcting previous "errors."

Like me, Gary Zukav says that we each have an immortal soul that exists outside of time, and those "souls that have chosen the physical experience of life as we know it as their path of evolution have incarnated their energies many times." But, writes Zukav: "All of the energy of the soul does not incarnate.... In the creation of a personality, the soul... reduces parts of itself, to take on the human experience.... It is a smaller soul self." He says that while the "five-sensory personality" is unaware of its soul and its guidance the "multi-sensory personality" not only "is aware of its soul—it seeks to align itself with its soul, to become the physical embodiment of its higher self—and it consciously invokes and receives the loving assistance of its own soul and of other souls that assist it."[448]

We all have a built-in need to seek fulfillment through loving connection to something higher that we intuitively know exists. No matter how happy and satisfied we may be in a relationship or a career, or how rich and famous we are, always something seems to be missing. Seeking that something, some people mistakenly strive for ever higher status and power; others turn to numbing or stimulating substances, gambling, sex, or other escapes or pleasurable things to do. But no external placebo will satisfy or even subdue our inner longing; it can't.

The Big Why

You may have expected something more momentous for the big WHY we created all this. But, the best answer to any question—to use the scientific metaphor called Occam's razor—is usually the simplest one. But while the answer is simple, and may be disappointing to you, the depth of it may be great. We had to have a way to see our individuality so we could know both it and our Oneness. We had to identify the many as aspects of the One, the multitude of the singularity. We had to limit the possibilities, had to create time, had to create material contrast.

Imagine: we did all this for that simple reason and for that simple purpose! It's true. At least that explanation is true for me.

Emanations

There's an important difference between something being "created from nothing," and something existing as an emanation of its source. When we think of creating something, we assume it didn't exist before and that it is separate from its creator. But when something is an emanation of its source, its attribute or face, it is entirely part of its greater Self, and has always existed in its source, whether manifest in the physical or not, and will always exist, at least as a possibility, inseparable from its source. It had no beginning, except as it was manifest as an expression of its source, shown to exist. It didn't come from "nothing," just nothing physical.

The pre-creation One (a term I'll use for the Whole Spirit Being of All That Is) was and still is a singularity, a single sea of luminescent, intelligent, consciousness, a blending of innumerable points of light. We, within that singularity, didn't feel a need for companions for we already had all the love of the multitude within us. We just hadn't yet identified it, so weren't able to appreciate it. The many were manifested to enable the singularity to know itself. Only through physical experience in multiple forms can the One know and appreciate its loving, giving nature, and its Oneness. The One learns, grows, expands its consciousness, evolves through the growth and awareness expansion of the many. But the many are never separate from the One. Before our vibrations were slowed to create form, we were aspects of the One; now some of us are faces of the One in manifest physicality.

We are all—everything—One, not just because we share the same One consciousness—which we do—but because we each literally are the One (the quantum hologram concept). The Kosmos, in its entirety, is the whole. But that whole has been shattered, so to speak, into the multitude of pieces—each containing and reflecting the image of the whole, and each piece of that multitude is also always the whole. As in a shattered hologram, all details of the whole may not be easily and clearly individualized in the pieces, but they are there. We each are a reflection of the ALL of us, so that anything that affects one of us automatically, simultaneously affects each and every other one of us in some way.

Each thing that happens to one of us becomes part of the pattern of vibrations that is the memory-field (called in Eastern terms, the Akashic record), of the whole, and then is extended to each and every part. This record is available for anyone's use, and we can draw on it for our experience as we choose.

Vibrations

Quantum physics, in agreement with the ancients, says everything is alive and vibrating, pulsating with life. And my higher Self tells me that by slowing energy vibrations, we "create" form, so that the slower the vibrations, the denser and more material a form seems, with minute differences in patterns of frequency making each entity unique.

As I understand it, that slowing also creates time, making events seem to occur in a linear fashion.

We humans, by choice, enter Earth life at considerably lower vibrations than is normal for us as spirit beings. At the slower vibration rates, identifying with the density of matter, we are unable to know what is going on at higher vibration levels. As we raise our consciousness to higher levels, we are raising our vibrations and coming closer in vibration rate to our soul, and are better able to see and understand more of the truth of our life.

Seeming Evil

The writings of Gnostics and some Pagans have been translated as having said that bodies and Earth life are evil, and the Buddha's words have been translated as "all is suffering." But these translations are inaccurate. The Kabbalah tradition probably has it most accurately. As we learned in an earlier chapter, they teach that there is no evil, as such, just as there is no darkness as such, being only the absence of light; so evil is simply a name for believing and acting as if good is not present.

All wisdom teachers have told us that Earth life is filled with seeming evil and suffering because that's how we experience contrast to our life in Reality. But they've told us, there is no such thing as true evil, and suffering is of our own making and always for our benefit. The purpose of these plays that we create is first to experience the contrast of the unfamiliar in order to realize, know, and appreciate ourselves and our unmanifest Reality. Then it is to experience the true loving us, in physicality, within its limits.

We take nothing back to our spiritual Reality but expanded awareness from our feelings and emotions as responses and reactions to our experiences and our interactive relationships. That means that there is no "judgment" or "punishment" or "evil" to atone for.

Extensions of Our Soul

Most doctrines of religions and the Metas consider our souls to be the experiencing, evolving entities, rather than regarding us humans as extensions of our eternal soul-Self. Some spiritual teachers, however, including Gary Zukav, many ancient Pagans, and students of the Kabbalah, say as I do that only a part of us enters physical life.

As an extension of our soul, each of us has its ongoing, personal connection to the One as the source of all truth and wisdom. Often unknowingly, we receive nearly constant help from our soul through intuition, which we couldn't get if we were an isolated soul rather than an extension. We are given spiritual feelings, hunches, or "inklings," as well as ideas, answers, insights, creative inspiration, and even things to say throughout every day. Sometimes we follow the advice and at other times we ignore it or defy it, but we always get it.

We each can develop a conscious awareness of the connection if we want to, so that we know when we're getting such help. Through inner communion, we can make it interactive. Each of us can also specifically get our own set of truths, if we want that.

No one is ever alone in this life. Our higher soul-Selves are the directors of our individual plays, coordinating the meetings and events that occur in our lives and helping us individually enact our roles in them. We each also have spirit guides and angels who help us with specific issues, and we have the souls of our soul group actors around us. We each have our own unique role to play for each of many others, mutually aiding each other's growth in awareness.

Planning Our Plays

We preplan our play scenarios and outline our intentions, but we don't use a script. We actors are caused to meet and interact; after that, our responses or reactions are strictly ours. How we perceive what is happening is colored by our beliefs and previous experiences of this life and, when we want, previous lives. Our choices are ours. The things we do and say are ours, in part dictated by the character each of us has donned for this play.

While we have a certain amount of free will, we also are constrained by our true loving nature as spirit beings and by the nature of our roles. For instance, unless it's part of our character's role and plot plan, we are unable to unnecessarily harm another being. To do so would be completely out of character and against our nature, so impossible. When it's in character to do harm we do it, *knowing* (on a higher level) whatever we do serves beneficial purposes and isn't really harm at all.

We have, by agreement prior to entering this life, chosen our family members, friends, lovers, teachers, co-workers, and villains. We've selected the time-frame and world conditions and the country, culture, and economic level in which we live. We've chosen our personal physical, mental, and emotional characteristics and capabilities, our ethnicity, belief system(s), and our gender and sexual orientation. And we've chosen our talents and achievements, as well as our afflictions, disabilities, challenges, heart-breaks, and the time and vehicle for our death.

Everyone and every event in our life is designed and enacted to enable us and others with whom we interact to experience emotions and feelings. The people and events themselves are of no real importance; only our reactions and responses—how we "feel" about them—make our experiences.

Only those feelings stay with us. Emotions help us expand our spiritual awareness, helping us raise our consciousness to increasingly higher levels. The higher we climb, the more we can see and appreciate of spiritual Reality, and the more compassion we have for our fellow Earth inhabitants. The higher we go, the closer we come to awakening. By higher, I don't mean higher in value or better than, I mean higher in vibration.

Our Challenging Experiences

We have chosen to experience challenges, failures, disappointments, and heartaches so we can know the emotional experiences of our reactions to them. We have planned such "bad" and "sad" experiences into our lives to provide awareness expansion.

Since in Reality we have love, joy, bliss, and harmony way beyond what we can now imagine, to experience mainly those in Earth life would give us little growth in awareness. But we will, in this life and/or future ones, experience in limited form those beautiful qualities, to know them through physical experience.

Some of us have agreed to enact villain roles to help others in their experience. When in those roles, we are not instruments of Satan—there is no such thing. Nor are we truly bad; we're merely playing that kind of role. Everything we do has love behind it and is only enacting a play. All of the actors are our loved ones—why Socrates and Jesus both said to love our enemies!

Tragedy is a central experience in many plots and scenarios of our plays, often taking the form of the early death of a loved one, or an illness or injury that causes lengthy, sometimes life-long, challenges. We may choose a tragic shock. A pivotal experience chosen by some of us is raising a child only to lose him or her at a very young age.

Part of that experience is the instrument of death, whether a lengthy illness, gangland shooting, a seeming accident, overdose of drugs, suicide, or perhaps abduction with fate unknown. It is pre-selected for its effect on loved ones—not by others, but by those involved, to serve our purpose of becoming more aware of what is Real.

Sometimes a child's lengthy illness provides us a great array of emotional experiences. Our interaction with the child and the child's handling of an illness or challenge provide the experience, and our handling of it adds to the experience of both.

The challenge of a personal disability, disfigurement, or loss of a body part also provides great experience opportunities. Our handling of such a challenge is not our experience alone, but is also for our loved ones.

Any healing that takes place, whether physical or emotional, or the absence of a physical or emotional healing, adds to the experience by raising the vibration and enhancing conscious awareness for all.

As aspects or expressions of the One, we are perfect love, always. We cannot err; to err implies accident or failure, and neither is possible. We humans may seem to make mistakes, but they are planned circumstances. We have no evil in us, so we don't deserve suffering as karmic justice. Stephan Hoeller says that Gnostics "see the cause of evil as ignorance." He adds: "By attaining enlightened consciousness and thus rising above all dualities, one is liberated from karma and from all conditions in which evil plays a role."[449]

We have chosen to enact plays in which we suffer and sometimes do bad things. We have deliberately put such suffering and evil into our lives to help us experience the dualistic states that provide contrasts so we can know our own divinity. As such, they are perfect. Without ever experiencing lack could we appreciate anything we have? Without fear could we know serenity? Without separation could we ever realize our

Oneness? Dualistic states are one of many continua enabling our experience of physicality and our realization of our spirituality and divine singularity.

We experience the necessary contrasts not only through our stage settings, cultures, and world conditions, but through the interactions and events in our plays. Before we enter human life, we contract with members of our soul group to provide each other such circumstances and evoke the emotions we each want to experience.

Occasionally, we provide mirrors for our fellow actors to view themselves. That is, we do or say something that provokes a strong reaction, and gives a friend an opportunity to deal with an issue. We probably don't do whatever it is knowingly, and may not know why we got such an explosive reaction. It has to do with us only to the extent we react to the other's reaction.

Our world conditions may be understood in part as the background scenery that we who have incarnated at this time wanted for our current play. But they also are what we collectively have created through our thinking, our beliefs, and our worldviews. Some of us have more directly created them by our actions, through greed, insensitivity, self-absorption, and corruption, as parts of our scenarios.

In my belief system, our current world conditions and dire problems are just as perfect as peace, prosperity, good health, and universal compassion. The materialist belief systems and the out-of-balance masculine energy have been our choices. We wanted all of it, in part as contrast to identify what we aren't and what we don't want. It all was perfect for the stage of our evolution from which we are moving away.

The extreme polarization of today—between religion and science, materialism and spirituality, the haves and have-nots—is all part of our plan, for our benefit in raising our consciousness. It is giving us choices and making those choices very clear. All of it is serving loving purposes, helping those of us who are ready for it to identify and become more certain of what we want in our lives.

Earth Angels

Throughout human history, loving beings have voluntarily entered Earth life to help humanity as a whole by enacting roles of mass victims, their loved ones, and their villains in horrible events of violence. Both victims and perpetrators of such as the Nazi Holocaust and all other genocide are such beings. People the world over, dying of Covid-19 and other disease, hunger, war, and terrorism all play victims to benefit humanity. I call them "Earth Angels." All such events are planned and enacted to raise humanity's consciousness.

Natural disasters, such as earthquakes, tsunamis, and hurricanes, are such events; as are airliner crashes, mine cave-ins, offshore oil spills, anything that gets our attention in a big way.

Substance abuse and addictions, as well as rampant physical and emotional abuse of women and children also serve such a purpose, as does the ever-widening gap between the haves and have-nots and the lack of adequate food and health care for so many.

The Global Consciousness Project, begun at Princeton University in 1998, is a scientific experiment to see if a global consciousness can be measured from interconnections among human beings. It's based on random number generators running on computers interconnected through the Internet. It's now in 70 sites around the world, and has accumulated data during more than 400 events like 9/11, hurricane Katrina, the Indonesian tsunami, and the Japanese earthquake. And, with a deviation from expectation at a billion to one odds against chance, it has answered "yes"! Director Roger Nelson writes,

> This indicates that human beings are interactive…. At some deep level, beneath our everyday consciousness, there is an interconnectedness that is brought into coherence when great events pull us all in the same direction.[450]

When we aren't in pain, devastated, or observing others' anguish, we're content to merely exist in a world of our own. But prod us with heartache, challenge, or a compassion-evoking event, like, most recently, the corona virus pandemic, and we become caring helpers, crusaders, or spiritual seekers. And computers register the change.

Terrible events and conditions get our attention, causing us to stop in our frenetic routine and think about what's happening. They grab our hearts and evoke outrage, sympathy, and caring. Sometimes they cause us to reach out and help our troubled neighbors. They bring out the best in us, the love. If only for a little while, all that's high in us surfaces. The greater the devastation, the more lives lost, the deeper is our response. Even when it's only temporary, such awareness-expansion to higher consciousness on some level is permanent. We may forget about the event and return to business as usual, but deep inside we've changed, at least a little. Those changes add up, and help in the evolution of our awareness to ever higher levels of consciousness, and we move toward individual awakening and the mass transformation of our collective consciousness.

The people who participate directly in such events also do so as parts of their individual scenarios, whether as villains or victims, or their loved ones. The so-called victims are not really such. They voluntarily enact their death scenes or other plight in those ways for the benefit of humanity's collective consciousness and also for the experiential benefit of their own individual awareness and of their loved ones. An early and seemingly unnatural death is always enacted for the benefit of loved ones, and often those involved in the event. Their benefit is individual.

We may want to know what deep sadness feels like, or how hatred feels. Such feelings may help us better understand others' anguish; or they may help us know joy and love when they come to us. Or we may want an opportunity to express forgiveness.

Children as victims, especially, get our attention and draw out the best in us. We see so much happening with children these days: Substance abuse, gangs, crime, disappearances, suicide, prostitution, school shootings, disease, starvation, parental neglect and abuse, peer abuse, low self esteem, autism, and other challenges. Those children raise both our individual consciousness and our collective unconscious more than we can imagine.

We all have been planned into each others' scenarios, yet we may never know our true involvement. Each of us sees the people and events in our life from our own perspective, which includes the demeanor of the role we are enacting, conditioning by our life-long beliefs and experiences, and our attitude toward life in general. No one can truly know another, nor what will please or displease them, nor how they will react to anything we do or say. All we can successfully do is satisfy ourselves in some way, without hurting another in the process. There is no good reason to judge either them or us; we don't know where they are coming from, or maybe our own motivation. But, since there are no accidents, we can be sure we each are doing or being only what we can in each moment.

Everything is perfect at all times. Maybe not ideal, as we would have it be, but perfect.

Even "death" isn't a bad thing. I know from reports of near-death experiences and what my soul-Self tells me that we don't suffer at death. Our body may seem to, but the real us, our consciousness, doesn't feel a thing. In death, our consciousness returns home to Reality, like awakening from a dream; the costume we've worn dies, taking with it our ego/intellect and the persona we've played. The actor is released from the confines of a limited human body and is free. Later, the actor may choose to return to enact another role in another play, or not. We leave this life only when the time is right, and the time is right only when we have finished what we came in to do, and often to fulfill a contract we've made with other beings.

Forgiveness

Since everything anyone does is perfect always, there's never any real need for forgiveness. Not only is it perfect but it actually (on a higher level) has love behind it. No one truly damages us anyway, maybe temporarily hurts our body or our emotions, but only for our benefit—and with our knowledge and complicity. Only our reaction to it affects us now. We can go through the motions of forgiving if we want to, but forgiveness implies blame in the first place, where there is no blame. Acceptance of the truth of its perfection is more appropriate and beneficial than forgiveness.

Each of us has a life mission. It may be to give life to another, or to cause a specific life-altering reaction in another, or to lead a nation, defend a particular client, write a book, compose a symphony, or help a student learn; or it may be to shoot children and teachers at school, hijack an airliner and fly it into a highly populated building, or participate in a war. Our mission may be lofty or mundane; it may seem truly good and honorable or immensely evil. It isn't ours to judge.

Enlightenment

Some of the experiences we plan into our personal scenario bring more light into our consciousness, helping us toward our awakening. Each bit of light expands exponentially as it adds to the light of love we already have within us.

Each such experience lifts us into a new level of consciousness at more rapid vibrations. It lightens the veil that hides Reality from us, revealing higher levels of understanding associated with the higher, lighter frequencies.

This is what we call en*light*enment. Each step expands our consciousness and brings us closer to awakening. The thrills of enlightenment are ones we would never enjoy had we not hidden truth from us and lived in darkness. Learning to remember, re-know, and reunite with our higher soul-Self is the most wonderful of experiences we have afforded ourselves through the devolution and evolution processes we've been going through.

Sharing Love

The Kabbalah, like many other spiritual paths, teaches that each of us has a built in need to give, to share. More than anything, we each have a need to share the love that fills us and is constantly pushing to flow outward.

We think that what we need is to receive love. But sharing is a two-way event—giving and receiving—and giving comes first. If we aren't emitting love from our self, any love coming from others has no way to be felt and truly appreciated. We may not even realize it's coming our way. Only by sending out love do we create the void, so to speak, to be filled by incoming love.

By love I don't necessarily mean romantic or sexual love, but any version of love: parental, sibling, friendship, nonjudgmental acceptance, a realization of the value of our relationship, or acknowledgment of the worth of each as a person. Our pets, too, help us know and express the feeling of love—through their unconditional love for us and as we experience our love for them. Love can also mean helping others find meaning, purpose, and compassion in their lives, and can include sharing wisdom.

When others aren't receptive to our love, we're frustrated in our efforts to share. Being receptive doesn't mean returning the love in like form or in the same degree; it merely means that a person is open to receiving love and enjoying it for what it is and the intent of it.

To be open to receive, a person has to be giving. Most people today aren't yet very heart centered and don't freely give of their love, so also aren't open to receiving. As we raise our consciousness ever higher, giving and receiving both get easier.

Meanwhile, our pets help us immensely through this whole process. Because they live at a higher, heart-centered level all the time, they are wonderfully open to receive our love, giving and receiving: true sharing. They provide us a release, someone with whom to share, in a balance of give and take.

Without such release, frustrations build and cause pain and sickness. We become angry and depressed, and all the things we really don't want to be. All of this is because we have naturally so very much love inside us that we want and actually need to be able to share.

Some of us, having felt hurt by the actions of someone we loved, protect ourselves from being hurt again. We close down our sharing feelings, don't allow ourselves to respond to any feelings of love we may have for another. Although those feelings come to us from our soul-Selves, we reject them, ignore them, even fight them, to keep from feeling vulnerable.

We think we are doing what's best for us, but we're really hurting ourselves. By not allowing ourselves to flow with divine love, and fighting our higher feelings, we cause internal conflict which may result in physical ailments. Those ailments are signals, trying to get our attention, wanting us to address this issue from our heart, not our head—from love, not fear. We may be robbing ourselves of an opportunity for true happiness, and wonder why we can't be happy. Until we learn to allow the flow of love, both in and out, and realize that control of it is fruitless and possibly destructive, we can't be fulfilled and truly happy.

We are affected by people and events in our life only to the extent we allow ourselves to react, and only in the manner we choose. Whatever occurs does so to give us an opportunity to experience emotions, giving us the choice of reacting or choosing a thoughtful response, to suffer or not.

Intellect/Ego

Intellect, related to ego, is a wonderful tool, but it is designed to react with emotions, and is conditioned by past experiences to automatically react to similar people and conditions as they come into our lives. So, without consciously thinking about it, we apply that conditioning. The higher our vibrations, the less apt we are to use intellect to react with an emotion and the more apt we are to use our heart to deliberately, lovingly respond to the situation, or to ignore it. The choice is always ours. If we rely too heavily on intellect, we may always be reacting to events and people in past ways, probably a deterrent to living in the now. And, too, intellect likes to be in control and will assert itself into our thinking.

It may also interfere with what we get from intuition, misinterpreting or overriding it. Still, it's possible to get intellect's cooperation. Life is a joint venture, and intellect can be made to understand that.

I see my intellect as a limited yet wonderful part of the God I Am. It's been a big help to me, especially in my journey of enlightenment toward awakening, asking innumerable questions. And it has helped immensely in my writing. So, I intend for it to rise to ever higher levels of awareness as a full partner in my awakening.

I'm not transcending my ego/intellect, I'm raising it to each higher level of my awareness. I've given it the choice: Rise with me or be left behind. Not wanting to be left out, my intellect has chosen to help me rise to higher levels. Of course, when I leave this life, my ego/intellect will be left behind as part of the physical me.

Meanwhile, we (all aspects of me) are enjoying this life as one.

Karma

Suffering and evil as major components of this life have to be explained, so the "fall" concept fills a need. Some say it's so we can "meet ourselves," often to "perfect" ourselves, or we need to experience the results of returning karma to cleanse our slate so we can gain freedom from reincarnation. I believe we come into Earth life because we want to and can leave, or stop reincarnating, anytime we choose.

Although many people view karma as making up for actions from past lives, I see it only as cause and effect, with the effect influential in the same life as the cause, unless we choose to use an experience of one life in a subsequent incarnation to serve some purpose in that life. That's strictly our choice, and has nothing to do with justice. I don't see the so-called "law of karma" as justice.

While believing in the law of karma as a form of justice may coerce some of us into more kind, thoughtful treatment of our fellow human beings, it seems to me to connote retribution or punishment. It also seems judgmental and subject to interpretation—what is bad karma or sin? Are our souls really lost in a maze of past-life transgressions and self-inflicted karmic reprisals? Are we destined to travel from one incarnation to another, never knowing what sins we committed in previous incarnations, how to atone for them, or what terrible tragedy may befall us as karmic justice? On what basis is it determined how we experience balancing karma or correcting *tikkun*? Must we pay for past-life sins of our family or of our culture? Is that really fair? Will our stockpile of negative karma ever be entirely exhausted? Maybe not, unless we assume a hermit's life, doing absolutely nothing. But then, what's the point of living such a life?

We don't need returning karma to awaken to our true Self. That teaching suggests we are alone in this life and get no help from our Self or from any spirit being. We each are in constant contact—usually unconsciously—with our Self, who guides us through the experiences of our life. When we have accomplished what we planned to at the lower levels in our veiled state of consciousness our soul-Self guides us to awakening.

All of us, whether human or other, are on a journey through the halls of experience. Some of us enjoy human experiences in Earth life; others enjoy nonhuman Earthly life, other physical life on other globes in the universe, or nonphysical life in other dimensions. The process or journey is everything.

Comments & Questions: My Philosophy

One criticism of my philosophy is that, since in it nothing is real and everything is already perfect, it could make one too passive to participate effectively and benefit from life's experiences. This would be a possibility if our roles, co-actors, or our souls would let us out so easily. But, there is so much more to learn and do to be the light and help our fellow humans see the light and make the shift, passivity isn't really an issue. Accepting this philosophy has greatly raised my feelings of responsibility to Earth and all of its inhabitants. To me, my philosophy is exciting and hopeful, making me want to share it.

Some readers have had trouble with my model of life as a play, for the most part unable to accept that they would have subjected themselves to the sufferings of their life. They can't accept that we each have chosen our scenario, with its afflictions, heartaches, challenges, failures, losses, and death.

I ask them: "If we didn't make those choices ourselves, who did? Why would someone else have done this to us? Who are we that someone else would be interested in either hurting us or seeing us enjoy happiness?" Or do they think everything happens by chance?

I ask them to think seriously about the events in their lives they consider terrible, think about how they reacted to those events and any people who may have harmed them. I suggest they consider whether, if they had ignored them or responded with love and peace, instead of reacting with fear, hatred, anger, or despair, the results would have seemed so terrible. I also ask if they are different in any way for having had the experience. I explain:

> It's our choice to be emotionally harmed or to appreciate and let those people and events help us learn more about ourselves—either way, we are learning. That's what life is about: learning through experience who and what we are, and learning to love and appreciate ourselves and everyone in our life.

Often a hurtful experience early in life or a later tragedy makes us stronger in some way or influences the direction of our future. Some of us choose to respond to such an event by playing the victim, and others by pursuing a life of anger, crime, abuse of others, or addiction. In either case our planned and innate nature, the role we decided to play in this lifetime, influences our response. The results are what we chose ahead of time and often contracted with co-actors to experience. We've just wiped such planning from our memory so we can realistically act it out.

Notice I said "influences" not "dictates." We always have options available to us and choices to make. Our future is not set in concrete, but neither is it random happenstance. Our choices are ours to make—but not ours alone—we each get help from our soul-Self. We can ignore that help, but our souls will let us get only so far afield.

We all have lived through considerable suffering in this life and previous ones. I *know* (intuitively) that at this point in humanity's experience, we have about completed that phase of our growth experience and can begin to enjoy more of our real nature in our experience of physicality. Our souls are leading us toward the shift in consciousness. They are helping us respond to our world with ever more compassion as part of that shift.

We are all on our own individual paths, each somewhat different from all others. We are also all on a collective path toward humanity's shift in consciousness that is our rapidly approaching destiny. Soon our vibrations will be high enough that our souls will be able to express directly through us, and enjoy Earth life as us, without extension, as other souls do with other life forms.

In *One Taste*, Ken Wilber concludes:

> ...when you realize that ordinary life is just a dream, just a movie, just a play... you don't feel less, you feel more—because you can afford to. You are no longer afraid of dying, and therefore you are not afraid of living.[451]

---

[448] Zukav, Gary, *The Seat of the Soul*. New York, NY: A Fireside Book by Simon & Schuster, 1990

[449] Hoeller, Stephan, *Gnosticism*. Wheaton, IL: Quest Books, Theosophical Publishing House, 2002.

[450] Nelson, Roger, "The Global Consciousness Project - An Update," *The Noetic Post*, Fall/Winter 2010. Petaluma, CA: Institute of Noetic Sciences.

[451] Wilber, Ken, *One Taste*, quoted in *The Essential Ken Wilber, an Introductory Reader*. Boston, MA: Shambhala Publications, Inc. 1998.

Consciousness

Introduction

Consciousness seems to be the least understood spiritual concept, second only to God. Webster limits its definition to "awareness of oneself and one's surroundings." Most people say humans (and maybe a few higher animals) are the only Earthly beings so aware, so the only ones with consciousness, that it's something we acquired at a particular point in our evolution, which makes us different from other animals.

Carter Phipps, writing of consciousness and challenges posed to science by our having it, quotes one scientist as asserting it's "easily reducible to brain function." He quotes another as arguing "You're not going to reduce consciousness to a process in the brain.... My own view is that consciousness itself is in some sense irreducible... fundamental in the world." A third scientist he quotes is "pushing for scientists to accept what mystics have long claimed: that there are inner dimensions of the human experience not ultimately reducible to matter."[452]

Consumed by materialism and naturalism and intent on avoiding dualism, orthodox scientists are forced to consider everything as part of matter, limiting their science. They have to find ways to associate the nonphysical sorts of things (thoughts, emotions, dreams, desires, imaginings, intuitions, and everyday perceptions) with the physical. As they do so, they insist those aspects of what it is to be human are either functions of our human brain, or its fantasies; they had to have emerged as we evolved to more complex beings, as abilities of our physical brains, not truly nonphysical.

A Nonphysical Quality

In *The Power of Premonition*, physician Larry Dossey tells us that although "many scientists concede there are huge gaps in their knowledge of how the brain makes consciousness," they are certain those gaps "will be filled in as science progresses."[453] He adds, though, that Nobel-prize-winning neurophysiologist John Eccles and philosopher of science Karl Popper, calling this attitude "promissory materialism," say it is "a superstition without a rational foundation... simply a religious belief held by dogmatic materialists... who confuse their religion with their science...."[454]

Despite the "absence of evidence," says Dossey, "the belief that the brain produces consciousness endures and has ossified into dogma."[455] He quotes astronomer Carl Sagan as saying: "My fundamental premise about the brain is that its workings—what we sometimes call mind—are a consequence of its anatomy and physiology, and nothing more."[456] And Francis Crick is quoted as saying that a person's "mental activities are entirely due to the behavior of nerve cells, glial cells, and the atoms, ions, and molecules that make up and influence them."[457]

I liken the brain to a computer, receiving input from the body, the environment, the mind (thoughts, questions, dreams and imaginings, daily perceptions, beliefs, emotions, and feelings), and it stores them for future reference. The brain doesn't do anything with that information other than accumulate it. Our intellect—which isn't in the brain but is part of our consciousness, is the software that uses that stored information throughout our daily life. It draws from the brain's database to address each new experience, applying conditioned impressions from past experiences—all that the intellect has from which to draw.

The Global Consciousness Project has made clear that human beings are "interactive and connected." Yet Roger Nelson, director of the project and author of the update article, materialistically concludes:

> We may be operating the way neurons do in the human brain. Neurons, without knowing anything about it, produce consciousness, a mind.... Maybe human beings similarly produce something through their interconnection and non-local interaction that is equivalent to a kind of collective consciousness...."[458]

I find this strange, coming from a noetic scientist, that he believes neurons produce consciousness! Fortunately, more and more scientists believe as Freeman Dyson does: "[T]he cosmos is suffused with consciousness, from the grandest level to the most minute dimensions." Hundreds of experiments—including those of the Global Consciousness Project—and "millions of testimonials affirm consciousness can and does operate beyond the brain, body, and the present."[459]

What Is Consciousness?

To orthodox science consciousness is merely the noun of the adjective conscious. For them, to have consciousness is to be aware of oneself and one's surroundings. They see consciousness as an awake state of human experience in which we are capable of thought, will, and perception. Such definitions limit science's understanding of human thinking processes, and those of other life forms on Earth.

Explaining the results of his own experiences with a concept from quantum mechanics, Dossey says:

> ...consciousness is not a thing or substance, but is a nonlocal phenomenon. Nonlocal is merely a fancy word for infinite. If something is nonlocal, it is not localized to specific points in space, such as brains or bodies, or to specific points in time, such as the present. Nonlocal events are immediate; they require no travel time. They are unmediated; they require no energetic signal to "carry" them. They are unmitigated; they do not become weaker with increasing distance.
>
> Nonlocal phenomena are omnipresent, everywhere at once. This means there is no necessity for them to go anywhere; they are already there. They are infinite in time as well, present at all moments, past, present, and future, meaning, they are eternal.... [N]onlocal events are no longer a matter of debate in physics; numerous experiments prove their existence.[460]

Conventional science's materialism, probably with the help of Western academic psychology, created Webster's definition of consciousness and orthodox science's—and the public's—restricted view of all life. But I see consciousness as so much more than merely being aware of ourselves and our surroundings.

The second most significant insight I received in my quest for enlightenment was that what most of us call God is consciousness. Since I already knew that God is everything, this meant that everything is consciousness.

Comprehending this truth finally made it possible for me to understand our Oneness. I had earlier accepted it as fact—because my soul and its intuition to my heart told me it was—but my intellect hadn't yet been able to accept it.

Now, in my philosophy, consciousness is irreducible and fundamental to the Kosmos in all its dimensions; it is, as Eastern traditions say, "the ground of being." As I understand it, consciousness is pure intelligence, creativity, love, light, and the energetic force field that permeates and entangles everything material, the quantum hologram.

It is the Gnostic "Fullness" containing all possibilities, Plato's "intelligences" as possibilities. It is the Mind of God; it is Goswami's "Self-Aware Universe," the Hindu Brahman, or ground of being. It is God, the One.

Consciousness brought the physical into existence and sustains all its forms. The physical is merely expressed thought of consciousness, made denser by slowing its vibrations to the level of matter and energy. *The physical is not outside of consciousness; it is consciousness incarnate.*

Consciousness is spirit, unmanifest and manifest: the Kosmos. We all, everything and everyone, are the same One consciousness. Spirit beings (souls) are individualized expressions of consciousness, and everything physical is an expression, face, or extension of one of those beings, their consciousness expressing in physicality, each defined by minutely differing rates of vibration. We are within consciousness and it is within us. It is our life force. We and everything that exists have and are consciousness in equal measure.

Nothing can have more or less consciousness than anything else. The wave isn't less ocean than its ocean; it's just a small, temporarily defined, individualized aspect of it. *Consciousness makes everything One. It is the ALL.*

Consciousness, Conscious, or Intellect?

Our understanding of consciousness is central to our under-standing of all life on Earth. Scientists want to understand consciousness but never will using their restrictive definitions. Nor will they understand our life.

Many scientists studying consciousness as a psychological phenomenon wonder how something unconscious—as they believe we humans were until some of our early ancestors "gained consciousness"—became aware of themselves as individuals. These scientists see that transformation occurring as a result of natural selection on gene mutations that led to increasing complexity in the structure of the brain. Some hardcore adherents of "scientism" therefore wonder if machines couldn't also become conscious (seriously!) in the same way, since, in their minds, we are nothing more than organic machines.

Noetic scientists and Metas, however, have come to understand that neither consciousness nor "being conscious" are brain functions. If being conscious is an awake state of awareness in which we use the intellect we acquired when we became modern humans, the use of the intellect affects the brain, not the other way around.

When intellect sleeps, or isn't in use (as may be the case in extreme autism, Alzheimer's, or coma) we aren't conscious, aren't capable of ordinary perception, reasoning, or will. But we are always, on some level, fully aware (to which near death experiences attest).

Intellect, not consciousness, is what humans acquired at a particular point in our evolution—our "mind's big bang." When our consciousness took on intellect, we became self-aware and began developing the traits science identifies with modern humans.

Intellect, with its perceiving, learning, and reasoning processes, is to materialist scientists all we have and use; it's what they call "mind." They see consciousness, along with meaning, values, and morality as produced by intellect; to them, intuition is fantasy.

There's so much more to consciousness than perceiving, thinking, gaining knowledge, reasoning, and reacting with emotions—they're merely functions and purview of intellect, part of our consciousness. To understand the nature of consciousness, then, we must define it as separate from intellect, not synonymous with it.

Most Metas think of the surrounding, interpenetrating energy as consciousness, yet many also say only humans have consciousness. If everything is interpenetrated by consciousness, how can anything lack it? They, too, may be thinking of intellect in such exclusion. If we identify them separately, we can see that only humans use intellect, while all life could be consciousness.

We humans use intellect as we enact our Earthly scenarios, and, yes, we are the only beings on Earth with this quality of intellect. It's a tool we use through which we experience interactions and dualistic states. Then as we apply judgment to those experiences, we evoke emotions.

Intellect is the questioner who helps us understand our life. It is our conscience. Intellect interprets what we receive as intuition and puts it into words we can use to express it. Intellect is what sleeps. We close down intellect when we die to this physical life, but we (our human selves) remain consciously aware; we remain as consciousness.

Levels of Consciousness

With intellect identified as part of our consciousness, here is my model of levels of human consciousness.

(1) Intellect/ego: most closely related to the physical; the rational thinking process; a tool we use in the role we are enacting; what sleeps and what dies.
(2) Human self: the spirit being; an extension of our soul; the actor in physicality; our awareness.
(3) Soul or higher Self: our unmanifest aspect; the director of our plays and provider of creativity, guidance, and wisdom through intuition; collectively the multiplicity within the One.
(4) One: the vast sea of consciousness; the single consciousness of us all; the singularity.

These are not separate levels, but identifiable aspects of our consciousness, delineated to help us understand.

A little different from most of the other models we've looked at, my model inserts "human self" between ego and soul. As an extension of its soul, the human self is also always whole, perfect, and spiritual, and it is always aware. It is the part that travels during physical sleep, surfacing in dreams.

The soul-Self is our individualized aspect of the One. Our souls have always existed and always will in that individualized state. They, along with other spirit beings, in the aggregate are the cause and designer of the manifest universe. They are the possibilities, the Intelligences. Because they are vibrational patterns, they resonate with each other, and those that resonate closely often function together, and are called "soul groups."

It would probably be my human self that Eastern traditions see as cycling on that nearly endless train of reincarnation seeking the freedom of release from its cycles. Most religions identify what I call the "human self" with the "soul."

Equating consciousness with intellect/ego, fundamentalists of both religion and science see only one level and believe only we humans have that; that all other beings function by instinct. Fundamentalist religions also see God as completely separate and in a place where angels, archangels, and maybe Satanic beings also dwell; this, though, is not seen as a level of human consciousness but as an entirely separate place, outside the manifest universe.

The more mystical arms of our Western religions probably see at least three levels of human consciousness: Ego, soul, God. (See Appendix A for comparison of these levels from the various perspectives we've examined.)

Are We Direct Expressions of the One?

Some people who accept the idea that consciousness is everywhere present seem to believe that we are direct expressions of the One, which is the Soul of us all. But I can't conceive of that. There must be more than one level of being.

If we come from and return directly to the Oneness, if our individuality exists only while we are in Earth life, then our personal experience would be the direct experience of the One. So why so much repetition of experiences? Why do so many people starve to death or have their lives cut short by war or genocide? Why would heartache, affliction, addiction, and challenge of every sort be such prevalent experiences? What is the point in the One experiencing all that, over and over again?

The only reason for repetitive experiences is that on some level the experience is not repetitious but serves another purpose. If there are two levels: the collective One—the singularity (the ocean of consciousness)—and the individualized possibilities—the multiplicity that comprise it (the droplets that make up the ocean)—then similar experiences by different souls serve different purposes. Each soul grows through its own extensions' experiences. And the One evolves through the growth of the many.

This is not to say that souls are separate from the One or from each other—fingers are not separate from their hand. It merely means that within the One there are unique, individualized aspects of consciousness, the pieces of the hologram.

Here's an analogy that may help in understanding my view of these levels:

> I put my hand inside a partially blown-up balloon, with the balloon covering my fist and held in place at my wrist. Then, without bursting the balloon, I jut out a finger, so the balloon now seems to have an appendage. I poke out another finger, and another. Outside the balloon is the stage where the appendages enact plays. I withdraw a finger

(die) and poke it out in another part of the balloon (reincarnate). As the hand and as the finger, I know the experience of each other finger and all appendages. But while I'm an appendage, I don't know the inner experience of other appendages because my view of them is obscured by the balloon, the veil surrounding us; I know only what I observe outside through the haze of my appendage eyes. Each time a finger becomes a new appendage it is a unique individual. It has its own life and varied experiences, gained through interaction with other appendages outside the balloon. The individual ego/intellect of each appendage believes in its separation, because that's all it can see; but all are inseparable in Reality. If the balloon were to burst, the hand would be bared to reveal the Oneness of what is inside, as what we will see when we re-awaken to Reality.

In my illustration our fingers are souls, ever conscious of the Oneness of the hand, arm, and body, and of each other. Each finger's tip, with its nail—a small extension of the finger—is the human actor playing its parts in plays. When it juts out the balloon as an appendage, it is a human self enacting its role. Each time a finger becomes an appendage, it's playing a different role, but is still the same fingertip (human self) and the same finger (soul) inside. And, like our physical fingernails, each human extension grows over time with experience.

Outside the balloon is the stage; inside is Reality and the un-manifest possibilities of everything. The balloon is the veil separating Earthly life from our Real life, distorting our perception of life and obscuring our view of Reality.

The fingers inside the balloon, fully aware of all that's going on, together work out the plays and coordinate enactment of them. The hand is a soul group, part of a greater whole that is ever conscious of that Reality.

A Continuum

Changes in vibration frequencies create our material experience. The energy of light, for example, vibrates faster than the energy of matter. So, as conscious souls, we slowed the vibration rate of our own being to create things material. The slower the vibrations are, the more solid things appear. This means there's another continuum: a range of vibrating levels exists between the obviously material and the never-seen.

Within human life, too, there's yet another continuum, as numerous levels of consciousness, from the lowest vibration levels to the highest.

These are neither qualitative nor quantitative; it's simply that, at the lower levels of consciousness it's nearly impossible to relate to anything at a higher level. As we become what some call "more enlightened," we raise our vibrations ever higher, gradually consciously awakening to more and more of our consciousness.

Where we are in the continuum in each moment is determined by our beliefs, intentions, and attitudes within our scenario. Some of us have deliberately become more enlightened than others have, so are better able to know and be consciousness. If you saw the movie, *What the Bleep Do We Know!?* you may remember that Native Americans weren't able to see the Spanish sailing ship because such a thing was not in their conscious awareness. Only after a native shaman observed its effect on the water, deduced its presence, and conveyed its reality to the other natives, did they also become aware of the ship. That shaman symbolically raised the other natives' consciousness to a higher level, enabling them to see the previously unseen.

The materialists, both orthodox scientists and religious fundamentalists, are currently at a level of consciousness from which they are unable to see the larger, more expansive, more holistic, spiritual picture. This in no way makes them less than those at a higher-vibrating level. They are pursuing other experiences, and are also helping the rest of us in our experiences, helping us all define our spirituality and discover our own level of consciousness.

Do Other Beings Have Consciousness?

Eastern traditions teach that only in a human life can beings achieve awakening, because awakening requires a merging of the physical and the nonphysical, and only humans have both consciousness and a physical body. Beings in animal and other physical forms cannot awaken, because although they have bodies, unlike humans, they don't possess consciousness. Likewise, angels can't awaken because, although they have consciousness, they don't have the requisite human bodies.[461]

I agree that awakening requires a physical/nonphysical merging, but I completely disagree that only humans have consciousness.

Many people believe it's consciousness that makes us different from and "more capable" than other animals. But, are we really the only beings aware of ourselves and our surroundings?

Throughout history animals have rescued both people and other animals from danger, some at great peril, even harm, to themselves. Don't such activities show greater awareness of the circumstances than science, religion, philosophy, and some Metas give animals credit for? I've heard of dolphins surrounding a swimmer until sharks moved away. And, when a child fell into a gorilla cage at a zoo, one of the gorillas picked him up and, protecting him from the other curious gorillas, took him to the back of the cage, where a handler was entering through a door. That gorilla handed over the child, leaving no doubt for observers that it was fully aware of the situation. You may have other stories.

There's another way of looking at all this. Consider the possibility that all other Earth creatures may be less material than humans, vibrating at higher frequencies. That's perhaps why cats and dogs, for example, are said to live seven years for every one of ours; they may vibrate seven times faster. It may also be why animal senses are sharper than ours, and why many are able to see colors and hear tones beyond our perception. Other life forms aren't saddled with intellect and can function from awareness and the pure intelligence we call consciousness.

They may all know exactly what's going on in this theater we call Earth, and are enacting their parts to help us in our experiences and growth, while enjoying other aspects of Earth life themselves. Other life forms with whom we share this Earth may observe us humans and scoff, thinking, "How primitively ignorant, how destructive!" Bees, who build beautiful, complex hives and sustain all life by spreading pollen and making nutritious and tasty honey, might be such advanced beings. Ants, who build extensive cities, might be more sophisticated than we can imagine. Cows, sheep, and horses, reposing in meadows, socializing with their families and friends, may be thinking far higher thoughts than our limited intellects can realize. They may be enjoying spiritual art and music we humans can't see or hear in our current state.

Most of us can't conceive such possibilities, because we believe in materialism, based on either the Genesis story of creation or the Darwinian theories of evolution. In either case, no other life forms could possibly be more advanced than we, or even equally so. According to both, we humans are the acme of life on Earth.

Stepping outside those stories and accepting intuition from my soul-Self, I'd say we humans intentionally replaced native intelligence with intellect, thus distinguishing us from all other beings, making us human.

It's not that we have consciousness and other animals don't, it's that we are the only ones who took on intellect and, in the process, hid our spirituality and natural intelligence. We are the only beings who are asleep, so to speak, so the only ones who need to awaken. The others are still awake, never having taken on intellect. We have to awaken in physicality because it's only in this form that we are asleep.

We are awakening to our spirituality, merging the physical and the nonphysical of our being. We didn't take away our native intelligence, but deliberately, temporarily covered it with intellect, and hid our extrasensory abilities and the knowledge of our spirituality.

If everything is consciousness, everything is both alive and intelligent, including the seemingly inanimate. All aspects of reality are ever consciousness, ever aware. Other life forms communicate through mental telepathy, sensing feelings, and reading auras, and most of us humans can't converse with them—but that's our problem, not theirs, although they probably wish we could. That doesn't make us less than others, nor does our intellect make us superior to others.

We use different tools to serve different purposes in our experience of Earth life.

Viewing consciousness as something only we humans have acquired denies Oneness, and causes disregard for the wellbeing of other forms of life. By realizing our interconnected Oneness, we can see all humans and all other life as equals. This has to be basic to our individual daily life for us to genuinely express love and compassion for all life. And, we need to be love and compassion to enable a better, peaceful world, with wellbeing for all life. We need to take to heart the fact that we all—everything—share the same One consciousness, the One, the hologram of which we each are a piece.

We are that consciousness. *There is nothing else.*

Monism

If consciousness is the only thing that exists, there is no dualism (other than the positive/negative dualism we use in Earth life). Pure consciousness can surely interact with what only appears to be material, that is, consciousness slowing its vibratory rate to create form. So my belief system, based on consciousness as God and therefore as everything, is monistic, not dualistic.

And, although my philosophy sees each of us as God, it is not polytheistic. I see us not as many different god-beings, but as a multitude of individualized expressions, emanations, or faces, of the One: God. My belief system is a form of monistic idealism in which there is no materiality; everything is spirit; spirit and consciousness are the same One

My beliefs are "pantheistic": all is God; or, maybe more specifically, my beliefs are what Fritz Ridenour refers to as "pantheistic monism," in which "all is one, one is all, and all is God," a concept which he says biblical Christians oppose.[462]

Comments & Questions on My Personal Belief System

I realize some aspects of my belief system are hard for others to accept. I don't intend to try to convince anyone that my truths are right for them or are the only correct ones. They are true and right for me, based on my exploration and experience, but not necessarily for anyone else based on theirs. The philosophy I offer here satisfactorily answers all of my questions and provides me a wonderful sense of this life. It doesn't have to do the same for anyone else. Each of us has to find our own truths and set our individual belief system.

There is no one path to awakening. I believe, though, that we're all headed in the same direction. Oneness, as consciousness, spirit, and love, is what we all will find we truly are. Call us God, if you want, or, if you prefer: The Universe, Kosmos, or the Ground of Being.

I hope that in expressing my view of life I've given you some things to think about which help you in solidifying your own philosophy of life. I want so much for you to enjoy the comfort of knowing truths that in fact set you free from the worries and fears of this life, as I have—not necessarily the same truths, but ones you can call your own.

My philosophy can be seen as a reflection of perennial wisdom, although I formed it through intuition, before reading most of the others' views presented here. All wisdom is available to anyone ready to receive it, asking for it, and willing to commit to furthering humanity's return to spirituality. This is the meaning for me of "Ask and you shall receive."

We are on the upward arc of our circular journey through the human experience. We are shifting our consciousness, waking up.

[452] Phipps, Carter, "Consciousness Rising," *What Is Enlightenment?* May-July 2004. Lennox, MA.
[453] Dossey, Larry, *The Power of Premonition, how knowing the future can shape our lives,* New York: Dutton, Penguin Group, Inc. 2009
[454] Ibid. quoting John Eccles and Karl Popper.
[455] Ibid.
[456] Ibid. quoting Carl Sagan.
[457] Ibid. quoting Francis Crick.
[458] Nelson, Roger, "The Global Consciousness Project - An Update," *The Noetic Post,* Fall/Winter 2010. Petaluma, CA: Institute of Noetic Sciences.
[459] Dyson, Freeman quoted in Larry Dossey's *The Power of Premonition, how knowing the future can shape our lives*, New York: Dutton, Penguin Group, Inc. 2009.
[460] Dossey, Larry, *The Power of Premonition, how knowing the future can shape our lives.* New York: Dutton, Penguin Group, Inc. 2009
[461] Wilber, Ken, *Kosmic Consciousness*, an audio presentation. Boulder, CO: Sounds True, 2004.
[462] Ridenour, Fritz, *So What's The Difference?* Ventura, CA: Regal Books from Gospel Light, 2001.

PART SIX: WHAT WE DO NOW

How We Get From the Outer to the Inner

You must be the change you wish to see in the world.
~ Mohandas K. Gandhi

Our Destiny

This final part is a recap. Its job is to help us pull all that we've covered together to get us to where we want to be.

Through this book, we've learned that our culture's prevailing destructive worldview is the result of outmoded and faulty belief systems, and that to the extent our personal belief system is materialist we need to change it to enable our shift in consciousness. We've seen that we *can* change our world conditions and resolve our problems by individually shifting our consciousness and working together as higher-level beings to create a new culture. We see that we are all, everything, One; that we are eternal spirit beings enjoying physical human existence on Earth. We've seen that all beings are interconnected, interdependent, entangled through a single consciousness. And we've learned that it is consciousness, slowed to manifest our material world and everything in it, that we can now think of as God, with ourselves as individualized extensions.

We are on the up-slope arc of the circle that will complete the cycle of human experience in which we have interacted with materiality from its level, as separate beings. We are now moving from a mode of living based on our outer material facade—in which we think of our inner self as merely part of the outer materiality—to one of spirituality—in which we know that our outer self is an important part of our inner being.

Our new mode of living will be based on knowing that our outer shell is not truly material nor truly real, but a modified spiritual vehicle for the real spiritual inner self to use through the experience of being human.

This isn't saying the old mode was "wrong" and the new one "right." Both are "perfect" in their time. We're merely shifting from one to the other. We're beginning to recognize our higher vibrating soul-Self and discern what's real and what's illusion. We're waking up.

It's time for more of us to commit to raising our consciousness to a higher level and then to help the rest of humanity do likewise. It's our destiny to return to the spirituality from which we began this journey called human life eons ago.

We didn't all begin our devolution from spirituality to materiality at the same time, but did so in sequential groups. That means we will also awaken in sequential groups until all of humanity has awakened. This process has been underway for decades and will continue on for many more decades. But, the progress of the first groups will facilitate the process for the following groups.

What's needed to bring all of this about is not terribly difficult, nor will it necessarily take a lot of effort or a long time. It's simply a matter of taking each step as it presents itself.

The first step is acceptance: acceptance of the necessity for change; acceptance that improving our world conditions and resolving our world problems is possible; acceptance that it's up to each of us, individually, our personal responsibility, to bring about the shift in consciousness; acceptance of the spiritual as real, actually more real than the material and this existence; acceptance of the Oneness of everything; acceptance that each of us is a part of the One, God, that you are God.

Once you have truly accepted these, you will not only be ready to shift but will find you have shifted. It's acceptance that causes the shift in consciousness. So think on these things and gauge your level of acceptance.

We don't really have a choice. At some point, each of us will accept all this, because it's our destiny to do so, to make this shift. We can't remain materialist forever. We are truly spiritual beings, and each of us will remember that fact, and probably without conscious effort. Our soul *will* get through to us, perhaps when we least expect it.

Shifting Our Beliefs and Behavior

Introduction

Of the great variety of life forms, only humans—by design and for a purpose—have been ignorant of our Oneness and our true symbiotic nature. We've created our own struggles, thinking we have to fight with power and control to survive, then we imposed that view on all life, thinking that life everywhere must exist under the same rules of behavior.

But it doesn't. Once we get past that conditioning, and open our eyes to other possibilities, we can see that life forms other than ours are cooperative—as more and more scientists are beginning to document. Our beliefs must change so we can make possible a unified, cooperative environment that includes us humans.

Cooperation and Unity or Competition and Division?

A major function of nature is to serve as our teacher and help us reflect its qualities in our own behavior. To Darwinists, all life on Earth is in competition for a limited food supply, so selfishness is natural—and our behavior has reflected that teaching. But to noetic scientists life on Earth is a cooperative venture shared by all. Bruce Lipton says: "Instead of invoking competition as a means of survival, the new view of nature is one driven by cooperation among species living in harmony with their physical environment."[463]

We can see this and learn so much by observing nature with our hearts and souls—our true consciousness—and by seeing everything as part of the same consciousness, not separate, but integral with us. Despite the prevalent Darwinistic view, we can see that cooperation and altruism are natural behaviors in all Earthly life, and sometimes even in us. Now our behavior must reflect this new understanding.

We live in a finely tuned ecosystem, where all other life forms interact in full cooperation and harmony—and so do we, on a higher level of consciousness. All forms live harmoniously together as one to create the whole of Earth life and to help each other experience this wonderful material existence. Other creatures help us in our experience. And we unconsciously help them in theirs, as unpleasant as it too often is for them. Because of our materialist beliefs, we humans don't know how to consciously cooperate with our fellow Earth inhabitants; instead, we exploit and abuse them.

Animals voluntarily provide our food, but instead of thanks, they get inhumane treatment from us. Fortunately, they don't really mind, as long as we learn something about ourselves from hurting them.

The food chain, which has larger animals, sea life, and birds preying on smaller ones, is cooperative. Often it's the unhealthy one that gets picked for food. And even when it's not, the one chosen volunteers on some level to provide sustenance in exchange for a ticket "home."

Death of one creature provides food for others, and other organic death produces loam that enables plants and insects to thrive. What we see as death is really a change in dimensional environment for the spirit being leaving Earth life; there's no real death. Besides, while some wild animal, fish, or bird ravaging its prey may be horrifying for us to watch, that deployment of the food chain is essential to maintaining a sustainable creature population.

War, disease, famine, and other devastating events are intended to do the same for our human population, but seem to be in a losing battle. Natural disasters are increasing and becoming more destructive, possibly to help reduce our human population while helping us raise our consciousness. As is also true of any pandemic.

Materialists have given us a false picture of life that we have allowed to dictate our social interactions and values, our laws, politics, and economics. Yet, while we wanted that picture to help us in our experiential growth, we no longer need to see life that way.

It's time to awaken to a new life paradigm, one that expresses unity, cooperation, and harmony among all Earth inhabitants, including humans. It's time to create a new picture, or remember a very ancient and more accurate picture of life on Earth that will enable new belief systems and worldviews. It's time for us humans to purposely join the other life forms in cooperative, harmonious living, as part of the shift in consciousness and transition to our new culture.

With quantum and noetic sciences demonstrating that ancient wisdom is relevant to the scientific view of life, we can see that a new direction is developing and a shift in consciousness is underway. We can see that cooperative behavior by us would be more productive and beneficial than continuing the competitive and conflict-oriented way of living. We can see that separation leads to competition, which leads to conflict, and is unnecessary. Using Mahatma Gandhi's directive to be the change we want to see in our world, Indian philosopher Jai Krishnamurti, says that it doesn't work to say "I'm going to become non-violent" to end violence; "going to" implies time, and in becoming, one is projecting from a place of violence. To end violence, we must *be* nonviolent. To end disorder, we must be order. To end conflict, we must be unified, for "where there is division there must be conflict.[464]

Identifying the dichotomy of materialism and spirituality, rather than adding to division as it may seem, reflects a shift in consciousness from a mode of living involving separation and divisive competition to one of unity and cooperation, both perfect in their time. I've highlighted these differences to identify what we need to change so we can individually enjoy the shift taking place in us collectively. When we realize the dualism in our thinking, we can begin to release it and experience the unity of the monistic One that is our destiny.

December Solstice 2012: Not the End But a Shift

The Mayan long count calendar completed its cycles on December 21, 2012. Produced over a thousand years ago, this calendar describes the interactions of the sun, the moon, the planets, certain stars, and Earth's cycles for every day of what some people believe is the past 5,135 years—which they see as the period of human history defined by the formation of cities and empires and the use of writing around the world.

Some people relate the calendar's ending to the end of the world, based on predicted earth changes and a possible polar shift.

I believe it signifies the end of a way of life on Earth as we have known it, the end of the materialist segment of humanity's existence.

The December solstice of 2012 was a point in Earth's process when our planet's axis was tilted in a particular direction while the sun was aligned with the center of the Milky Way galaxy, creating what is for us a once-every-26,000-years window of opportunity. At the same time, Earth's magnetic field was at its weakest in a very long time; and historically, when that field is weak the greatest changes on the planet occur.[465] The changes we experience can be physical or they can mean a leap in our collective consciousness. So, on that date, the Kosmos extended an opportunity to choose for ourselves before choosing for us.

The Mayan calendar is circular, reflecting the true nature of life. It chronicles the evolution of human consciousness through the physical cycles of our development on Earth. As we grow ever more conscious of our spirituality and our unity, we conclude our primarily material evolution. That's when the calendar ends and we are ready for a new spiritual segment of our journey.

P. M. H. Atwater writes of Mayan worlds or, as they call them "suns," that each end in catastrophe, which is recognized as necessary for new forms and new growth to emerge. The "death of the old, birth of the new... ensuring... not only a fresh start but a world better than the one before." [466]

She adds that Kabbalah, Hindu, and Hopi traditions all use time keeping eerily similar to that of the Mayans, and all "predict the fifth world as soon to come." [467] Most sacred traditions report this "galactic alignment," and our forebears realized that "the human family was no accident upon this Earth, that there was a plan created by a source above and beyond things visible and invisible."[468] Rather than depicting doomsday, Atwater says, the Mayan calendar "illustrates a gateway we will cross through—like a time-space portal into new ways of living, new worlds of opportunity."[469]

The Shift

What is this Shift? It's a change in our attitudes and behavior. In the compilation of studies described in *Living Deeply, the Art and Science of Transformation in Everyday Life* researchers under the direction of Marilyn Schlitz at the Institute of Noetic Sciences say it is

> a transformation that... dramatically and permanently changes the person's worldview to one of being more loving, kind, compassionate,

altruistic, connected to others, and dedicated toward creating a more just, sustainable, and peaceful world for all.[470]

Spiritual teacher Owen Waters says "The Shift is the awakening of humanity's heart."[471]

Part of the Shift is realizing that everything is one interconnected consciousness. From that comes a change in our way of being to heart-based kindness, cooperation, trust, and loving nonjudgmental acceptance. With a shift in our consciousness, our outer reality reflects, not our intellectual belief system, but our spiritual inner being.

As a result of the Shift we will seek to ensure wellbeing, comfort, and dignity for every Earthly entity. While recognizing our Oneness, we will appreciate the diversity in all life and among human cultures. Feminine energy will once again take its place in our consciousness to balance the masculine and restore our reverence for nature. This shift is part of our circular evolution in which we are revolving back to a new level of the spirituality with which we began this journey.

Balancing Our Energy and Restoring Our Relationship with Nature

We were originally born into an energy state that was balanced between the masculine and feminine. But experiencing from that state could not give us all the contrasts we wanted to help us know ourselves and our Reality. Had we chosen a feminine imbalance, all of humanity might be like the fictional Stepford wives, compliant and bland, accepting whatever happens, caught up in weakness and an inability to act or make decisions.

By contrast, the masculine energy state that the Chinese and Japanese call *yang*, which has dominated the Western world for over 3,000 years, has been active, interesting, and productive.

As spirit-beings, we want the balance of both masculine and feminine energies, which supports the pleasant world conditions and happier individual emotional states that we know are possible. Therefore, in the absence of balance in the Western world, this generation of spirit beings has chosen intense low-frequency experiences to help us move in that direction.

But we've nearly completed that phase of our growth and it's all about to change. When we originally created the unbalanced condition, we limited its duration, and now it's coming to its planned end. Our experiences throughout these past millennia have brought us purposefully to this point. We are ready to move on.

In *The Journey Beyond Enlightenment*, spiritual teacher Stewart Wilde says that Gaia (one of the Greek names for Earth) is an evolving spirit like us, and that rebalancing Gaia's energy through rebirth of the feminine principle "is in the master plan...." He says that the dominance of the masculine energy is nearing its end and calls on us to embrace the feminine and join the plan.[472]

Restored reverence for nature is also part of the feminine and of spirituality, and will return naturally as we accept more of both; it will add immeasurably to a glorious future for all life on Earth.

Saying that everything in and about life is relationship, Krishnamurti tells us: "If you lose relationship with nature, you lose relationship with man."[473] Once we realize our Oneness and begin to re-balance our energy, we will restore a relationship with nature, and automatically improve our human relationships. We will realize that life on Earth can be shared in cooperation and love and be enjoyed by all life in joint participation and fullness.

Will Our Shift be Forced or Voluntary?

Ancient Mediterranean cultures believed that the total destruction end-time of humanity and Earth, with a divine judgment-day, were immanent, and many based their religions on finding salvation from the agony of such a time. We call their writings "apocalyptic" because they "raise the veil" of people's awareness, which is the meaning of the Greek word, *apocalypsis*.

The Hebrew prophet Isaiah wrote of an Armageddon-type event but he also wrote of another kind of change, one of consciousness. By offering us both prophecies, he implied we have a choice. We can choose to continue destructive ways and end in utter annihilation, or we can choose a new route toward spiritual consciousness. Humanity, today, is at that crossroads.

All sorts of aberrations of nature are occurring, with natural disasters increasing in number and severity—the chaos that always comes before creation of the new. We can let those devastating earth changes drastically reduce our numbers until remaining survivors awaken to their destiny; or we can choose to actively participate in a spiritual renaissance and its associated shift in consciousness.

The Kosmos won't let us completely self-destruct; annihilation is not our destiny; a shift in consciousness is. We are to become enlightened, and need to do so only in physical form. Our transformation *will* occur; it's only a matter of how and when. Our choice is not whether to make the shift, but whether to do it ourselves or to require the Kosmos to bring us to it—to do whatever it takes to get us to change. If we shift on our own, disasters will no longer be needed. It's up to us individually and collectively to make the shift.

The whole issue of global climate change—both natural and manmade aspects—is an example of higher-level planning to help us see the larger picture and to realize we are all interconnected and interdependent. It's part of the efforts of the Kosmos to get our attention and to instigate our shift in consciousness, first individually, then collectively. Other disasters serve the same purpose (including the recent pandemic). Through horror, anguish, and compassion, they help us raise our consciousness to ever higher levels. As we ponder our choices, destruction and death will continue, prodding us; so the longer it takes for us to choose, the more devastation, death, and chaos we'll see. Some of us may have to lose everything we value and be brought to the depths of despair before we allow ourselves to consider changing. All of us will shift, eventually.

Moving to a Parallel Universe

I see the two totally different experiences prophesied by Isaiah—the self-destructive, material reality manifest to our senses and the heart-based, spiritual reality that we experience beyond those senses through higher consciousness—as in a sense two parallel universes, both existing here on Earth. All of us oscillate between them all the time, moving from our unmanifest spirituality to the manifest reality of Earth and back again to the unmanifest.

Some of us are already focusing ever more of our attention toward the more spiritual experience, spending more of our time and energy in an alternative universe which is very real, but not to our normal senses. When we're ready, we'll shift our awareness from the material fully to the spiritual, from the manifest to the presently unmanifest. The unmanifest is very real, maybe even more so than the world of the material; it's just vibrating at higher frequencies and so seems unmanifest from the lower levels of our normal senses. As we raise our consciousness we spend more time in that universe.

When ready, we each will make the quantum leap and be fully and permanently in the new universe, observing and manifesting it to enjoy at a new level.

In this model, the old reality will continue on for those not yet ready to shift, with world conditions worsening, greed the driving energy, and global warming and natural disasters increasing and becoming more severe. Eventually materialists, too, will tire of those conditions and begin shifting. All of humanity *will* ultimately make that quantum leap into a new world, but still here on Earth; the shift is in our awareness, not physicality—from one parallel reality to another.

How does this shift and parallel universe notion affect those who have died? They are already home in that spiritual reality; and just because their actor selves were enacting roles steeped in materialism or preshift ignorance doesn't mean that's what's happening where they are now. That was only their self-chosen posture for the experiences of their play of life. If they choose future reincarnations they will choose whatever physical reality and scenario they wish to experience. In Reality, they know what it's all about and can do or be anything they want.

You may be concerned that in making the shift into the new universe, you will be leaving behind your loved ones who are stuck in materialism. But that's not the case; you aren't going anywhere; there's nowhere else to go; everything is occurring right here, right now. That parallel universe is not a physical place; it's in consciousness, in awareness. As you shift you are expanding your awareness to know things others can't yet see. And, from your new vantage point you can better help others toward the shift. Besides, we are evolving in groups and our loved ones are in our same group, so those loved ones who seem stuck in materiality are probably more ready to shift than either you or they realize—and your hesitancy may be holding them back.

A Spiritual Renaissance

The shift, earnestly under way in the mid 1960s, proceeds with ever-increasing fervor, progressing quietly. No one is directing it, or at least no human is. Many of us have already made the shift. Some of us are writing books, encouraging greater compassion, holism, and spirituality, which many others are reading. Before the pandemic, people the world over participated in conferences to further spirituality, world peace, environmental welfare, and recognition of the interconnected unity of our body, mind, and spirit, and each of us to the Whole. Small community groups met regularly to share their spiritual experiences with likeminded people. The energy put into our collective consciousness by such gatherings was filled with love, compassion, and harmony. These conditions will be even stronger after and a result of the pandemic, and we'll be spending more of our time and energy in the new universe. Humanity is changing from within. We *are* evolving, naturally.

Much more than most of us realize is going on right now to help us reclaim our spiritual roots, move from separation and competition to unity and cooperation, and balance our energy.

We're not transcending life on Earth; we are shifting from an outmoded way of life into, or rather we are remembering, a long-hidden awareness. We are waking up, coming full circle.

Our vibrations are increasing, as we can tell by the way time is speeding up. Our days go by more quickly and our year flies by. Summer is here before we realize spring has begun and suddenly the winter holidays are upon us. This is no illusion; our vibrations are, in fact, increasing and we are rising ever higher with them. The faster our vibrations, the more we can know of higher levels and dimensions, other parallel universes. The higher we rise individually, the closer we come to attunement with our soul-Self and awakening.

And that's what the rest of our Earthly lives will be about. We are returning to the consciously spiritual beings we were initially, only with greatly expanded awareness of possibilities. Soon, we will no longer need to hide our wholeness, our unity, from ourselves. There will be no intermediate level of consciousness, and our souls will be able to experience physicality directly.

This consciousness shift, this attitudinal change, wasn't dramatically different and discernible on December 21, 2012 for most people. It's been taking place in us gradually for decades—for centuries, truly—and most likely, we'll wake up one day several months, years or decades from now and realize the extent of our change, maybe into the parallel universe I described above. We'll look back and see the end of 2012 as when humanity's evolution became clearly discernible.

The wonderful part of this shift is not in its culmination, but in living and observing it, seeing the new reality gradually manifest for everyone. The processes of life are far more enjoyable and important to our growth than any end result. By becoming more consciously aware, we can enjoy every little change we and others around us make. It's an exciting and thrilling time to be experiencing life on Earth, one of hope and joy, in which everyone can participate to the extent we choose.

[463] Lipton, Bruce, "Embracing the Immaterial Universe," *Shift: at the Frontiers of Consciousness*, December 2005-February 2006. Petaluma, CA: Institute of Noetic Sciences.
[464] Krishnamurti, J., *Truth is a Pathless Land*, an audio program. Boulder CO: Sounds True.
[465] Braden, Gregg, "Choice Point 2012, our date with the window of emergence," *The Mystery of 2012: Predictions, Prophecies and Possibilities*. Boulder, CO: Sounds True, 2007.
[466] Atwater, P. M. H., *Beyond the Indigo Children*. Rochester, VT: Bear & Company, 2005.
[467] Ibid.
[468] Ibid.
[469] Ibid.
[470] Schlitz, Marilyn; Mandala, Cassandra; Vieten, Tina; Amorok, *Living Deeply, the Art and Science of Transformation in Everyday Life*. Petaluma, CA: Institute of Noetic Sciences, 2009.
[471] Waters, Owen, *The Shift, the Revolution in Human Consciousness*. Delaware: Infinite Being Publishing, 2006.
[472] Wilde, Stewart, *The Journey Beyond Enlightenment*. Niles, IL: Nightingale Conant audiobooks.
[473] Krishnamurti, J., *Truth is a Pathless Land*, an audio program. Boulder CO: Sounds True.

Wake Up! Shift Your Consciousness

Introduction

When I say "Wake Up!" I mean several things. Wake up to the fact that our culture is destructive and not working well for life on this planet, and it must change. Wake up to the fact that it can change, and that you personally have an important role in that change. Wake up to our Oneness; realize that everything you see and don't see shares in this Oneness and has an equal right to fully enjoy this life. Wake up to your need to know who you truly are, what you are doing here on this stage we call Earth, what the meaning of this life is for you, and what your destiny is; set your life to getting answers, becoming enlightened, and wake up to your own divinity. Finally, wake up to your own Self; make conscious contact with your own higher-vibrating soul-Self, that larger part of you that wants to help you make the shift; get to know your Self and live as the complete One that you truly are.

Although the above are in order of a common developmental pattern, if you were to go straight to the last two steps, you'd soon find you had accomplished the others as well. Once all these steps have been experienced, you can wake up to your need to be part of humanity's evolution to a higher level of consciousness.

It's a natural outcome: once shifted, you will naturally want others to shift too. In Buddhism, this is called "the *bhodisattva* vow." This is not about "helping others;" it's recognizing that they are part of you in consciousness. All of our experiences throughout our human lives have brought each of us to the cusp of this shift, reminding us of our hidden spirituality and giving us tools to assist others—by which we lift our selves even higher. Now it's time to demonstrate the highest in us, and as part of humanity let surface what's highest in us collectively.

As our personal destiny, we each will reach ever higher to realize the Oneness of which we are a vital part. In each next moment we can be an ever higher expression of the God we are.

Change and Transformation

There's a difference between trying to control life and guiding the direction of inevitable change. Change is constant in Earth life, but it doesn't have to happen in a particular way. We guide the change through our intent, letting life flow in that direction. Rather than trying to control the process, we allow it and realize the manifestation of our intent.

To transform the world, we have to want our world to be different, then we have to positively envision and intentionally *be* a new world in which all life is healthy, free, and expressing its highest, cooperative nature. In this, we give our souls freedom to express their highest in material form through us.

Why, if we are always consciousness, do many of us refer to humanity's transformation as a shift in consciousness? What is shifting? Our outward expression of our internal consciousness, our conscious thinking and behavior in our daily lives, are shifting from old, apparently harmful ways to new ways of holism, love, and compassion. We are awakening to ever more of our consciousness. We are spending ever more time in the higher-vibrating yet unmanifest universe, shifting our awareness into that other universe. We are manifesting a new reality.

A New God and A New Spirituality

In Neale Donald Walsch's *Tomorrow's God*, God says humanity needs a "new version of God. A larger version ...not the God of your present understanding." God urges us to expand our "awareness and come to a more complete understanding of who and what God is, and of what is true about Life." God explains: "From your thought springs your reality. From your ideas your future emerges. Thus, your beliefs create your behaviors, and your behaviors create your experience. What you believe, therefore, becomes a most important thing."[474] God adds:

> God is separate from nothing, but is Everywhere Present, the All in All... the Sum Total of Everything that ever was, is now, and ever shall be....
>
> [This truth] is the one element that is missing from most of the world's theologies. Because this message has been missing, humanity has been missing the mark in its attempts to create a world of peace and harmony and happiness, and religions have been missing the point of Life

itself, causing millions of people to be missing the experience of Oneness with the Creator—and with each other. If humanity adopted this Missing Message as its next new truth in religion ... the world could change overnight.[475]

Walsch's God talks also about a new spirituality. He says "It will be the Evolution Revolution. A... 'revolving'... from Oneness to Separation to Oneness again. From Total Consciousness to Unconsciousness to Total Consciousness again."[476]

In *The Human Cycle*, the Hindu philosopher Sri Aurobindo writes:

The coming of a spiritual age must be preceded by the appearance of an increasing number of individuals who are no longer satisfied with the normal intellectual, vital, and physical existence of man, but perceive that a greater evolution is the real goal of humanity and attempt to effect it in themselves, to lead others to it, and to make it the recognized goal of the race. In proportion as they succeed and to the degree to which they carry this evolution, the yet unrealized potentiality which they represent will become an actual possibility of the future.[477]

Each of us has a role to play in our culture's shift. Our energy overlaps like petals in a blossom, and each one who reawakens to their spirituality affects numerous others, who in turn affect others. Once enough of us have accepted our responsibility in the collective shift, we will create the spiritual environment necessary to cause a leap in our culture's consciousness—in effect, creating our new culture.

Fortunately, we don't all have to reach that acceptance for the shift to occur: the effectiveness of a relative few can be phenomenal, in what's called "the hundredth monkey effect." The power of the few with heart-based intentions outweighs the many, exponentially.

As Ken Keyes explains in *The Hundredth Monkey*, the "hundredth monkey effect" arose from a 1950s study of behavior in Japanese monkeys. As some monkeys on one island learned to wash their food (sand-covered sweet potatoes) before eating, their new behavior attracted the attention of others in their group. Soon, many monkeys were washing their food. Suddenly, scientists observed, when the number reached a critical mass (when the hundredth monkey tipped the scale), not only did nearly all of that island's monkeys behave the new way, but monkeys on other islands and the mainland also began washing their food before eating it, without having seen it done by others. [478]

We can intentionally cause this same phenomenon in our human population by focusing our consciousness, our intention, in a uniform direction—for instance, toward Oneness, toward Love. We don't just let love happen; we actively love everyone and everything in a nonjudgmentally accepting way. We don't have to be obvious and don't have to be organized. We just each individually need to be dedicated and sincere in our intent.

As more and more evidence demonstrates, a relative few of us can spread love, spirituality, and compassion around the world, and so encourage a global shift in consciousness. So be love! As we each personally shift our consciousness, we add our weight to the amassing energy of like consciousness.

We don't have to and won't all shift at once. Since we are evolving toward this, our destiny, in groups, the number of "monkeys" necessary to tip the scales of the first wave of the shift isn't really very large at all. Then, before we know it we will have reached the critical mass when the totality of humanity's consciousness can collectively shift.

We Won't All Shift at Once

Not all of humanity is ready to change their belief system or their ways of facing life. Not all are ready for the concept of God as One, or to accept that they are God, or for the individual introspection of communion or gnosis. Only a relatively small percentage is ready now.

People in non-industrialized countries, where few are educated in either their own indigenous ways or in Western spirituality, and most live with poverty, disease, and death as constants, have needs they won't know can be met by spirituality. Not until the rest of us transform our consciousness and move into the mode of living fostered by the concept of Oneness, can we help those people end starvation and disease and a new spirituality will be available as a path for them.

This holds true also for inner-city people everywhere, who also live with poverty and death as constants. They have no way of relating to the concept of a higher level of consciousness, much less that we all are God. These are some of the hoards of humanity I call Earth Angels, who by their obvious plight help the rest of us raise our consciousness.

People stuck in the old ways of materialism, militarism, greed, separation, and self-absorption are represented by Amanda in the film *What the Bleep Do We Know!?*, who, like the Native Americans, couldn't see, among other things, a sailing ship because it wasn't in her level of consciousness. Such people are in Gary Zukav's "five-sensory" mode of behavior, unaware of the holism and compassion of "multi-sensory" spirituality. Spiritual concepts are not part of their reality, because they are not yet at a level of consciousness where they can use them.

Those committed to materialist religion will be slow to shift, their leaders fighting it with their very being, calling it Satanic. One by one, though, they, too, will transform, as more and more see God as love that is everywhere present, leaving no room for the evil they've been taught to fear.

Atheistic orthodox scientists will be slow to shift. They won't easily accept any view of God or spirituality. Maybe they will eventually acknowledge the evidence denied by their theories and realize that consciousness, not matter, is the ground of being.

As our "monkey" population grows and shows the love and compassion of spirituality, materialists of all walks of life will begin to see the light and reach out to it. Their higher Selves will help them do so when they, too, are no longer needed in the role they are currently playing for the benefit of the rest of us.

What about the people who want to maintain the status quo, for fear of jeopardizing their perceived power and wealth, what they consider their security? They are people who prioritize their wants and pleasures above the needs of other cultures and other species; they think war is sometimes necessary; they believe (what they call "understand") that the costs of curtailing pollution or selectively cutting our forests are too high to do practically; they want consumers to buy ever more of their technological goodies, without concern for their toxic waste or their products' ultimate disposal; they want to keep people dependent and buying their prescription drugs rather than provide for good health naturally; they think global warming is an environmentalist fantasy, and not something to which we contribute; they think it's more important to drill for a small amount of oil in wilderness areas and oceans than to protect the species who live there; they think their corporation's bottom line is more important than allowing for new inventions which run on less energy and new types of energy. These people will shift, but slowly. If we want to reach them, we have to lovingly expand their thinking into new ways and priorities, based, not in separation and fear, but in love and unity. We need to help them understand the Oneness of us all.

It might help them wake up if the rest of us were to boycott their products or businesses to get their attention. Earth changes may be needed to shock some people into less self-absorbed, more compassionate behavior. As have so many before, they may have to lose everything they think important before they notice and reach for the light.

Each of these groups is awaiting their turn to shift. Each is helping us and the other groups to approach and further our shift. When those of us in this first big wave have made the shift, another group will be ready, then another, until all of humanity is awakening to our spirituality and our Oneness. We all will know ourselves and what to do to make everything right. Then our problems will no longer exist and our world conditions will be what we all want them to be.

The final group to make this shift may have been the group that was the last to devolve, the higher-level beings of Atlantis who were the original deified heroes, the ones who became the gods of the primitive "children" who became the first civilizations.

Those "children" were in the first wave of the devolution process and are probably those of us who either have already shifted or are now ready to shift. We were the first in, so are the first out, so to speak.

Experiencing Intuition

The Aquarian Age of light is one of knowing. This is the meaning of the term, enlightenment. It's time for our enlightenment, when we each go within to gather our own truths. It's time for the deep introspection, to know ourselves, and for the conscious communion with our Selves that the ancient Pagans and Gnostics encouraged.

An ancient legend tells of the gods arguing a long time, trying to agree where best to hide Truth from man:

> Some said, 'We cannot hide it in the mountains, for he would scale vast peaks to find it.' Others said, 'Nor can we bury Truth in the depths of the earth, for he would dig until he discovered it. Nor should we cast Truth to the bottom of the sea, for there, too, he would search it out.' They were in a quandary until the wisest god proposed the answer: 'We will hide Truth within man, himself. He will never think of looking there.'

Deep inside, we already know all truths. That's why we ask questions; we are beginning to remember. Why do we seek enlightenment in our journey toward awakening? We want to know whether we are physical beings or the eternal spirit beings we think we might be. We want to know what our life is about, why there's so much suffering and evil. We want to know we aren't as separate as we seem. We need to awaken. Our souls are prodding us to question.

Gary Zukav says: "As our personality becomes multi-sensory [our soul's] intuitions—its hunches and subtle feelings—become important to it." He elaborates:

> [W]hen the energy of the soul is recognized... and valued, it begins to infuse the life of the personality. When the personality comes fully to serve the energy of its soul, that is authentic empowerment.... Every experience that you have and will have upon the Earth encourages the alignment of your personality with your soul.
>
> Every circumstance and situation gives you the opportunity to choose this path, to allow your soul to shine through you.[479]

There is no single path to awakening. Some find meditation satisfying; others prefer a life of devotion and service. Some need the dogma, rites, and rituals of organized religion, whether fundamentalist, mainstream, or mystic. Others are directed on their path through the awe-inspiring beauty and orderly perfection of the physical cosmos and its workings seen through scientific study. Many of us find enlightenment through communion with our "voice within" most effective and satisfying.

True Communion

Communion, I think, is the ancient Gnostic way of going within to know the soul-Self and thereby know God. It assumes there is something in spirit with which we can communicate and from which we can gain wisdom. Its goal is to establish a conscious link between our little, thinking self, and that higher intelligence that will help us better understand our life. It's a case of consciously filling the mind and heart with the light that is God, a light of love and truth that is always within, awaiting our acceptance. Ralph Waldo Emerson said of it:

> The soul's communication of truth is the highest event in nature... and the communication is an influx of the Divine Mind into our mind.... Every moment when the individual feels invaded by it is memorable.[480]

Communion can also soothe and heal. It aligns us with our soul-Self, our "still small voice within."

Much of the wisdom we get from our ancient ancestors instructs us to go within to be enlightened, and it's time we paid attention. We each need to go within, and find God and truth.

While there are several paths to awakening, the enlightenment path is the most direct and the one most needed now. Your soul is waiting, ready, eager for you to make the necessary commitment.

Do you know you are a unique, eternal spirit being, yet not separate from the All? Do you know that you are consciousness and the mind of God? Are you aware that as a piece of the quantum hologram you are God, the One?

If you know these things you have only to live them. But if you don't believe these or aren't certain, you have work to do. Go within, and learn of them. If you don't already commune with your soul, or voice within (however you think of it), and want to, here is a fairly easy way to start the communion process that I found helpful:

(1) Sit quietly with eyes closed, and take a few deep, relaxing breaths. Get as relaxed and quiet as possible, through meditation if you want. Focus your attention in your heart center or in your third eye, your divinity.

(2) Once quiet and relaxed, by thinking ask your inner voice to help you by answering yes or no to your questions. Specifically say you want your head to nod up and down for "yes" and to shake from side to side for "no." Ask a question, phrasing it to be answered yes or no.

(3) Then sit quietly, and be aware of any movement with your head; it may be only an internal sense of nodding or shaking. Ask another question, or verify the answer you got by repeating it back and asking if it's correct. The more often you do this, the easier it will be to discern answers.

(4) Once you're comfortable with the process, ask for a word which will usually be the first one that pops into your head. Verify if that was the word sent, then ponder it. Look it up in the dictionary. Think about how and why it would be important to you, for there's a message for you in each such word. This can lead to phrases, then sentences and, finally, full communion.

For detailed steps to inner communication, see my website, at www.OurJourneytoAwakening.com.

Don't leave it as merely yes or no to your questions or positive or negative to your feelings; with that you have to come up with the questions or conditions. If what you want is wisdom and a solid conscious connection with your soul within, you need more than yes or no answers; you need truths from higher intelligence, not merely whatever your intellect can think up to question.

Our souls constantly communicate with and guide us through a process we call intuition. We are becoming ever more aware of them as they prod us from within toward greater spirituality. We each individually reach a point in our lives when we need to know. We begin asking the big questions, and have to pursue answers, somehow knowing they are ours to find.

You, too, can have conversations with God. Some people have a keen sense of intuition, and just seem to know, without going through questions and answers.

What's called "Automatic writing" works well for some to tap into this deeper knowing. With a conscious intention to receive answers from the higher Self, pick up a pen or pencil and allow it to write whatever letters or words enter your mind. Some people find using their non-dominant hand to write with assists the process. Alternatively, you can allow your fingers on the keyboard to type randomly until letters, words, or phrases start flowing through you.

While learning communion, it's important to get to know your thinking mind, or "little self" and its way of operating. The better you know the way your intellect functions (thinks and reacts), the better able you are to discern when your higher Self, rather than your intellect, speaks to you.

Your intellect, limited to this material existence, may be relatively knowledgeable but is not particularly wise and tends to be self-serving. If you don't want to mistake advice of your intellect for wisdom from your all-knowing Self, you have to distinguish one from the other. Only by knowing your self (intellect) can you know your real, soul-Self. As you proceed on this path discernment will come more easily. Your soul-Self will help you. But you have to personally want to become more enlightened and want your Self's help. You have to "knock," then your Self will make it very clear with whom you are communing, and open the door wide.

Once on this path, you are more aware of your moment-to-moment thoughts and reactions; you learn about yourself and your ways of responding to your interactions and experiences of this life.

This helps you to be less critically judgmental of yourself and others and more compassionate. The more aware you are of your self without judging your thoughts and reactions, the more generally aware you are.

It's fun to watch the self in this process; it's almost like being outside yourself, dispassionately observing. You are more multi-sensory and more attuned to feminine energy, gaining the benefits of balance. You see the cooperative, harmonious unity of life and are empowered from within.

Our inner voice will help us to the extent we let it. Each of us has it, our own spirit guide, our personal God. It gives us what it knows we need and can best learn from. Through communion, it gives us insights in the best way for us to assimilate and use them. Some of us get words, maybe questions and answers in conversations, or in automatic writing. Some get feelings, while others see mind pictures.

For me, it's inner *knowing*: infusion of thought into my mind, which I usually translate into words. Often my Self gives me an experience as a tangible explanation—truly thrilling spiritual experiences. All of it is thrilling.

Were we to actively listen for our inner voice, life would be so much easier and more satisfying. We would be more apt to follow those subtle beneficial hints and inner longings we get but often ignore. Besides, the destiny of each of us in human existence is to reunite with our soul and enable our whole Self to experience human life. The more we commune with our voice within the closer we come to that re-union, awakening our self to our Self.

Sacred Community

Such alternative methods don't have to compete with attending a place of worship. Most of us need a community relationship, and many find the sacred ritual very satisfying. We all want to be able to cope with this life, and both our belief system and the unique things a sacred community can offer help us do that.

The less rigid, more mystic denominations may make integration easier. For Christians, New Thought churches like Centers for Spiritual Living (formerly Religious Science), Unity, and Divine Science are more spiritual than most, as are many Quaker and modern Christian Gnostic meetings. They lean more toward the teachings of Jesus in Christ Consciousness than on worshiping the person of Jesus as the only Son of God. For Jews Kabbalah and for Muslims Sufism are mystic paths. Bahai, Ananda (Self Realization Fellowships) and Eckankar also focus on the spiritual path.

Being the Shift

Some people individually just wake up one day knowing they are different, having made the shift overnight without concerted effort, or even knowledge, on their part. It's startling to them, and irreversible. Their soul-Self decided it was time for them to transform and saw no reason to go through it gradually. John Van Auken sees this as a kind of reincarnation, in which a new part of a person's soul joins their little self in this life.[481] Some people reach the depths of despair and are given a foot-hold to help them climb out to the light. Neale Walsch says this was his experience[482] and IONS researchers report many such experiences.[483] Maybe you, too, shifted this way or will in the near future.

This book is a call to consciously be exactly what we are: spirit beings enjoying physical experience. We are the One experiencing as the many, each of us contributing uniquely to each other and the experience of the One.

What I suggest has little to do with doing. We are so used to doing rather than being, but, again, I'll remind you of the Occam's razor concept: usually the best solution is the simplest one. Proactive seems to be a by-word these days, but we're too active much of the time. It's hard to "hear" the wisdom and guidance of our inner Self when rushing here and there, busily doing. What I'm encouraging is more passive than active, and the only thing we must do is commit to making our own personal shift in consciousness, then helping humanity collectively make the shift will follow naturally.

The spiritual path is a life commitment that is being felt today more than ever, probably because we are nearing that shift in consciousness. Our souls are pushing us. Movements and organizations have emerged to help us in this most important effort: Craig Hamilton's Academy for "Evolutionaries," Amit Goswami's "Quantum Activism," and Barbara Marx Hubbard's Foundation for Conscious Evolution are movements well worth looking into. An internet search would surely unearth many more.

The important thing in this process is that we aren't being enlightened for ourselves alone; we are becoming so for the sake of the whole of humanity. Once we individually have made our shift, our whole being automatically seeks to help all of humanity evolve to the next level. We all have an inner longing to share with fellow humans. We are One, and what we do and accomplish we also want others to do and accomplish. When we shift, we want others to shift, too. People are rising to higher levels and getting unstuck, waking up.

As ever more of us move into that light, humanity gets closer to mass awakening. We are being the quantum observer who will enable all other humans to bring the light into their consciousness. Calling this "Quantum Activism," Goswami says:

> An ordinary activist tries to change the world without making any change in himself or herself; the spiritual activist tries to transform himself or herself, believing that the world will take care of itself. The quantum activist undertakes the journey of personal trans-formation with the transformation of the whole world also in mind.[484]

In this sense, we all are to become quantum activists. We need to honestly, objectively, examine our personal worldview and the beliefs that constitute it. Then, depending on what we find, many of us may need to take the step of actively changing our belief system. Once we've accepted the need for change, here are some steps we each can take:

- Assess your beliefs and worldview to see if they are completely heart based, and if not, work to change them.
- Think, behave, and conduct your life to allow wellbeing and dignity for all Earth's inhabitants; approach all of life with compassion. Be heart-centered!
- Encourage restoration of balance in your energy between the masculine and feminine. Be personally balanced!
- Find yourself some truly spiritual beliefs; have or develop a belief system in which you recognize the spirituality and unity of everyone and everything, seen and unseen, manifest and unmanifest.
- Make a commitment to be enlightened by going within, and devote your life to your awakening;
- Go Within, often! Make conscious intercourse with your Self within a constant in your everyday life.

- Form a group of like-minded thinkers to discuss spirituality and the shift in consciousness.
- When possible and appropriate, encourage others—family, friends, co-workers, religious leaders and congregants—to take these steps.

And, when in a position to do so, encourage:
- corporate officers to conduct their business responsibly and with compassion and to see quality of life for all Earth's inhabitants rather than profit as their bottom line;
- responsible technology, a return to natural organic foods and clothing; responsible use of natural resources, and better, more sustainable, more environmentally friendly energy, any way you can (Be responsible!);
- restoration of our spiritual roots and improved spiritual interpretation of ancient texts and better understanding of their spiritual content and symbols;
- your place of worship to study the wisdom teaching in your sacred book(s) rather than the fantastic, miraculous stories about their heroes;
- secular academia to change its ways of teaching and conducting research to better address subjects holistically through interdisciplinary approaches, with true learning in mind; get funding mechanisms changed to allow new, unconstrained thinking, study, and teaching.

You might also
- Boycott media until they report what's actually happening in our world rather than merely sensationalism.
- Help people everywhere to learn and understand that they, too, are God.
- Encourage others to join together altruistically in harmony and cooperation to create the larger being, the new culture.

Doing these successfully, we can resolve all our national and worldly problems, and more easily than we may think. Remember, it takes only a relative few to change the collective consciousness, and as each of us makes the shift, the process gets ever easier for others.

Be what you want to see in the world!

Whatever it takes, these are exciting times. I eagerly await the shift, but am thoroughly enjoying the journey toward it, being one of the "hundred monkeys." We are about to produce our own next evolutionary step, the greatest yet, into the parallel universe of the 5th world. There is a gloriously beautiful, love-filled future awaiting our choice, our observation, and awareness of it.

---

[474] Walsch, Neale Donald, *Tomorrow's God*. New York: Atria Books, 2004.
[475] Ibid.
[476] Ibid.
[477] "The Writings of Sri Aurobindo" compiled and edited with Introduction and Afterword by Roberty McDermott, *The Essential Aurobindo*. Lindisfarne Books, 1987, 2001.
[478] Keyes, Ken, *The Hundredth Monkey*. Coos Bay, OR: Vision Books, 1982. [editor's note: This is a lovely allegory, but it turns out that behavior was not new to that species of monkey.]
[479] Zukov, Gary, *The Seat of the Soul*. New York, NY: A Fireside Book, by Simon & Schuster, 1990.
[480] Emerson, Ralph W. "The Oversoul", an essay to be found in most collections of his writings, including *Natural Abundance, Ralph Waldo Emerson's Guide to Prosperity*, with a "translation" and summary by Ruth L. Miller. New York: Beyond Words/Atria; 2011.
[481] Van Auken, John, *Edgar Cayce and the Kabbalah*. Virginia Beach, VA: A.R.E. Press, 2010.
[482] Walsch, Neale Donald, *Conversations with God (Vols 1-4)* and *Tomorrow's God*; also www/nealedonaldwalsch.com.
[483] Schlitz, Marilyn; Mandala, Cassandra; Vieten, Tina; Amorok , *Living Deeply, the Art and Science of Transformation in Everyday Life*. Petaluma, CA: Institute of Noetic Sciences, 2009.
[484] Goswami, Amit, *How Quantum Activism Can Save Civilization*. Charlottesville, VA: Hampton Roads Publishing Company, Inc., 2011

Afterword

Everything is perfect as it is, in its time. My criticism of materialist belief systems is not denying their perfection, but is intended to help people see the need for either affirming or changing their beliefs and to help them better understand the shift taking place in our consciousness. Our new ways are not qualitatively "better" than our old ways. Each, both past and present, is what we have chosen as part of our experiential growth and conscious awareness expansion—in its time. When I write words such as "fortunately" or "unfortunately," I do so as a being in the world, responding to it with human emotions and opinions.

It's not my intention to transcend the world. I'm here to experience it fully and to understand it from both a human and a spiritual perspective, with a balance in my life between the two. While we are spirit beings, we are in this physical human life for experiential growth, and all that we experience—the pre-shift materialism, the shift itself, and the post-shift spirituality—adds greatly to our growth.

Everything works out for the best, whether or not we ever recognize it as such. We often won't let ourselves see the good in what appears disastrous. But, given time, we may later look back and realize the great value we gained from those events which, at their time, broke our hearts. In fact, they broke our hearts open: each such experience makes room for something better in the long run, whether a different direction in life and a little awakening or a significant relationship, a special challenge, a different environment, or a stronger character.

In his website newsletter/blog, Neale Donald Walsch writes:

> We have our ups and our downs, our hills and our valleys, our celebrations and our sorrows. What I didn't know as a younger person is that the valleys were necessary in order for the hills to have any meaning. I'm a little older now, and one advantage to having grown older is the added wisdom and increased awareness which has come to me.... Not nearly the number of things that I thought would hurt me—and

perhaps damage me forever—have done any such thing. In fact, a startling number of those "bad things" have turned out, in the end, to have been the greatest gifts. Perhaps more importantly, I've come to see clearly that without any "downs" at all in my life, the "ups" would mean nothing. It is Contrast that creates the Context within which anything at all can be known Experientially....

If Life is presenting you with showers right now, just know, just trust, that there will be flowers. Nothing happens to us by chance, there are no accidents, and there is no such thing as coincidence. Everything proceeds in God's Universe in perfect order.[485]

Everyone and everything in existence are all interconnected and interdependent: all one consciousness. Most of us just don't realize it, don't yet remember it. It's time for us to at least begin to remember and to behave accordingly. When we are aware of our Oneness, we also are aware of the love that is around us and that we truly are. When we put our attention to it, we can be that love, and think love and kindness before we act or speak. Love awaits our awareness of it.

Because all other beings are always consciously aware—never having devolved, never going to sleep—they don't have to awaken. Only we humans have the thrilling experiences of the upward evolutionary process to remember our spirituality and Oneness, reinstate extrasensory abilities and other capabilities natural to us, and reunite consciously with our souls. All other beings, including Earth, eagerly await the day when we can understand and communicate with them and realize what wonderful loved ones they've been to us. They await the day when we no longer abuse them but respect and value them as equals. They look forward to restoration of the interspecies cooperation and creativity that we had before we devolved. Our individual job now is to evolve to a higher level. It is to allow our consciousness to express at its highest in physicality, and in this way to help the whole of humanity make the shift. Some of us are already being the greater compassion of spirituality, and daily ever more are joining us. We're nearing the critical mass when the shift will occur.

Many of us have made the shift to "multi-sensory" beings, and are more intuitive and more heart-centered with more balanced energy. The "new children," who were mentioned above, in the chapter on academia, come into Earth life with a more balanced nature, joining those of us who have already shifted, so a growing portion of humanity is realizing the balanced energy state. Some of us realize love is more powerful than any external possession or control ever could be; and we needn't fear losing it, for we can't. We are being the love we truly are.

As we awaken to the Oneness, we realize how unreal material existence is and at the same time how wonderful it is. We see the perfection in the suffering and "bad" things that have happened to us, and appreciate them for their help in our experiencing human life and in making us who we are. We realize there are no coincidences, no accidents, no victims, no death, no villains, nothing to fear; there is only love, harmony, and cooperation unfolding in new and different ways, and so we seek to express those ourselves. We recognize that the life of all other beings is based on cooperation in harmony with others and the environment, and we seek to live the same way. We seek to ensure well-being, comfort, and dignity for every Earthly inhabitant. We revere all of nature, are more aware, and enjoy more of the beauty and goodness in everything, seeing it with clarity.

Empowered with balanced energy, we're more sensitive to others' feelings and emotions and more compassionate. We are active and creative, but don't unnecessarily harm or exploit any life. We are peaceful inside and out for our world to reflect. We respect and honor all cultures, all belief systems, and others' ways of living this life. We bask in our diversity.

When humanity, generally and collectively, begins to accept a new version of God and build a new spirituality around our Oneness, we can turn our fearful, destructive, and divisive ways into harmonious, heart-based behavior virtually overnight. Once we recognize our interconnected unity and choose that reality, we will make it so and then act accordingly, with love in our hearts for all.

When we replace fear with love, we become empowered from within. It's our individual choice. It's all up to us, each of us, personally.

Our culture is at a crossroads, and will either remain on the same path toward destruction that we've been traveling or choose a new version of a very old path. Our choice is to proceed according to materialist beliefs on a linear path of fear and death or to take a "quantum leap" onto the route of love and life to the conscious knowledge that our ancient ancestors possessed.

In many ways, humanity has progressed substantially in the last few decades, but we are not yet as wise as those from whose wisdom we

Our Old Beliefs Don't Work Anymore

moved away. Those ancients knew so much that many of us are finally now seeking to learn.

While the ancient mythic stories may have been altered through public word-of-mouth transmission or interpretation and publication of their written word, the underlying wisdom is there, hidden in metaphor, symbol, parable, and aphorism. Because humanity is becoming more spiritual and as such more heart-based, we are being allowed to see more and more of the truths of ancient perennial wisdom. As ever more of us make the shift to heart-centered spirituality, more of that wisdom is being more accurately interpreted and made available for understanding.

Although we know some of what the ancients believed, we may have only scratched the surface of their beliefs, and have probably misinterpreted or misunderstood many of the ones we think we know. Interpretation of ancient language when made from a spiritual perspective is very different from that made from the standpoint of materialist religion or conventional science. There is always more than one way of understanding the meaning of nearly any story, or even verse, in all ancient writings. Biblical stories, when seen as metaphor, can paint an entirely different picture from the one seen through literalism. The truths of the ancients must be studied with open minds and hearts; then—and only then—will they reveal what we need to know.

Actually, were we to take seriously and act on the truths we already know, we could have peace and wellbeing throughout our world. In addition to those biblical ones mentioned earlier—"I am that I AM" and "Be still and know that I am God"—here are a few other truths (biblical, Gnostic, or mystic and generally attributed to Jesus) that tell us everything:

- Know yourself;
- know that you and God are One;
- know that you are gods;
- go within to find God;
- the kingdom of God is within you and around you.

Think on these. Learn who you are and know the truth for yourself.

While I want to see our Western culture's worldviews change and believe that replacing materialist beliefs with spiritual ones would be in the best interests of all life on Earth, I also know that beliefs are individual and shouldn't be dictated by anything or anyone outside of the individual. I believe that our destiny as actors in these earthly plays is to awaken to our spirituality and our Oneness. But, it's not my intention to impose my beliefs on anyone else. And I don't think such imposition is needed anyway, for I also believe that eventually every-one will come to a similar conclusion.

Every human will awaken to their spirituality, without undo influence from me or any spiritual teacher. Everyone will come to this realization on their own, with only the help and direction of their own higher-vibrating soul-Self. This is why I encourage going within to commune with the inner, higher vibrating you.

The Mayan and Aztec calendars are circular, like the seasons, with the sun and its rising and setting, the moon and its waxing and waning and the shape of our beautiful globe. Were we to look for it, we would see circular form or pattern of movement everywhere. Our evolution is no different; we are revolving from full spirituality to nearly full materiality and back now toward full spirituality. That's what our evolutionary path is and always has been, only spiral, because we will return to a level far higher than the one on which we began this great journey, a level realized through human experience.

So many things are happening to help us make our shift in consciousness: Discoveries of ancient scriptural texts, disclosure of the mythic nature of the foundational basis of our Western religions, and improved understanding of ancient perennial wisdom about our existence. These are all bringing us to the realization of both a new spirituality and a new God. The changes within science toward broader, integral, and holistic approaches, mean that science, too, is no longer denying spirituality. Everything seems to be converging on spiritual consciousness as the One and ground of all being. We are coming close to the necessary critical mass

No Superman, Wonder Woman, Lone Ranger, or Christ is coming to rescue us, nor would we truly want them to. Our salvation lies within ourselves, and we need it only to the extent we live in ignorance. Each of us individually has to find our own way out of ignorance; no savior can do it for us. Shifting our consciousness is part of our journey of enlightenment toward awakening, and only through it do we find true joy and fulfillment.

Once we have made that shift, we naturally assume responsibility for helping others to make the shift in consciousness. All humanity eventually will transform and that will be the wonderful final chapter of the strictly material part of the human story on Earth.

We are nearing the time when we individually and collectively bring heart-based compassion and cooperation into our regular ways of thinking and behaving. A new culture and a new world are before us. We are the observer and creator of our reality and of our own evolution. We are following our own plan, realizing both our uniqueness and our Oneness, becoming enlightened, waking up.

We are awakening to our soul's communication, replacing faith with gnosis, and becoming enlightened. While faith seems to involve devotion to someone or something outside and apart from us, Gnosis, communion, and enlightenment involve understanding and acceptance of the knowledge that is inside of and part of us. The shift I encourage is to move from the outer to the inner.

I contend that materialist beliefs must change to spiritual knowledge to enable our awakening to the spiritual. Meta writers such as Neale Donald Walsch, Bruce Lipton, Gregg Braden, and Wayne Dyer write about changing our beliefs, and many others imply a change in beliefs when they teach their brand of spirituality. But I believe we need to specifically focus our attention on and deliberately change any limiting, materialist beliefs to more expansive, heart-based ones.

Our beliefs help us experience what we want to think of as real. But, while right for us in the past, our materialist beliefs are now insufficient for us. We need to realize our own spirituality, bring it into our worldviews to express the peace, compassion, and holism we want to experience in every aspect of our life.

We are balancing our energy, allowing the sacred feminine to return to our consciousness to balance the masculine power we've been living with. Many of us are beginning to act more like caretakers of Earth and its varied inhabitants, valuing them rather than exploiting and abusing them. More of us every day are going within to find God. We are reuniting with our higher soul-Selves, and are being empowered from within. We are quietly being more spiritual.

But the time for quiet is over. Those of us who have made the choice for greater spiritual understanding and have perhaps shifted must now shout: "Wake Up! You are spirit! You are God! I am spirit! I am God! We are One! We all share the same consciousness!"

It's time to be evolutionaries and quantum activists. It's time for all of humanity to gather into a cooperative harmonious higher level being. It's time to be part of the shift. It's time for all of us to wake up.

What will your choice be? Will you choose enlightenment, love, and spirituality? Will you be the hundredth monkey? How do you see yourself, as a mortal physical being, perhaps thinking spiritually while fighting to survive, or as an eternal spirit being enjoying the wonders of human life in physicality as a learning experience, co-creating with loved ones this marvelous experience? Are you raising your consciousness to a higher level? Are you becoming a higher level being? Are you waking up?

Words from Jesus, as offered by Baird Spalding in his six-volume set of books, *Life and Teaching of the Masters of the Far East*, seem appropriate to close this book:

> [Y]ou are an especially designed creation, you have a particular mission, you have a light to give, a work to do that no other can give or accomplish; and if you will open your heart, mind, and soul wide to spirit, you will learn of it in your own heart.... you may accept others as brother helpers, but you are always instructed and led from within; the truth is there for you and you will find it.[486]

I wish you a wonderful journey of enlightenment toward your own personal awakening.

With a great deal of love,
    Andrée (Dee) Cuenod

---

[485] Walsch, Neale Donald, Newsletter, April 5, 2009 www/nealedonaldwalsch.com.
[486] Spalding, Baird T. *Life and Teaching of the Masters of the Far East*. Marina Del Rey, CA: DeVorss & Company, 1927, 1944.

APPENDIX A

Comparisons of Levels of Consciousness

PERSPECTIVE	1	2	3	4
MODELS	ASSOCIATED WITH THE BODY	SPIRITUAL - REINCARNATES	SPIRITUAL - NEVER INCARNATES	ULTIMATE
Orthodox Science	Ego/Intellect/Brain/Consciousness			
Western Fundamentalist Religions	Ego/Intellect/Consciousness/ human soul			Spirit realm, residence of God and angels. (A separate place.)
Cohen, Andrew	Ego/self	self	Authentic Self/Impersonal True Self/First Cause	Self Absolute/One self-aware Being/God/Perfection
Wilber, Ken	Ego/Gross/Matter/mind	Deeper Psychic/Soul/Subtle	Atman Self/Causal/spirit	Kosmos/Emptiness unbound
Cayce, Edgar	Ego/Earthly self	Soul/"entity"	Spirit/divine spark/consciousness w/individualness/"superconscious"	Whole of God consciousness/Vast sea of mind force
Edge, Henry Travers for Theosophy	Animal soul	Human Soul	Spiritual Soul	Divine Monad, as part of ONE
Kabbalah	Nefesh: soul of atomic structure	Ruach: holy spirit	Neshama: higher awareness and angelic realms	Chayah: realm of wisdom, source of all understanding.
Cuenod, Andree	Ego/Intellect/personality/mortal/ role in this life	Human self/Actor/Soul's Extension eternal	Soul/ Higher-Self/Immortal/individualization of ONE	Consciousness/One All/Kosmos/singularity
Gnostics, as described by Stephan Hoeller	Personality	Soul - human self	Spirit - part of the Great Generation /Aeons	Great One/True God
Gnostics and Pagans, as described by Freke and Gandy	Counterfeit self; Eidolon/embodied lower self/personality/ mortal	Daemon: Immortal Spirit or Individual Higher True Self/spiritual connection to God	Guardian Angel/Higher Self/Light Power/ Universal Self, shared by all /Soul of God	One/God
Indian *Upanishads*, as reported by Amit Goswami	Vital - blueprint of biological form manifested physically	Mental - made of mana, mind substance, software	Supramental, Intellect - theme body	Spiritual Joy or Bliss - unlimited, ground of all being

APPENDIX B

Time Line

bya = billion years ago	
20-14bya	Big Bang, or beginning of the universe and time
8-6bya	Formation of the Earth
4bya	Oxygen atmosphere and first life - single-celled organism
2bya	One-celled organisms begin splitting
1bya	Groupings of cells - eukaryotes
mya = million years ago	
600-500mya	Cambrian explosion of invertebrates
500-400mya	Fish (vertebrates); land life: scorpions and plants
408-360mya	Amphibians, forests
300-200mya	Reptiles, large mammals; single land mass: Pangaea
245-200mya	Dinosaurs; small mammals
130-20mya	Birds; Pangaea begins splitting into Laurasia and Gondwanaland
66mya	Dinosaurs become extinct
65mya	Mammals, flowering plants; Africa and South America split
9-7mya	Primates (apes and monkeys)
11-7mya	Chad Man, possibly first hominid (prehuman)
2.5mya	"Lucy", Homo habilis: upright, tool-using hominid
tya = thousand years ago	
600tya	Neanderthal characteristics appear - Europe; Old Stone Age
300-250tya	Archaic Homo sapiens with features like modern humans; last Ice Age begins

130tya	Neanderthal complete characteristics - Europe
50tya	Homo sapiens sapiens - Humans become self-aware
24tya	Neanderthal characteristics disappear
40-23tya	North American and Mesoamerican Indians appear
18tya	Last Ice Age peaks
15-12tya	Sphinx, Great Pyramid may have been built - Egypt; Gobekli Tepe - Turkey
12-10tya	river villages established - Mesopotamia, Anatolia, Asia Minor; Ice Age ends
m = millennium	*(thousand-year period)*
11th - 6th m	Catal Huyuk town with running water - Turkey; Sumeria; sunken cities/world; Neolithic (New Stone Age)
5th – 4th m	Mesopotamian City-states; Biblical creation date
3rd m	Egyptian Empire; Great Pyramid built; Indus/Harrapan Civilization; Bronze Age (3500 – 1000BCE); Vedas/Hinduism – Iran & India
c = century	*(hundred-year period)*
Mid-7th - 6th c	Hebrew God conceptualized, religion defined; Siddhartha, Buddhism - India; Confucianism, Taoism - China; Iron Age begins (1100 – 500BCE) – Mediterranean region
6th - 3rd c	Genesis written; Greek city-states and philosophers: Pythagoras, Plato, Socrates, Aristotle
CE = in the Common Era	*(used to be called AD)*
0-33	Roman empire established; Birth of Jesus; Paul begins Christianity - Asia Minor
70-150	Jerusalem temple destroyed; New Testament gospels written; Christianity
early 2nd c	Anasazi culture - SW North America; Ptolomeic system puts Earth at the center of the universe
220	Hebrew Bible set; Judaism becomes Rabbinic

325	Nicene Council establishes Church as arm of Roman empire; Nicene Creed sets Godliness of Jesus
7th c	Muhammad, Islam - Arabia
9th - 10th c.	Mayan civ. - Central America; Medieval period - Europe
11th - 13th c	Crusades - Europe, Asia Minor, Israel/Palestine
Mid-15th c	Aztec Civ. - Central America, Mexico; Inca Civ. - South America; Renaissance begins - Europe
mid-16th c	Copernicus and Sun-Centered Astronomy; Protestant Reformation
17th - 18th c	Galileo, Descartes, Newton; Scientific Revolution, Age of Enlightenment – Europe; Industrial Age begins
1832	Emerson publishes *Nature*
1859	Darwin publishes The Origin of Species
1875-1925	Modern Metaphysical philosophies and religions begin
1975-2025	Beginning of the New Age of Aquarius, Aeon of Horus, Fifth World

APPENDIX C

The Botanical Society of America Statement on Evolution[487]

The Botanical Society of America has as its members professional scientists, scholars, and educators from across the United States and Canada, and from over 50 other countries. Most of us call ourselves botanists, plant biologists, or plant scientists, and members of our profession teach and learn about botanical organisms using well established principles and practices of science.

Evolution represents one of the broadest, most inclusive theories used in pursuit of and in teaching this knowledge, but it is, by no means the only theory involved. Scientific theories are used in two ways: to explain what we know, and to pursue new knowledge. Evolution explains observations of shared characteristics (the result of common ancestry and descent with modification) and adaptations (the result of natural selection acting to maximize reproductive success), as well as explaining pollen: ovule ratios, weeds, deceptive pollination strategies, differences in sexual expression, idiocy, and a myriad of other biological phenomena. Far from being merely a speculative notion, as implied when someone says, "evolution is just a theory," the core concepts of evolution are well documented and well confirmed. Natural selection has been repeatedly demonstrated in both field and laboratory, and descent with modification is so well documented that scientists are justified in saying that evolution is true.

Some people contend that creationism and its surrogate, "Intelligent Design," offers an alternative explanation: that organisms are well adapted and have common characteristics because they were created just so, and they exhibit the hallmarks of Intelligent Design. As such creationism is an all-inclusive explanation for every biological phenomenon. So why do we support and teach evolution and not creationism? "Intelligent Design" if both explain the same phenomena? Are botanists just dogmatic, atheistic materialists, as some critics of science imply? Hardly, although scientists are routinely portrayed by creationists as dogmatic. We are asked, "Why, in all fairness, don't we teach both explanations and let students decide?"

The fairness argument implies that creationism is a scientifically valid alternative to evolution, and that is not true. Science is not about fairness, and all explanations are highly speculative with little in the way of supporting evidence, and they will stand or fall based upon rigorous testing. The history of science is littered with discarded explanations, e.g., inheritance of acquired characters, but these weren't discarded because of public opinion or general popularity; each one earned that distinction by being scientifically falsified. Scientists may jump on a "bandwagon" for some new explanation, particularly if it has tremendous explanatory power, something that makes sense out of previously unexplained phenomena. But for an explanation to become a mainstream component of a theory, it must be tested and found useful in doing science.

To make progress, to learn more about botanical organisms, hypotheses, the subcomponents of theories, are tested by attempting to falsify logically derived predictions. This is why scientists use and teach evolution; evolution offers testable explanations of observed biological phenomena. Evolution continues to be of paramount usefulness, and so, based on simple pragmatism, scientists use this theory to improve our understanding of the biology of organisms. Over and over again, evolutionary theory has generated predictions that have proven to be true.

Any hypothesis that doesn't prove true is discarded in favor of a new one, and so the component hypotheses of evolutionary theory change as knowledge and understanding grow. Phylogenetic hypo-theses, patterns of ancestral relatedness, based on one set of data, for example, base sequences in DNA, are generated, and when the results make logical sense out of formerly disparate observations, confidence in the truth of the hypothesis increases. The theory of evolution so permeates botany that frequently it is not mentioned explicitly, but the overwhelming majority of published studies are based upon evolutionary hypotheses, each of which constitutes a test of an hypothesis.

Evolution has been very successful as a scientific explanation because it has been useful in advancing our understanding of organisms and applying that knowledge to the solution of many human problems, e.g., host-pathogen interactions, origin of crop plants, herbicide resistance, disease susceptibility of crops, and invasive plants. For example, plant biologists have long been interested in the origins of crop plants. (There follows a lengthy discourse on an hypothesis regarding wheat species, too technically detailed to include here.)

The actual work was done by many plant biologists over many years, little by little, gathering data and testing ideas, until these evolutionary events were understood as generally described above. The hypothesized speciation events were actually recreated, an accomplishment that allows plant biologists to breed new varieties of emmer and breadwheats. Using this speciation mechanism, plant biologists hybridized wheat and rye, producing a new, vigorous, high protein cereal grain, triticale.

What would the creationist paradigm have done? No telling. Perhaps nothing, because observing three wheat species created to feed humans would not have generated any questions that needed answering. No predictions are made, so there is no reason or direction for seeking further knowledge. This demonstrates the scientific uselessness of creationism.

While creationism explains everything, it offers no understanding beyond, 'that's the way it was created.' No testable predictions can be derived from the creationism explanation. Creationism has not made a single contribution to agriculture, medicine, conservation, forestry, pathology, or any other applied area of biology.

Creationism has yielded no classifications, no unifying concepts with which to study organisms or life. In those few instances where prediction can be inferred from biblical passages (e.g., groups of related organisms, migration of all animals from the resting place of the ark on Mt. Ararat to their present locations, genetic diversity derived from small founder populations, dispersal ability of organisms in direct proportion to their distance from eastern Turkey), creationism has been scientifically falsified.

Is it fair or good science education to teach about an unsuccessfully, scientifically useless explanation just because it pleases people with a particular religious belief? Is it unfair to ignore scientifically useless explanations, particularly if they have played no role in the development of modern scientific concepts? Science education is about teaching valid concepts and those that led to the development of new explanations.

Creationism is the modern manifestation of a long-standing conflict between science and religion in Western Civilization. Prior to science, and in all non-scientific cultures, myths were the only viable explanations for a myriad of natural phenomena, and these myths became incorporated into diverse religious beliefs. Following the rise and spread of science, where ideas are tested against nature rather than being decided by religious authority and sacred texts, many phenomena previously attributed to the supernatural (disease, genetic defects, lightning, blights and plagues, epilepsy, comets, mental illness, etc.) became known to have natural causes and explanations. Recognizing this, the Catholic Church finally admitted, after 451 years, that Galileo was correct; the Earth was not the unmoving center of the Universe. Mental illness, birth defects, and disease are no longer considered the mark of evil or of God's displeasure or punishment.

Epileptics and people intoxicated by ergot-infected rye are no longer burned at the stake as witches. As natural causes were discovered and understood, religious authorities were forced to alter long-held positions in the face of growing scientific knowledge. This does not mean science has disproved the supernatural. The methodology of science only deals with the material world.

Science as a way of knowing has been extremely successful, although people may not like all the changes science and its handmaiden, technology, have wrought. But people who oppose evolution, and seek to have creationism or Intelligent Design included in science curricula, seek to dismiss and change the most successful way of knowing ever discovered.

They wish to substitute opinion and belief for evidence and testing. The proponents of creationism/Intelligent Design promote scientific ignorance in the guise of learning. As professional scientists and educators, we strongly assert that such efforts are both misguided and flawed, presenting an incorrect view of science, its understanding, and it processes.

---

[487] Armstrong, J. E. and Jernstedt, J., "A Statement on Evolution" - The Botanical Society of America, "Special Report," *Skeptical Inquirer*, November/December 2003. Amherst, NY: CSICOP.

APPENDIX D

American Association for the Advancement of Sciences Board Resolution on Intelligent Design (ID) Theory[488]

The contemporary theory of biological evolution is one of the most robust products of scientific inquiry. It is the foundation for research in many areas of biology as well as an essential element of science education.

To become informed and responsible citizens in our contemporary technological world, students need to study the theories and empirical evidence central to current scientific understanding.

Over the past several years proponents of so-called "Intelligent Design theory," also known as ID, have challenged the accepted scientific theory of biological evolution. As part of this effort they have sought to introduce the teaching of "Intelligent Design theory" into the science curricula of the public schools. The movement presents "Intelligent Design theory" to the public as a theoretical innovation, supported by scientific evidence, that offers a more adequate explanation for the origin of the diversity of living organisms than the current scientifically accepted theory of evolution. In response to this effort, individual scientists and philosophers of science have provided substantive critiques of "Intelligent Design," demonstrating significant conceptual flaws in its formulation, a lack of credible scientific evidence, and misrepresentations of scientific facts.

Recognizing that the "Intelligent Design theory" represents a challenge to the quality of science education, the Board of Directors of the AAAS unanimously adopts the following resolution: Whereas, ID Proponents claim that contemporary evolutionary theory is incapable of explaining the origin of the diversity of living organisms;

Whereas, to date, the ID movement has failed to offer credible scientific evidence to support their claim that ID undermines the current scientifically accepted theory of evolution;

Whereas, the ID movement has not proposed a scientific means of testing its claims;

Therefore Be It Resolved, that AAAS urges citizens across the nation to oppose the establishment of policies that would permit the teaching of "Intelligent Design theory" as part of the science curricula of the public schools;

Therefore Be It Further Resolved, that AAAS calls upon its members to assist those engaged in overseeing science education policy to understand the nature of science, the content of contemporary evolutionary theory and the inappropriateness of "Intelligent Design theory" as subject matter for science education;

Therefore Be It Further Resolved, that AAAS encourages its affiliated societies to endorse this resolution and to communicate their support to appropriate parties at the federal, state and local levels of the government.

Approved by the AAAS Board of Directors on October 18, 2002

---

[488] "AAAS Board Resolution on Intelligent Design Theory," *Skeptical Inquirer*, March/April 2003. Amherst, NY: CSICOP

BIBLIOGRAPHY

Audio/Video Presentations

The Biology of Perception & The Psychology of Change, with Bruce Lipton & Rob Williams, Spirit, 2000.

Braden, Gregg, *Beyond Zero Point, The Journey to Compassion, an abridgment of walking between the worlds* (Conscious Wave). Sounds True, 2000.

——————, *Speaking The Lost Language of God*. Injoi Corporation, 2004.

——————, *The Science of Miracles, the quantum language of healing, peace, feeling, and belief.* Hay House, Inc., 2009

Cohen, Andrew, *Awakening the Authentic Self, the path & practice of evolutionary enlightenment*. EnlightenNext Media, 2007

Dyer, Wayne, *Excuses Begone*. Hay House, Inc., 2009

The Gospel of Judas. National Geographic, 2006

Goswami, Amit, *The Quantum Activist.* Quantum Activations, 2010

Krishnamurti, J., *Truth is a Pathless Land*. Sounds True, 2003

Mind Walk. Produced by Fritjof Capra, The Atlas Production Company, with Mindwalk Productions, 1990

Technologies of the Gods. Mystic Fire Video, Inc., 1998.

What The Bleep Do We Know!? Captured Light & Lord of the Wind Films LLC, 2004

What the Bleep!? Further Down The Rabbit Hole. Captured Light & Lord of the Wind Films LLC, 2006

Wilber, Ken, *Kosmic Consciousness*. Sounds True, 2004

Wilde, Stewart, *A Journey Beyond Enlightenment*. Nightengale-Conant, 2007

Zukav, Gary, *Soul to Soul*. Sound Ideas, 2007

Books

Allen, James, *As a Man Thinketh*, self-published, 1903

Atwater, P.M.H, *Beyond the Indigo Children*. Bear & Co., 2005

Baigent, Michael, *The Jesus Papers*. HarperCollins, 2006

Barnstone, Willis, editor, *The Other Bible*. HarperSanFrancisco, 1984

Barnstone, Willis & Marvin Meyer, editors, *The Gnostic Bible*. Shambhala, 2003

Baumann, T. Lee, *God at the Speed of Light, the Melding of Science and Spirituality*. Association for Research and Enlightenment, 2001

Blavatsky, H. P., *An Abridgement of The Secret Doctrine*. Theosophical Publishing House, 1967

Braden, Gregg, *The Isaiah Effect: decoding the lost science of prayer and prophecy*. Three Rivers Press, 2000

_____, *The God Code*. Hay House, Inc., 2006

_____, *The Divine Matrix, bridging time, space, miracles, and belierf*. Hay House, Inc., 2007

_____, *The Spontaneous Healing of Belief, shattering the paradigm of false limits*. Hay House, Inc., 2008

_____, *Deep Truth: igniting the memory of our origin, history, destiny and fate*, Hay House, Inc., 2012

Carey, Ken, *The Starseed Transmissions: an extraterrestrial report*. Uni*Sun, 1982

Carroll, Lee and Jan Tober, *The Indigo Children, the new kids have arrived*. Hay House, Inc., 1999

Chapman, Carole A. P., *Golden Ones, from Atlantis to New World*. Mystic Children's Studio, 2001

Church, W. H., *Edgar Cayce's Story of the Soul*. A.R.E., 1989

Cohen, Andrew, *Embracing Heaven & Earth*. EnlightenNext Media, 2000

_____, *Living Enlightenment, a call for evolution beyond ego*, EnlightenNext Media, 2002

_____, *Evolution as Enlightenment*. EnlightenNext Media, 2011

Cooper, Rabbi David A., *God is a Verb*. Riverhead Books, 1997

Cremo, Michael A., *Human Devolution*. Bhaktivedanta Book Publishing Inc., 2003

_____ and Richard L. Thompson, *Forbidden Archaeology: the Hidden History of the Human Race*. Bhaktivedanta Book Publishing Inc., 1993, revised 1996, 1998

_____, *Hidden History of the Human Race*. Bhaktivedanta Book Publishing Inc., 1996

Dalai Lama, *The Universe in a Single Atom*. Morgan Road Books, 2005

Darwin, Charles, *On the Origin of Species*, 1859. Univ. of Chicago Pres, 1957

_____, *The Descent of Man*, 1871. Univ. of Chicago Press, 1957

Davis, Jimmy H. & Harry L. Poe, *Designer Universe: Intelligent Design and the existence of God*. Broadman & Holman, 2002

Dawking, Richard, *The God Delusion*. Mariner Books, 2006

Dembski, William A., *Intelligent Design, the bridge between science & theology*. IVP Academic, 1999

Dossey, Larry, *The Power of Premonition*. Dutton, Penguin Group, Inc. 2009

Duerk, Judith, *Circle of Stones, Woman's Journey to Herself*. Lura Media, 1989

Dunn, Christopher, *The Giza Power Plant*. Inner Traditions/Bear, 2002

_____, *Lost Technologies of Ancient Egypt*. Inner Traditions/Bear, 2010

Dyer, Wayne, *Excuses Begone*. Hay House, Inc., 2009

Edge, Henry Travers, *Evolution: Who and What is Man?* Point Loma Publications, 1979

_____, *Design and Purpose, a Study in the Drama of Evolution*. Point Loma Publications, 1979

Flew, Anthony and Roy Abraham Varghese, *There is a God: how the world's most notorious atheist changed his mind*. Harper One, 2007

Friedman, Richard Elliott, *Who Wrote the Bible?* HarperCollins Publishers, 1987

Freke, Timothy & Peter Gandy, *The Jesus Mysteries: was the original Jesus a pagan god?*. Random House Publishing, 1999

Gaffney, Mark H., *Gnostic Secrets of the Naassenes*. Inner Traditions, 2004

Giberson, Karl W. & Donald A. Yerxa, *Species of Origins: America's search for a creation story*. Rowan & Littlefield, 2002

Gordon, John, *Egypt Child of Atlantis*. Bear & Co., 1997

Goswami, Amit, *The Self-Aware Universe: how consciousness creates the material world.*. Tarcher/Putnam, 1995

_____, *The Visionary Window*. Quest Books, Theosophical Publishing House, 2000

_____, *Creative Evolution, a physicist's resolution between Darwinism and Intelligent Design*. Quest Books, Theosophical Publishing House, 2008

_____, *How Quantum Activism Can Save Civilization*. Hampton Roads Publishing, 2011

Gould, Stephen Jay, *Ever Since Darwin, Reflections in Natural History*. W.W. Norton & Company, 1977

Hall, Manly P., *The Secret Teachings of All Ages*. Tarcher/Penguin, 2003

Hitching, Francis, *The Neck of the Giraffe*, New American Library, 1982

Hoeller, Stephen A., Gnosticism, *New Light on The Ancient Tradition of Inner Knowing*. Quest Books, Theosophical Publishing House, 2002

Jastrow, Robert, *The Enchanted Loom: Man in the Universe*. Simon & Schuster, 1981

_____, *Red Giants and White Dwarfs*, W.W. Norton, 1979.

Joseph, Frank, *Edgar Cayce's Atlantis and Lemuria*. A.R.E., 2001

_____, *Atlantis and 2012*, Bear & Company, 2010

Keyes, Ken Jr., *The Hundredth Monkey*. Vision Books, 1982

King, Ursula, *Pierre Teilhard De Chardin*. Orbis Books, 1999

Kryon, channeled and written by Lee Carroll, *Lifting the Veil (The New Energy Apocalypse)*, The Kryon Writings, Inc., 2007

Lamsa, George M., *Gems of Wisdom*. Unity School of Christianity, 1966

Lipton, Bruce, *The Biology of Belief: unleashing the power of consciousness, matter, and mind.*. Mountain of Love/Elite Books, 2005 and Hay House, 2008.

_____, and Steve Bhaerman, *Spontaneous Evolution, Our Positive Future*. Carlsbad, CA: Hay House, Inc., 2009

Mack, Burton L., *The Lost Gospel, the book of Q & Christian origins.* HarperSanFrancisco, 1993

Marciniak, Barbara, *Family of Light, Channeled Pleiadians.* Bear & Co., 1999

Margulis, Lynn, *Symbiosis in Cell Evolution: microbial communities in the Archean and Proterozoic eons.* W H Freeman, 1993.

McDermott, Robert, Introduction, Afterword, and compiler of *The Essential Aurobindo,* Lindisfarne Books, 1987

Miller, Ruth L., *Unveiling Your Hidden Power, Emma Curtis Hopkins' Metaphysics for the 21st Century,* WiseWoman Press, 2005.

_____, *Mary's Power: embracing the divine feminine as the age of invasion and empire* ends. Portal Center Press, 2010.

_____, *Make The World Go Away, The Gift of 2012.* Portal Center Press, 2011.

_____, *Natural Abundance,* Ralph Waldo Emerson's *guide to prosperity,* Beyond Words/Atria/Simon & Schuster, 2011.

Pagels, Elaine, *The Gnostic Gospels.* Random House, 1979

_____, *Beyond Belief.* Random House, 2003

Ridenour, Fritz, *So What's the Difference?* Gospel Light, 2001

Robinson, Lytle, *Edgar Cayce's Story of The Origin and Destiny of Man.* Berkeley Publishing, 1972

Robinson, James, *Nag Hammadi Library.* HarperSanFrancisco, 1978

Ruggles, Michael, *Quantum Conversations, how thoughts, feelings, and beliefs shape and create your reality.* Fast Pencil, Inc., 2011

Schlitz, Marilyn, Cassandra Vieten, Tina Amorak, *Living Deeply, the Art and Science of Transforming Everyday Life.* New Harbinger Publications, Inc. 2007

Sharma, I. C., Cayce, *Karma and Reincarnation.* Harper & Row, Publishers, 1975

Smith, Huston, *The Religions of Man.* New American Library, 1963.

_____, *Why Religion Matters.* HarperSanFrancisco, 2001

Spalding, Baird T., *Life and Teaching of the Masters of the Far East,* Vols I-V. DeVorss & Company, 1922-1944

Talbot, Michael, *The Holographic Universe.* HarperCollins, 1991

Van Auken, John, *Ancient Egyptian Mysticism and Its Relevance Today*. ARE Press, 1999

_____, *Edgar Cayce and the Kabbalah*, ARE Press 2010.

Van Pelt, Gertrude W., *Doctrine of Karma, Chance or Choice?* Point Loma Publications, 1974

Walsch, Neale Donald, *Conversations with God*, Book One. Putnam, 1995

_____, *Conversations with God*, Books Two and Three. Hampton Roads Publishing Company, Inc., 1997 and 1998

_____, *Tomorrow's God*. Atria Books, 2004

Watch Tower, *Life - How did it get here? By evolution or by creation?* Watch Tower, 1985

Waters, Owen, *The Shift, the Revolution in Human Consciousness*. Infinite Being Publishing LLC, 2006

Wilber, Ken, *The Essential Ken Wilber*. Shambhala, 1998

_____, *A Brief History of Everything*. Shambhala, 2000

_____, *Quantum Questions, mystical writings of the world's greatest physicists*, Shambhala, 2001

Wilson, Collin, *Atlantis and the Kingdom of the Neanderthals*, 100,000 Years of Lost History. Bear & Company, 2006

Wise, Micheal, Walter Abegg, Jr. & Edward Cook, *The Dead Sea Scrolls: a New Translation*. HarperSanFrancisco, 1996

Woodward, Mary Ann, E*dgar Cayce's Story of Karma*. Berkeley Publishing, 1971

Zukav, Gary, *The Seat of the Soul*. A Fireside Book by Simon & Schuster, 1990

Anthologies

The Essence of Wisdom: words from the masters to illuminate the spiritual path. Stephen Mitchell, ed., Broadway Books, 1998

Forbidden History. Kenyon, Douglas K., ed., Bear & Co., 2005

Forbidden Religion. Kenyon, Douglas K., ed., Bear & Co., 2006

Forbidden Science. Kenyon, Douglas K., ed., Bear & Co., 2008

Intelligent Design Creationism & Its Critics. Robert Pennock, ed, MIT Press, 2001

Mere Creation, Science, Faith & Intelligent Design. Dembski, William A., editor. InterVarsity Press, 1998

The Mystery of 2012, predictions, prophecies, & possibilities. Tami Simon, ed. Sounds True, 2007

The Search for Lost Origins, a collection of reports on today's breakthrough research, from the editors of Atlantis Rising Magazine. Atlantis Rising Books, 1996

Magazines (printed & on-line)

Atlantis Rising, Atlantis Rising Publications
EnlightenNext (formerly *What Is Enlightenment?*) EnlightenNext Media
National Geographic. National Geographic Society
Science & Theology News. (no longer published)
Science & Spirit. Heldref Publications (no longer published)
Science of Mind. Science of Mind Publications
Shift. Institute of Noetic Sciences
Skeptical Inquirer. CSICOP
SuperConsciousness. SuperConsciousness Media
Venture Inward. A.R.E.

Newsletters (many on-line)

Hamilton, Craig
Houston, Jean
Hubbard, Barbara Marx
Van Auken, John, Ancient Mysteries. A.R.E.
Van Auken, John, Personal Spirituality. A.R.E.
Walsch, Neale Donald
Waters, Owen, Infinite Being

Atlases & Encyclopedias (on-line & CDRom)

Funk and Wagnalls New Encyclopedia, on Infopedia CD-Rom. SoftKey, 1996

Phillip's Atlas of World History, edited by Patrick K. O'Brien. George Phillips Limited, 1999

The Stanford Encyclopedia of Philosophy, www.stanford.edu

Wikipedia, the free on-line Encyclopedia, www.wikibedia.com.

Presentations in *The Great Courses* Series by The Teaching Company

Brier, Bob, The History of Ancient Egypt, 2004

Cary, Phillip, Philosophy & Religion in the West, 1999

Cherry, Shai, Introduction to Judaism, 2004

Ehrman, Bart D., Lost Christianities: Christian Scriptures and the Battles over Authentication, 2002

_____, From Jesus to Constantine: A History of Early Christianity, 2004

Harl, Keneth W., Origins of Great Ancient Civilizations, 2005

_____, Great Ancient Civilizations of Asia Minor, 2005

Higgins, Kathleen, World Philosophy, 2001

Holland, Glenn S., Religion in the Ancient Mediterranean World, 2002

Larson, Edward J., Theory of Evolution: History of Controversy, 2002

Oden, Robert, God and Mankind: Comparative Religion,

Principe, Lawrence M., Science and Religion, 2006

Schumacher, Benjamin, Quantum Mechanics: The Physics of the Microscopic World, 2009

Wolfson, Richard. Einstein's Relativity and the Quantum Revolution.

INDEX

aborigines vi, 199, 251
Age of Darkness...................... ix
Age of Light .... ix, 7
Akasha 225, 229, 230
Alternative researchers 147, 149, 150, 178
alternative scientists... 147, 162
ancient ancestors iv, ix, x, 5, 143, 144, 146, 195, 330, 341
Aristotle 7, 51, 52, 53, 55, 95, 167, 173, 195, 349
assumptions 3, 5, 27, 30, 41, 208
Authentic Self 215, 216, 217, 357
Buddhist....................... 186, 200
Christian bishops............ 15, 68
Christianity v, vi, ix, 15-18, 20, 21, 50, 51, 57, 60, 65-74, 78-82, 85-90, 134, 144, 146, 167, 179, 181, 185, 190, 192, 195, 199, 203, 219, 233, 249, 349, 361, 364
creation story 57, 63, 100, 125, 360
creative evolution 210, 215, 221
Dead Sea scrolls 64, 175
December 21, 2012 viii, 315, 321
Descartes ...52-55, 94, 196, 202
devolution 236, 271, 274, 288, 312, 328

Discovery Institute 127, 131, 133, 136, 139, 140
DNA 8, 96, 102, 107, 108, 116, 128, 131, 209
Einstein iii, 1, 30, 36, 38, 114, 115, 123, 136, 193, 364
enlightenment viii, xii, xiii, 6, 31, 143, 144, 169, 172, 183, 186, 201, 213-218, 221, 245, 256, 257, 288, 290, 297, 329, 330, 344, 345, 357, 371
feminine ix, 11- 13, 20, 22, 46, 78, 79, 195, 317, 318, 332, 335, 344
fossil record 96, 98, 99, 102, 105, 107, 112, 136, 204
fundamentalist Christianity .vi, 8, 17-20, 136
Gnostics 71, 78, 84, 181-187, 199, 200, 250, 257, 280, 283, 329
Gondwanaland 157, 158, 163, 348
Gospel of Judas............ 176, 357
Gospel of Thomas 81, 83, 178, 183, 184
ground of being vi, 113, 118, 199, 205, 206, 210, 216, 257, 298, 327
Hebrew 19, 30, 57, 58, 60, 62-68, 71, 72, 80, 84, 86, 88, 176-

181, 189, 239, 242, 259, 318, 349
Hindu Vedas 186, 199
holistic iv, ix, xii, 12, 36, 42, 117, 138, 147, 178, 195, 203, 209, 217, 225, 303, 343
holographic model.............. 114
illusion 30, 36, 84, 134, 183, 193, 220, 241, 242, 248, 269, 275, 277, 311, 321
Institute of Noetic Sciences .. 3, 10, 32, 39, 44, 117, 123, 138, 293, 307, 316, 322, 333, 337, 363
Islam vi, 16, 17, 21, 50, 60, 63, 65, 72, 78, 79, 199, 200, 350
Judaism vi, 17, 21, 50, 59, 65, 68, 72, 74, 78, 79, 89, 179, 199, 239, 245, 349, 364
masculine ix, 11-13, 16, 20, 22, 28, 45, 46, 78, 195, 273, 284, 317, 318, 335, 344
materialism v, viii-xii, 7, 8, 25, 37, 39, 45, 49, 94, 100, 119, 127, 132, 133, 136, 137, 187, 210, 284, 295-297, 305, 315, 320, 327, 339
media................. 7, 8, 9, 41, 336
Metas ix-xii, 6, 16, 18, 19, 44, 143, 144, 156, 195, 197-203, 220, 250, 256, 257, 281, 299, 304
monad 175, 236
monism vi, 54, 196, 199, 205, 306
monistic idealism 115, 196, 197, 206, 306
monotheism .... vi, 66, 199
multisensory beings 45
Mysteries 16, 18, 63, 90, 91, 153, 165, 168, 169, 171, 172, 176, 179-181, 187-192, 230, 257, 360, 364
mystics vi, 21, 115, 175, 240, 295
Nag Hammadi 70, 81, 176, 178, 183, 361
new sciences x, 10, 40, 196, 197
New Testament 19, 66, 68-75, 80-84, 177, 183, 189, 242, 349
New Thought 10, 22, 74, 333
Newton 25, 52, 54, 94, 175, 350
noetic scientists vi, vii, 8, 117, 296 313
Orthodox 25, 26, 29, 73, 77, 96, 104, 109, 110, 136, 145, 148, 149, 160, 185, 209
Osiris.... 169, 171, 189, 190, 192
Pagans 16, 62, 65, 67, 78, 167, 191, 199, 250, 280, 281, 329
pantheism .... vi, 63
philosophers vi, ix, xi, 7, 50, 54, 131, 143, 167, 168, 170, 173, 179, 195-197, 218, 255, 256, 349, 355
Plato xi, 7, 16, 51, 52, 119, 125, 152, 153, 167, 168, 170, 171, 173, 179, 182, 196, 210, 237, 265, 298, 349
Plotinus xi, 173, 174, 180, 196
prayers 9, 61
Pythagoras xi, 7, 16, 51, 167, 168, 169, 171-175, 349
Qur'an........ 19, 59, 72, 177, 199
reality v, viii, ix, 4, 9, 10, 13, 25, 29, 43, 45, 53, 93, 113-118, 130, 132, 137, 148, 152, 173,

182, 195-197, 237, 239, 241-244, 248, 249, 251, 305, 317, 319, 320, 322, 324, 327, 341, 344
reductionism.................... 29, 30
Reformation.................. 73, 350
Renaissance..... 73, 94, 321, 350
resurrection 65-67, 70, 75, 76, 87, 169, 171, 190, 191, 243, 244, 245
Roman church 7, 15, 16, 27, 51, 52, 54, 69-74, 143, 190, 219
scientific method.... 27, 51, 117
Shift viii-xii, 3, 45, 46, 119, 201, 210, 245, 248, 250, 255, 273, 274, 291, 293, 311-328, 333-336, 339, 340, 342-345, 370
spiritual teachers vii, 5, 143, 255, 281
Sri Aurobindo xi, 206, 213, 218, 219, 222, 325, 337
Taoist.............................. 11, 12
Teilhard de Chardin xi, 206, 213, 218, 221
tikkun.................. 242, 243, 291
YHWH..................... 60- 63, 259

ACKNOWLEDGMENTS

I thank the many publishers who gave me permission to use material from their books, magazines, and audio and video presentations. These are in the reference notes throughout this book. I have drawn from a few other sources for information to use more briefly, without citing them in the notes. In most cases, I've identified at least the author, if not also the specific source. Some are old quotes of famous people, and others add tidbits of color to my presentation. I have listed in the Bibliography all of these sources, as well as a few others I enjoyed, and recommend them to my readers.

CONTINUING THE CONVERSATION

My website is www.OurJourneytoAwakening.com. There you will find many articles expressing my spiritual philosophy and talking about the Shift in consciousness. There is also a link to a glossary of words I've used in this book and other writings whose definition might help in understanding what I mean by them. Other links contain interesting quotes from other people, things I think you should know, my philosophy of life in a nutshell, and a list of steps I used to attain good communication with my higher-vibrating, always in spirit guidance, my soul-Self.

ABOUT THE AUTHOR

With an MBA for women executives from UCLA, Andrée (Dee) Cuenod rose to management in the Los Angeles space industry. She was then recruited to help start UCLA's pioneering Planning Office, responsible for academic planning and serving as associate director.

After leaving academia, drawn to spiritual/metaphysical philosophy, Cuenod pursued a spiritual journey of enlightenment. She learned to commune intuitively with her inner, soul-Self and got personal answers to her numerous questions. Wanting to share the positive philosophy she developed from those answers, she began writing spiritual/metaphysical philosophy articles for new age publications, then books, and saw the first, *Awakening, a Journey of Enlightenment*, published in 1995. Cuenod has since studied the wisdom of ancient cultures, world religions, science (both classical orthodox and quantum), and contemporary spiritual wisdom. She found that Indian Vedic teaching, the "Mysteries" of most ancient cultures, worldwide indigenous traditions, and certain quantum physicists all express a similar spirituality, one in agreement with her own and which has a very different view of life from that of orthodox science's materialism or of fundamentalist religions. She has written and taught about spirituality, circular evolution, and the illusory nature of this life for over 40 years.

Cuenod teaches spiritual metaphysics and privately mentors individuals and groups. She has e-mailed more than 150 articles expressing her spirituality and philosophy of life and posted them on her website at www.OurJourneytoAwakening.com. Cuenod is author of *Wake Up! Our old beliefs don't work anymore!* (2013), updated second edition (2020), *Awakening: A Journey of Enlightenment*, updated second edition (2015), and *Beyond Materialism, Change Beliefs, Change the World*, and *Our Human Journey: Random Happenstance, Alien-Assisted, or Circular?*, both awaiting publication.

Related Titles from Portal Center Press

Awakening, a Journey of Enlightenment, by Andrée Cuenod

Discovering A New Way, possibilities for a peaceful future in the patterns of the past, by Ruth L. Miller

Language of Life, answers to modern issues in an ancient way of speaking, by Milt Markewitz, Ruth L. Miller and Batya Podos

Madonna, Magdalene, & Beyond: Feminine Power Hidden in our Empire Culture, by Ruth L Miller

Miracles through Music, tools learned by a harpist healer by Joel Andrews

Views from the Pew, moving beyond religion & discovering truth within, by J C Pedigo and friends

www.portalcenterpress.com

www.ingramcontent.com/pod-product-compliance
Lightning Source LLC
Chambersburg PA
CBHW022058120526
44592CB00033B/132